Music in the Baroque World

Music in the Baroque World: History, Culture, and Performance offers an interdisciplinary study of the music of Europe and the Americas in the seventeenth and first half of the eighteenth centuries. It balances culture, history, and musical analysis, with an emphasis on performance considerations such as notation, instruments, and performance techniques. It enables in-depth discussion and critical analysis and serves as a complete course with a website that hosts an anthology and audio/video links. Through stories of local traditions, performance trends, and artistic mixing *Music in the Baroque World* illuminates representative works through the lens of politics, visual arts, theology, print technology, gender, domesticity, commerce, and cultural exchange.

Features:

- An interdisciplinary approach that balances detailed analysis of specific pieces of music and broader historical overview and relevance
- A selection of historical documents at the end of each chapter that position musical works and events in their cultural context
- Extensive musical examples that show the melodic, textural, harmonic, or structural features of baroque music and enhance the utility of the textbook for undergraduate and graduate music majors
- A global perspective with a chapter on Music in the Americas
- A companion score anthology and website with links to audio/video content of key performances and research and writing guides

Susan Lewis is Director of the School of Music and Associate Professor of Musicology at the University of Victoria, Canada.

Music in the Baroque World

History, Culture, and Performance

Susan Lewis

**University of Victoria,
Canada**

Routledge
Taylor & Francis Group

NEW YORK AND LONDON

First published 2016
by Routledge
711 Third Avenue, New York, NY 10017

and by Routledge
2 Park Square, Milton Park, Abingdon, Oxon, OX14 4RN

Routledge is an imprint of the Taylor & Francis Group, an informa business

Library of Congress Cataloging-in-Publication Data
Lewis Hammond, Susan, 1972– author.
   Music in the baroque world : history, culture, and performance /
Susan Lewis Hammond.
      pages cm
   Includes index.
   1. Music—17th century—History and criticism.   2. Music—18th century—History
and criticism.   I. Title.
   ML193.L49 2016
   780.9'032—dc23
   2014048789

ISBN: 978-0-415-84275-4 (hbk)
ISBN: 978-0-415-84276-1 (pbk)
ISBN: 978-0-203-75843-4 (ebk)

Typeset in Sabon
by Apex CoVantage, LLC

Front cover image: NETHERLANDS - CIRCA 2002: Lute, 1667–1670, by Gerard ter
Borch the Younger (1617–81), oil on canvas, 53×39 cm. Netherlands, 17th century.
Kassel, Neue Galerie (Modern Art Museum) (Photo by DeAgostini/Getty Images
159827069

MIX
Paper from
responsible sources
FSC® C014174
www.fsc.org

Printed and bound in the United States of America by Sheridan Books, Inc. (a Sheridan Group Company).

For Zachary and Abigail

Timeline of Important Works, Composers, and World Events—Compiled by Elissa Poole

1573   The Florentine Camerata meets at the home of Count Giovanni de Bardi

1581   Vincenzo Gallilei, *Dialogo della musica antica et della moderna*

1587   Claudio Monteverdi, *Madrigali, libro primo*, 5vv

1588   *Musica Transalpina* introduces Italian madrigals to England
       Maddalena Casulana, *Il primo libro de madrigal*, 4vv

1589   Intermedi performed for wedding of Christine of Lorraine and Grand Duke Ferdinando de' Medici

1590   Edmund Spenser, *The Faerie Queene*

1594   Carlo Gesualdo, *Madrigali libro primo*, 5vv

1597   Giovanni Gabrielli, *Symphone Sacrae*
       Jacopo Peri, *Dafne*

1600   John Dowland, *Second Booke of Songs or Ayres*
       Peri, *Eurydice* performed for wedding of Henry IV of France and Maria de Medici
       Guilio Caccini, *Eurydice* staged in Florence
       Emilio de' Cavalieri, *La rappresentazione di anima e di corpo* performed in Rome

1601   Giulio Caccini, *Le nuove musiche*
       Shakespeare, *Hamlet*

1603   James I crowned King in England

1604   John Dowland, *Lachrimae or Seven Teares*

1605   Claudio Monteverdi, *Il quinto libro de madrigali*, 5vv

1607   Monteverdi's *Orfeo* performed in Mantua
       Jamestown colony founded in Virginia

1608   Girolamo Frescobaldi made organist at St. Peter's, Rome
       Samuel Champlain founds Quebec

1609   Heinrich Schütz studies with Giovanni Gabrieli in Venice
       Johannes Kepler, *Astronomia Nova*
       Tea from China shipped to Europe for first time (Dutch East India Company)

1610   Louis XIII crowned (until 1643)

1611   *Parthenia*, music for virginals printed in London
       Publication of the *King James Bible*
       Dutch merchants permitted to trade in Japan

1612   Tobacco planted in Virginia

1614   *Fitzwilliam Virginal Book* of English keyboard music
       Sir Walter Raleigh, *The History of the World*
       Peter Paul Rubens, *The Descent from the Cross (Die Kreuzaufrichtung)*

1617   Johann Hermann Schein, *Banchetto musicale*
       Ben Jonson appointed first poet laureate by James I

1618   Francesca Caccini, *Il primo libro delle musiche*
       Thirty Years War begins
       First African slaves arrive in Virginia

1620	Pilgrims arrive in Massachusetts
1621	Philip IV crowned King of Spain (until 1665)
	Robert Burton, *Anatomy of Melancholy*
	Potatoes planted in Germany for first time
1623	François De Lauze, *Apologie de la danse*
1624	Samuel Scheidt, *Tabulatura nova*
	Cardinal Richelieu made first minister in France (until 1642)
1625	Francesca Caccini, *La liberazione di Ruggiero dall'isola d'Alcina*, first opera by a woman composer
	Charles I crowned King of England (until 1649)
1626	Dutch colony of New Amsterdam founded
1627	Heinrich Schütz, *Dafne* performed, first Germany opera
1633	Galilei tried by the Inquisition for supporting Copernicus' theory that the earth revolves around the sun
1634	Ground broken for the *Taj Mahal*
1635	Girolamo Frescobaldi, *Fiori musicali*
1636	Marin Mersenne, *Harmonie Universelle*
	Dutch settle in Ceylon
1637	Johann Froberger organist at court chapel in Vienna
	First public opera theater opens in Venice
	Ferdinand III is Holy Roman Emperor (until 1657)
	Collapse of the Dutch tulip trade
1640	First European café opens in Venice
1642	Monteverdi, *L'incoronazione di Poppea*, opens in Venice
	English Civil War; theaters closed by Puritans
1643	Louis XIV crowned King of France (until 1715)
	Molière founds *Comédie française*
	Dutch explorer Abel Tasman discovers New Zealand and Tasmania
1644	Giovanni Lorenzo Bernini, *The Ecstasy of Saint Teresa*, sculpture series for the Cornaro Chapel, Santa Maria della Vittoria, Rome
1645	Heinrich Schütz, *Die sieben Worte Jesu Christi*
1647	Luigi Rossi's *Orfeo* produced in Paris
1648	Treaty of Westphalia and end of *Thirty Years War*: Germany's population down to 8 million from 17 million in 1618
1649	René Descartes, *Les passions de l'âme*
	Francesco Cavalli, *Giasone*
	Charles I beheaded and Commonwealth established in England (until 1660)
1651	Barbara Strozzi, *Cantate, ariette e duetti, Op. 2*
	Thomas Hobbes, *Leviathan*
	Dutch settle Cape Town in South Africa
1653	Jean-Baptiste Lully appointed court composer in Paris
	Oliver Cromwell dissolves Parliament
1654	Teatro di San Bartolomeo, the first opera house in Naples, opens
1656	Christian Huygens builds the first accurate pendulum clock
1659	Harvest of first grapes in Cape Town, South Africa for wine
1660	Restoration of the Monarchy and Charles II in England (until 1685)
	Samuel Pepys, *Diary*
1661	The Dutch relinquish Brazil to Portugal
1665	Heinrich Schütz, *Johannes-Passion*
	Baruch Spinoza, *Ethica*
	Johannes Vermeer, *The Girl with a Pearl Earring* (*Het meisje met de parel*)
1666	Great Fire of London

1667	Marc Antonio Cesti, *Il pomo d'oro*
	John Milton, *Paradise Lost*
1670	Jacques Chambonnières, *Pièces de claveçin*
1671	The French lay claim to all land west of Montreal
1678	John Bunyan, *The Pilgrim's Progress*
	Niagara Falls discovered by Louis Hennepin
1681	Arcangelo Corelli, *Trio Sonatas, Op. 1*
1682	Peter the Great becomes Tsar of Russia
1683	John Blow composes *Venus and Adonis*
	Alessandro Scarlatti in Naples
1685	Johann Sebastian Bach, George Frideric Handel, and Domenico Scarlatti born
	Revocation of the Edict of Nantes
1687	Isaac Newton, *Principia mathematica*
	Henry Purcell's *Dido and Aeneas* performed at court of James II
	Elisabeth Jacquet de la Guerre, *Premier livre de pièces de clavessin*
1689	Richard de Lalande, *De profundus*
1690	British East India Company establishes trading base in Calcutta
1692	Purcell, *The Fairy Queen* performed in London
	Benedictine monk Dom Pérignon invents champagne
1695	Georg Muffat, *Florilegium*
1697	Etienne Loulié uses an adjustable pendulum to construct the first mechanical metronome
1698	Philip V of Spain crowned (until 1746)
1700	London is Europe's largest city with population of 700,000
	The West African Asante nation sells slaves to Europeans for guns
1703	St. Petersburg founded by Peter the Great
1707	Mount Fuji in Japan erupts for 16 days
1709	Coldest winter in 500 years (Little Ice Age ca. 1550–1850)
	Bartolomeo Cristofori invents pianoforte
1711	Handel's *Rinaldo* in England
	Vivaldi, *L'estro armonico*
	Bubonic plague kills half a million people in Europe
1713	François Couperin, *Pièces de claveçin … premier livre*
	Bach in Weimar
	Treaty of Utrecht ends War of the Spanish Succession
1715	Death of Louis XIV
1717	Lady Mary Wortly introduces inoculation against smallpox into England
	The French establish trading post New Orleans
1719	Daniel Defoe, *Robinson Crusoe*
1721	Sweden cedes Estonia and most of Latvia to Russia in treaty of Nystad
1722	Jean-Philippe Rameau, *Traité de l'harmonie*
	The Iroquois League becomes known as the Six Nations
	Dutch discover Easter Island in the South Pacific
1725	*Concerts Spirituels* founded in Paris
	Vivaldi, *Le quattro stagioni*
	Catherine the Great assumes power in Russia
	New crops from the Americas such as maize and sweet potatoes fuel huge population growth in China
1727	Coffee planted in Brazil
	Quakers denounce slavery

1728	John Gay, *Beggar's Opera*
	Vitus Bering discovers the passage between Russia and Alaska
1730	Metastasio becomes court poet in Vienna
1731	Johann Sebastian Bach, *Clavier-Übung I*
	Treaty of Vienna
1732	Johan Gottfried Walther, *Musik-Lexikon*
1733	Giovanni Pergolesi, *La serva padrona*
	Rameau, *Hippolyte et Aricie* performed in Paris
1734	George Sale translates *Koran* into English
1736	Pope Clement XII condemns Freemasonry
1737	Rameau, *Castor et Pollux,* premieres in Paris
	Florence loses its independence when the last Medici duke of Tuscany dies
	The great castrato Farinelli retires from public singing and joins Spanish court of King Philip V
1738	Domenico Scarlatti, *30 Essercizi*
1740	Maria Theresa crowned Holy Roman Empress
	Frederick II crowned King of Prussia
	Frederick II invades Silesia, initiating War of the Austrian Succession
	Venezuela, Columbia and Ecuador become Spanish viceroyalty of New Granada
1742	Premiere of Handel's *Messiah,* in Dublin
1744	The first golf club founded in Scotland
1745	Johann Stamitz court Kapellmeister in Mannheim
1746	Frederick the Great begins palace of *Sans Souci* in Potsdam
1747	Tribal leader Ahmad Shah Abdali elected king of newly-founded Afghan nation
1748	The treaty of Aix-la-Chapelle ends the War of the Austrian Succession
	Ruins of Pompeii are excavated
1750	Denis Diderot and Jean le Rond d'Alembert found the *Encyclopédie*
	Death of Johann Sebastian Bach
	Population of the world estimated at 750 million
	China invades Tibet, establishing control over the Dalai Lama
1751	Francesco Geminiani, *The Art of Playing on the Violin*
	China invades Tibet
1752	*Querelle des bouffons,* dispute over merits of French and Italian opera
	Johann Joachim Quantz, *Versuch einer Anweisung die Flöte traversiere zu spielen*
	Benjamin Franklin invents lightning conductor
	Dorothea Erxleben becomes first qualified female medical doctor in Germany
	Great Britain and colonies adopt Gregorian calendar
1753	C.P.E. Bach, *Versuch über die wahre Art das Clavier zu spielen*
	Jean-Jacques Rousseau, *Lettre sur la musique française*
	Jewish Naturalization Act protests discrimination against Jews in Britain
1755	Samuel Johnson, *Dictionary of the English Language*
1754	War breaks out between French and British in North America
1755	First outbreak of smallpox in southern Africa
1756	Wolfgang Amadeus Mozart born
	Leopold Mozart, *Versuch einer gründlichen Violinschule*
	First chocolate factory in Germany
	England formally declares war on France (Seven Years War)
	First Jewish settlement in North America, in South Carolina

Contents

Detailed Contents

Preface

Music in the Baroque World: History, Culture, and Performance offers an interdisciplinary study of the music of Europe and the Americas in the seventeenth and first half of the eighteenth centuries. It answers calls for an approach that balances culture, history, and musical analysis, with an emphasis on performance considerations such as notation, instruments, and performance techniques. It situates musical events in their intellectual, social, religious, and political contexts and enables in-depth discussion and critical analysis. The package features a single-volume textbook with ample musical examples and source readings from the time period, and a companion website with links to online audio content and full scores of major works under study.

My approach to writing the textbook is one that emphasizes the meaning of music, to its performers, composers, patrons, and present-day audiences. The interest shifts from looking for historical causation—why something happened—to studying the meaning of an event. What was the impact of the first performance of Claudio Monteverdi's opera *Orfeo*? What did it mean for the reputation of its patron? And for the guests and diplomats in attendance at the north-Italian court of Mantua? Such an approach is especially important for it supports an instructional environment that is responsive to diverse learning styles and background experiences. Woven throughout the textbook are illustrations that reinforce the stories of Baroque music visually by giving students access to paintings and engravings of composers and musicians. Images of title pages and notation from period music books bring the world of Baroque music-making a bit closer to college and university students. The timeline of major cultural, historical, musical, and political events provides both a reference tool and a framework for what follows. Entries for a given year, such as 1725, range from the founding of the *Concerts Spirituels* series in Paris, to Vivaldi's *The Four Seasons*, to the huge population growth in China.

Features

- An interdisciplinary approach that balances detailed analysis of specific pieces of music and broader historical overview and relevance
- Engaging illustrations and historical documents that position musical works and events in their cultural context
- Extensive musical examples that show the melodic, textural, harmonic, and structural features of Baroque music and enhance the utility of the textbook for undergraduate and graduate music majors
- A global perspective with a chapter on music in the Americas
- Emphasis on performance practices in the textbook and companion website, which features performance tips for major works
- Student-learning aids such as a timeline of key musical, artistic, political, and historical events, and a glossary
- Convenience: listen when and where you want, to top performances of Baroque music from the companion website with links to audio content and music scores

Organization

The main form of organization is both chronological and idea-oriented to encourage links across genres, historical concepts, and cultural themes in the Baroque period. The opening two chapters familiarize students with key concepts and materials that are essential to an understanding of Baroque music and culture. Chapter 1 addresses the fundamental questions: What is Baroque music? How does a cultural approach illuminate our understanding of Baroque music? Students get an overview of the geopolitical situation of early modern Europe and how geopolitics impacted the mobility of musicians and the transfer of cultural ideas across regions. Issues of performance are raised throughout the book, but demand special treatment in the introductory chapters. Chapter 1 introduces students to the complexities of notation, improvisation, and performance conventions in the Baroque period. Print technology is explored both as a conduit for the circulation of music, and for the potential challenges it brings for the interpretation of Baroque music. Chapter 2 opens with a discussion of musical rhetoric and the role of the performer, likened to an orator, in articulating the structure and emotional content of musical works.

The layout follows a chronological approach that lends coherence to the narrative, yet offers opportunities for thematic-based discussions and the reinforcement of central concepts and ideas that instructors want to impart on the period as a whole. Part One comprises Chapters which address dramatic, sacred, and instrumental music up to the end of the Thirty Years' War (1618). Part Two (Chapters) addresses secular and sacred music of the second half of the seventeenth century with a chapter each on opera in Italy, the French court under Louis XIV, and Restoration England. Chapters comprise Part Three and concentrate on music from the first half of the eighteenth century, including a wide range of dramatic music, the concerto, and the pivotal composer and organist, Johann Sebastian Bach. Part Four (Chapter 12) extends the book's reach beyond Europe by adopting a global view that assesses the role of music in European efforts to colonize and convert the Americas.

Music in the Baroque World: History, Culture, Performance tells stories of local traditions, cultural exchange, performance trends, and artistic mixing. It illuminates representative works through the lens of politics, visual arts, theology, print culture, gender, commerce, and cultural influence.

Source Documents

Central to *Music in the Baroque World* are readings drawn from letters, political records, music books, business contracts, and religious works that illustrate musical culture in the broad sense. My choice of documents balances geographic and linguistic regions, amateur, domestic, and professional repertories, vocal and instrumental genres, modes of patronage, and issues of music theory, performance, and commerce. The selection expands and complements the collections by Piero Weiss and Richard Taruskin in *Music in the Western World: A History in Documents* (2nd ed., Independence, KY: Cengage Learning, 2007) and *Strunk's Source Readings in Music History* (revised edition, ed. Leo Treitler, New York: Norton, 1998).

Online Resources

www.routledge.com/cw/lewis

The companion website is a vital part of *Music in the Baroque World*. The website connects all music analyzed in the textbook with recordings and scores. The website houses links to fifty-three tracks from Spotify and iTunes (with option to download). The recordings are chosen on the basis of their historical and artistic importance and feature top performers of early music. Audio files are accompanied by full scores linked from the companion website. Performance tips offer advice on how to interpret Baroque music, including information on ornamentation and choice of instruments.

Acknowledgments

I extend sincere thanks and appreciation to the many people who helped me see this book to its completion. Routledge Music Acquisitions Editor Constance Ditzel approached me with the idea of writing a textbook on Baroque music, and guided me through its development and completion. Routledge embarked on an extensive review process and I thank the anonymous reviewers for their candid feedback and critique, which improved the textbook in many ways, including the addition of more musical examples and analysis and the priority given to issues of performance. I thank the editorial team of Denny Tek, Aurora Montgomery, and Denise File for their careful review of the manuscript and attention to detail, in addition to Mhairi Bennett the production editor

The University of Victoria provided a wonderful workplace with funding to support assistance with research, writing, and manuscript production. To my students, I thank you for inspiring me with your thoughtful questions and observations about Baroque music and culture. Student research assistants Konstantin Bozhinov, Michael Dias, and Bradley Pickard directly assisted with musical examples, copyright permissions, and the companion website, respectively. My thanks to graduate research assistant Rena Roussin for her assistance with the final stages of manuscript preparation. I thank David Foley for transcribing the many musical examples that appear in the textbook. Music and reference librarian, William Blair, and his team at the University of Victoria offered constant support and invaluable assistance at all junctures of my research and writing. Elissa Poole deserves special thanks as my primary research assistant and editor. Her insight into Baroque music has informed and improved the book in countless ways. Staff and colleagues in the School of Music at the University of Victoria assisted me at various points, and offer ongoing support and inspiration.

Finally, I thank my family for their love and support and especially my children, Zachary and Abigail, for making life so enjoyable and rewarding.

Susan Lewis
Victoria, BC, Canada April 2015

1   What Is Baroque Music?

Western European musicians in 1700 would have been surprised to discover that the age in which they lived would eventually be known as the Baroque, and that this term would be applied to a stretch of time they would have considered so multifarious, so full of change and contradiction, as to make the idea of it falling under a single rubric an absurdity.

Unlike many historical terms that have been invented by scholars after the fact, the term *baroque* was applied to music as early as 1733. But that is almost the end of the age it describes, a 150-year period from approximately 1600 to 1750. Moreover, for eighteenth-century commentators, *baroque* was always a derogatory term. Anything considered grotesque, bizarre, excessive, or preposterous—whether it was a piece of music, a poem, a painting, or a building—was labelled *baroque*. To call an entire era "Baroque" would not have been a compliment.

Certainly the visual arts of the Baroque period—home to master painters Caravaggio, Rubens, and Rembrandt, the sculptor and set designer Bernini, and architects Borromini and Wren—tended to extravagance and excess. Churches from Rome to Krakow, in Poland, were outfitted with opulent ornaments, gilded *putti* or marble detail, dramatic contrasts of light-and-shade (*chiaroscuro* effects), and large ceiling frescoes featuring *trompe l'oeil* images rendered in so realistic a fashion that they tricked the eye into seeing what was depicted in three dimensions. Marian columns became a fashionable addition to church streetscapes and a vital display of public faith in Catholic Europe. One of the earliest is in the Piazza Santa Maria Maggiore in Rome, which features a column from the ancient Roman Basilica of Constantine that was crowned in 1614 with a bronze statue honoring the Virgin and Child. Ornate versions of this column were erected in Munich, Prague, and Vienna, as a symbol of gratitude to the Virgin for her aid in ending plague or safeguarding the city from invasion or destruction during the Thirty Years' War (1618–48).

In one of the earliest applications of the term *baroque* to music, a reviewer of Jean-Philippe Rameau's opera *Hippolyte et Aricie* (1733) complains of its extravagant modulations, excessive repetitions, and whimsical metrical changes. The writer labels the opera *baroque*. Similarly, Jean-Jacques Rousseau's *Dictionary of Music* (1778) defined *baroque* music as dissonant, unnatural, and having sudden changes in tempo and harmony. It is worth noting, however, that Rameau's opera dates from the latter years of the Baroque era. The writer may be judging Rameau's music by a standard that is already out of date; or he—like Rousseau—may be writing from the perspective of a new generation whose aesthetic preferences lie with the emerging, Classical style (another term that is equally convenient but imprecise).

Early historians continued to wind that negative thread through their writings on the Baroque period. The Swiss historian, Jacob Burckhard, who used *baroque* as both a stylistic-historical term and as a qualitative term, is a good example. In 1855, Burckhard—who would have had no trouble finding writers at the beginning of the seventeenth century who agreed with him—described the Baroque as the Renaissance "gone wild."

From the early twentieth century onward, however, historians generally retreated from such pejorative judgments. The most influential application of the term *baroque* to music came from German musicologist Friedrich Blume (1893–1975). Blume believed that Baroque music was part of a larger Baroque *Zeitgeist* or spirit of the times. His "Fitness and Need of the Word 'Baroque' in Music History" (Document 1) was

Figure 1.1 The piazza and basilica of Santa Maria Maggiore, Rome.

one of his most important writings to appear in *Die Musik in Geschichte und Gegenwart* (Music in History and the Present), a comprehensive music dictionary of 9,414 articles under Blume's editorship. Blume raised fundamental questions about how we *do* history, and about the implications and validity of borrowing terms from other arts:

> All future music historiography will be faced with the choice of either setting up purely musical style-categories labelled in purely musical terms that do indeed stand unequivocally for specific musical matter but remain dissociated from the intellectual ambiance and origin of these styles and intelligible only to the professional musician, or using to characterize its own style-periods and style-forms terms that are at the same time applicable in other fields and familiar to the non-musician also, even though because of this they suffer from a certain ambiguity. (Document 1)

For Blume, the advantages of *baroque* music outweighed the disadvantages of borrowed terminology.

It remains fair to ask: Why use the term now? Is it merely a convenience or are there common denominators that run through the art, music, literature, and architecture of this period that testify to an overarching unity of purpose?

Indeed the Baroque period does manifest a central code of aesthetics. It placed value on abundance, pleasure, variety, and the emulation of past masters. It also embraced the fundamental assumption that composers, artists, sculptors, architects, painters, and performers could (and ought to) influence the emotions of the audience, whether those emotions were in the service of the church, the state, an individual patron, or society at large. But we might also note that the means of swaying the audience was through representing an emotion: The viewers, or listeners, were not expected to be swept away by their feelings. Rather, emotions were objectified; one experienced them as states, and they were thus subject to rationalization and control—a very different way of looking at art and emotion than what one finds in the Romantic era, for instance.

In music, we mark the start of the Baroque period with a number of important innovations: the invention of opera, the transformation of the polyphonic madrigal into solo and ensemble settings with instruments, the rise of solo singing, and a greater focus on natural declamation and expressing the meaning of the words. We see as well a shift towards chordal harmony, a freer treatment of dissonance, and a gradual disintegration of the modal system as composers begin to understand and exploit harmonic progressions in terms of what we call functional harmony. At the time, these changes appeared so radical that they incited heated debates. The madrigals of Claudio Monteverdi (1567–1643), a young composer working at the ducal court in Mantua at the beginning of the seventeenth century, were especially contentious in the way they challenged conventional compositional practice, particularly as it pertained to dissonance. His madrigal "Cruda Amarilli" (Cruel Amaryllis) was immediately understood as a standard bearer for the new style. In it, Monteverdi deliberately wrote dissonant clashes between the soprano and bass to portray the cruelty of Amaryllis, whose bitterness is reflected in her very name (the Italian *amare* can mean either bitterness or love). He also left dissonances unresolved at cadences—a breach of harmonic protocol no Renaissance composer would have dared.

Such departures from standard practice so outraged the conservative theorist Giovanni Maria Artusi (1540–1613) that he protested against Monteverdi's music in a series of pamphlets published to discredit the young composer. Monteverdi fought back with a rebuttal, released through his brother Giulio, and published as a preface to the composer's Fifth Book of madrigals (1605) and, in expanded form, the *Scherzi musicali* (1607). Here, the Monteverdis argue that the text was paramount: "in this kind of music, it is his goal to make the words the mistress of the harmony and not its servant, and it is from this point of view that his work should be judged."[1] Textual meaning could only be captured by using more expressive harmonies, regardless of rules of counterpoint and voice leading. To distinguish the old style from the new, Monteverdi coined the terms first and second practice. The first practice referred to music that made "the harmony the mistress of the words," thereby following stylistic norms of the Renaissance period. The second practice referred to music governed by the text: harmony "becomes the servant of the words."[2] The public nature of the dispute, and the obvious awareness that the earlier style was under siege by the modern, reinforces the general acceptance among musical scholars for starting the Baroque period around 1600.

When did the Baroque period end? As with those eras labelled Medieval, Renaissance, and Classical, the Baroque period did not end at a clearly demarcated point. New and old overlapped, and styles lasted longer in some regions than others. Italy, for instance, quickly adopted the concerto styles of Antonio Vivaldi (1678–1741) in the eighteenth century, while English composers continued to enjoy concertos based on earlier models by Arcangelo Corelli (1653–1713). Similarly, the dense, polyphonic fabric of German contrapuntalists like Johann Sebastian Bach (1685–1750) overlapped with a new aesthetic that privileged melody and balanced phrasing. Issues of stylistic overlap and longevity were only heightened in the Americas, where European colonialism brought concerted and operatic idioms to Mexico in the early eighteenth century, decades after the genres' induction on the Continent. Even as late as 1762, Christoph Willibald Gluck's opera *Orfeo ed Euridice* was essentially a reaction to Baroque style, which survived in the institution of

Example 1.1 Monteverdi, "Cruda Amarilli," mm. 1–14.

opera seria long after the *galant* had made serious headway in lighter forms of opera. But Gluck's reform was also a return to opera's roots. In sharp contrast to the elaborate but dramatically static *da capo* arias (ABA form) that dominated Baroque stages in the decades around 1700, Gluck's simpler, less flamboyant music attempted to emulate the union of poetry and music the creators of opera at the beginning of the Baroque era had idealized as the ancient Greek theatrical practice.

Geopolitics and Musical Style

The political and religious landscape of Baroque Europe was complicated and diverse, with multiple and competing models of governance. This situation was only enhanced when European powers embarked on a vast program of overseas colonization during the Baroque period, one that had profound impacts on the world economy and population.

Italy was the undisputed stronghold of Catholicism, which united a political hodgepodge of courts, city-states, foreign-held territories and the Papacy, with Rome at its center and the Pope at its head. Among the independent territories, the Republic of Venice enjoyed the greatest prominence, offering a unique governing model that was famous across Europe for its innovative approach to democracy. A similar range of political models characterized German-speaking lands, although there was far less agreement in religious affiliation.

The German-speaking lands were a political and religious mosaic of Lutheran, Calvinist, and Catholic dukedoms, princedoms, electorates, and free imperial cities. The region was held together under a nominal allegiance to the "Holy Roman Empire of the German Nation," a territorial affiliation that was born with the coronation of the Frankish King Charlemagne as Roman emperor in 800 and lasted until the aftermath of the Napoleonic Wars in 1806. Dynastic marriages and religious tolerance enhanced regional stability until controversy over succession erupted upon the death of Emperor Matthias (ruled 1612–19), who had no heir. The crisis sparked the Thirty Years' War (1618–48), a bitter series of conflicts that drained the population and left many towns and cities in turmoil. France, Spain, Sweden, and Denmark joined the dispute in an effort to gain territory and wealth. The conflict finally ended with the signing of the Peace of Westphalia on October 24, 1648; the treaty granted the principle of *cuius regio, eius religio*: "Whoever rules the territory determines the religion."

Under Louis XIV (1638–1715), France strengthened its monarchy and secured its position as a Catholic power in the Baroque period. Across the Channel, England underwent immense political, social, and religious change, overturning the political instability of the first half of the seventeenth century with the Restoration of the Stuart monarchy in 1660; by the end of the Seven Years' War (1763) England was the leading state power. The most important political change for Spain, a vast territory that included Portugal, the southern Netherlands, and the kingdoms of Sardinia, Sicily, and Naples, was the transfer from Habsburg to Bourbon rule. With no offspring, Spanish king Charles II (ruled 1665–1700) willed his inheritance to Philip (1683–1746), grandson of Maria Teresa and Louis XIV.

Europe's geopolitical landscape had a direct impact on the cultivation of music and culture during the Baroque period. Political crisis and instability brought with them reductions in musical personnel in England and parts of Germany during the Thirty Years' War; in France, however, where musical establishments were considered part of the cultural machinery designed to strengthen the monarchy, they grew. Pockets of regional styles coexisted with international trends that swept across national, linguistic, and religious boundaries. The Catholic courts of Salzburg, Vienna, and Munich had especially close ties with Venice and Rome, where rulers sent agents to recruit the best singers and artists. Conflicts over religion and territory at times strengthened and at other times weakened cultural ties and musical migration. A good example of the former is the strong network of Lutheran courts operating in northern Europe. Bound by ties of marriage and religion, the Lutheran courts of northern Germany exchanged musicians with the court of King Christian IV of Denmark in the first half of the seventeenth century. Heinrich Schütz (1585–1672), chapel master at the electoral court of Dresden, traveled to Copenhagen to participate in the wedding festivities for Crown Prince Christian in 1634 and may have introduced Italian operatic singing to the far north during this visit. Musical practices in England at times worked independently of Continental influence but were at other times deeply engaged with European styles, whether in emulation or in an effort to mark a distinctly English path.

Europe's geopolitical situation ensured a large pool of competing patrons: courts, churches, town councils, and cities. But why, despite the continual wars, religious tension, and the challenges of daily living, did patrons invest so heavily in music? In fact, periods of political and religious tension may have fuelled patronage. Art, whether it was music, theater, paintings, visual arts, or architecture, offered ruling powers a means of advertising not only their wealth and good taste, but the fact that theirs was a state secure enough to provide the leisure time for enjoying art. Cultural display was thus akin to modern-day public relations. Glorifying the ruler was the central strategy for artistic patronage. Then as now, glory was best bestowed through brilliant spectacle and lasting tributes.

By the eighteenth century, patterns of musical migration and competition forged with political and emerging nationalistic sentiments to create distinct and easily recognized musical profiles that are commonly referred to as national styles. An emblem of French style, for instance, was the stately overture that originated at the French court of Louis XIV, which was known and imitated across Europe by Johann Sebastian Bach, George Frideric Handel (1685–1757), and Georg Philipp Telemann (1681–1767). Similarly, dense counterpoint came to be associated with German composers, particularly in the organ music of Dietrich Buxtehude (*ca.* 1637–1707) and Bach, while Italian music was praised for its melodiousness.

Musicians recognized and even debated the merits of national styles. The strongest clash came between proponents of the French and Italian styles, a battle waged off and on in print for decades. French cultural commentator Charles de Saint-Évremond (1613–1703) claimed that "the expressiveness of the Italians is false or at least exaggerated. . . . As to the manner of singing . . . no nation can rival ours."[3] This did not stop François Couperin (1668–1733) from combining the French and Italian styles to create a sophisticated stylistic hybrid in *Les goûts réunis* (The Styles Reunited, 1724). In the preface to the collection, Couperin diplomatically asserts his own neutrality, stating, "The Italian and the French styles have for a long time shared the Republic of Music in France. For myself, I have always highly regarded the things which merited esteem, without considering either composer or nation."[4] In his influential treatise, *Versuch einer Anweisung der Flöte Traversiere zu spielen* (On Playing the Flute, 1752), German theorist and composer Johann Quantz (1697–1773) further acknowledged such stylistic amalgamation, claiming for his homeland, and for the court of Frederick the Great in Berlin in particular, a preeminent role in the union of national styles.

Employment Opportunities

What professional options were available to Baroque musicians? The typical career trajectory for a Baroque musician was early training in the hometown, a study trip or foreign travel, and a series of court or church positions. For musicians, court employment offered relative job security, the chance to compose in a variety of genres and styles—from church to chamber to opera—and a network of artists, poets, and musicians with whom to collaborate. Job contracts specified the duties and responsibilities of court musicians, who provided music for meals, festivals, celebrations, leisure, dancing, worship, and outdoor events. These contracts also shed light on a musician's life, providing information about status and reputation, the strategies used to obtain and improve working conditions, and even how the music was to be performed.

The contract for Christoph Bernhard (1628–92) for the position of vice chapel master at the court of the Elector of Saxony in Dresden is a good example. Bernhard, a pupil of Heinrich Schütz (1585–1672), was first hired by the court as an alto and as singing instructor to the choirboys in 1649. His letters to Elector Johann Georg I show his increasing frustration at the preferential treatment of Italian musicians at court and his desire to leave his post. Bernhard's appointment as vice chapel master in 1655 may have been an effort to appease him (Document 2). Certainly he must have considered himself next in line for the post of chapel master, which became vacant in 1663. But when the job went to the Italian singer Paranda, Bernhard left his post to take a job in Hamburg as cantor of the Johannisschule. This type of musical migration—no doubt fuelled by a desire for status as well as career advancement—typified the hiring and firing of musicians in the Baroque period.

Churches employed singers, composers, and instrumentalists to lend structure and splendor to religious music. Large churches had a choir of singers and instrumentalists under the direction of a chapel master. Such groups comprised male singers (or female singers in convents), an organ, and additional instruments as the prestige of the church, court chapel, or setting demanded. The Basilica of St. Mark's in Venice, which hired eminent composers like Claudio Monteverdi and Francesco Cavalli (1602–76) for the post of chapel master, employed as many as seventy musicians in the eighteenth century. Smaller churches, such as those in Bologna, hired a string band led by a concert master, normally the principal violinist. In 1663, the Basilica of San Petronio in Bologna employed sixteen singers and twelve instrumentalists, a total of twenty-eight musicians. Even very modest churches hired an organist and a small choir that could perform works such as *Cento concerti ecclesiastici* (One Hundred Sacred Concertos, 1602), a collection of sacred music for one to several singers with keyboard by Lodovico Viadana (*ca.* 1560–1627).

Towns and cities hired musicians to perform a wide range of practical functions. Major commercial centers in German-speaking lands employed a town band for civic events and private ceremonies such as weddings. Civic governments hired professional musicians, known in German-speaking lands as *Stadtpfeifer*, whose roles might include tower duty, or serving as organist, school teacher, instrument maker, or concert director, depending upon the size of the town and its governing structure (court, imperial city, small town, or university town). As competition from freelance musicians encroached on their employment, *Stadtpfeifer* from northern and central Germany formed a musicians' union in 1653, with statutes ratified by Emperor Ferdinand III. The city cantor *(Stadtkantor)* organized music at all the main churches and was responsible for the town's musical life that came under the jurisdiction of the town council. The Hamburg cantor coordinated music for the city's five parish churches, which were serviced by four organists, from eight to ten singers, and, when needed, instrumentalists from the *Stadtpfeifer*. The city cantor taught at the Latin school and directed music at all major civic and religious events. The most famous city cantor of the Baroque period was Johann Sebastian Bach, who held the post of cantor at the St. Thomas School and civic director of music in Leipzig from 1723 until his death in 1750.

The Baroque period saw a growing demand for musicians' services in homes, salons, and concert series. Florentine patrons Giovanni de'Bardi (1534–1612) and Jacopo Corsi (1561–1602) employed Giulio Caccini (1551–1618) and Jacopo Peri (1561–1633) to sing at their gatherings, where poets, intellectuals, and musicians discussed ancient Greek music and experimented with operatic style. In a similar vein, the city of Rome was home to many wealthy aristocratic families that were active patrons of the arts. Most prominent was Queen Christina of Sweden, who, during her periods of self-imposed exile, hosted regular *conversazioni* in her palace for learned audiences who savored the display of erudition and skill. The salon culture continued after her death in meetings of the Arcadian Academy, a group of poets and musicians, founded in 1690, whose members shared a passion for pastoral love poetry ripe for musical setting.

Concerts of instrumental music also first appeared in the Baroque period. The *Abendmusik* organ concerts in the north German town of Lübeck in the 1620s and 1630s are early examples of concerts in which instrumental music took the center stage rather than serving an accompanimental role. The Collegium Musicum in Hamburg, founded in 1660, gave public concerts every week that featured up to fifty musicians performing fashionable music from Italy and Germany. England proved a prime ground for the development of public concerts; the closure of theaters under Puritan influence left non-theatrical music relatively free from governmental control. Violinist and flageolet player John Banister (1624/5–1679) promoted a series of concerts in London newspapers in the 1670s that featured an array of local musicians, including himself on the flageolet (a small flute that became popular in London in the second half of the seventeenth century).

Music for a paying public appeared on a grand scale with commercial opera. Opera for ticket buyers started in Venice in 1637 and its subsequent growth in the 1640s increased demand for professional troupes and a range of occupations, including dancers, machinists, poets, costume designers, instrumentalists, set designers, and entrepreneurs (Chapter 6). Commercial opera took hold across Europe, with London, Paris, and Hamburg emerging as established centers for the genre in the late Baroque (Chapter 9). As the public for opera and concerts grew and diversified, there was a greater role for cultural critics to play, and commentators became important arbiters of Baroque taste.

The emergence of public concerts and opera was due, in part, to a growing appreciation for the solo performer. The performer grew in status during the Baroque period. For the first time in history, it was possible for a singer to make a career as a freelance artist. This phenomenon was seen first in opera. The success of Italian Baroque opera was indebted to specific singers, to the voices of Francesco Rasi, who sang the title role in Monteverdi's *Orfeo*, for example, and Anna Renzi, who performed the role of Ottavia to great acclaim in Monteverdi's *L'incoronazione di Poppea* (The Coronation of Poppea, 1643). The importance of the singers in ensuring the success of an opera became more pronounced with commercial opera, and top singers regularly earned more than librettists and composers. The popularity of the singers also affected the structure of the operas: Arias, embellished with exuberant repeats, increased in number in direct response to audience demand. Singers were the Baroque era's celebrities, even inspiring outright mania in the case of the castrato Carlo Broschi (1705–82, Fig. 1.2). Known by his stage name, Farinelli, he established his career on the operatic stages of Rome, Naples, Venice, and Milan, and he dominated the London stage in the 1730s. According to *The Daily Post* (1737), the Queen of Spain pleaded with Farinelli to come to Madrid in the hopes that his singing would cure the depressed King Philip V. Farinelli complied, serenading the king every night until the ruler's death in 1746.

Though less prominent than singers, instrumentalists were attracting more attention, too. English lutenist John Dowland (1563–1626) had a strong following outside his native England; in 1599 King Christian IV secured him for 500 daler, making Dowland one of the highest paid servants at the Danish court. Arcangelo Corelli made his career entirely as a composer of instrumental music (amazingly, he left no vocal works in this operatic age), and his Opus 1 sonatas went through thirty-nine editions between 1681 and 1790.

Corelli's Opus 5 surpassed even that, and there were at least forty-two editions circulating within Europe by 1800. The period saw the continuation of musical dynasties: families of instrumentalists who passed down the profession from generation to generation. Prominent examples from across Europe include the Couperins in France, the Purcells in England, and the Neusidler and Bach families in Germany.

The instrumentalist's rise in status was made possible, in part, by a strong industry of instrument builders and craftsmen and their many improvements to the instruments. Instrument building, too, passed from generation to generation in family businesses—the Stradivari violin makers in Cremona, in northern Italy, for example. Tremendous improvements to the violin were made at the hands of Antonio Stradivari (1644–1737), whose violins were known for their beauty, tonal quality, and fine workmanship. From about 1575 until 1675, the Ruckers family in Antwerp built harpsichords and virginals whose designs influenced keyboard manufacturing for the entire Baroque period (they remain important models for modern replicas). French organ builders Thierry and Clicquot solidified the reputation of Paris as a major center for organ building from the early decades of the seventeenth century until the nineteenth century. The Hotteterre family, also in France, were responsible for revolutionary improvements in wind instruments.

The Baroque period saw the continued professionalization of the music industry and greater appreciation for expertise and specialization. These trends can be seen in the career of Giovanni Rovetta (1595/7–1668).

Figure 1.2 Portrait of Carlo Brioschi, known as Farinelli (Andria, 1705–Bologna, 1782).

Rovetta started out as an instrumentalist at St. Mark's Basilica in Venice in 1614. In the preface to his 1626 collection of concerted motets, Rovetta makes a special attempt to convince the reader that even if he is better known as an instrumentalist, he is still a valid candidate for a composing position. Indeed he published his motets to prove just how good a composer he was. Successful in his application, Rovetta accepted a permanent post as vice chapel master on November 22, 1627. Rovetta's defensive tone suggests the growing degree of specialization within the music world as performers, instrumentalists, and composers firmly establish professional identities.

The working conditions of composers, musicians, poets, and performers had a direct impact on their livelihood, mobility, and contact with fellow artists. From a historical perspective, the social status of musicians in the Baroque period strengthened trends seen from about 1500. Patronage institutions remained intact: courts, churches, and civic councils formed the mainstay of employment options. But newer developments in music and technology, from music printing to the emergence of the virtuosic solo performer, opened up exciting new avenues for musicians and entrepreneurs.

Music Printing

The invention of music printing in 1501 made the circulation of music a profit-bearing initiative that created many jobs along the chain, from the composer who produced the music to the client who purchased it. Many composers, Orlande de Lassus (1532–94), Johann Hermann Schein (1586–1630), and Henry Purcell (1659–95), for instance, developed close relationships with printing houses and directly oversaw the printing of their music. Music printing was a complex task—there were staffs to position, words to align

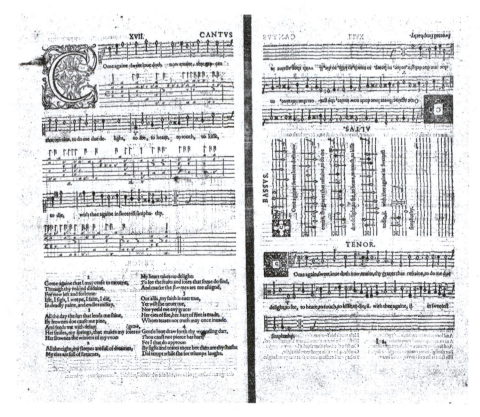

Figure 1.3 John Dowland, "Come Again," *The Firste Booke of Songes*. London, 1600.

under the correct notes, accidentals, symbols and other performance indications to add—and it involved numerous craftsmen, from the composer or engraver who copied the music onto paper to the printer who printed it and the proof-reader or editor who made corrections.

Some publications presented particular challenges. In repertories like the lute song, for example, it was fashionable to print music for four different players as a single book. This surely complicated the typesetting process, and it may have led to errors and stop-press corrections. "Come Again" by John Dowland, England's most famous lutenist and composer in the years around 1600, required the typesetter to coordinate notation, words, and lute tablature for four performers (Fig. 1.3).

This repertory is a good example of technology's effort to accommodate a social and performance desiderata: positioning a group of players closely together so they can play from a single book.

Once a book was printed, it had to be marketed and sold to as many buyers as possible. Such activity was undertaken either by the printer or a separate publisher who specialized in distributing books. One strategy undertaken by printers, publishers, or professional editors was to compile music by different composers, in various styles and genres, and to market it as an anthology. Titles refer to musical flowers, gardens, and banquets; they even specifically name "variety," as in Robert Dowland's *Varietie of Lute Lessons* (1610), reminding us that pleasure and variety were important aesthetic attributes of the Baroque period. The publications were indeed attractive to a wide public: Anthologies increased in popularity in the decades around 1600 and remained an effective means of circulating music throughout the Baroque period.

Publishers advertised music in catalogues and journals, selling it in store fronts, at book fairs in Frankfurt and Leipzig, and through agents. Lawyers dealt with disputes that arose between composers, printers, and publishers over jurisdiction (who could print what and where), authors' rights, and fees. At the final stage of the process came the clients who bought the music books: musicians, teachers, students, elites, nobles, churches, schools, and courts. In addition to the standing demand for music by students, professional musicians, and amateur players, the Baroque period saw the emergence of an elite class that bought books—or art, coins, and other cultural objects—to enhance their private collections and libraries. Music was included in the collecting mania. For example, the library of Duke August the Younger (1579–1666) forms the core of the present Herzog August Bibliothek in Wolfenbüttel, Germany.

Interpreting Baroque Music Scores

Performance traditions are perhaps the largest variable when it comes to answering the question, "What did Baroque music sound like?" The answer is more complicated than a score might suggest. It was common, for instance, for music to be revised or rewritten to suit different performers and listeners. Iconic works such as Monteverdi's *L'incoronazione di Poppea* survive in multiple versions with significant differences in text and music. We also find differences between the manuscripts and printed editions of the same music that relate to where they were copied or printed and when. Nor do scores always include the many performance conventions that were taken for granted at the time and thus were never written down. Not only were ornaments often left to the discretion of the performer, but the type of ornamentation varied from place to place; indeed, it was one of the fundamental characteristics that distinguished one national style from another. France, for instance, had a distinct vocabulary of ornaments (usually indicated with small symbols). Discussions of these ornaments (called *agréments*) abound, from Bénigne de Bacilly's (1668) wonderfully nuanced discussion of ornaments in vocal music to the many tables published in the decades around 1700, especially in keyboard works, and they do not agree on all the particulars. The preface to Jean Jean Henry D'Anglebert's *Pièces de clavecin* alone includes a table of twenty-nine ornaments that explains the many ornament signs found in his keyboard works (Chapter 7, Figure 7.9). His preface would be of little use, however, for music composed in Italy, or even composed in France fifty years earlier.

Various rhythmic practices were also aligned to specific national styles. Particular to the French style as it was consolidated during the reign of Louis XIV are the overdotted rhythms associated with French overtures. Played exactly as notated, one of Lully's opera overtures sounds stiff and banal; interpret the dotted rhythms as Lully would have expected, however, and the music has more panache and more sparkle. *Notes inégales* (unequal notes) are another unwritten French convention: Here, the practice of giving notes moving by step a slightly dotted or lilting rhythm can turn a stodgy minuet into a graceful one.

Vocal scores, such as opera, also present myriad unwritten demands. Singers would automatically have known to deliver recitative with a certain amount of rhythmic freedom, to embellish the repeats in a da capo aria, or to improvise a cadenza (a display of vocal virtuosity) at a fermata or important cadence. In fact, writing that down would have only gotten in the singer's way. A Baroque score is often only a skeletal representation of what was heard in performance.

The performance of the *basso continuo*—a type of quasi-improvised accompaniment in which the bass line is provided with figures (numbers, flats and sharps) written above or below the relevant note that tell the player what harmony is needed to make the correct realization—is a case in point. Basso continuo was arguably the most important innovation at the start of the Baroque period, and it was present in opera and accompanied solo songs, concertos, oratorios, sonatas, and cantatas throughout the period and to the end of the eighteenth century. Some composers were meticulous about indicating each interval above the bass; other composers, especially in the early Baroque, left the figures out altogether and expected the performer to determine the harmony from the other parts. Viadana's *Cento concerti ecclesiastici*, a collection of sacred concertos for a few voices, is one of the earliest scores with continuo. With or without figures, continuo realization was largely an improvised art and could thus accommodate different performers and performing situations; the bass line provided only the scaffolding for the harmonies, while the voicing of the chords and sometimes even the harmonies themselves were left to the performer, along with the rhythm, certain conventions in interpreting the cadences, and whether or not to arpeggiate (play the notes in a series rather than simultaneously) or repeat the chords.

The choice of the continuo instruments also had to be compatible with the principles of stylistic decorum: Context, such as whether the music was sacred or secular or in a chamber or theatrical setting, determined the size and composition of the continuo group. In *Del sonare sopra 'l basso* (On Playing upon the Thoroughbass, 1607), Agostino Agazzari (1578–1640) divided instruments into chordal ones (instruments of foundation), such as the organ, harpsichord, chitarrone, theorbo, or lute, that play or support all voices or parts of a work; and ornamental or single-line instruments, such as the violin. Michael Praetorius (*ca.* 1570–1621) retained this distinction in his influential treatise, *De Organographia* (On Musical Instruments, 1619). Any chordal instrument might be utilized in the continuo group, depending upon the situation, along with any instrument that could provide or double the bass line. The instrument of choice for accompanying solo song in the early Baroque period was the theorbo, an extended lute with longer bass strings. Artist Gerard Ter Borch included a double neck theorbo in his painting of an idyllic domestic music-making scene, along with an open music book and a singer dressed in rich fabrics that convey her stature (see book cover). Church settings suggested just organ for continuo, but spectacular theatrical events demanded a large continuo group. In *Orfeo*, for example, Monteverdi specified a continuo group of two harpsichords, two pipe organs, two or three chitarrone, a double harp, three bass *violas da gamba*, and a small reed organ.

Lodovico Viadana, the first to actually use the term basso continuo, remains the most authoritative source on how to perform it at this time. Viadana prefaced his *Cento concerti ecclesiastici . . . con il basso continuo* with twelve rules for continuo players. These mix general aesthetic principles, such as the importance of singing tastefully, with practical advice. Viadana starts with a general admonition against singers ornamenting to the score: "Concertos of this kind must be sung with refinement, discretion, and elegance, using accents with reason and embellishments (*passaggi*) with moderation and in their proper place: above all, not adding anything beyond what is printed in them."[5] By contrast, Viadana gave organists much more freedom. Point three advises that "The organist should first cast an eye over the concerto which is to be sung, since, by understanding the nature of the music, he will always execute the accompaniments better."[6] As Viadana notes, there was much left to the interpretive and creative skill of the organist:

(5) When a concerto begins after the manner of a fugue, the organist begins also with a single note, and, on the entry of the several parts, it is at his discretion to accompany them as he pleases.[7]

Discrepancies between scores; ambiguities in our understanding of ornamentation, time signatures and tempo words; and divergent local practices (including how much some of the more prevalent conventions might apply outside of their home territory) remain vital areas of research in the field of historical performance practice, often called period performance. By examining treatises and prefaces in which composers describe how to play their music, and by combing libraries and archives for descriptions of specific performances and general writings from the period, scholars and performers have assembled a picture of Baroque performance that is very different from the one we had fifty years ago. But there are still many gaps.

Even the sound of Baroque music can surprise the modern ear. The clarity and vivid colors of historical instruments (gut strings and differently shaped bows, one-keyed wooden flutes, brass mouthpieces with small bores); the purity of boys' voices in Bach's choral works; the differences in pitch in various regions (French pitch, for example, was as much as a whole tone lower than modern pitch, while Italian pitch was often higher); non-equal tuning systems, which can give a piece in F minor a significantly different character from one in B minor; ideals of vocal timbre and projection that are vastly different from today's voluptuous voices; and a less consistently applied vibrato: All of these change the way we hear and experience Baroque music.

Documents

Document 1. From *Renaissance and Baroque Music: A Comprehensive Survey* by Friedrich Blume, translated by M.D. Herter. New York: W.W. Norton. Copyright © 1967 by W.W. Norton & Company, Inc. Used by permission of W.W. Norton & Company, Inc.

Fitness and Need of the Word "Baroque" in Music History

Despite a profound similarity in the psycho-spiritual bases out of which the stylistic forms and expressions of the so-called "Baroque" age grew in all the arts, it may appear questionable whether purely as a matter of terminology it is suitable or necessary to introduce into the history of music this designation or others taken over from the plastic arts (like "Gothic," say) or from the history of literature (like "Romantic") on the assumption that they are scientifically valid classifications—that is, style-categories of precisely definable content. Certain it is that music would be perfectly capable of suggesting words from the vocabulary of its own terminology that could characterize a style period with adequate clarity, as happened successfully with, for example, the generally accepted concept *ars nova*. Yet it will always be difficult to find a nomenclature for styles in music history that would be broad enough not to bog down in merely technical designations (as in Riemann's *Handbuch der Musikgeschichte*) and definite enough not to get lost in the ambiguity of general categories like "Classic" and "Renaissance." That music historiography today has developed most of the terminology for its classifications not from the stylistic criteria of music itself but by adopting analogies is due not to the lack of sufficiently sharply profiled musical style-concepts but to its always having, as a late-comer among the disciplines, more or less admittedly tried to place the music of a given period in relation to that period's other forms of expression. Thus it was that Riemann, for example, came to explain the music history of the 14th century as a parallel to the "Renaissance" in [Jules] Michelet's sense of the "discovering" of man and the world.

In music history some ambiguity will of necessity continue to cling to all extraneous terminologies applied to its styles, whereas all terminologies formed from intrinsically musical criteria, while they may be more pregnant, must isolate music from its inherent relationship to other spiritual activities. All future music historiography will be faced with the choice of either setting up purely musical style-categories labelled in purely musical terms that do indeed stand unequivocally for specific musical matter but remain dissociated from the intellectual ambiance and origin of these styles and intelligible only to the professional musician, or using to characterize its own style-periods and style-forms terms that are at the same time applicable in other fields and familiar to the non-musician also, even though because of this they suffer from a certain ambiguity. But since in the last analysis every categorization of spiritual phenomena is a belated abstraction from the versatile fullness of real life, such ambiguity can be accepted into the bargain if it helps overcome the isolation of music within its own technical history and makes this art comprehensible as a product of the impelling spiritual forces of its time. Hence it comes about that the introduction of the concept "Baroque" into music history, while in no way necessary, is useful since through the precedence of historical research in art and literature the word stands for certain definite currents and forces in man's spiritual history.

This is not the decisive point, however. The application of borrowed terms to the history of musical style is questionable only when, through the analogy between certain external style-forms, connections are set up that may not meet the nature of the case (see the preceding chapter), or when the taking over of extramusical concepts drags in a structural system that cannot serve as a scaffolding for the subject-matter of music. Now it is incontestable that at the same point of time when the pictorial and plastic arts and literature begin to develop the new style-forms today called "Baroque"—i.e., sometime in the last two to three decades of the 16th century—a similar process begins in music: the nature of the Baroque style in music consists not in opposition to the style-forms of the Renaissance but, as with the other arts, in a revaluation and further development of these forms corresponding to the new sense of life. And it is equally incontestable that in all the arts at the same point of time—namely somewhere in the second or third decade of the 18th century—there is to be observed in part a dissolution of these style-forms, in part their conquest by new forms. The taking over of the concept "Baroque" therefore does not introduce a forced periodic structure into music history.

Document 2. Christoph Bernhard's Contract as Vice-Kapellmeister. Heinrich Taube to Johann Georg I. Dresden, August 1, 1655. In Gina Spagnoli, *Letters and Documents of Heinrich Schütz, 1656–1672: An Annotated Translation.* Ann Arbor, MI: UMI Research Press, 1990. pp. 167.

Heinrich Taube[8] to Johann Georg I

The most serene elector of Saxony and burgrave of Magdeburg, etc. and my most gracious lord, accordingly appointed the former alto Christoph Bernhard as your vice-Kapellmeister, and ordered that now or in future, in the absence of [either] the electoral Kapellmeister Heinrich Schütz or the elector apparent's Kapellmeister, or else at their command, he direct and organize the music both in church and at the electoral and princely table. In particular, however (whether he himself or a Kapellmeister conducts), he shall always beat time from the lectern for the *choraliter* singing, and always communicate the texts of the musical pieces beforehand to the senior court preacher or to whoever delivers the sermon. Furthermore, when a Kapellmeister conducts and needs his voice, he shall serve willingly; and, in addition, should choir boys be entrusted to him, he shall instruct them in music.

This will be officially announced to the elector's rightfully designated lords of the exchequer, and these will have his appointment, after the ceremonial handshake has taken place on the above points, and his salary drawn and handed out to him according to the appointment of the previous vice-Kapellmeister. Indeed, his salary as alto shall cease from this date forward and will be, in addition to the open table, which had been given to the previous vice-Kapellmeister, granted to the future Hofkantor for his pleasure.

Signed Dresden. August 1, 1655.

Notes

1   Giulio Cesare Monteverdi, "Declaration," in *Scherzi musicali* (Venice, 1607), trans. in *Music in the Western World*, ed. Piero Weiss and Richard Taruskin, 2nd ed. (Belmont, CA: Thomson/Schirmer, 2008), p. 146.
2   Giulio Cesare Monteverdi, "Giulio Cesare Monteverdi's Explanation of the Letter," in *Source Readings in Music History*, part IV, ed. Margaret Murata (New York: W.W. Norton, 1998), p. 538.
3   Charles de Saint-Érremond, "Letter on the Opera," in Carol MacClintock, ed., *Readings in the History of Music and Performance* (Bloomington: University of Indiana Press, 1979), pp. 253–4.
4   François Couperin, Preface to *Les goûts-réunis*, trans. in David Ponsford, *French Organ Music in the Reign of Louis XIV* (New York: Cambridge University Press, 2011), p. 123.
5   Lodovico Viadana, Preface to *Cento concerti ecclesiastici* (Venice, 1602), in F.T. Arnold, *The Art of Accompaniment from a Thorough-Bass as Practised in the XVIIth & XVIIIth Centuries* (London: The Holland Press, 1961), p. 10.
6   Lodovico Viadana, Preface to *Cento concerti ecclesiastici* (Venice, 1602), in F.T. Arnold, *The Art of Accompaniment from a Thorough-Bass as Practised in the XVIIth & XVIIIth Centuries* (London: The Holland Press, 1961), p. 11.
7   Lodovico Viadana, Preface to *Cento concerti ecclesiastici* (Venice, 1602), in F.T. Arnold, *The Art of Accompaniment from a Thorough-Bass as Practised in the XVIIth & XVIIIth Centuries* (London: The Holland Press, 1961), p. 14.
8   Taube served as Senior Court Marshall at the Dresden court.

2 Music and Meaning in the Baroque Era

An essential component of interpreting Baroque music is an understanding of contemporary notions of meaning in music. Of course, music served various utilitarian functions: as entertainment, for religious services, and for marking important ceremonies and events. Nonetheless, underlying much of Baroque music, independent of its function and genre, was an attempt to align the goals of music composition and performance with those of rhetoric. Like orators, performers and composers attempted to elicit an emotional response from listeners, often with specific objectives in mind: spiritual union in the case of religious music, desire and ecstasy in some theatrical scenes and solo songs, or even rage in the case of the *stile concitato* or agitated style—a device consisting of rapid repeating sixteenth notes used by Claudio Monteverdi (1567–1643) and his contemporaries.

The notion that music swayed the emotions of listeners has a venerable history. Ancient philosophers, including Aristotle, proposed that fear, anger, sorrow, and joy were discrete emotional states or affections. According to Aristotle, Quintilian, and Cicero, orators used tone, speech, and hesitation as persuasive means to control the emotions of their audiences, thereby retaining or changing their emotional state. In a similar fashion, music could encourage bravery, instill anger, calm the nerves, or inspire joy. Renaissance and Baroque writers perpetuated these notions, often in very general terms and with copious Classical references. A prominent source for early modern attitudes toward madness and melancholy is the Oxford academic Robert Burton, whose *The Anatomy of Melancholy* (London, 1621) builds on the legacies of the influential late-ancient physician Galen (*ca.* 129–99 CE), for whom madness and melancholy were physical illnesses; and Plato, who proposed a spiritual or mental model. For this reason, music proved a doubly valuable cure for its effects on the body and the spirit. Burton writes:

> Musick is a tonick to the saddened soul, a Roaring Meg [a powerful cannon] against Melancholy, to rear and revive the languishing soul, affecting not only the ears, but the very arteries, the vital and animal spirits; it erects the mind, and makes it nimble. This it will effect in the most dull, severe, and sorrowful souls, expel grief with mirth, and if there be any clouds, dust, or dregs of cares yet lurking in our thoughts, most powerfully it wipes them all away, and that which is more, it will perform all this in an instant: cheer up the countenance, expel austerity, bring in hilarity, inform our manners, mitigate anger. . . . But to leave all declamatory speeches in praise of divine Musick, I will confine myself to my proper subject: besides that excellent power it hath to expel many other diseases, it is a sovereign remedy against Despair and Melancholy, and will drive away the Devil himself.[1]

Burton's theory met practice in such music as the popular *Lachrime pavane* by John Dowland (1563–1626). First published as an instrumental piece in 1596, the text "Flow My Tears" was added in *The Second Booke of Songs or Ayres* (London, 1600); the piece survives in more than a hundred manuscripts and printed books in solo and ensemble versions. The opening descending motif from A by step down to E was immediately recognizable as a musical symbol of grief.

Example 2.1 Dowland, "Flow My Tears," opening motif, soprano and bass.

Dowland's "Flow my tears" is an iconic example of the strong links between music and rhetoric; here Dowland uses the opening descent as a musical figure, much like a writer or orator adopts figures of speech to articulate an argument's content and structure.

Music and Rhetoric around 1600

Music's ties with rhetoric were particularly close in the Baroque period, when rhetorical principles of structure, argumentation, and design served as models for musical composition and performance. Baroque theorists drew on the writings of Aristotle, Cicero, and Quintilian, who divided the art of verbal discourse into five parts: *inventio* (the invention of the argument), *dispositio* (disposition or the arrangement of the argument), *elocutio* (elocution or style), *memoria* and *pronuntiatio* (both pertaining to the delivery of speeches). At the start of the Baroque period, German theorist Johann Burmeister (1564–1629) adopted the names and numbering of the parts of an oration from Classical authors, drawing specifically on Aristotle's three-part division of beginning, middle, end:

> A piece has three parts: (1) the exordium, (2) the body of the piece, (3) the ending. . . . The body of the musical piece is the series of affections or periods between the exordium and the ending. In this section, textual passages similar to the various arguments of the confirmation in rhetoric are instilled in the listener's mind in order that the proposition [*sentential*] be more clearly grasped and considered. (Document 1)[2]

Burmeister's account appeared in *Musica poetica* (Musical Poetics, 1606) along with chapters on notation, harmony, melody, and musical figures or ornaments.

A full account of the rhetorical structure of music came in the eighteenth century from German composer and theorist Johann Mattheson (1681–1764), who offered one of the most extensive discussions of rhetoric and music in *Der Vollkommene Capellmeister* (The Complete Chapel Master, 1739). Mattheson proposed a rhetorical model for musical composition that drew a direct parallel between the orator's use of grammar and rhetorical figures and the composer's organization of music into phrases and longer units that are articulated by cadences and differentiated by various musical figures. The analogy between figures of rhetoric and music was already well established in German circles, dating back at least to Burmeister's *Musica poetica*. In *Der Vollkommene Capellmeister*, Mattheson applied standard oratorical techniques—invention, arrangement, elaboration, and the presentation of an argument—to the art of musical composition. Mattheson's description of musical rhetoric is infused with metaphors that have to do with language. In fact, he structures his chapter "On the Sections and Caesuras of Musical Rhetoric" as a series of points that pair a linguistic phenomenon with its musical equivalent. For example, Mattheson describes a paragraph and its component parts, then makes a parallel with a musical melody that, like a paragraph, is made up of shorter phrases and pauses:

5. Every idea, be it verbal or written, consists then in certain word-phrases, or periods; but every such phrase also consists in smaller caesuras up to the close with a period. A whole structure or paragraph is developed from such phrases, and from various of these paragraphs a main part or a chapter is finally developed. That very briefly is the stepwise outline or climax of all that which can really be spoken, written, sung, or played.

6. In melody, as in musical speech, we usually employ only one paragraph at a time, a whole structure and section, which commonly forms the bounds of an aria, and, as stated, must consist of and join together at least two different smaller sentences or short statements. Though occasionally there is an exception in pedagogy, if clarity requires it.[3]

The Performer as Orator

More than any other historical period in music, Baroque composers and theorists were fully aware of the novelty of their ideas and the need to define and defend them in relation to what had come before. As we have seen, Mattheson emphasized the structural aspects of oration—in keeping with a practice that extended from Antiquity to the Medieval period. However, commentators from the Renaissance and Baroque periods had also started to give more attention to issues of elocution and style, a domain controlled not just by the composer, but by the performer as well. Just as the orator was critical for the articulation of a work's structure and emotional qualities, so, in the case of music, was the performer.

The very fact that music had the power to evoke emotion in the listener was both a guide and an inspiration to performers. The earliest operas by Jacopo Peri (1561–1633), Giulio Caccini (*ca.* 1550–1618), and Monteverdi showcase the power of music through the tale of Orpheus, the mythic Greek hero whose beautiful music permits him to retrieve his beloved Eurydice from the Underworld. The performer turned orator exploits harmonic language, various rhythmic devices, and ornamentation to control the emotions of listeners. Such attention to rhetoric helps explain the transformation of the madrigal around 1600 from a polyphonic style into solo forms. Talented singer and composer Giulio Caccini explained the new path and provided practical examples at a new level of refinement in *Le nuove musiche* (The New Music, 1601), a collection of solo madrigals, strophic canzonettas, and strophic variations. Caccini prefaced the collection with a virtual manifesto for solo song that highlights his new approach, one that turns away from counterpoint to melody:

> In both madrigals and airs I have always sought to imitate the ideas behind the words, trying to find those notes of greater or lesser affect (depending on the feelings of the texts) and of particular grace. As much as possible I have hidden the art of counterpoint. . . . But to compose and sing well in this style, understanding of the [poet's] conception and sensitivity to the text (plus imitating them through affective music and expressing them through affective singing) are much more useful than counterpoint. The latter I use only to adjust the two parts to each other, to avoid certain egregious errors, and to link certain dissonances—and more to match the affect than to be artful.[4]

Caccini ends with practical advice for singers: He warns against excessive ornamentation and empty virtuosity, calling for good judgment in the use of ornaments *(passaggi)* in order to better "move the affect of the soul." To this end, Caccini often specified ornamentation that might otherwise have been left to chance. A good example is the solo madrigal "Amarilli mia bella," where Caccini writes out the ornamentation in the final line, an expansion of the key phrase "Amarillis is my love."

Amarilli mia bella   Amarillis is my love

To enhance the persuasive quality of performance, Caccini intended the singers to accompany themselves with a "graceful neglect" of the strictly notated rhythms, an effect referred to as *sprezzatura*. When done well, *sprezzatura* lent an elegant and unstudied nonchalance to a performance.

Example 2.2 Caccini, "Amarilli mia bella," mm. 37–50.

*articulations & ornaments in parentheses are editorial suggestions

Further evidence that performance techniques and styles grew in significance in the Baroque period can be found in the many instruction manuals on singing and playing instruments; in guides to ornamentation; and in the many improvements made to instruments, which gave the performer greater control over sound production. Descriptive accounts of performers, such as the castrato Carlo Broschi (1705–82, known by his stage name Farinelli) and George Frideric Handel (1685–1759) and Johann Sebastian Bach (1685–1750) on the organ, also acknowledge the greater role of the performer. The chapters that follow address all of these trends as they trace the development of Baroque music across Europe and the Americas.

Baroque Elocution or Style

Stylistic decorum dictates that the style of music should suit its performance setting. Would you go to a fine dining restaurant in jeans, or to the beach in a tuxedo? Just as we pay attention to occasion and setting, so, too, did Baroque theorists, composers, and performers. Stylistic decorum embraces issues of general style as well as particular features of rhythm, texture, melody, harmony, form, and text expression. Music creates the desired effect only if its style matches its venue and occasion. Conversely, a mismatch between style and venue dilutes music's power of persuasion.

The stylistic distinction of old and new became a relevant means of describing and defending one's musical choices. Monteverdi's use of the terms first and second practice—the first referring to sixteenth-century harmonic protocol and the second to the new fashion of tailoring harmony to text—make it clear that the changes in the harmonic language of the Baroque period were known and acknowledged. Monteverdi's debate with Giovanni Maria Artusi, a proponent of the old school, created an artistic protocol for distinguishing text-based harmonic language, with greater freedom for employing dissonance, with an older style that preserved the rules of contrapuntal writing as laid out by theorists Gioseffo Zarlino in the sixteenth century.

Italian theorist and master of the royal chapel at Warsaw, Marco Scacchi (*ca.* 1600–62), built on this system by correlating harmonic language with genre and performance venue. Scacchi divided music into the categories of sacred, chamber, and theatrical music, arguing that each implied a corresponding harmonic practice:

The modern consists in two practices and three styles, that is, the church, chamber, and theater styles. The practices are: the first, which is *ut Harmonia sit Domina Orationis* [that harmony governs the words], and the second, which is *ut Oratio sit Domina Harmoniae* [that the words govern the harmony].[5]

Like the Monteverdis, Scacchi developed his classification system in defense of modern music. As such, stylistic categories became a convenient way to delineate rhetorical purpose, whereby diverse genres and styles could be accommodated within a central rhetorical framework.

Scacchi's theory was taken up by Christoph Bernhard (1628–92), a German theorist, composer, and singer who may have studied with Scacchi in Warsaw. Bernhard's major theoretical writing, *Tractatus compositionis augmentatus* (*ca.* 1657), maps the notions of Monteverdi's first and second practices onto Scacchi's stylistic categories. Bernhard's fundamental distinction between *stylus gravis* (*stylus antiquus*, ancient style) and *stylus luxurians* (*stylus modernus*, modern style) recalls Monteverdi's first and second practices; he further divides *stylus luxurians* into *communis* and *theatralis*, to create a tripartite division of church, chamber, and theater music. According to Bernhard, the first and second practices were relevant to both church and chamber music, whereas only the second practice was suitable to theatrical music. Both practices coexisted, since conventions of stylistic decorum often precluded the use in church settings of the more brazen dissonances and unorthodox harmonies common to secular opera and cantatas. Bernhard reformulated Quintilian's theory of imitation, calling for the emulation of distinguished authors: He recommended Giovanni Pierluigi da Palestrina (1525/6–94) as a model for sacred music, and Claudio Monteverdi, Francesco Cavalli (1602–76), and Giovanni Rovetta (1595/7–1668) for theatrical music and *stylus luxurians communis*—the common style of music for which the text and harmony are on equal footing.

Style classification systems framed both the creation of "modern" music and the continuation of the *stile antico* (ancient style) as exemplified in the music of Palestrina. Prized for their elegant lines, the clarity of the text-settings, and the judicious treatment of dissonance, Palestrina's masses and motets represented, for Catholic composers, the ideal union of function and style. A typical example of what became known in the Baroque period as *stile antico* is the opening of Palestrina's motet "Ave maris stella" (Hail, Star of the Sea). Written in honor of the Virgin Mary, Palestrina opens the motet with a string of overlapping phrases of imitative polyphony and consonant harmonies. Despite the cascading lines, Palestrina maintains text clarity through the reiteration of key words and phrases across the voices (Ex. 2.3).

Ave maris stella,	Hail, star of the sea,
Dei mater alma,	Portal of the sky,
atque semper virgo	Ever Virgin Mother
felix coeli porta.	Of the Lord most high.[6]

The *stile antico* was still the standard model for sacred music by such Roman composers of the early seventeenth century as Felice Anerio (*ca.* 1560–1614) and Gregorio Allegri (1582–1652). When Pope Urban VIII revised the texts to Palestrina's hymns, Allegri, in his role as guardian of the *stile antico*, was chosen by his colleagues in the papal choir to undertake the musical revisions. Characteristics of *stile antico* can be found in Allegri's motet, "Christus resurgens ex mortuis" (Christ, Rising from the Dead). Cast for unaccompanied choir, the motet features a homophonic texture, clear lines, and consonant harmonies.

Baroque theorists connected categories of old and new with the notion of genera or genre. Burmeister was among the first German theorists to consider this pairing. Writing in 1606, Burmeister describes imitation in relation to four genera of style: (1) lowly (characterized by stepwise motion and consonant harmonies), (2) grand (with wider intervals and more dissonance), (3) middle (a balance between the two), and (4) mixed ("that which adopts the other three styles . . . according to the nature of the text").[7] Here Burmeister transfers the principles of tone and register (low, medium, high) from classical rhetoric to musical practice.

More than a century later, Jean-Philippe Rameau used strikingly similar language in his *Traité de l'harmonie* (Treatise on Harmony, 1727) to describe his very different concept of harmony, one that acknowledged the

Example 2.3 Palestrina, "Ave maris stella," mm. 1–21.

eclipse of what had been a basically modal worldview up to that point. Yet in laying the foundation for the theories of tonality that were to underpin harmonic thinking for years to come, Rameau cast his discussion against the backdrop of the affections:

> Harmony can arouse in us different passions. . . . Consonant harmonies are to be found everywhere but should be employed most frequently in music expressing gaity and magnificence; . . . Languishings and sufferings are perfectly expressed by dissonances "by supposition" [9th and 11th chords created by placing a "supposed" bass below the root of the chord] and especially by chromatic progressions.[8]

Rameau would have been well aware that making the music expressive involved breaking the old rules on dissonance, so firmly rooted in the *stile antico*, and so painstakingly outlined in every major treatise from Heinrich Glarean's *Dodecachordon* (Twelve Modes, 1547) to the various French composition treatises published before 1700. He would also have taken it for granted that breaking the rules was not only justified but necessary as it suited the occasion, the genre of music, and the affect.

Music and the Passions

Matching style, tone, and genre all contributed to the central goals of musical rhetoric: to move the emotions, to delight the senses, and to teach. Understanding *how* to direct the emotions to these ends required a grasp of the ancient theories of emotional states, which date back to Aristotle. One of the most influential translators of the ancient theory of emotional states to Baroque readers was René Descartes (1596–1650), a French philosopher and mathematician, who laid the foundations for a philosophy of the affections in Baroque art in *Les passions de l'âme* (The Passions of the Soul, 1649). In three parts, Descartes outlines general principles, describes the six main passions of wonder, love, joy, hatred, desire, and sadness, and ends with descriptions of particular passions such as esteem and scorn. For Descartes, emotions had a physical basis rooted in the body. He writes:

> So there is no better path for arriving at an understanding of our Passions than to examine the difference between the soul and the body, in order to understand to which of the two each of the functions within us should be attributed.[9]

Descartes' descriptions link the physical connection in the body (a reaction in the heart or blood, for instance) that triggers a change in the soul, which resided in "the brain, or perhaps the heart–the brain because the sense organs are related thereto, and the heart because the passions are felt as if therein."[10]

One of Descartes' most influential followers was painter and theorist Charles Le Brun (1619–90), who argued that facial expression showed the emotion of the soul and made the passions visible to the audience. In *Méthode pour apprendre à dessiner les passions propose dans une conference sur l'expression générale et particulière* (A Method of Learning to Draw the Passions as Proposed in a Lecture on Expression, In General and In Particular, 1698), Le Brun gave young painters precise depictions of emotional states and instructions to help them reach their expressive goals. Le Brun describes anger *(La colere)* as an impassioned state (Document 2):

> *Anger.* When anger takes possession of the soul, he who experiences this emotion has red and inflamed eyes, a wandering and sparkling pupil, both eyebrows now lowered, now raised, the forehead deeply creased, creases between the eyes, wide-open nostrils, lips pressed tightly together, and the lower lip pushed up over the upper, leaving the corners of the mouth a little open to form a cruel and disdainful laugh. He seems to grind his teeth, his mouth fills with saliva, his face is swollen, pale in spots and inflamed in others, the veins of his temples and forehead and neck are swollen and protruding, his hair bristling, and one who experiences this passion seems more to blow himself up rather than to breathe because the heart is oppressed by the abundance of blood which comes to his aid.[11]

Figure 2.1 Charles Le Brun, The head of a man screaming in terror, a study for the figure of Darius in 'The Battle of Arbela' (charcoal on paper).

Le Brun's work was critical, not only for painting, but for the cultivation of gesture in theatrical works, including opera. His influence remained strong in the eighteenth century, particularly in England, where Robert Sayer issued engravings based on Le Brun's seminal series.

The specific means of harnessing music's powers varied from theorist to theorist, and from performer to performer; there was no single set of guidelines or instructions for making music expressive. Most often a single emotion, whether sadness, anger, joy, or love, formed the basis of an entire piece of music or a section within a larger work. Composers for the voice wrote music specifically aimed at expressing the emotional content of the text, but the particular melodic, harmonic, or rhythmic formula for doing so might vary among composers, locales, or genres.

Claudio Monteverdi provides one of the clearest descriptions and examples of presenting emotional states in *Madrigali guerrieri et amorosi* (Madrigals of Love and War, 1638), his eighth book of madrigals. Monteverdi's preface remains the composer's most extensive writing on music. Given the esteemed tradition of setting love poetry to music (*canti amorosi*), Monteverdi focuses on explaining the new *stile concitato* (agitated style) used in the *canti guerrieri* (songs of war). Monteverdi explained the musical content of this new style as follows:

I therefore began to cogitate upon the semibreve [whole note], which I defined as a spondee beat when sounded uninterruptedly. When it was then divided into sixteen semiquavers [sixteenth notes] that were sounded one after another, and when text was added that expressed anger and vexation, I heard in this small example the similitude of the emotion that I was seeking. . . . To perform a better experiment, I seized upon the divine Tasso as a poet who in his text expresses with perfect suitability and naturalness all the passions he wishes to describe, and I hit upon the description he makes of the combat between Tancredi and Clorinda, so that I would have the two contrary passions to set to music, that is, war, supplication and death. (Document 3)

Monteverdi included the *Combattimento di Tancredi e Clorinda* (Combat of Tancredi and Clorinda, 1624; published 1638) as the centerpiece of the war-like music in *The Eighth Book of Madrigals*. Example 2.4 typifies the *stile agitato* with its steady repeated sixteenth notes and violent text.

Testo	Narrator
L'onta irrita lo sdegno alla vendetta e la vendetta poi e la vendetta poi l'ontra rinova onde sempre al ferir, sempre alla fretta stimol novo s'aggiunge e piaga nova.	Shame spurs anger into vengeance and vengeance then renews the shame, so that constantly as they strike, constantly as they hasten new stimulus is added and new wounds.[12]

Monteverdi makes a clear link between style and genre at the close of his preface:

And, since the musical forces of great princes are employed in their royal chambers in three ways for their delicate tastes theatrical, chamber and dance therefore in the present book I have indicated the said three styles with the titles of warlike, amorous and dramatic [*guerriera, amorosa et rapresentativa*]. (Document 3)

Describing emotional states and finding ways of conveying them musically became a preoccupation in the Baroque period. Theorists, especially in Germany, devoted large parts of their treatises to explaining and categorizing the various types of affections and the musical means—such as keys, rhythms, formal structures, melodic figures and styles—for evoking them. A comprehensive theory of affections, known as the Doctrine of Affections (or *Affektenlehre* in German) evolved during the Baroque period, according to which composers—no less than painters and orators—could control the emotions of their audiences. German composer and theorist Johann Mattheson (1681–1764) offered one of the most extensive accounts of the affections in *Der Vollkommene Capellmeister* (The Complete Chapel Master, 1739). Though Mattheson's descriptions of emotions are straightforward, his advice on how to express them in music is vague and simplistic. In regards to the connection between affect and tempo, he writes:

Adagio distinguishes Grief
Lamento distinguishes Lamentation
Lento distinguishes Alleviation
Andante distinguishes Hope
Affettuoso distinguishes Love
Allegro distinguishes Comfort
Presto distinguishes Desire
Whether the composer has thought on this or not, it can occur when his genius is truly effective; this may very often happen without our knowledge or cooperation.[13]

Writing in the mid-eighteenth century, composer, flutist, and theorist Johann Joachim Quantz (1697–1773) attests to the longevity of these ideas, although he also seems to suggest that some listeners

Example 2.4 Monteverdi, *Combattimento di Tancredi e Clorinda*, mm. 164–171.

were constitutionally more comfortable "feeling" certain types of music than others. He recommends learning about listeners' humors, advising that:

> A choleric person may be satisfied with majestic and serious pieces; one inclined to melancholy with thoughtful, chromatic pieces, and those set in minor keys; and a gay, wide-awake person with gay and jocular pieces.[14]

Quantz takes it for granted that emotional states can be produced in the listener by the music and that the composer can manipulate the phenomenon (even if it is for so self-serving a purpose as to flatter the person who paid for the concert). Quantz's assumptions may seem simplistic, but current theories grounded in contemporary research in psychology and neurology may one day seem as inadequate as those of the seventeenth and eighteenth century in explaining music and meaning, music and emotion. It remains the case

Example 2.4 (continued)

On - de sem-pre al fer - ir sem-pre al fer - ir sem-pre al-la fret - ta

sti-mol no - vo s'ag - guin - ge e pia - ga no - va

that in the Baroque era the relationship between music and feeling was held to be quite direct. Sound, they believed, affected the listener *physically*, causing the body to respond as if it were experiencing an actual emotional stimulus: Music in a slow tempo proceeding by tiny steps mimics the way the body feels when it is weary; when the body feels weary, the body's vapors touch the soul and the corresponding emotional state is created. It sounds backwards to modern minds, but this rationale explains why such "physical" gestures in music as descending or ascending scales, leaps, running notes, musical sighs, and rapid tremolos were such strong cues for defining affect. We might think such gestures resonate as metaphors; but Baroque musicians believed their presence in the music could actually fool the body into thinking it was reacting to a real emotional situation. We shall keep this in mind in our discussions of individual pieces throughout this text, for it explains not only why certain formulae appear again and again—readying the body for a calculated emotional response, as it were—but why novel affects were also cultivated and prized for their capacity to shock, surprise, or delight.

Documents

Document 1. Johann Burmeister, *Musical Poetics*. Trans. Benito V. Rivera and ed. Claude V. Palisca. New Haven, CT: Yale University Press, 1993. pp. 201, 203, 205. Copyright © 1993 by Yale University Press. Used by permission of Yale University Press.

Chapter 15. *The Analysis or Arrangement of a Musical Piece*

Musical analysis is the examination of a piece belonging to a certain mode and to a certain type of polyphony. The piece is to be divided into its affections or periods, so that the artfulness with which each period takes shape can be studied and adopted for imitation. There are five areas of analysis: (1) investigation of the mode; (2) investigation of the melodic genus; (3) investigation of the type of polyphony; (4) consideration of the quality; (5) sectioning of the piece into affections or periods. . . .

Sectioning of the piece into affections means its division into periods for the purpose of studying its artfulness and using it as a model for imitation. A piece has three parts: (1) the exordium, (2) the body of the piece, (3) the ending.

The exordium is the first period or affection of the piece. It is often adorned by fugue, so that the ears and mind of the listener are rendered attentive to the song, and his good will is won over. The exordium extends up to the point where the fugal subject ends with the introduction of a true cadence [*clausula vera*] or of a harmonic passage having the marks of a cadence. This is seen to happen where a new subject definitely different from the fugal subject is introduced. However, examples do not confirm that all musical pieces should always begin with the ornament of fugue. With this in mind, let the music student follow common practice and what it allows. Sometimes *noëma* takes place in the exordium. When this happens, it should be for the sake of an aphoristic text [*textus sententiosus*] or for other purposes which common practice will show.

The body of the musical piece is the series of affections or periods between the exordium and the ending. In this section, textual passages similar to the various arguments of the confirmation in rhetoric are instilled in the listener's mind in order that the proposition [*sentential*] be more clearly grasped and considered.

The body should not be protracted too much, lest that which is overextended arouse the listener's displeasure. For everything that is excessive is odious and usually turns into a vice.

The ending is the principal cadence where either all the musical movement [*modulation*] ceases or where one or two voices stop while the others continue with a brief passage called *supplementum*. By means of this, the forthcoming close in the music is more clearly impressed on the listener's awareness.

Document 2. Charles Le Brun, "Concerning Expression In General and In Particular." In *A Documentary History of Art, Volume 2: Michelangelo and the Mannerists. The Baroque and the Eighteenth Century*. Ed. Elizabeth Gilmore Holt. New York: Doubleday Anchor Books, 1958. pp. 161–3.

Expression, in my opinion, is a naïve and natural resemblance of the things which are to be represented. It is necessary and appears in all aspects of painting and a picture could not be perfect without expression. It is expression that marks the true character of each thing; by means of it is the nature of bodies discerned, the figures seem to have movement and all that is pretense appears to be truth.

In the first place, passion is an emotion of the soul, which lies in the sensitive part [of the body]. It pursues what the soul thinks is good for it, or flees what it thinks bad for it; ordinarily whatever causes passion in the soul evokes action in the body.

Since, then, it is true that most of the passions of the soul produce bodily action, we should know which actions of the body express the passions and what those actions are. . . .

Anger. When anger takes possession of the soul, he who experiences this emotion has red and inflamed eyes, a wandering and sparkling pupil, both eyebrows now lowered, now raised, the forehead deeply creased, creases between the eyes, wide-open nostrils, lips pressed tightly together, and the lower lip pushed up over the upper, leaving the corners of the mouth a little open to form a cruel and disdainful laugh. He seems to grind his teeth, his mouth fills with saliva, his face is swollen, pale in spots and inflamed in others, the veins of his temples and forehead and neck are swollen and protruding, his hair bristling, and one who experiences this passion seems more to blow himself up rather than to breathe because the heart is oppressed by the abundance of blood which comes to his aid.

Rage and despair sometimes follow anger.

Document 3. Claudio Monteverde to the Reader, Preface to Claudio Monteverdi, *Madrigals Book VIII (Madrigali Guerrieri et Amorosi)*. Ed. Gian Francesco Malpiero with preface and new literal translations of the texts by Stanley Appelbaum. New York: Dover, 1991. Copyright 1991 by Dover Publications. Used by permission of Dover Publications.

Having considered that our mind has three principal passions or affections anger, temperance, and humility or supplication as the best philosophers affirm, and, indeed, considering that the very nature of our voice falls into a high, low and medium range and musical theory describes this clearly with the three terms of agitated [*concitato*], languid [*molle*] and temperate [*temperato*]; and never having been able to find in all the compositions of past composers an example of the agitated style [*genere*] as described by Plato in his third book *On Rhetoric*[15] in these words [in Latin]: "Take up that harmony which, as it should, imitates the voice and accents of a man going bravely into battle"; and, knowing that it is contraries that deeply affect our mind, the goal of the effect that good music ought to have, as Boethius affirms when he says [in Latin]: "Music is associated with our lives, either to lend honor to our manners or to overthrow them," I therefore, with no little research and effort, set myself the task of discovering it. And having considered that the pyrrhic metrical foot is a quick tempo, to which all the best philosophers affirm that the agitated dances of war were performed, and the opposite type of dance was done to the spondee [a metrical foot comprised of two accented syllables], a slow tempo, I therefore began to cogitate upon the semibreve [whole note], which I defined as a spondee beat when sounded uninterruptedly. When it was then divided into sixteen semiquavers [sixteenth notes] that were sounded one after another, and when text was added that expressed anger and vexation, I heard in this small example the similitude of the emotion that I was seeking, even though the voice did not attain the velocity of the instrument. To perform a better experiment, I seized upon the divine Tasso as a poet who in his text expresses with perfect suitability and naturalness all the passions he wishes to describe, and I hit upon the description he makes of the combat between Tancredi and Clorinda, so that I would have the two contrary passions to set to music, that is, war, supplication and death. And then in the year 1624, when I performed it before the best people of the noble city of Venice in a noble room in the home of the illustrious and excellent Girolamo Mocenigo, a foremost nobleman who is among the leaders of the Most Serene Republic and my special patron and obliging protector, it was listened to with great applause and praised. Having seen this trial succeed in imitating wrath, I pushed my investigation further with greater zeal and wrote various other compositions, some for the church and some for the chamber. This style was so pleasing even to composers of music that they not only praised it aloud but also imitated me by using it in their works, much to my pleasure and honor. Therefore I felt it was right to make it known that I was responsible for the investigation and first trial of this style, so necessary to the musical art, which it may be truly said was incomplete without it up to now, having possessed only the two styles languid and temperate. And because at the outset the musicians, especially those who were to play the basso continuo, found the necessity to strike a single string sixteen times in one measure more laughable than praiseworthy, they reduced that multiplicity to a single stroke per measure, and, while supposed to be performing a pyrrhic foot, actually performed a spondee and destroyed the similitude of the agitated style. Therefore I instruct that the basso continuo and its accompaniment be played in manner and form according to the written style. In this will likewise be found the procedure that must be maintained in other compositions in other styles, because the manners of playing should be of three sorts: oratorical [based on the verbal text], harmonic [referring to the combination of notes] and rhythmic. The manner discovered by me of that warlike style gave me the opportunity to write several madrigals that I called madrigals of war. And, since the musical forces of great princes are employed in their royal chambers in three ways for their delicate tastes theatrical, chamber and dance therefore in the present book I have indicated the said three styles with the titles of warlike, amorous and dramatic [*guerriera, amorosa et rapresentativa*]. I know that the book will be imperfect, because I am not much good at anything, but especially at the warlike style since it is new and since [in Latin] "all beginnings are feeble." Therefore I beg the kind reader to accept the will for the deed. I shall await from his learned pen greater perfection in the nature of the above-mentioned style, because [in Latin] "it is easy to add to things already discovered." May you live in happiness.

Notes

1 Robert Burton, *The Anatomy of Melancholy* (New York: Tudor, 1955), pp. 478–9.
2 Aristotle, *Poetics* 7.3 and 23.1, cited in Johann Burmeister, *Musical Poetics*, trans. Benito V. Rivera and ed. Claude V. Palisca (New Haven, CT: Yale University Press, 1993), p. 203, note 2.
3 Ernest C. Harriss, *Johann Mattheson's Der vollkommene Capellmeister: A Revised Translation with Critical Commentary* (Ann Arbor, MI: UMI Research Press, 1981), p. 381.
4 Oliver Strunk, *Source Readings in Music History* (New York: W.W. Norton, 1950), p.
5 Marco Scacchi, *Breve discorso sopra la musica moderna* (Warsaw, 1649), C3v-C4r, quoted in Claude V. Palisca, "Marco Scacchi's Defence of Modern Music (1649)," in Claude V. Palisca, *Studies in the History of Italian Music and Music Theory* (London: Clarendon Press, 1994), p. 111.
6 Adapted from Edward Caswall, *Hymns & Poems*, 2nd ed. (London, 1873), p. 105.
7 Johann Burmeister, *Musical Poetics*, trans. Benito V. Rivera and ed. Claude V. Palisca (New Haven, CT: Yale University Press, 1993), p. 209.
8 Walter Gerboth, Robert L. Sanders, Robert Starer, and Frances Steiner, eds., *An Introduction to Music: Selected Readings* (New York: Norton, 1964), pp. 49–50.
9 René Descartes, *The Passions of the Soul*, trans. Stephen Voss (Indianapolis, IN: Hackett, 1989), p. 19.
10 René Descartes, *The Passions of the Soul*, trans. Stephen Voss (Indianapolis, IN: Hackett, 1989), p. 36.
11 Charles Le Brun, "Concerning Expression In General and In Particular," in *The Documentary History of Art, Volume II: Michelangelo and the Mannerists. The Baroque and the Eighteenth Century*, ed. Elizabeth Gilmore Holt (New York: Doubleday, 1963), p. 163.
12 Claudio Monteverdi, *Madrigals Book VIII (Madrigali Guerrieri et Amorosi)*, trans. Stanley Appelbaum and ed. Gian Francesco Malpiero (New York: Dover, 1991), p. xxiii.
13 Ernest C. Harriss, *Johann Mattheson's Der vollkommene Capellmeister: A Revised Translation with Critical Commentary* (Ann Arbor, MI: UMI Research Press, 1981), p. 208, quoted in George J. Buelow, "Johann Mattheson and the Invention of the *Affektenlehre*," in *New Mattheson Studies*, ed. George J. Buelow and Hans Joachim Marx (Cambridge: Cambridge University Press, 1983), p. 407.
14 Johann Joachim Quantz, *On Playing the Flute*, 2nd ed., trans. Edward R. Reilly (London: Faber and Faber, 2001), p. 201.
15 Monteverdi mistakes Plato for the author of *On Rhetoric*, a text by Aristotle.

Part I

Music in Years of Transition, Experimentation, and Crisis, 1580–1648

3 Opera's Beginnings

Words and Music

Nothing marks the start of the Baroque period in music more clearly than the birth of opera. That first opera, for us at any rate, is *Euridice*, based on a text by Ottavio Rinuccini (1562–1621), with music by Jacopo Peri (1561–1633), for it is the first opera for which the complete music survives. *Euridice* was performed at the court of Florence in 1600, where both Rinuccini and Peri held appointments at the Medici court of Grand Duke Ferdinando I. By all accounts, Florence, whose literary and musical reputation rivalled that of any city, was a hotbed for discussions and stagings of this new art form—a performance of *Dafne*, with text by Rinuccini and music by Peri and Jacopo Corsi, had already taken place there in 1598, although its music is now lost. All told, about twenty-five operas were performed at the courts of Florence, Mantua, and Rome between 1598 and 1640. Together, they constitute the first phase of early opera.

Early Baroque opera was a multimedia event that required great resources, demanding the collaboration of poets, musicians, set designers, engineers and publicists. Experts in these fields worked together to instill a state of wonder, or *meraviglia*, in the audience. Early operas honored state weddings, royal births, and diplomatic events, attracting influential guests, diplomats, and their entourages from across Europe. Published accounts and commemorative librettos and scores spread the news of a lavish theatrical performance far and wide. As we will see in Chapter 6, the means of production and patronage had considerable impact on the style and sound of opera, and these changed significantly with the start of public opera, for paying audiences, in Venice in 1637.

The producers of early opera knew there was something special about what they were doing, and the primary feature that distinguished opera from the theatrical forms that had preceded it was its use of a novel type of speech-song called *stile recitativo* or *stile rappresentativo*. Both terms refer to a mode of singing that imitated the natural accentuation and emotional intensity of impassioned speech.

The relationship of words to music is a crucial aesthetic distinction, and in early opera the balance of power lay with the words. Most opera aficionados today love an opera for its arias—they relish the music, not the words. But the key moments of musical passion and persuasion in these first operas were sung in *stile recitativo*, and *stile recitativo* was nothing without its text. At the time, the idea of music dominated by text was so revolutionary that Claudio Monteverdi coined the terms first and second practice *(prima* and *seconda pratica)* to distinguish the Renaissance art of layered polyphony, where musical concerns were primary, from the new, text-based style of the early Baroque.

The first century of Italian opera witnessed a constant battle over which was to have supremacy: words or music. This aesthetic debate had implications for the status of the patron, librettist, composer, and singer. But at opera's birth, under the protection of princely patronage, the words reigned supreme.

Humanist Court Opera in Florence

Florence was the ideal home for the years of artistic activity that led up to opera. The city and its court offered the necessary intellectual, musical, and poetic backdrop for the new genre. The Medici family dominated political and cultural affairs in the city and its territories from the early fifteenth century until 1737. A policy of marital alliances with royal houses of Europe secured the Medici dynasty a vital role in Catholic lands. The Medici produced several popes and cardinals, ruling Rome under Giovanni de'Medici's pontificate as Pope Leo X (1513–21) and Giulio de'Medici's service as Pope Clement VII (1523–34). In 1569 Cosimo I de'Medici was granted the coveted hereditary title Grand Duke of Tuscany, a title held by the Medici family until the death of the last male, Gian Gastone, in 1737.

The intellectual ethos of the Florentine court, and, indeed, of much of Italy at this time, is encompassed by the term humanism. Humanism refers to the broad range of study in classical grammar, rhetoric, poetics, history, and moral philosophy that informed Renaissance thought from about 1400 onward. In the closing decades of the sixteenth century, these humanist pursuits inclined towards the study of ancient Greek music theory and drama. One center of humanist activity was the salon hosted by the Florentine courtier Count Giovanni de'Bardi, which was dedicated to exploring the links between modern and ancient music and poetry. Known as the Camerata, Bardi's group of scholars, musicians, and amateurs met between about 1573 and 1587. Girolamo Mei (1519–94) served as the group's cultural advisor. Working in Rome, Mei edited Greek texts and studied ancient Greek music, sending letters to Bardi that detailed his findings.

Figure 3.1 Buontalenti, *La pellegrina*, 1589. Costume designs: Dorian Harmony

In Book 4 of his monumental *De modis musicis antiquorum* (On the Musical Modes of the Ancients, 1567–73), Mei presented his most critical theory for the new genre of opera: that ancient Greek tragedies and comedies were sung in their entirety and accompanied in unison by a wind instrument called the aulos. Vincenzo Galilei, father of the famous astronomer and member of Bardi's Camerata, furthered Mei's theory in his own *Dialogo della musica antica et della moderna* (Dialogue on Music Ancient and Modern) of 1581, which became the most important aesthetic manifesto of the Camerata. In it, Galilei condemned the complexity of contrapuntal music, calling for composers to imitate the ancients with solo songs set to simple accompaniment. These theories were critical for experimenting with a new style called monody, a catch-all term from the late sixteenth century to about 1640 for accompanied Italian solo song. Composers of monody sought to unite poetry and music according to what they believed was an ancient Greek ideal. The rhythm of the text inspired the musical line, which was cast in the low, middle, or high register depending on the level of emotional intensity of the text. The vocal line was provided with a simple chordal accompaniment.

When Bardi departed for Rome in 1592, Jacopo Corsi, a wealthy aristocrat, banker and composer, replaced him as chief patron of the arts in Florence. Corsi assembled a group of poets and musicians to enact Mei's ideals of speech-like music and dramatic poetry, and it was Corsi's circle that sponsored the earliest known operas. Building on the popularity of pastoral plays such as Torquato Tasso's *Aminta* (1581) and Giovanni Battista Guarini's *Il pastor fido* (The Faithful Shepherd, 1589), librettists turned to sources with

Example 3.1 Cavalieri, "Dalle più alte sfere," mm. 1–14.

Example 3.1 (continued)

pastoral themes for opera subjects. Librettist Ottavio Rinuccini and composer Jacopo Peri based *Dafne* (1598) on Ovid's *Metamorphoses*. Their next contribution, *Euridice* (1600), draws from the same Ovidian source. Both plots combine depictions of rural life with ancient Greek ideals of musical poetry. The Orpheus myth in particular was popular throughout the Baroque, and important operas based on the myth bookend the period: Claudio Monteverdi's *Orfeo* (1607) at the start of the Baroque, and Christoph Willibald Gluck's *Orfeo ed Euridice* (1762) at its finish.

Early opera had an important predecessor in the *intermedio*, a type of musico-dramatic entertainment placed between the acts of a play. These *intermedi* were a means of diverting the audience during scene changes, since once the curtain had been drawn, the stage remained open for the duration of a play. The *intermedi* fit the bill, with music, choruses, dances, and spectacular effects. The genre reached its height with the 1589 festivities for the wedding of Grand Duke Ferdinando de'Medici and Christine of Lorraine in Florence. The event featured Girolamo Bargagli's comedy, *La pellegrina*, and the play was provided with six separate *intermedi* under the direction of Giovanni de'Bardi, featuring texts by Rinuccini, Bardi, and Laura Guidiccioni Lucchesini. Bardi chose to link the interludes with a single theme, one close to the heart of Camerata thought—the power of ancient music. Among the many composers who contributed music were Antonio Archilei, Cristofano Malvezzi (chapel master to Grand Duke Ferinando), Luca

Example 3.1 (continued)

Marenzio, Jacopo Peri, Giulio Caccini, and the recently hired superintendent of music at the court, Emilio de'Cavalieri. Details of the performances survive in letters, diaries, printed booklets, and a commemorative edition of the music printed in 1591.

The Florentine appetite for scenic display was accommodated from the opening moments of Bardi's (Fig. 3.1. First *intermedio*, a visually striking scene in which Harmony floats down from heaven to earth on a cloud. The backcloth rises to reveal a darker, starry sky, with the Sirens disposed on four clouds. They sing first as two groups, and later as three. Contemporary accounts stress the magical quality of Harmony's descent, and Bernardo's costumes and set design can no doubt take credit for much of this.

The effect was well calculated in every respect, from the casting of the famous Vittoria Achilei as (Doric) Harmony to the virtuosic melody lines and carefully notated ornamentation of Cavalieri's opening song for her (ornaments that would earlier have been left to improvisation). The music itself even seems to float—a metaphorical alignment of sight and sound that surely contributed to the *meraviglio* of this scene (Ex. 3.1).

Dalle più alte sfere	From the highest spheres[1]
Di celesti sirene amica scorta	Of the heavenly sirens, a friendly escort,
Son l'armonia ch'a voi vengo mortali	I, Harmony, come to you mortals

This style of song-writing developed in Florence and was made famous by Giulio Caccini in his collection *Il nuove musiche* (The New Music, 1602).

The Myth of Orpheus

Jacopo Peri, Giulio Caccini, and Claudio Monteverdi all set music to the plot of Orpheus. Why was the story so appealing? Perhaps it is because the myth presented opportunities to combine spectacle—in the underworld scenes, for example—with both the Italian pastoral tradition and Greek theatrical practice. Furthermore, the Orpheus legend centers on the power of music: Orpheus summons his voice to sing for his beloved Euridice's return from death, and his lament captures the poignancy of his suffering. The myth

Figure 3.2 Title page, Monteverdi, *L'Orfeo*. Venice, 1609.

thus epitomized the central tenet of humanist and Camerata thought: modern music inspired by ancient Greek ideals.

The Orpheus myth would have been well known to spectators of early opera, having inspired the first secular Italian vernacular drama, *Fabula di Orfeo* (Fable of Orpheus, 1480), by Angelo Poliziano (1454–94). Poliziano drew most heavily from the versions of the Orpheus myth in Ovid's *Metamorphoses* and Virgil's *Georgics*. His *Fabula* was partly sung, partly spoken, and by casting the musical numbers in regular stanzas, Poliziano set a model for future opera librettists, distinguishing recitative with irregular lines, from arias and short songs with regular, poetic rhyme.

Of the various Orpheus operatic treatments, Claudio Monteverdi's is by far the most famous. It was first performed at the ducal palace at Mantua, a city ruled by the Gonzaga family from 1328 to 1707. Mantua, like Florence, was an extravagant court in the decades around 1600. The Gonzaga family employed as many as eight hundred writers, artists, musicians, and even a troop of *commedia dell'arte* actors. The years around 1600 were especially lavish, with artist Peter Paul Rubens, composer Claudio Monteverdi, and the poet Guarini all active at the Gonzaga court.

Orfeo was commissioned by the Accademia degli Invaghiti, an aristocratic club whose members included librettist Alessandro Striggio, Francesco Gonzaga, and his father, Duke Vincenzo Gonzaga. It was performed at the Carnival of 1607. The printed libretto of 1607 retains the original tragic outcome: Orpheus loses Euridice forever and is torn apart by the Bacchantes. However, for the extravagant printed score of 1609, Striggio substituted a happy ending to reflect the prevailing aesthetic taste of the day. In his dedication of the score to Duke Francesco Gonzaga, Monteverdi writes that he brings the Fable of Orpheus to "the Great Theater of the Universe for all mankind to see." As the score circulated, it acquainted the rest of Europe with the new genre and the new style, promoting the reputation of the opera's patron as it did so.

The canonical status of *Orfeo* attests to the talents of its principal creators. *Orfeo*'s text was by Alessandro Striggio (1573?–1630), one of Monteverdi's most important collaborators—Striggio probably also provided texts for the ballet *Tirsi e Clori* (1616) and the lost dramatic cantata *Apollo*. Their collaboration is further documented in a series of letters from the 1610s, following Monteverdi's move to Venice in 1613. Striggio's libretto for *Orfeo* was not without precedent, however. In 1600 Striggio had seen Rinuccini's *Euridice* in Florence, while attending Duke Vincenzo Gonzaga as court secretary and poet. He then used *Euridice* as the model for *Orfeo*.

Claudio Monteverdi

Praised by contemporaries as a "great man" whose works were "set to last as long as they can resist the ravages of time," Claudio Monteverdi (1567–1643) remains one of the most important composers before 1700. Equally adept in both the older and newer styles, Monteverdi transformed and mastered the principal genres of his day—madrigals (secular settings of poetry), operas, and sacred music—and his works influenced generations of musicians and other artists. By proposing a new relationship between poetry and harmony, he initiated one of the most important aesthetic debates of the era.

Monteverdi's life and works are emblematic of the debate that surrounds the decades around 1600. Are these years best viewed as the end of the Renaissance or as the beginning of the Baroque? Scholars still grapple with the question.

Monteverdi's life and works straddle both eras. He spent his early years in his birthplace of Cremona, in northern Italy, where he studied with the music director of the local cathedral, Marc'Antonio Ingegneri. He became proficient on string instruments, entering the court of Duke Vincenzo Gonzaga as a string player in 1591, remaining for twenty-one years at Mantua. In 1601 he was appointed head of the chapel at the Mantuan court. This was a productive period for Monteverdi, who completed madrigal Books 3–5, the operas *Orfeo* and *Arianna*, the *Vespers* of 1610, and two ballets. However, when Vincenzo died in 1612, his son Francesco dismissed many court artists, including Monteverdi, initiating the composer's move to Venice and the last phase of his career. From 1613 Monteverdi held the prominent post of music director at the Basilica of St Mark's, and his landmark operas of the 1640s, *L'incoronazione di Poppea* and *Il ritorno d'Ulisse*, had a significant impact on the rise of commercial opera in Venice. Monteverdi thus played a key role in the beginnings of both courtly and public opera, the former at the start of his career, the latter at its finish.

The years around 1600 at the Mantuan court were critical for Monteverdi's development as a dramatist. Madrigal Books 4–5 (1603, 1605) featured settings of texts drawn from Guarini's *Il pastor fido*, and he set several passages from them as dialogues to exploit the full dramatic potential of the madrigal genre. By the time he turned to Striggio's libretto for *Orfeo*, Monteverdi's musical language was mature. Persuasive in the fullest sense of the word, it could encourage, cajole, urge, wheedle, shock, and sadden. In other words, it could represent emotion, and it could evoke it.

The First Performances of Claudio Monteverdi's *Orfeo*

We know much more about the first performances of *Orfeo* than we do about most musical events of the Baroque period. *Orfeo* was performed on February 24 and March 1, 1607, at the ducal palace at Mantua. Information about *Orfeo* survives in printed librettos, diplomatic correspondence, diary entries, and commemorative scores printed in 1609 and 1615. To these materials can be added contemporary treatises on set design and theater production. Taken together, these sources shed light on what it was like to attend early opera.

Then as now, operatic success depended upon patronage. Today, productions are funded by ticket sales and the support of dedicated donors and government arts councils. In the early Baroque period, it was the patron who determined whether a production happened and whether it was repeated. And since the production's success also reflected positively back on the person who sponsored it, each staging of *Orfeo* essentially celebrated the patronage and credibility of Francesco Gonzaga.

This style of princely patronage had a profound impact on the operatic end product. Theater and set designers were mindful of the needs of patrons. It was important to arrange seating at theatrical events with attention to the prestige and status of the attendees. Stage and theater design tell us a lot about the status of the spectators and the patronage market for early opera. We know very little about the actual stage layout for *Orfeo* beyond the fact that it was at the ducal palace and that the space was crowded. But we do know a great deal about Italian stage practice of the early Baroque period in general, thanks to Nicola Sabbatini's *Pratica di fabricar scene e machine ne' teatri* (Manual for Constructing Theatrical Scenes and Machines, 1638). Sabbatini's manual addresses the architect, whose job it was to turn a hall into a theater with scenery, machines, and lighting (Document 1). The first book covers theater construction, audience arrangement, scene building, painting, and lighting. Sabbatini offers a unique take on locating the prince's chair in relation to the vanishing point, and provides the ground plan for scenery, wings, and shutters. Sabbatini also discusses the demands for moving scenery, and the incorporation of *intermezzi*, set pieces and spectacle, all of which gives us a sense of just how complex early Baroque operatic production was.

There are many cases in early Baroque opera where the patron took particular interest in musical matters. Francesco Gonzaga not only sponsored *Orfeo;* he also oversaw the hiring of singers. The degree of Francesco's involvement may have been motivated by rivalry with the Florentine court and with his brother, Ferdinando, who left Mantua in 1605 to study in Pisa. A series of letters from Francesco in Mantua to his brother in Pisa show the great effort taken to recruit the best singers from the Florentine court (Document 2). Furthermore, the urgency of the letters suggests how crucial the *castrato* part was deemed for a successful first performance. *Castrati*, who first appeared in church music to replace the falsettists from the 1580s and 1590s, often sang female roles in Papal States, where women were forbidden to appear on stage (young boys were also useful for this purpose). In *Orfeo*, "a little priest" (Girolamo Bacchini?) sang the part of Eurydice, while the young *castrato* Giovanni Gualberto Magli sang the prologue and one other unspecified role (Speranza?); he was subsequently given the part of Proserpina as well. The singer-composer Francesco Rasi performed the title role.

Surviving accounts of the performance make it clear that the history of early Baroque opera is as much a history of the libretto as a history of the music. As Francesco Gonzaga reported on February 23, 1607, printed libretti were to be distributed at the performances of *Orfeo* so that spectators could follow the action on stage. Libretti may have been studied at leisure or given dramatic readings at academies and social gatherings, such as the Accademia degli Invaghiti. The novelty of setting an entire libretto text to music would not have escaped the first operatic audiences.

Musical Persuasion in Early Opera

Groups like the Accademia degli Invaghiti and the Florentine Camerata were intensely interested in the idea that music could move the affections of listeners. The theory that music held special power over listeners—which dates back to antiquity—resonates twofold in Monteverdi's *Orfeo*, for it provides both the plot line of the opera and, in a broader sense, the rationale for Monteverdi's musical style.

Early Baroque opera used four types of music: recitative, chorus, arias, and instrumental passages or *ritornelli*. Monteverdi used recitative, or speech-song, for key moments in the drama. Following the tradition of Greek tragedy, the chorus served to comment on the drama. "Arias" at this phase of opera's development were often short songs that came at points of reflection in the libretto. They are self-contained works for one or a few singers with instrumental accompaniment, and arise from the long tradition of solo song and monody in the Renaissance. Regular rhyme and metrical schemes in the text make the arias more structured than recitative.

Instrumental passages provided transition material, support for singers, and a continuous soundscape. In *Orfeo*, Monteverdi called for a total of forty-two individual instruments, including strings, wind, and continuo. The continuo group alone consisted of two harpsichords, one double harp, three *chitarroni*, two *ceteroni*, two *organi di legno*, two regals, and one *basso de viola da brazzo*. The diversity of instruments created a unique sound world that fused elements borrowed from the *intermedi*, the pastorals, and the new *cori spezzati* style popularized in Venice.

The most famous passage of *Orfeo* is the messenger scene and Orfeo's lament from Act 2, "Tu se'morta mia vita" (You Are Dead, My life). This is the point where Orpheus first learns of Euridice's untimely death. In the reception of the opera, particularly in Romain Rolland's review of Vincent d'Indy's historic revival of *Orfeo* in 1904 (Document 3), it is singled out as one of the opera's highpoints.

The scene is remarkable not only for its harmonic and structural coherence, but for the way Monteverdi builds emotional tension. (Examples 3.2–3.4 include a part for the keyboard player's right hand so that the harmonies are easier to see, although this version represents only one of many possible ways the chords of the basso continuo can be realized.)

The Messenger's opening cry "Ahi, caso acerbo" (Ah, bitter chance) recurs and functions as structural glue, even as it reaches a new level of intensity with each repetition. Monteverdi even specifies adding an organ to the continuo group to lend weight to the Messenger's speeches.

Example 3.2 Monteverdi, Messenger scene from Act 2, "Ahi caso acerbo," mm. 172–175.

Example 3.3 Monteverdi, Messenger scene from Act 2, mm. 226–233.

Example 3.4 Monteverdi, Messenger scene from Act 2, "Ahi caso acerbo," mm. 287–289.

Throughout, Monteverdi borrows a common strategy from his madrigals, allowing the words to dictate harmonic shifts in the music. A jarring clash between the minor mode of the Messenger's speech and the major mode of the shepherds—who have yet to comprehend the despatch—reflects their opposing emotional perspectives. Orpheus, attuned to the Messenger's concern, responds with interjections in G minor and C minor. As the Messenger recounts the events leading to Euridice's death in music that ranges from simple narration on repeated notes to highly charged recitative, Monteverdi mirrors the drama in his music with wandering harmonies, chromaticism, and quick changes in tonal center. The music gains momentum in parallel with the drama, making its most abrupt harmonic turn at the crucial, climactic moment when Orpheus finally realizes that Euridice is dead (Ex. 3.3).

Messenger	To you I come, Orpheus,
A te ne vengo Orfeo,	miserable messenger of tidings yet more
Messaggiera infelice,	miserable and more tragic.
di caso più infelice e più funestro	Your lovely Euridice
la tua bella Euridice	

Orfeo	
Oimè che odo?	

Orpheus then laments his loss in the poignant "Tu se'morta mia vita" (You Are Dead, My Life). In this piece, Monteverdi draws upon the rich tradition of laments that extends back to Greek drama, where the lament occupied the central affective moment. The genre reached a privileged status in European literature in the epic poetry of Torquato Tasso's *Gerusalemme liberata* (Jerusalem Liberated) and in Olimpia's lament from Ariosto's *Orlando furioso*. Girolamo Mei singled out the lament as a defining feature of the new monodic style, and the lament added legitimacy to early opera: Its emotional intensity moved listeners to pity.

Monteverdi casts the lament scene as a recitative soliloquy, a style whose flexibility mirrors the mercurial quality of an extreme emotional state. Tension builds as pitch rises and the level of chromaticism increases, and Monteverdi maintains this tension across an overarching structural plan, even repeating words and phrases from the libretto in the first four lines of the lament to control the rate of escalating intensity. The example shows Striggio's libretto with Monteverdi's expansions in brackets.

Tu se'morta [*se'morta*], mia vita, ed io respire?	You are dead, my life, and I breathe?
Tu se'da me partita [*se'da me partita*]	You are gone from me
Per mai più [*mai più*] non tornare, ed io ri-mango?	Never to return, and do I remain?
Nò [*nò*], che se'i versi alcuna cosa ponno,	No, for if my verses can do anything,
N'andrò sicuro a'più profondi abissi,	I will go surely to the deepest abysses,
E intenerito il cor del Rè de l'ombre,	And having softened the heart of the Shades,
Meco trarrotti a riveder le stelle:	I will bring her back to see again the stars:
O, se ciò negherammi empio destino,	Oh, if wicked destiny refuses me this,
Rimarrò teco, in compagnia di morte.	I will stay with you in the company of death.
Addio, terra, addio cielo e sole, addio.	Farewell earth, heaven, sun, farewell.

Monteverdi employs the skills he honed as a madrigalist in his approach to setting the text. He hits the lowest note on "abysses," rises upwards for the "stars," and ends with a final descent of a seventh for the "farewell." Literal depiction of the text in this way is called word painting, and it is a common characteristic of Italian madrigals. Monteverdi even sets the final line of text in four parts to reflect Orpheus's farewell to earth, heaven, sun, and a closing departure.

Example 3.5 Monteverdi, *Orfeo*, Act 2, "Tu se'morta," mm. 312–352.

How might this scene have been performed? Recitative had such extraordinary rhetorical power that the style was fervently discussed in the writings of composers, theorists, and commentators. Compelling advice on how to perform recitative comes from an anonymous treatise titled *The Choragus*. The treatise's title refers to the professional charged with directing theatrical works, the choragus (or director). *The Choragus* likely dates from the 1630s and captures the aesthetic concerns of theatrical production from the early seventeenth century. The author reserves a chapter for recitation, in which he advises that singing should not be continuous; instead, the singer should pause at the end of each thought. Ever the dramatist, Monteverdi incorporates these moments of pause and repose directly in the music.

Orpheus's lament ends with a choral reprise of the Messenger's central warning, "Ahi caso acerbo," (Ex. 3.6) Reminiscent of ancient Greek practice, Monteverdi's chorus represents a specific body of characters, in this case the shepherds and shepherdesses. Monteverdi positions the Messenger's opening cry in the bass part, which ties the lament to the earlier part of the scene. Monteverdi adds four parts above the bass line, and the result combines features of recitative and madrigal with group declamation.

Example 3.5 (continued)

Ahi, caso ascerbo,	Ah, bitter chance,
Fato empio e crudele	Ah, fate wicked and cruel,
Ahi, stele	Ah, stars

How did composers determine whether to use aria or recitative? Composers took cues from their librettists. Striggio set off passages intended for arias in the libretto to *Orfeo*.

Monteverdi responded to Striggio's aria markings, and even expanded them to allow for text repetitions and moments of repose.

Orpheus's confrontation in Act 3 with Charon, ferryman of the River Styx, is a central dramatic moment in the opera. When Charon forbids Orpheus's entry to the underworld, a domain ruled by Pluto, Orpheus responds with the aria "Possente spirto" (Mighty Spirit). Monteverdi cast "Possente spirto," which appears at the midpoint of the five-act opera, as a set of strophic variations. Here Orpheus employs all of his devices as a singer to persuade Charon to ferry him across the Styx. In theatrical terms, this is a "real" song, naturally occasioned by dramatic events. It demonstrates the power of singing to effect change in the spectator, in this case Charon (and, by extension, the audience).

Monteverdi included two versions of Orpheus's "Possente spirto" in the 1609 printed score (Fig. 3.3): One gives the original, unadorned vocal line; the other shows the melody with a great deal of ornamentation. What do these ornaments imply? Can we take them as evidence of the version performed by the famous tenor, Francesco Rasi, in Mantua? Indeed, Rasi may well have performed such ornaments, or *passaggi*, as the singer's own books of secular songs or monodies suggest: Rasi's *Vaghezze di musica* (1608) contains *passaggi* and written-out embellishments very similar in style to those in "Possente spirto."

Monteverdi also achieves remarkable spatial effects in this scene by drawing upon the new *concertato* style associated with the Venetian *cori spezzati* technique. As Orpheus's music reverberates in the cavernous underworld, the vocal line is echoed by virtuosic instrumental interjections and ritornellos. Monteverdi's instrumentation is often quite specific, and was clearly designed to define character and enhance the ambience of particular types of scenes. For example, his instructions in the printed score of 1609 for "Possente spirto" stipulate organ and chitarrone as the accompanying instruments (Monteverdi also clarifies that Orpheus is to sing only one of the two notated vocal parts). Similar directions appear throughout the score: Pastoral scenes are represented by the merry sounds of treble and descant recorders, hell by darker tones of regal and trombones, and Orpheus, with his lyre (Act 3), is paired with virtuoso ritornellos for violins, cornets, and double harp. Monteverdi's training as a string player may have made him particularly sensitive to the role that instruments play in moving the emotions of listeners.

Example 3.6 Monteverdi, *Orfeo*, Act 1, Scene 2, choral reprise, mm. 353–358.

Figure 3.3 Monteverdi, *L'Orfeo*, "Possente spirto."

Modern Revivals of *Orfeo*

The superior quality of Monteverdi's instrumental, choral, solo, and ensemble writing grants *Orfeo* special status as the first masterpiece in the new genre of opera. But despite the musical and dramatic heights it reaches, *Orfeo* received only two performances in Mantua in 1607 and a possible revival at Genoa some time before 1646. It then lay virtually dormant until the early twentieth century. English historians Charles

Figure 3.3 (continued)

Burney and John Hawkins studied the score in the eighteenth century, but Monteverdi's audacious harmonies and colorful orchestra remained more of a curiosity than a model. In the late nineteenth century, however, research on Baroque music and early opera in particular played a crucial role in the nascent field of musicology in Germany. As musicology sought to establish itself as a legitimate form of scholarly inquiry, the revival of early music in the academy spawned the publication of new musical editions, theoretical writings, histories, monographs, and articles. The first modern edition of *Orfeo*, published in 1881 in an edition by Robert Eitner, was a fruit of that revival. However, the many significant changes that Eitner made to the original score—and these include substantial cuts, toning down Monteverdi's bold harmonies, and an overly simplistic continuo realization—confirm that the study of early music performance was still in its infancy.

A revival of interest in Claudio Monteverdi in the twentieth century sparked a number of new editions of *Orfeo*, and these divide roughly into two streams—arrangements and adaptations on the one hand, and scholarly attempts to respect the composer's original intentions on the other. Composers Vincent d'Indy, Carl Orff, Ottorino Respighi, and Luciano Berio are among those who made free adaptations or modern arrangements of Monteverdi's masterpiece. Romain Rolland's account of concert performances of *Orfeo* at the Schola Cantorum in Paris in 1904 (the performance was based on Vincent d'Indy's edition of 1905 and used d'Indy's own French translation) suggests that the renewed interest in Monteverdi's music reflected the social, cultural, and political times. Part history lesson, part music review, Rolland's essay reveals the nationalist sentiment surrounding the Monteverdi revival of the early twentieth century (Document 3).

Perhaps the most influential of these composer-editions of *Orfeo* is the remake by Carl Orff (1895–1982). Orff departed in significant ways from Monteverdi's original, using modern orchestra and compressing the action into three acts. Orff's interest in combining music, dance, and text was central to his compositional thought in general—his best-known stage work, *Carmina burana* (1937), is a good example of this—but Orff also drew inspiration from classical Greek tragedy and Italian Baroque stage music. His fascination with Monteverdi's *Orfeo* spanned much of his career: Orff made an early version with German text titled

Figure 3.4 Rehearsal of Monteverdi's *Orfeo*, June 22, 2007, Theatre de l'archeveche, Aix-en-*Provence de l'opera.*

Orpheus in 1923, a second version in 1929, and a third (now considered the definitive version) in 1939. In 1957, this latter version was published as part of a triptych, entitled *Lamenti*, that also includes Orff's settings of the laments from *Arianna* and the *Ballo delle ingrate*. In the program for the 1940 Dresden production under conductor Karl Böhm, Orff argued that a modern orchestra, rather than a historical replica of Monteverdi's Mantuan ensemble, enhanced the work, allowing this "masterpiece of a past age" to speak to contemporary listeners "in our language."

Free adaptations of *Orfeo* brought new attention to Monteverdi's work but they also inspired attempts at more historically accurate interpretations. Editions by Francesco Malipiero, John A. Westrup, Paul Hindemith, Thurston Dart, and Denis Stevens gave scholars and performers a fresh starting-point for performances staged in the United States and Britain in the mid-twentieth century. By the late 1960s, *Orfeo* had entered the standard repertory of the major opera houses, with influential productions led by Raymond Leppard (London, 1965), Nikolaus Harnoncourt (recording issued 1969), Roger Norrington (Kent Opera, 1976, and Florence, 1984), and John Eliot Gardiner (London, 1981). The Aix-en-Provence (2007) performance adopted a stark minimalist approach, with a huge white box designed by Toland Aeschlimann encasing the action (Fig. 3.4).

There is thus no single *Orfeo*, and each revival of *Orfeo* is both a product and a reflection of its own era. Audiences of Monteverdi's day would have experienced the opera as part of a continuum of court *intermedi* and pastoral plays, but perhaps they would also have seen *Orfeo*, with its novel, vivifying, speech-like recitative, as a culmination of that continuum. Perhaps they would have seen it as well as a window onto ancient Greece, as false as that window may have been. For us today, *Orfeo* is iconic. We, too, see it as a window onto the past, as a glimpse of a particularly pregnant moment in the cultural and musical history of the early Baroque. Certainly the historically informed, period performances of the opera are a manifestation of our age's obsession with history and with placing art in its historical and cultural context. But each era has brought different values and different perspectives to *Orfeo*. The fact that *Orfeo* has resonated so powerfully as a work of art for so many different types of audiences and in so many different guises speaks to its quality, yes. It also tells us something about ourselves.

Documents

Document 1. Nicola Sabbatini, *Manual for Constructing Theatrical Scenes and Machines* (1638). In *The Renaissance Stage: Documents of Serlio, Sabbattini and Furtenbach*. Trans. Allardyce Nicoll, John H. McDowell, and George R. Kernodle. Ed. Barnard Hewitt. Coral Gables, FL: University of Miami Press, 1958. pp. 87–8, 96–7. Reprinted with the permission of the University of Miami Press.

Set Design

How to Place the Prince's Seat

It seems reasonable to me, after having described the stage setting, to discuss how and in what position should be located the seat of the prince or other dignitary who is to witness the performance. You will have to choose a location as near as possible to the point of distance, and elevated sufficiently from the floor of the hall so that when seated his eye will be as high as the vanishing point, for all the objects in the scene appear better from that position than from any other place. You then make a kind of palisade, fixed to the ground with strong beams and secured with stout pegs and nailed, so that the crowd of people, who on these occasions show little discretion, cannot injure it. Around this may be placed seats for the courtiers, or for the soldiers of his guard, as desired. . . .

How and in What Order to Accommodate the Audience

The accommodating of an audience is a matter of much importance and trouble. Yet, at these performances there is never a lack of willing helpers, especially those who seek the job of showing the ladies to their seats. Were the performances given daily, there would still be plenty of those. You must take care, however, to select for this purpose, persons of years of discretion, so that no suspicion or scandal arise. The ladies are to be placed in the orchestra, or as we say, in the third of the hall nearest the stage, taking care to place the least important in the first rows nearest the parapet and proceeding in the other rows according to rank. Care should be taken always to place the most beautiful ladies in the middle so that those who are acting and striving to please, gaining inspiration from this lovely prospect, perform more gaily, with greater assurance, and with greater zest.

The more elderly ladies should be seated in the last rows on account of the proximity of the men, so that every shadow of scandal may be avoided. Those who are responsible for seating the men should be persons of authority and, if possible, should be acquainted with all or at least part of them. In giving them the seats, it will be necessary to see that the common or less cultivated persons are set on the tiers and at the sides, since the machines give a less perfect appearance in these places, and because such people do not observe them minutely. The persons of culture and taste should be seated on the floor of the hall, as near the middle as possible, in the second or third rows. They will have the greatest pleasure there, since in such a position all the parts of the scenery and the machines are displayed in their perfection, and they will not be able to see the defects which are sometimes discerned by those on the steps or at the sides.

Document 2. Recruiting Singers: Letter of Francesco Gonzaga, Mantua, January 5, 1607, to Ferdinando Gonzaga in Pisa. Trans. Stephen Botterill. In *Claudio Monteverdi, Orfeo*. Ed. John Whenham, Cambridge Opera Handbooks. Cambridge: Cambridge University Press, 1986. pp. 167–9. Reprinted with the permission of Cambridge University Press.

I have decided to have a play in music performed at Carnival this year, but as we have very few sopranos here, and those few not good, I should be grateful if Your Excellency would be kind enough to tell me if those *castrati* I heard when I was in Tuscany are still there. I mean the ones in the Grand Duke's service, whom I so much enjoyed hearing during my visit. My intention is to borrow one of them (whichever Your Excellency thinks the best), so long as you agree that the Grand Duke will not refuse to lend him, if you yourself do the asking, for a fortnight at most. Please will Your Excellency let me know about this, so that if I do decide to use one of these singers I can write to you asking for your support in my approach to the Grand Duke.

* * *

Letter of Ferdinando Gonzaga, Pisa, January 14, 1607, to Francesco Gonzaga in Mantua.

In accordance with Your Highness's orders I have engaged a *castrato*, who is, in fact, not one of those whom Your Highness heard; but he has performed with great success in musical plays on two or three occasions. He is a pupil of Giulio Romano [Giulio Caccini] and receives a stipend from the Grand Duke.

* * *

Letter of Francesco Gonzaga, Mantua, January 17, 1607, to Ferdinando Gonzaga in Pisa.

Because I hope that His Highness will be good enough not to refuse my request [for a *castrato*], and in order not to waste time waiting for your reply, I am sending you the said *castrato's* part, so that he can study it and learn it thoroughly, should the Grand Duke lend him to me. He should be able to set out at the beginning of next month; on this occasion I must ask Your Excellency to give him some money to cover the expenses of his journey, which I will repay by being of service to you here in any way that I can.

* * *

Letter of Francesco Gonzaga, Mantua, February 2, 1607, to Ferdinando Gonzaga in Pisa

By the time Your Excellency receives this, my much-needed *castrato* will have arrived here, or will at least be on his way. . . . Without this soprano it would be quite impossible to stage [the play] at all.

* * *

Letter of Ferdinando Gonzaga, Pisa, February 5, 1607, to Francesco Gonzaga in Mantua.

This is to introduce Giovanni Gualberto, a young *castrato* whom I am sending to your Highness to take part in the performance of your play. You will hear from his own lips of the difficulty he has had in learning the part which was given him; so far he has managed to commit only the prologue to memory, the rest proving impossible because it contains too many notes.

* * *

Letter of Francesco Gonzaga, Mantua, February 9, 1607, to Ferdinando Gonzaga in Pisa.

I would have expected that the *castrato* would have arrived by now, and indeed it is essential that he should be here as soon as possible. He will now have not only to play the part that was sent to him, but also to learn that of Proserpine, as the singer who was to take the role can no longer do so. So I am awaiting him from day to day with great eagerness, as without him the play would be a complete failure. Meanwhile, I must ask Your Excellency to thank the Grand Duke for the kindness he has shown me; I will thank him myself by letter when the *castrato* returns to you.

Document 3. A Review of Vincent d'Indy's Performance. Paris, February 25 and March 2, 1904. Romain Rolland, "A Review of Vincent d'Indy's Performance (Paris, 1904)." Trans. Wendy Perkins. In *Claudio Monteverdi, Orfeo*. Ed. John Whenham, Cambridge Opera Handbooks. Cambridge: Cambridge University Press, 1986. pp. 119, 122, 123, 124. Reprinted with the permission of Cambridge University Press.

The outstanding musical event of this month (I do not mean the one that has most struck the public, but if we were to concern ourselves with the opinion of the public! . . .), the most significant event has been the performance of Monteverdi's *Orfeo* at the *Schola*. For all the musicians who heard it this performance was a revelation. In *Orfeo* we have not merely an historical curiosity, but a masterpiece that is virtually the only example of a vanished art. Vanished? Who knows? For, strange to say, this art seems on the point of being reborn in our midst, and this *favola in musica* from the beginning of the seventeenth century may offer precious ideas, even models, for those among our young composers who are, at this moment, trying to create a more supple, more realistic style of lyrical declamation, and one that is free from Germanic influences. . . .

Four or five pages seem to me divine: Orpheus's air at the beginning of the second act, when he greets the fields and the woods with joyful tenderness—'Ecco pur ch'a voi ritorno, care selve e piaggie amate'; his lamentations in the Underworld—'Orfeo son'io' (Act III), containing those passages of vocalisation without words, strange and inspired, close to sobbing; the proud, youthful exuberance of the fourth act, when he emerges from the Underworld, leading Eurydice —'Qual honor di te fia degno, mia ctra onnipotente'; and, above all, in the second act, the recitative of the Messenger who announces the death of Eurydice to Orpheus. This is, to my mind, truly the highest point which musical declamation has ever reached. The artistry is so great that it is forgotten; heart speaks to heart, and one in penetrated by grief both profound and chaste, of sublime innocence.

Our new school of composers might look for models and arguments here to support them in their conviction that there exists, that there must exist, a musical art superior to that which has been imposed on us for two centuries by a degenerate Italy and her pupil Germany: an art less solemn, less constrained, less subservient to the formalism of classical rhetoric, to the tyranny of the bar-line, to the conventions of a theater of declaiming puppets; in their conviction, too, that the emancipation of music envisaged and desired by the impetuous nature of a Beethoven, or by the inspired ignorance of a Berlioz, is far from being accomplished, and that this dream of a freer, more human art is not a chimera; for, many centuries ago, the young and audacious genius of the Renaissance had, for a moment, achieved it. A moment so fleeting! . . .

I believe that the liberating reform of Monteverdi came to nothing, like so many other inspired ideas of the Italian Renaissance, because the Italian Renaissance was itself slowly dying at that moment, crushed by all kinds of political and religious despotisms, which is not my purpose to discuss here. The free spirit of Italy longs for subjection; music, in common with the other arts, tends towards domestication. It is clear that, in this order of things, the France of Louis XIV and the Germany of the Prussian Sergeant-Major [Friedrich Wilhelm I] ought to have the prize. Now that our minds are struggling for emancipation once again, they are rediscovering the way for themselves and trying to take up the unfinished task of the world's most liberated age.

Note

1 Giovanni de'Bardi, "Dalle più alte sfere," trans. in Claude V. Palisca, ed. *Norton Anthology of Western Music*, 2nd ed. (New York: W. W. Norton, 1988) vol. 1, p. 344.

4   Music and Religion to the End of the Thirty Years' War

One of the hardest concepts for us to grasp today is the firm hold that religion had on virtually all aspects of society, culture, and politics in the Baroque period. The sixteenth through mid-seventeenth centuries was a period of extreme religious unrest in the wake of the gradual consolidation of Lutheran, Calvinist, Protestant, and Catholic denominations across Europe and England. The role of music in worship was hotly debated, as it had been for centuries. St. Augustine (354–400) identified the crux of the argument in his autobiographical *Confessions*, where he admits to being at times "more moved by the singing than by what is sung." Sacred texts that are sung, according to Augustine, can certainly inspire "greater religious fervor." But music can also distract the mind away from the words, away from pious thoughts. Religious leaders, scholars, and congregants continue to disagree about what type of music is most conducive to worship.

This chapter examines the writings of theologians and religious laymen within the socio-economic conditions of the early Baroque period for evidence of their influence on religious and musical practices. We will also examine a series of case studies from Italy, France, England, and German-speaking lands to explore sacred music from the late sixteenth century to the end of the Thirty Years' War in 1648. The thread that connects these case studies is the shared belief across the continent that music could have a profound impact on its listeners, an idea that was no less relevant to sacred music than to secular music in the Baroque. Although we can trace the idea back to antiquity, its prominence distinguishes the Baroque era from the past. Theorists referred to it as the Doctrine of Affections, an aesthetic concept derived from ancient Greek and Latin rhetoric. Essentially the Doctrine of Affections transposed the highly sophisticated rhetorical techniques of oration to musical composition and performance. Orators used their skill in rhetoric to control and direct the emotions of their audiences; Baroque composers and performers believed they could do the same. In sacred music, their goal was to direct those emotions towards devotion and piety.

Music and the Arts after the Council of Trent

The sixteenth century was a turbulent one for the Catholic Church, with attacks from Martin Luther, Jean Calvin, and King Henry VIII. In response to calls for a "general free Christian council" to reform the church, Pope Paul III (reigned 1534–49) convened the Council of Trent in 1545 to provide direction for the future of the Catholic Church (Fig. 4.1). The Council met in twenty-six sessions through 1563 under Pope Pius IV. The ensuing church reform established the parameters for debates on music and religion in the early Baroque period. It also revived Baroque Catholicism.

The Council formulated a central doctrine for the arts in Catholic worship that offered a context for the production of music in the post-Tridentine period. That doctrine is set out in a decree that defines the appropriate use of images and paintings in the service of the Church, and in it we can see direct parallels between decoration in religious architecture and the visual arts and in music. For instance, the Council called for the veneration of images of Christ, the Virgin, and the saints, all of whom were the focus of musical elaboration as well. Holy images also served a pedagogical purpose, bringing biblical stories "before the eyes of the faithful." Music, too, was considered a pedagogical tool; simple music helped people learn religious texts, such as the psalms. Further, the Council instructed that "images shall not be painted and

SACRO CONCILIO GENERALE DI TRENTO

Incominciato sotto il Pontificato di Paolo III. Regnando l'Imperatore Carlo V. l'Anno 1545. terminato l'Anno 1564. Intervennero 7 Cardinali, 4 Arcivescovi, 7 Prelati, 227 Vescovi, 12 Generali di tutte le Regioni, 12 Dottori e Teologi, 8 Ambasciatori di Principi.

Trento presso Giuseppe Anton Morietti Librajo

Figure 4.1 The inaugural meeting of the Council of Trent, *ca.* 1555.

adorned with a seductive charm, or the celebration of saints and the visitation of relics be perverted by the people into boisterous festivities and drunkenness." So too, music: Post-Tridentine reforms called for the removal of excessive melismas (embellishments) and secular melodies.

The high altar was the focal point for visual display. Giacomo della Porta's design of the Gesu Church in Rome typifies Baroque interest in decoration, visual splendor, and magnificence (Fig. 4.2).

Statements of the Roman Catholic Church guided artistic production during the Baroque period and marked points of differentiation from competing faiths. Remarkably, however, the Council said very little about musical style itself. The single decree on music appeared in the canons and decrees of the twenty-second session of the Council, Abuses in the Sacrifice of the Mass, celebrated on September 17, 1562. This decree affirmed the primacy of Gregorian chant; it also banned secular music and music whose sole intent was the listener's pleasure.

But if the Council gave only limited direction in terms of musical style, its liturgical reforms certainly determined the types of music cultivated in the Baroque period. The Council revised the liturgy to create a more uniform celebration of both the Mass and the Divine Office, and editions of the reformed breviary and missal soon appeared. Entrusting composers Giovanni Pierluigi da Palestrina (1525/6–94) and Annibale Zoilo (*ca.* 1537–92) with the necessary liturgical and stylistic updates, Pope Gregory XIII (1502–85) set about ridding the plainsong melodies of excessive melismas, correcting Latin accentuation, and removing awkward melodic intervals. Complementing the new breviary and missal was the *Caeremoniale episcoporum*, issued in 1600, which codified much of the Tridentine ritual, including the use of organ. The resultant *Editio Medicaea* was published in 1614.

Musically speaking, the most important change was the new demand for specifically liturgical music, such as psalms and hymn cycles for the Office of Vespers, and Magnificats. The reforms made these a

Figure 4.2 Main altar at Chiesa del Gesu, Rome. Designed by architects Giacomo della Porta and Giacomo Barozzi da Vignola.

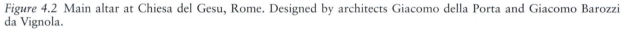

standard part of the Roman Catholic liturgy, as it was now celebrated across Europe. Composers such as Giovanni Rovetta (1595/7–1668), Claudio Monteverdi (1567–1643), and Alessandro Grandi (1586–1630) responded with publications of vespers and concerted psalms. In addition to set liturgical pieces, the reforms allowed for a more flexible utilization of motets and even for organ music within the Mass. Complete settings of the Mass Ordinary—Kyrie, Gloria, Credo, Sanctus-Benedictus, and Agnus Dei—continued to be composed. At the same time, free motets on texts that combined scriptural and even non-scriptural sources were written for informal devotional worship and for liturgical services where their heterogeneous texts made them suitable for various feast days. Free motets became venues for musical exploration and experimentation in harmonic language, text expression, and, in the concerted motets, instrumentation.

Motets Big and Small

The first half of the seventeenth century saw two basic styles of motet writing. The choral motet style of the sixteenth century, which continued to be cultivated in the Baroque period, is exemplified in the motets of Palestrina, whose music served as a model for such Roman composers of the early seventeenth century as Ruggiero Giovannelli (*ca.* 1560–1625), Felice Anerio (*ca.* 1560–1614), and Francesco Soriano (1548/9–1621). In its later guise, the style became known as the *stile antico* (old style), in reference to its *a capella* settings, conservative harmonies, textual clarity, and homophonic textures—all Renaissance traits.

The vocal concerto or motet concerto of the Baroque period drew on the newer styles of writing for voices and instruments that originated with the *cori spezzati* (split choirs) of the mid-sixteenth century. The *cori spezzati*, common in both Venice and Rome, exploited the spatial separation of multiple choirs through call-and-response forms and short imitative dialogues. In Venice, Adrian Willaert's (*ca.* 1490–1562) settings of double-choir vesper psalms for St. Mark's Basilica, where he served as chapel master from 1527 until his death, survive in *Di Adriano et di Jachet: I salmi . . . a uno et a duoi chori* (Psalms, for One and Two Choirs, Venice, 1550). Palestrina's *Motettorum . . . liber tertius* (Motets, Book 3, Venice, 1575) exemplify the Roman practice of polychoral music. The syllabic text settings common to the polychoral style aligned nicely with the Council of Trent's insistence on textual clarity, while the multiple choirs projected an unmistakable message of religious splendor.

The practice of adding instruments to the *cori spezzati* for an even grander sonic display started in Venice under Andrea Gabrieli (1532/3?–85) and his nephew and student, Giovanni Gabrieli (*ca.* 1554/7–1612). Both had prominent careers as organists at St. Mark's Cathedral in Venice, where famed music theorist Gioseffo Zarlino served as chapel master from 1565 until his death. Andrea Gabrieli probably assumed his appointment as permanent organist there at the start of 1566; Giovanni competed for an organist position on January 1, 1585, won, and retained the position all his life. At the time of their service, St. Mark's was the undisputed musical and religious capital of Venice, and the Basilica's status was matched by the magnificence of a collection of large-scale motets by both Andrea and Giovanni Gabrieli issued under the title *Concerti di Andrea, et di Gio[vanni] Gabrieli* (Venice, 1587). The scale of these motets made them ideal for special feasts and ceremonies, where they were performed at the Offertory, Elevation, and Post-Communion of the Mass.

Giovanni Gabrieli published two collections of "sacred symphonies" (*Sacrae Symphoniae*, 1597, 1615) in the new mixed concertato idiom. Each volume contains works for large groups of instruments and multiple choirs. The motet "Hodie completi sunt" for the Feast of Pentecost from the second book of *Sacrae Symphoniae* is typical of the set. Gabrieli divides the text into sections that accord with the structure and meaning of the text. Each section is demarcated by a change in texture: Gabrieli shifts from homophonic, call-and-response passages to imitative sections and then to overlapping choirs for the words "qui crediderit, et baptizatus fuerit" (he who believes, and has been baptized, will be saved (Ex. 4.1)). This passage is from the Vulgate (Latin version of the Bible authorized for use in the Roman Catholic Church), St. Mark 16:16. A feature of this and other large works by Gabrieli is an Alleluia refrain in triple meter—symbolic of the Trinity of Father, Son, and Holy Ghost. Gabrieli restricts himself to harmonies of the *prima pratica*, although the setting of the baptismal text, which oscillates on the chords of G major, C minor, and F major, is more adventurous.

The physical layout of St. Mark's enhanced the distribution of the text across the space. Groups of musicians were positioned amidst the main choir on the ground level of the Basilica and in its famous upper galleries.

The Venetian fascination with musical sonority outweighed the obsession with textual clarity that dominated Roman polychoral works. By adding instruments, Venetian-based composers essentially announced the city's musical independence, mirroring the city's efforts to gain political independence from Rome. Tension between these two territories was rife, erupting with the Interdict of 1606–7 that brought Venice to the brink of excommunication for its failure to respect Roman rule on land and legal disputes.

The stature of the Republic was partially responsible for the popularity of the Venetian polychoral style outside of Italy. It was a major center for music printing, an international marketplace, an artistic capital, and a political inspiration—its constitution, which included elements of monarchy, aristocracy and republican process, attracted the interest of philosophers and political strategists across Europe and even in America, among its founders of the eighteenth century. Projecting an image of both political and musical sovereignty to the rest of Europe was essential if Venice was to maintain its stature: The splendor of Gabrieli's opulent polychoral music played no small role in this. In Venice, religious ritual was also state ritual: Glorifying God went hand in hand with glorifying the Republic.

The Gabrielis had strong ties to southern Germany, with periods of service at Duke Albrecht V's court at Munich during Orlande de Lassus's tenure as chapel master. Giovanni's reputation in the north was further enhanced by his status as a teacher, and he played host to a string of young musicians who traveled to Venice to study with him. Among them was Heinrich Schütz (1585–1672), who became the most important

Figure 4.3 Title page, *Concerti di Andrea, et di Giovanni Gabrieli*, 1587.

successor of Gabrieli's style. Schütz cultivated the polychoral idiom in three volumes of *Sacrae Symphoniae* (1629, 1647, 1650), collections whose title paid homage to Gabrieli's earlier volumes of the same name. Venetian polychoral style thus established a prototype for religious splendor for all of Europe, Catholic and Protestant alike.

The social and economic decline of the 1620s caused by the protracted conflicts of the Thirty Years' War (1618–48) led to the production of smaller-scale sacred works. Many chapels and smaller parish churches were forced to reduce the number of singers and instrumentalists in their musical establishments, creating a market for motets for one to four voices that is clearly reflected in the Venetian presses. These compact motets featured the new basso continuo, which provided harmonic and rhythmic scaffolding for concertato

Example 4.1 Giovanni Gabrieli, "Hodie completi sunt," mm. 52–60.

Example 4.1 (continued)

solo, duet, and trio singers. "Exaudi me, Domine" (Here Me, O Lord), from Lodovico Viadana's *Centi concerti ecclesiastici* (One Hundred Sacred Concertos, 1600), is typical of this genre.

The small-scale motet remained a popular medium for the next generation of northern Italian composers as well, including Alessandro Grandi and Giovanni Rovetta. Rovetta served as vice chapel master at St. Mark's Basilica in Venice from 1627 and succeeded Monteverdi as chapel master in 1644, remaining in that post for the rest of his life. Among his four volumes of motets, five books of psalms (including one with masses), three books of concerted madrigals, and the opera *Ercole in Lidia*, is the duet "O quam tu pulchra es" (How Beautiful Art Thou), which first appeared in Rovetta's *Motetti concertati*, op. 3 (1635). It offers a snapshot of sacred music-making in Venice in the generation after Gabrieli. Rovetta sets a passionate passage from chapter four of the Old Testament's *Song of Solomon*.

The opening and closing phrase, "Quam pulchra es amica mea" (How beautiful art thou, my love) is cast homophonically. The intervening duet section is imitative, and its lyrical, *arioso* writing and urgent, overlapping phrases are clearly indebted to contemporary opera (Ex. 4.2).

Rovetta punctuates the syntax of the text with abrupt harmonic shifts that signal a pause or full stop, such as the shift from G major for "eloquium tuum dulce" (your sweet speech) to E major with the sudden change in the text's mood at "Vulnerasti cor meum" (Thou has wounded my heart).

As the singers praise the eyes, hair, lips, teeth, speech, and tongue of the beloved, the ornamentation recalls secular theatrical styles of the 1630s (Ex. 4.4).

Example 4.2 Rovetta, "Quam pulchra es," mm. 51–55.

mel et lac sublingual tua   Honey and milk are under thy tongue[1]

Example 4.3 Rovetta, "Quam pulchra es," mm. 28–33.

Favus distillans labia tua, sponsa mea;   Thy lips, my spouse, are as a dripping honeycomb,

Example 4.4 Rovetta, "Quam pulchra es," mm. 46–50.

Example 4.5 Rovetta, "Quam pulchra es," mm. 80–84.

Rovetta closes with a traditional, extended, triple-meter Alleluia. Rovetta uses a common rhythmic technique called hemiola here, in which two units of triple meter are articulated as three units of duple meter. The square brackets in m. 83 indicate coloration in the original source; this switch in the color of the notes (to black, for instance) signaled to the singer a change of rhythmic values. Hemiolas energize the music by suggesting, momentarily, a faster pulse.

While such sensuous love poetry might strike us as an odd choice for church music, "Quam pulchra es" was considered an ideal text for the feast days of female saints and virgins or for devotional singing in less formal settings.

Free motets in the new concerted idiom were controversial, however. Jesuit dramatist and preacher Jeremias Drexel (1581–1638) warned that the concerted idiom was "showy" and "more suitable for theater or dance than for the temple." He pleaded for "the old religiosity of sacred music to be revived."[2] On the other hand, Giovanni Battista Doni (*ca.* 1593–1647) insisted that the new style met the demands of the Council of Trent.

The Congregation of Sacred Rites, one of the Curial bodies established to oversee post-Tridentine reform, issued its most important decree on polyphony in 1643. The decree was part of a reintroduction of more rigorous control over religious life and a repurification of ritual. The decree makes explicit reference to the problem of textual clarity in sacred music of the time:

> The text of the Sacred Scriptures is notably altered, by mutilating, interchanging, and altering the words and their sense, and by adapting them to the modulation so that the music does not seem to be the slave of the Sacred Scripture, but the Sacred Scripture of the music.[3]

Textual clarity remained a huge concern for the rest of the seventeenth century: The decree was reinstated in 1657, 1665, 1674, and 1692.

The Catholic reforms were often at odds with contemporary musical practices and taste, and by 1650 the composition of sacred music had lost considerable status. The book industry, too, suffered with the economic decline experienced in Venice in the early decades of the seventeenth century, leaving a vacuum in the printing of sacred music books. Furthermore, the rise of public opera in Venice from 1640 onward drew such talented composers as Claudio Monteverdi and Francesco Cavalli to the theater. By 1700, Roman Catholic sacred music had reached a crisis point.

Emilio de'Cavalieri's *Rappresentazione di Anima e di Corpo*

Liturgical and para-liturgical music were complemented by an active devotional repertory of music for churches, homes, and religious gatherings. Some of this music was simple: The songs of praise known as *laude*, for instance, were syllabic settings for group singing. But some of the devotional music was also more adventurous, and various genres provided opportunities for composers to adopt modern stylistic trends and even break new ground.

In Rome, innovation entered via the confraternities, Oratorians, and Jesuits. The city was in the process of embracing a new sensuousness in its religious arts. We see it in both its architecture and in the visual arts, in the strategies artists used to exploit space, to contrast darkness and light, and in the vast ceiling frescoes designed to lift the gaze up to the heavens. Musically, there was a new attitude toward expressing the meaning of a text that cannot be divorced from the novel style of declaiming that had captured the imagination of poets and literati in Florence at the end of the sixteenth century. The new idiom, known as the *stile moderno*, was introduced to Roman circles by Emilio de'Cavalieri (*ca.* 1560–1602) in his *Rappresentatione di Anima e di Corpo* (Representation of Body and Soul). This exceptional musical event was Rome's first taste of the new recitative style.

Rappresentatione di Anima e di Corpo takes its place in music history as the first surviving play set entirely to music. It features a new style of sung dialogue (or *recitar cantando*, as Cavalieri called it in the preface to the printed score), along with arias, songs in dance meters, strophic songs, madrigals, and choruses. Is *Rappresentatione di Anima e di Corpo* an oratorio or an opera? Perhaps the term sacred opera best captures both its content and the context in which it was performed.

We know a great deal about the first performance of the *Rappresentatione* because it coincided with the festive occasion of the Holy Year of 1600. Indeed, an illustration on the title page of the *Rappresentatione* shows Clement VIII proclaiming the Holy Year 1600 and opening the *porta santa*, or Holy Gate. The Jubilee Year spurred travel to Rome as news of the festivities spread across Europe through diplomatic channels. Writing from Rome to the affluent Fugger family in Augsburg, a correspondent reported on January 1, 1600, that:

> Although the Pope was not quite free from gout, he was yet unwilling to put off the opening of the Holy Gate any longer on account of the large sums which the Hospital of the Holy Trinity was spending on the great mass of Pilgrims who have crowded the town. Therefore, on the last day of December, he had himself carried in Pontifical vestments to the Church of St. Peter, accompanied by all his cardinals, bishops, the foreign ambassadors, his clergy and retinue. There, after he had reached the other door with great difficulty, and after the Antiphones had been sung, he opened the Holy Gate with the usual ceremonies. Although the Swiss Guards had beaten back crowds with their staves, the journey of the Pope was very tedious. Whereupon the cardinals also opened the gates of the Churches of St. Paul, St. John and Our Blessed Lady under a great concourse of people.[4]

A letter from Cavalieri to Cardinal Benedetto Accolti adds to this image of festive hub-hub. Dated December 28, 1600, Cavalieri states, "On Christmas day the Pope gave the blessing and granted the indulgences; and I believe there are 130,000 [people] in Rome, where normally there are 106,000."[5]

The high traffic of pilgrims to Rome was a manifestation of this era's intense preoccupation with spiritual salvation. Heavenly rewards and infernal punishments were not just abstract ideas; they were real and topical. These themes were central to the devotional practices of the city's confraternities, which formed an important performance context for the *Rappresentatione*. And they are central to the *Rappresentatione*'s story itself, an allegory of the Soul and the Body, torn between the temptations of the World and the promise of Heaven.

The work was performed in February 1600, in a small oratorio off the right transept of the Chiesa Nuova, the Church of Santa Maria in Vallicella. There were a reported thirty-five cardinals in attendance. The Chiesa Nuova was the seat of the *congregazione dell'oratorio*, a confraternity founded in 1575 by Filippo Neri. Padre Agostino Manni, a member of the *congregazione dell'oratorio*, was probably the librettist for the *Rappresentatione*. Manni specialized in devotional poetry filled with depictions of heaven and hell, and many composers set his texts as *laude*—simple syllabic songs of praise suitable for congregational singing. Between 1563 and 1600, nine books of *laude* by Giovanni Animuccia, Francesco Soto de Langa, and Giovanni Giovenale Ancina were published to meet the new demands of the Oratorians and related groups. Their devotional services abandoned Latin, taking place in vernacular Italian instead, and a normal service included silent prayer, a series of lessons and homilies, and the singing of *laude*.

Cavalieri had firm ties to Rome's confraternities. He served as organist and coordinator of Lenten music from 1578 until at least 1584 at the Oratorio del SS Crocifisso in S Marcello, prior to his service at the Medici court at Florence in 1588. Cavalieri had overseen the staging of the lavish *intermedi* occasioned for the 1589 wedding of Ferdinando Medici to Christine of Lorraine, which brought him into close contact with the top artists, musicians, and literati of the day. Among these were the poets Ottavio Rinuccini, Giovanni Battista Strozzi, and Laura Guidiccioni; set and costume designer Bernardo Buontalenti; Giovanni de'Bardi, who conceived the allegorical plan and wrote some of the music and poetry; and the composers Alberigo Malvezzi, Luca Marenzio, Giulio Caccini, and Jacopo Peri. Cavalieri's years in Florence had also introduced him to the new musical idioms he brought to Rome in the *Rappresentatione*.

The core dialogue between the Soul and the Body provides an example of Cavalieri's merging of familiar and novel musical styles. "Anima mi ache pensa" (My Soul, What Are You Thinking?), from Act 1, Scene 4, first appeared as a popular religious song text in a collection of *laude* for the Congregazione dell'Oratorio in 1577. With a nod towards the oratories, where dialogues with an allegorical, hagiographic, or biblical content were highly prized, Cavalieri set the text as a dialogue in the *Rappresentatione*. He gave each character a contrasting vocal style—a conventional *lauda* singing style for the Soul, and the new recitative style for the Body. The syllabic setting and predictable rhythmic flow of the Soul's music, often accompanied with a note-against-note basso continuo, is in sharp contrast to the pliant rhythmic inflections of the Body's music, where shifts in harmony and intensity track the Body's progress from conviction to doubt and on to conversion.

The harmonic language underscores the contrast in musical styles. Cavalieri assigns the key of G major to the Soul and G minor to the Body, maintaining harmonic unity across the work even as the tension between the two modes essentially defines the action. The dialogue begins with the Body's attempt to seduce the Soul to worldly pleasures in a series of entries on B♭ above a G minor chord (nos. 4, 6, 8, 10, 12, 14). When the speaker changes, so does the mode, and the Soul's responses are on G major chords (nos. 5, 7, 9, 11 (Ex. 4.6)).

Corpo	Body[6]
Anima mia, che pensi?	My soul, what are you thinking?
Perchè dogliosa stai.	Why are you so occupied.
Sempre trahendo guai?	Always sighing woefully?

Anima	Soul
Vorei riposo, e pace;	I would have repose and peace;
Vorrei diletto, e gioia,	I would have love and joy,
E trovo affanno, e noia.	And I find anxiety and trouble.

Doubtful, the Body answers with the downward leap of a diminished fourth on "Lasso" (Alas).

Lasso, che di noi sia	Then what can we do!

The Soul persists, and a series of long notes reflect her desire for "rest in God," but the Body continues to question, with a cross relation—"che far deggio" (What should I do).

The turning point occurs when the Body utters, "Yes, my Soul" (Sì che hormai, alma mia), and the music begins its modulation towards G major, the Soul's key. Even the stage directions highlight the moment of conversion: The preface instructs the Body to "remove some vain ornament, such as a gold necklace, the plume of a hat, or something else."

Example 4.6 Cavalieri, *Rappresentatione di Anima e di Corpo*, Act 1, Scene 4, mm. 1–13.

Example 4.7 Cavalieri, *Rappresentatione di Anima e di Corpo*, Act 1, Scene 4, mm 50–52.

The preface to the printed score offers advice on how to perform the work that is relevant to performing early opera in general (Document 1). Primary concerns are how to instill variety and how to enhance the emotional impact of the music and poetry. Variety could be attained by having lots of different characters and costumes, through instrumentation, and by positioning *intermedi* between the acts. The greatest impact on emotions comes when the singer performs so that the text is understood "and that she accompany it with gestures and motions not only of the hands but also of steps, which are very effective means to move the affections" (Document 1).

The preface also contains the earliest description of figured bass with numbers and accidentals. According to the preface, the singers are to perform the dialogue "senza diminutioni" without excessive ornamentation. Cavalieri's rhetorical precedent for this was close to home, for the earliest followers of Filippo

Example 4.8 Cavalieri, *Rappresentatione di Anima e di Corpo*, Act 1, Scene 4, mm. 89–92.

Example 4.9 Cavalieri, *Rappresentatione di Anima e di Corpo*, preface.

Neri had already established a tradition of delivering a sermon "senz'alcuno ornamento." The composer describes only four short ornaments in his brief instructions to musicians—the *groppolo*, *monachina*, *trillo*, and *zimbelo*. These are notated in the score by the abbreviations *g, m, t, z* and written out in staff notation at the end of the preface (Ex. 4.9). In keeping with the rhetorical tradition of simple presentation, the dialogue contains only one such ornament, a *monachina* on the word "deggio" of the Body's text, "What should I do?" (see Ex. 4.8).

Did Cavalieri succeed in creating a work that could both move its audience and inspire it to piety? To judge from the preface to the printed score, yes, he did. In Alessandro Guidotti's dedication, the editor makes a special point of distinguishing between the pastoral dramas produced in Florence in the 1590s—which please the audience—and the *Rappresentatione*, which offers "clear proof of how this style could move one also to devotion." Indeed Guidotti singles out as the best means of moving the affections the very features present in the dialogue between the Body and the Soul: textual clarity, gestures, motions, and a variety of musical styles. When he returned to Rome in November 1600, Cavalieri boasted that those who had seen both the modest production of his *Rappresentatione* in Rome and the more elaborate wedding production of *Euridice* in Florence preferred the *Rappresentatione*. Why? "Because the music moved them to tears and laughter and pleased them greatly, unlike this music of Florence, which did not move them at all, unless to boredom and irritation."[7]

Sacred Music in Lutheran Germany

When Martin Luther (1483–1546) nailed his 95 Theses to the door of the castle church in Wittenberg to protest the Catholic Church's practice of selling indulgences, the news soon spread across Europe. Asked to recant, Luther refused and was excommunicated in 1521. Nine years later, after years of isolation, Luther emerged with the central doctrine of the new Lutheran church, presenting the Augsburg Confession to Emperor Charles V in 1530.

The core tenet of Luther's faith was the privileging of the Word of God—the scriptural texts—over the traditions of the church. This distinguished Lutheranism from competing confessions. The main theological difference between the Catholic Mass and the Lutheran Sunday morning *Gottesdienst* was the shift in emphasis away from the sacramental part of the service—the communion—to the liturgy of the Word, which, in the Lutheran tradition, contained the sermon.

The Formula and the Book of Concord of 1580 consolidated Lutheran doctrine and documents into a single volume: "For it seemed exceedingly necessary that, amidst so many errors that had arisen in our times, as well as causes of offense, variances, and these long-continued dissensions, there should exist a godly explanation and agreement concerning all these controversies, derived from God's Word, according to the terms of which the pure doctrine might be discriminated and separated from the false" (Document 2). The publication, symbolically fifty years after the Augsburg Confession, marks the beginning of the period of Lutheran Orthodoxy, which lasted until about 1680. Throughout the period, the writings of Martin Luther were of vital relevance to the way in which Baroque composers such as Michael Praetorius, Johann Hermann Schein, and Johann Sebastian Bach approached music.

Luther's liturgical reforms in the *Formula missae* (1523) and the *Deutsche Messe und Ordnung Gottesdienstes* (German Mass and Order of Service, 1526) called for two principal services: the Sunday morning *Gottesdienst* and the afternoon service of Vespers, held on Saturdays and Sundays. The services were conducted in Latin and German, although the use of German increased over the course of the Baroque period. The *Formula missae* retained most of the Latin Mass and its associated plainchant. But in keeping with Luther's theology, the celebration of the Mass was downplayed in favor of chorales and vernacular hymns.

Luther was a skilled musician, lutenist, singer, and composer. More than any other reformer, Luther proclaimed the value of music for the praise of God in his letters, writings, and hymnal prefaces, and his psalm-hymns, or chorales, circulated on cheap broadsheets, in letters, and by word-of-mouth.

Much of what we know about Luther's thoughts on music is included in his preface to the motet collection *Symphoniae iuncundae atque adea breves* (Rhau, 1538). This became one of Luther's most influential statements on music, for it was reprinted in sacred music books throughout the seventeenth century.

Luther's philosophy of music asserted three basic beliefs. First, music was God's gift to humanity, subordinate only to theology. Second, music had the power to move the affections and guide the spirit, a fundamentally Christian interpretation of the Greek ethical teachings of Plato and Aristotle. This conviction in particular—that music could play a fundamental role in spiritual formation—gave urgency to debates about the type of music that was appropriate for worship. For Luther, music amplified the textual message:

> Thus it was not without reason that the fathers and prophets wanted nothing else to be associated as closely with the Word of God as music. Therefore, we have so many hymns and Psalms where message and music join to move the listener's soul, while in other living beings and instruments music remains a language without words. After all, the gift of language combined with the gift of song was only given to man to let him know that he should praise God with both word and music, namely, by proclaiming [the Word of God] through and by providing sweet melodies with words.[8]

Finally, Luther regarded music as a pedagogical and edifying tool, again following ideas formulated in Plato's *Republic* and Aristotle's *Politics*. For that reason music held an esteemed intellectual and artistic position within the Protestant Latin school curriculum. Luther's preface to the *Symphoniae* encapsulated his affect-based theology of music as follows:

> We can mention only one point (which experience confirms), namely, that next to the Word of God, music deserves the highest praise. She is a mistress and governess of those human emotions—to pass over the animals—which as masters govern men or more often overwhelm them. No greater commendation than this can be found—at least not by us. For whether you wish to comfort the sad, to terrify the happy, to encourage the despairing, to humble the proud, to calm the passionate, or to appease those full of hate—and who could number all these masters of the human heart, namely, the emotions, inclinations, and affections that impel men to evil or good?—what more effective means than music could you find?[9]

How did Luther's writings play out in music for the Lutheran church? In keeping with Luther's theology, simple chorales or vernacular hymns were given prominence over the celebration of the Mass. These formed the mainstay of the music after the Gradual, before the sermon, and during Communion. Chorale settings were sung by the choir and congregation, in alternation, in unison, or in homophonic settings for four or five voices with the chorale tune in the top voice. This *musica choralis* alternated with more complex polyphony that was sung by professional singers called *musica figuralis*. The congregation's participation in hymn and psalm-singing, which was intended as a means of enhancing the participant's spiritual engagement on both an individual and communal level, is a key distinction between Protestant and Catholic liturgies. This simple and often unison singing framed more complex polyphonic motets and psalm settings for large choirs and instruments. For the larger-scale religious works, Lutheran composers such as Johann Hermann Schein and Heinrich Schütz turned to Italian models. It is a testament to musical taste and fashion that Italian musical styles of the early seventeenth century were favored across Europe, regardless of confessional alignment.

Heinrich Schütz

The works of Heinrich Schütz, who stands out among a talented group of German musicians and composers of the first half of the seventeenth century, exemplify the principles of the Lutheran doctrine of music. Schütz's music, along with that of Michael Praetorius (1571–1621), Samuel Scheidt (1587–1654), Johann Hermann Schein (1586–1630), and Hans Leo Hassler (1564–1612), shows the impact of cultural exchange with Italy. Elements of secular and sacred styles converge, and there is some experimentation in new styles within the context of the Lutheran chorale tradition. In German musicology, Schütz and Johann Sebastian Bach have long been considered the pillars of Lutheran music.

Figure 4.4 Portrait og Heinrich Schütz, engraving.

Schütz left letters, book prefaces, and documents that shed light on his life, musical style, and career. His life spanned the entire Thirty Years' War (1618–48) and its aftermath, a turbulent time for religion, politics, and the arts in German-speaking lands. Two extended stays in Italy were among his most formative artistic experiences. At the urging and financial expense of Landgrave Moritz of Kassel, Schütz made his first trip to Venice to study with Giovanni Gabrieli between 1609 and 1612. Schütz paid homage to his teacher, naming him in the dedication of his first book of madrigals (1611) to Landgrave Moritz. Elector Johann Georg I made his first attempt to lure Schütz to the Saxon court at Dresden in 1614. Schütz finally assumed the post of chapel master there on a permanent basis in 1621, and remained affiliated with the Dresden court for much of his career. His second trip to Italy (1628–9) proved equally valuable, for it was then that Schütz heard Monteverdi's music, setting the stage for his introduction of *seconda pratica* harmonic language to German-speaking lands. Schütz took the newer Italian styles to Denmark as well, in the course of two Danish tours. The first was occasioned by the festivities around the 1634 wedding of the crown prince of Denmark to Johann Georg's daughter, Magdalena Sibylla, for which Schütz directed the music; the second took place in 1642–4. After a brief period at the court of Wolfenbüttel in northern Germany, Schütz returned to Dresden in 1645 and remained there until his death in 1672.

Schütz was influenced by both types of sacred concertos common to the early seventeenth century: the concerto for few voices with basso continuo, modeled on Viadana's *Centi concerti ecclesiastici*; and those in which the polychoral interplay of voices and instruments is paramount, typified in Andrea and Giovanni Gabrieli's *Concerti* (1587) and Giovanni Gabrieli's *Sacrae Symphoniae* (1597).

Viadana's sacred concertos were very popular in German-speaking lands. All three volumes of his *concerti* were printed in Frankfurt by Nikolaus Stein (1609, 1610), a businessman known for specializing in Italian music. Stein issued a complete edition in 1613 with reprints in 1620 and 1626, along with a German translation of Viadana's preface and its valuable instructions on continuo playing. Viadana's music was an especially opportune model for composers who faced restrictions on chapel expenditures during the Thirty Years' War. As the effects of the war spread through the empire (the Treaty of Westphalia was not signed until October 24, 1648), composers were forced to abandon large-scale concertos in favor of reduced formats for only a small number of voices and basso continuo. Between 1618 and 1648, German composers produced a distinguished series of sacred concertos, scored for one to six voices and continuo, that includes Schein's *Opella nova* (New Works), Valentini's *Sacri concerti* (Sacred Concertos), Scheidt's *Newe geistliche Concerten* (New Sacred Concertos), and Schütz's *Kleine geistliche Conzerte* (Small Sacred Concertos).

"Eile mich, Gott, zu erretten" (Make Haste, O God, to Save Me, SWV 282) from Schütz's first volume of *Kleine geistliche Conzerte* is representative of the smaller-scale, sacred concertos. The text, drawn from

Example 4.10 Schütz, "Eile mich, Gott, zu erretten," SWV 282, mm 1–4.

Psalm 40, verses 14–17, explores central themes of Lutheranism: praise, devotion, and moral instruction. The setting, for soprano and basso continuo, is in a style marked *oratorio*. Schütz took great care in setting the text, adopting the speech-like style of the *stile rappresentativo*, although the setting is more restrained harmonically and rhythmically than its theatrical counterpart. Schütz's student, Christoph Bernhard, in describing *stylo oratorio* in his "Tractatus," (chapter 35), may be referring to Schütz when he writes that "today it [the stylo oratorio] has been admirably refined and polished through the efforts of considerable talent, so that I hardly believe that the ancient Greeks possessed this species of music."[10]

Schütz sets the opening lines in a declamatory style on many repeated pitches (Ex. 4.10). Rests reinforce the syntax of the line and off-beat chords provide places for the singer to breathe. The setting is a classic example of textual illustration—of depicting the words through the music—a key feature of musical rhetoric as Johann Burmeister described it in his *Musica poetica* (1606).

The most poignant example of textual illustration—or *hypotyposis*, as Burmeister referred to it—is Schütz's setting of the final lines of the psalm, which intensifies to an emotionally charged plea for God's help at the words "Ich aber bin elend ein arm" (Yet I am poor and wretched). This is cast in E major—a key that is sometimes associated with heightened emotional states in the Baroque—and the closing line of text, "mein Gott verzeuch nicht" (My God, do not delay), is treated to successive repetitions and ascending sequences that drive home the urgency of the speaker's plea (Ex. 4.11). Scarce though resources may have been during the Thirty Years' War, this compact setting shows no sacrifice in expressive power.

Schütz's three volumes of *Sacrae Symphoniae* (Sacred Symphonies, 1629, 1647, 1650) pay homage to Giovanni Gabrieli and Caspar Hassler, both of whom published collections entitled *Sacrae Symphoniae* before 1600. As the title implies, these are sacred concertos with obbligato instruments. Schütz published his first volume in Venice at the end of his second visit to the Republic. The final volume stands out from the earlier ones for its grand forces: from five to eight *obbligato* parts and a "Complementum" choir of from four to eight parts, to be "included at one's discretion" according to the title page. In the preface to the

Example 4.11 Schütz, "Eile mich, Gott, zu erretten," SWV 282, mm. 28–35.

Bassus ad organum partbook, Schütz provided "a few reminders" on how to perform the music, informing the reader that he has indicated figures "with all possible care above the bass." Unlike Italian composers, who often left the harmonic realization to the discretion of the performer, Schütz followed the precept: *Abundans cautela non nocet* (Abundant caution does not harm).

"Mein Sohn, warum hast du uns das getan?" (My Son, Why Have You Done This to Us? SWV 401) shows Schütz at his most expressive. The piece is a setting of a dialogue between the twelve-year-old Jesus and his parents, based on a passage from the Gospel of St. Luke. Luke's account takes place at the Temple in Jerusalem, where Jesus and his parents have attended the festival of Passover. When Mary and Joseph return to Galilee, they discover that Jesus has remained at the Temple. Schütz set Mary's reprimand of Jesus from chapter 2, verses 48–9, adapting the original text to include a part for Joseph—a savvy dramatic move, and one that also gave him the added resource of a bass voice. Conceived in two parts, the piece ends with a closing song of praise for full choir, a setting of verses 2, 3, and 5 of Psalm 84. The operatic style and high level of chromaticism forecast debates on musical style and decorum that heat up in Lutheran circles of the late seventeenth century.

After an opening Symphonia (for two violins, *Complementum* instruments, and continuo), Mary enters with her plea, "My son, why have you done this to us?" (Mein Sohn, warum hast du uns das getan?) (Ex. 4.12). Joseph joins her, and at the words, "Behold, your father [your mother] and I have searched for you with sorrow" (Siehe, dein Vater [deine Mutter] und ich haben dich mit Schmerzen gesucht), an abrupt shift from A minor to G minor vividly communicates their anxiety.

Jesus's question, "Was ist's, daß ihr mich gesuchethabet?" (Why is it that you search for me?), is a model of effective text setting. Set as a rising fifth, the phrase repeats, rises in pitch, and occurs in sequence, all techniques with clear parallels in expressive, rhetorical speech. Together they bestow a confident authority on Jesus' response to his parents.

Schütz used the entire four-part vocal and instrumental forces in the closing section. Their luxuriant sound is especially apt for the praise text of Psalm 84.

Schütz's 1650 volume, dedicated to Johann Georg, his long-term patron, includes a "Memorial," dated January 14, 1651, in which he summarized his career. In it the sixty-five-year-old composer pleaded to be "released into more peaceful circumstances." Evidently Schütz was unsuccessful in his request, for he did not retire until the Elector died in 1656. It is thanks to Schütz, however, and to the international breadth of his career, that Lutheran sacred music of the early Baroque period is graced with such expressive text settings, harmonic ingenuity, and rhetorical sophistication.

Example 4.12 Schütz, "Mein Sohn, warum hast du uns das getan?" SWV 401, mm. 39–42.

Example 4.13 Schütz, "Mein Sohn, warum hast du uns das getan?" SWV 401, mm. 79–87.

England to the End of the Commonwealth

England was the site of violent disruption and change in the sixteenth and seventeenth centuries, sparked by the pope's refusal to grant King Henry VIII an annulment of his marriage to Catherine of Aragon and Henry's subsequent proclamation of the Church of England in 1533. The Act of Supremacy (1534) proclaimed Henry supreme head of the Church of England. But although Henry's subsequent reforms included an attack on the cult of saints and images, he remained faithful to the central pillars of the Roman Catholic faith, not excepting the sacrament of Holy Communion at Mass. The short rule of young Edward VI (ruled 1547–53) was another matter, however, for the influence of austere Calvinist ideology during his realm increased the differences—and the enmity—between the Catholic Church and the Church of England. When Edward's sudden death left the throne open to Queen Mary (ruled 1553–8), a fierce Catholic, she reinstated Catholicism, restoring altars and images to parish churches. Her reign, too, was short, if brutal, and when Elizabeth I ascended to the throne in 1558, the pendulum once again swung back to Protestantism. Another Act of Supremacy (1559) made Elizabeth supreme governor of the Church. That same year Parliament passed the Act of Uniformity, which fixed the Anglican liturgy in the form of *The Book of Common Prayer*.

Nonetheless, Elizabeth preferred Catholic approaches to ceremony and ritual, and she was antipathetic to the reform spirit of many Protestants that contributed to the rise of the Elizabethan Puritan movement. Puritans, or "the godly" as they called themselves, sought an intense spiritual experience. Their religious practice was characterized by attendance at sermons during the week, demands for quality preaching, and complete devotion to God on the Sabbath. They also held that God's law as stated in Scripture is the one true law, a clear attack on the Act of Royal Supremacy. Despite this, Elizabeth and her successor, King James I (ruled 1603–25), permitted this diversity of faith, containing it under the single umbrella of the Church of England.

But tolerance did not suppress division, and both the Church of England and its Puritan challengers responded with a flurry of tracts. Richard Hooker penned *The Laws of Ecclesiastical Polity* (1593–1662) at the request of Archbishop Whitgift as a defense of the Elizabethan religious establishment. In Book 8, Hooker discusses the validity of the Royal Supremacy in ecclesiastical affairs. James I, in his famous 1609 speech to Parliament, drew directly from Hooker in proclaiming the monarchy an institution responsible only to God: "The state of monarchy is the supremest thing upon earth; for kings are not only God's lieu-tenants upon earth, and sit upon God's throne, but even by God himself they are called gods."

Such bold statements brought the king into conflict with powerful parliamentary interests. The impo-sition of elaborate stone altars in parish churches and the revival of the Elizabethan prayer book under Charles I further outraged reformers and led to Civil War (1642–9).

Despite doctrinal debates within the Church of England, there was some consensus on the role of music in worship. Following the writings of Plato and Aristotle, Elizabethans honored the notion that musical harmony is a correlation of the proportionality of God's creation. Furthermore, they acknowledged music's affective powers; it could educate, ennoble, corrupt or destroy nature, animals, and humanity. Not even the Puritan social reformer Philip Stubbes denied the power of music. In his popular Puritan tract, *The Anatomie of Abuses* (1583), Stubbes affirms that "music is a good gift of God" that "comforteth the heart, and maketh it ready to serve God." Yet he warns that "being used in public assemblies and private conventicles . . . it corrupteth good minds, maketh them womannith and inclined to all kind of whordom and mischief."

The English Anthem

The Anglican liturgy permitted anthems—broadly defined as an English religious text set to music—during the Offertory and Post-Communion of the English Communion Service, and for the canticles of Matins and Evensong (Venite, Te Deum, Benedicte, Benedictus, Jubilate, Magnificat, Cantate Domino, Nunc dimitis, Deus misereatur). Full anthems used the full choir throughout, while verse anthems alternated between the full choir and soloists with instrumental accompaniment.

The anthem was the cornerstone of religious music at English cathedrals of the Baroque period. The Anglican liturgy retained firm links to Catholicism: Communion corresponds to the Catholic Mass, Matins is a conflation of Catholic Matins and Lauds, and Evensong or Evening Prayer is an amalgam of Catholic Vespers and Compline. Thus the anthem is essentially the English equivalent of the motet in the Catho-lic service. The early Baroque church under James I advanced a more Catholic approach to ritual, and the Hampton Court Conference of January, 1604, granted renewed importance to vestments, religious objects, and music in cathedrals and collegiate churches. While these so-called ornaments of worship were criticized as popish—ultimately they contributed to the execution Charles I in 1649—the atmosphere of Jacobean England was a fertile one for the English anthem, which reached its final flowering at the hands of Orlando Gibbons (1583–1625), Thomas Tomkins (1572–1656), Thomas Morley (1557/8–1602), and Thomas Weelkes (1576–1623).

Orlando Gibbons spent his career in his native England, where he served as chorister at King's College, Cambridge (1596–9). He entered the university in 1598, joining the Chapel Royal in 1603 and staying until his death. Renowned as a keyboard player and composer of vocal and instrumental music by his contem-poraries, his reputation as a composer rests with his anthems. Many of these have been in the repertory of English cathedral choirs since the Restoration.

Gibbons wrote the verse anthem "This Is the Record of John" in 1611 or later, and dedicated it in two manuscripts to clergyman and archbishop of Canterbury, Dr. William Laud, "presedent" of St. John's, Oxford. Laud later served as Bishop of London in 1628 and dean of the King's chapel (1626–33). He was executed in 1645 for his crypto-Catholic, anti-Puritan views. Gibbons set text from the Gospel of John, 1:19–23, as found in the Geneva Bible of 1586; verses 19–23 tell of John the Baptist's confrontation with

Example 4.14 Gibbons, "This Is the Record of John," mm. 3–9.

Jewish authorities. When the priests and Levites are sent from Jerusalem by the Jews to question him, John rejects their attempts to label him as either prophet or Messiah, insisting, instead, that he is only a voice "crying in the wilderness" (cf. Mark 1:3). The solo-chorus division of the verse anthem is an apt and powerful dramatic format for this particular text, which pits group interrogation against a single individual.

Gibbons sets the text in six sections that alternate solo and choir. The narrator sings in a style that shows the influence of declamatory song, with decorative figuration at cadences (Ex. 4.14). Rather than repeating large chunks of material, however, Gibbons repeats smaller musical figures, or motives, both at pitch and in sequence, to create momentum. Repetition of small groups of notes in this fashion—in the organ, the untexted parts and the voices—confers a sense of unity. For instance, the three-note ascending motive featured at the outset recurs throughout the anthem in descending, inverted, or normal forms. The harmonic language responds at the local level to fluctuations in emotional intensity. It is not clear how the anthem would have been accompanied, as there are parts for both organ and for instruments, presumably viol consort. Whether they played separately or together is impossible to determine from the existing scores. Perhaps viols and organ alternated; perhaps only the verse sections were accompanied; or perhaps the entire piece was accompanied.

In *The Principles of Musik* (1636), Charles Butler praised Gibbons's piece as "a solemn Anthem" that is "pleasing unto God and Man." "This Is the Record of John" is representative of the final highpoint of the Elizabethan tradition in the years around 1600. Both sacred and secular music suffered a decline with the Civil War and the subsequent interregnum, although the restoration of the monarchy from 1660 brought about the resumption of Anglican worship and a revival of its musical traditions.

Psalm Singing

Vernacular metrical psalmody, sung by the congregation, had been a feature of English Protestant worship at parish and cathedral churches since the Reformation, replacing the elaborate polyphony associated with Roman Catholicism. Jean Calvin (1509–64) established the practice in his two collections of psalms. The first edition of Calvin's psalter appeared under the title *Aulcun pseaulmes et cantiques mys en chant* (Psalms and Hymns Made into Song, 1539), and comprised settings of psalms translated by both Clément Marot and Calvin, along with several tunes from earlier Strasbourg hymnbooks. Working in Geneva, Calvin produced a new psalter in 1542. This volume is the core of Calvinist music still practiced today.

Like their Lutheran and Calvinist counterparts in Germany, Switzerland, and France, English reformers believed psalm texts to be divinely inspired, and thus granted psalms special status. Court poet Thomas Sternhold (1500–49) made verse translations of the psalms, and his *Certayne Psalmes Drawen into Englishe Metre* (*ca.* 1549) formed the basis of English and Scottish psalm books. Metrical translations facilitated the transformation of the psalms into sacred music suitable for congregational singing. During the reign of Catholic Mary I (1553–8), English psalmody developed in exile in Frankfurt, Geneva, and Strasbourg. Beginning in the late 1550s, publications with tunes gradually appeared, and by 1562 the entire psalter had been versified in English and printed in a single volume by John Day. The Queen's Injunction (1559) allowed for "an hymne, or such like songue" at the beginning or the end of common prayers at cathedral and parish churches. The Injunction was commonly used to justify not just the singing of psalms in parish churches, but the singing of anthems in cathedrals as well. However, in periods when the reforming impetus was at its most intense, metrical psalm singing was the only music used in churches.

Outside the church, metrical psalms were seen as a tool for musical devotion in the home in the sixteenth and seventeenth centuries. According to *The Practise of Pietie* (1613) by staunch Puritan Lewis Bayly, psalms were to be sung for "mercy after sinning, in sickness, on recovery, in times of joy, after being wronged or deceived or for spiritual solace." Drawing on the long-standing tension between the beauty of music and the intent of the text, Bayly cautions singers to "be sure that the *matter* makes more melodie in your *hearts*, then the *Musicke* in your *eares*" (Document 3). Private psalm singing continued in the seventeenth century, in both unison settings and simple note-against-note harmonizations. Harmonized settings were suitable for cathedral, church, or home use, making them especially versatile. John Day (1563), William Daman (1579), John Cosyn (1585), William Swayne (1591), Thomas East (1592), and Thomas Ravenscroft (1621) authored books of harmonized psalms that show the influence of harmonized versions of the French psalms by Goudimel and Claude Le Jeune on the Continent. East's *The Whole Booke of Psalmes . . . Composed into Foure Parts* (1592) contains the entire texts of the standard psalms and hymns originally versified by Sternhold and Hopkins in 1562.

Ravenscroft's *The Whole Booke of Psalmes* (1621) was an especially influential psalter of the Baroque period; it contained four-part settings of 105 pieces that became a fixture of domestic piety among the musically literate. Thomas Ravenscroft (1592?–*ca*. 1635) received training as a chorister at St Paul's Cathedral and took his degree in music from Cambridge in 1605. Ravenscroft's preface to *The Whole Booke of Psalmes* makes a strong case for the role of psalm singing in the cultivation of a pious spirit. He advocated that:

> The singing of Psalms (as say the Doctors) comforts the sorrowful, pacifies the angry, strengthens the weak, humbles the proud, gladdens the humble, stirs up the flow, reconciles enemies, lifts up the heart

Example 4.15 Tenor line from Ravenscroft's Psalm 100 showing the "French tune."

Figure 4.5 Ravenscroft, Psalm 100 from *The Whole Booke of Psalmes*, 1621.

to heavenly things, and unites the Creature to his Creator, for whatsoever is in the Psalms, is conducive to the edification, benefit, and consolation of mankind.[11]

The perceived affective power of psalm singing united the Lutheran, Calvinist, and Catholic faiths in their approach to music's role in worship. Although Martin Luther, Calvin, and Catholic theologians set out distinct views on how (and what) religious music might best be utilized, all agreed that it could move the emotions of listeners, and, by extension, nourish their spirituality.

Musically, Ravenscroft's settings reflect the turn away from eight-line melodies (typical of Sternhold-Hopkins) to four-line melodies that matched the typical length of a psalm verse. Ravenscroft, who gleaned many settings from earlier publications of John Day, Archbishop Parker, Thomas East, and Barley, positioned the melodies in the tenor part. He named them (often after historic towns or cities), and provided a handy index to the tunes at the front of the book. Not all the settings were borrowed ones,

Example 4.16 Ravenscroft, Psalm 100 from *The Whole Booke of Psalmes,* 1621.

however. He included some of his own compositions, and he also featured new settings by several of his contemporaries, including John and Thomas Tomkins, Martin Peerson, Robert Palmer, John Milton the Elder, and Simon Stubbes.

Psalm 100, from Ravenscroft's *The Whole Booke of Psalmes*, is typical of the genre of harmonized psalmody. Psalm 100 is the culmination or final doxology for a set of ten psalms (Psalms 91–99) that constitute a booklet for worship on Sabbaths and important feasts. Its steady rhythm, homophonic texture, and memorable melody—Ravenscroft labeled it a French tune (Ex. 4.15)—are features of the period.

Ravenscroft set the music in part form with the cantus and tenor parts on the left side and the "medius" and bassus parts on the right side of an open page, a format that facilitated sight-reading in the intimate setting of home or church (Fig. 4.5).

In its expression of praise and thanksgiving, both central themes of worship in all faiths, this setting of Psalm 100 epitomizes the ease with which harmonized psalmody answered a variety of devotional needs, regardless of confession or locale.

Psalm 100 had a lasting following, for it appeared in Playford's list of "The Most Usual Common Tunes Sung in Parish Churches" from *A Breefe Introduction to the Skill of Musick* (1658).

Conclusions

We often assume that sacred music is conservative, and indeed much of the sacred music of the Baroque—the choral motets, for instance, and the English anthems—maintains continuity with the Renaissance. But sacred music in the Baroque made consistent forays into what was considered then novel territory. Sacred opera, oratorio, the lush concerted motets of the Venetians and Schütz's smaller motets with basso continuo are very much in step with the new styles and new attitudes of the early Baroque. As we have seen from the source readings in this chapter, composers were extremely careful to make sure their works were positioned and performed according to their intentions. They were also influenced in many ways by current religious doctrine on music; various religious perspectives favored—and fostered—different styles and genres of sacred music. Only the singing of psalms received unilateral praise from commentators on music and theologians of all religious stripes.

Shifting economic, social, religious, and cultural circumstances all contributed to a temporary slump in the production, scale, and quality of sacred music in the second half of the seventeenth century. The demise of the Venetian book trade had a massive impact on the publication of music books. The economic devastation of the Thirty Year's War left much of the German-speaking lands in turmoil. The decline of sacred music in England during the Civil War was reversed only toward the end of the seventeenth century, with the anthems of Henry Purcell. Only France under Louis XIV—which will be addressed in Chapter 7—remained a vital focal point for Catholic music.

Documents

Document 1. Emilio de'Cavalieri? (unsigned), "Address to the Reader" from *Rappresentatione di Anima, et di Corpo.* **Rome, 1600.** *Miscellanea 5, Early Sacred Monody, Vol. 4.* **Ed. Murray C. Bradshaw. Middleton, WI: American Institute of Musicology, 2007, p. 7.**

Wishing to stage the present work, or others like it, and to follow the instructions of Signor Emilio de'Cavalieri, and to see to it that this sort of music, revived by him, moves the different affections, like pity and joy, weeping and laugher, and the like . . . it is necessary that everything should be excellent, that the singer should have a beautiful voice, good intonation, and carry a steady tone, that she sing with feeling, softly and loudly, and without embellishments, and above all that she sing with the text so that it be understood, and that she accompany it with gestures and motions not only of the hands but also of steps, which are very effective means to move the affections.

The instruments should be well played, and in number more or less according to the place, whether it is a theater or a hall, which should be of a size suitable for this kind of musical performance. . . . In performances in very large halls it is impossible for everyone to hear the words, and hence the singer would have to force his voice, the affect would be lessened, and all the music, with the words not being heard, would become boring. The instruments, in order not to be seen, should be played behind the stage curtain, and by performers who should follow the singing, with a full sound and without diminutions. To give some suggestions from what has proved useful in a similar place, a double lyre, a harpsichord, a chitarone or theorbo (as they say) together make a very good effect, as do a sweet-sounding organ along with a chitarone. Signor Emilio would recommend changing the instruments according to the affect of the recitation.

Document 2. Preface to the Christian Book of Concord. Articles 20–21. From *Triglot Concordia: The Symbolical Books of the Evangelical Lutheran Church: German–Latin–English.* **Published as a memorial of the quadricentenary jubilee of the Reformation anno Domini 1917 by resolution of the Evangelical Lutheran Synod of Missouri, Ohio, and Other States. St. Louis: Concordia Publishing House, 1921. http://bookofconcord.org/boc-intro.php (accessed April 13, 2015).**

20. [. . .] For we have no doubt whatever that even in those churches which have hitherto not agreed with us in all things many godly and by no means wicked men are found who follow their own simplicity, and do not understand aright the matter itself, but in no way approve the blasphemies which are cast forth against the Holy Supper as it is administered in our churches, according to Christ's institution, and, with the unanimous approval of all good men, is taught in accordance with the words of the testament itself. We are also in great hope that, if they would be taught aright concerning all these things, the Spirit of the Lord aiding them, they would agree with us, and with our churches and schools, to the infallible truth of God's Word. And assuredly, the duty is especially incumbent upon all the theologians and ministers of the Church, that with such moderation as is becoming they teach from the Word of God also those who either from a certain simplicity or ignorance have erred from the truth, concerning the peril of their salvation, and that they fortify them against corruptions lest perhaps, while the blind are leaders of the blind, all may perish. Wherefore, by this writing of ours, we testify in the sight of Almighty God and before the entire Church that it has never been our purpose, by means of this godly formula for union to create trouble or danger to the godly who today are suffering persecution. For, as we have already entered into the fellowship of grief with them, moved by Christian love, so we are shocked at the persecution and most grievous tyranny which with such severity is exercised against these poor men, and sincerely detest it. For in no way do we consent to the shedding of that innocent blood, which undoubtedly will be required with great severity from the persecutors at the awful judgment of the Lord and before the tribunal of Christ, and they will then certainly render a most strict account, and suffer fearful punishment.

21. In regard to these matters (as we have mentioned above) it has always been our purpose that in our lands, dominions, schools, and churches no other doctrine be proclaimed and accurately set forth than that which is founded upon the Word of God, and contained in the Augsburg Confession and the Apology, (and that, too, when understood properly in its genuine sense,) and that opinions conflicting with these be not admitted; and indeed, with this design, this formula of agreement was begun and completed. Therefore before God and all mortals we once more declare and testify that in the declaration of the controverted articles, of which mention has already been made several times, we are not introducing a new confession, or one different from that which was presented in the year 1530 to Charles V, of happy memory, but that we wished indeed to lead our churches and schools, first of all, to the fountains of Holy Scripture, and to the Creeds, and then to the Augsburg Confession, of which we have before made mention. We most earnestly exhort that especially the young men who are being educated for the holy ministry of the churches and schools be instructed in this faithfully and diligently, in order that the pure doctrine and profession of our faith may, by the help of the Holy Ghost, be preserved and propagated also to our posterity, until the glorious advent of Jesus Christ, our only Redeemer and Savior. Since, therefore, such is the case, and being instructed from the Prophetic and Apostolic Scriptures, we are sure concerning our doctrine and confession, and by the grace of the Holy Ghost our minds and consciences have been confirmed to a greater degree, we have thought that this Book of Concord ought to be published. For it seemed exceedingly necessary that, amidst so many errors that had arisen in our times, as well as causes of offense, variances, and these long-continued dissensions, there should exist a godly explanation and agreement concerning all these controversies, derived from God's Word, according to the terms of which the pure doctrine might be discriminated and separated from the false.

Document 3. Adapted from Lewis Bayly, *The Practise of Pietie*. London, 1613. The Practise of Pietie at Evening, pp. 464–6.

At evening when the due time of repairing to rest approaches, call together again all thy Family. Read a chapter in the same manner that was prescribed in the morning. Then (in the holy imitation of our Lord and his Disciples) sing a Psalm. But in singing of Psalms either after Supper, or at any other time, observe these Rules.

Rules to be observed in singing of Psalmes

> Beware of singing divine Psalms for an ordinary recreation, as do men of impure spirits, who sing holy Psalms intermingled with profane Ballads. They are Gods word, take them not in thy mouth in vain.
>
> Remember to sing David's Psalms with David's spirits.
>
> Practise Saint Paul's rule: I will sing with the spirit, but I will sing with the understanding, also.
>
> As you sing uncover your heads, and behave yourselves in comely reverence, as in the sight of God, singing to God, in Gods own words. But be sure that the matter makes more melody in your hearts, then the music in your ears: for the singing with a grace in our hearts, is that which the Lord is delighted with all, according to that old verse: . . . [Latin verse] It's not the voice, but vow: Sound hart, not sounding string: True zeal, not outward show, That in Gods ear doth ring.
>
> Thou may, if thou think good, sing all the Psalms over in order: for all are most divine and comfortable. But if thou wilt choose some special Psalms, as more fit for some times and purposes: and such as by the oft usage, thy people may the easier commit to memory.

Notes

1 Translations for Examples 4.2–4.5 are from Giovanni Rovetta, *Quam pulchra es amica mea*, ed. Dennis Collins (Arbroath, UK: Prima la musica!, 2005).

2 Jeremias Drexel, *Caelum, beatorum civitas aeternitatis*, pars III (Antwerp, 1636), p. 66, quoted in Karl Gustav Fellerer and Moses Hadas, "Church Music and the Council of Trent," *The Musical Quarterly* 39/4 (1953), p. 589.

3 Craig Monson, "Renewal, Reform, and Reaction in Catholic Music," in *European Music, 1520–1640*, ed. James Haar (Woodbridge, UK: Boydell Press, 2006), p. 405.

4 Victor von Klarwill, ed., *The Fugger News-Letters: Being a Selection of Unpublished Letters from the Correspondents of the House of Fugger during the Years 1568–1605*, trans. Pauline de Chary (London: John Lane the Bodley Head, 1925), p. 226.

5 Warren Kirkendale, *Emilio de' Cavalieri "gentiluomo romano": His Life and Letters, His Role as Superintendent of All the Arts at the Medici Court, and His Musical Compositions* (Florence: Leo. Olschki, 2001), p. 235.

6 Trans. adapted from Emilio de'Cavalieri, *Rappresentatione di Anima e di Corpo*, Cappella Musicale di San Petronio di Bologna, cond. Sergio Vartolo, Early Music/Alte Musik, trans. Keith Anderson (Naxos, 855409697), pp. 21–2.

7 Howard E. Smither, *History of the Oratorio: Vol. 1: The Oratorio in the Baroque Era: Italy, Vienna, Paris* (Chapel Hill: University of North Carolina Press, 1977), p. 82.

8 Martin Luther, Preface to *Symphoniae iuncundae atque adea breves quattuor vocum* (Rhau, 1538), in Ulrich S. Leopold (ed. and trans.), *Luther's Works. Vol. 53: Liturgy and Hymns* (Minneapolis, MN: Fortress Press, 1965), pp. 321–4.

9 Martin Luther, Preface to *Symphoniae iuncundae atque adea breves quattuor vocum* (Rhau, 1538), in Ulrich S. Leopold (ed. and trans.), *Luther's Works. Vol. 53: Liturgy and Hymns* (Minneapolis, MN: Fortress Press, 1965), p. 323.

10 Christoph Bernhard, "Tractatus compositionis augmentatus," in Walter Hilse, trans., "The Treatises of Christoph Bernhard," *The Music Forum* 3 (1973), p. 110.

11 Adapted from Thomas Ravenscroft, *The Whole Booke of Psalmes* (London, 1624), signature A4.

5 Instrumental Music

Instrumental music thrived in homes, palaces, courts, and churches during the early Baroque period. Instruments supplied music for dancing, domestic recreation, court festivities and entertainment, and religious worship. The function the music was intended to serve was a significant factor in a composer's choice of instruments, in addition to timbre and volume, extra-musical associations, and the size of instrumental groupings. Ideal for domestic settings were consorts (groups of from three to six musicians), solo lute, clavichord or virginal. Religious settings had their own sound world. Small churches might employ only a single organist and a handful of singers, while large centers, such as Venice, had the performing resources for much more opulent instrumentation. The polychoral works of Giovanni Gabrieli not only had multiple groups of singers and instruments, but multiple organs as well. Instrumental music at courts was diverse and dependent upon the patron's taste and wealth. Michael Praetorius's beautifully illustrated treatise *De Organographia* (On Musical Instruments, 1618) sheds light on how these instruments might have looked. Produced by a court printer, *De Organographia* featured scaled drawings, lavishly engraved, of brass, woodwind, keyboard, and percussion instruments, as well as some novel instruments. It was the most authoritative and thorough account of instruments to date, and ends with an elaborate "Theater of Instruments" comprised of forty-two woodcuts illustrating the families of instruments.

Various factors raised the status of both instrumental music and instrumentalists in the Baroque period. Kings and queens played instruments and their courts followed suit, hiring expensive foreign tutors to educate their offspring. Men and women across the social classes sought to reach a level of competence in instrumental performance, not the least because it often served as a critical measurement of one's social skills and status. Henry Peacham's popular *The Compleat Gentleman* (1622) captured the role of instrumental music for young men of good birth. Peacham advised: "I desire no more in you then to sing your part sure, and at the first sight, withal, to play the same upon your Violl, or the exercise of the Lute, privately to your self."[1]

A major function of instrumental music, one relevant across Europe and England and embracing virtually all instruments, was the provision of dance music. The instrumental sound world of the early Baroque was regionally diverse and rich in local tradition, but there was also a great deal of international cross-fertilization, for instrumentalists moved fluidly among the courts, cities, and chapels of England and the Continent. The popularity of court and theatrical dance and the influence of dance styles on instrumental music at large was a common thread throughout the period, regardless of locale.

Dance Music

Dancing, then as now, functioned on several levels: as entertainment (to watch), as enjoyment (to participate in), and as a means of making subtle social distinctions (how well do you dance, and what do you tell us about yourself in the *way* that you dance). Theatrical productions such as English masques, Italian *intermedi*, and French *ballets de cour* were opportunities to display the wealth of the patron and the skill of the courtiers who participated as dancers. Even the monarchs took part: King Louis XIV was an avid dancer,

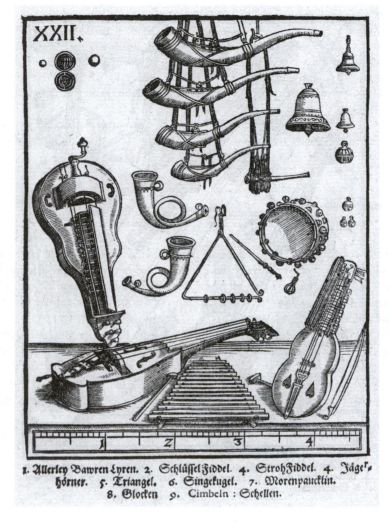

Figure 5.1 Praetorius, *Syntagmatis Musici. 2. De Organographia*, 1619.

reputedly taking dance lessons throughout his life. As a young man he took part in many of the early court theatrical entertainments and ballets, most famously, perhaps, the role of Apollo in the court *Ballet de la nuit* (1653). Dance was thus an important marker of social, political, and cultural success across Europe throughout the Baroque period.

The broad appeal of dancing supported a growing market for dance manuals. The most informative source from the late sixteenth century is *Orchésographie* (1589) by Thoinot Arbeau, a cleric, astronomer, lawyer and dancer at Langres in eastern France. Written as a dialogue between the master, Arbeau, and his student, Capriol, *Orchésographie* is important for its descriptions of styles, illustrations of dance steps, and advice on etiquette. Arbeau distinguished forty-seven choreographies or dance types by their tempo, meter, and rhythmic patterns, features intimately linked to the choreography and patterns of movement associated with each dance. Arbeau also developed an innovative system for notating the music with the corresponding dance steps.

Arbeau lays out the basic dance steps in a series of diagrams and patterns. Capriol asks Arbeau to teach him each dance in turn, and the manual progresses from simple pavans to more complex double branles, gavottes, the Canary, and regional versions of the principal dances. The branle is the most common dance pattern in the

Orchésographie, with regional types and a proto-suite that gains momentum as it progresses from branle double, simple, gay, and bourgoigne. Arbeau describes the double branle as a straightforward piece danced sideways, with dancers holding hands; it may be accompanied by the violin and is suitable for all ages (Fig. 5.2).

Present day performers must still determine the most suitable instrumentation. Arbeau noted that the *pavan* and *bassedanse* could be sung or played by "violins, spinets, transverse flutes, and flutes with nine holes, *hautboys* and all sorts of instruments."[2] This amount of flexibility and variety is typical for dance music of the Baroque period.

In addition to practical advice on dance steps, Arbeau ventures into broader issues of social decorum and manners. He argues that dancing is a vital form of socialization and an acceptable means of selecting a mate. He writes:

> Dancing is practised to reveal whether lovers are in good health and sound of limb, after which they are permitted to kiss their mistresses in order that they may touch and savour one another, thus to ascertain if they are shapely or emit an unpleasant odour as of bad meat.[3]

The French continued to dominate the European dance scene for the seventeenth century. Duke Friedrich Ulrich of Brunswick and Lüneburg hired French dance instructor, Antoine Emerauld, whose influence can be detected in *Terpsichore* (1612), a collection of dance suites by Brunswick court musician and composer Michael Praetorius (1571–1621). In 1663 English patron and cultural commentator Samuel Pepys (1633–1703) hired a French dancing master at his wife's urgings to learn the new French *coranto*. French influence reached its height with *Apologie de la danse* (1623) by dance master François De Lauze; the volume had actually appeared earlier in 1623 in a version that one of De Lauze's colleagues, choreographer B. de Montagut, had plagiarized from De Lauze's manuscript-in-progress. In the opening chapter of "In

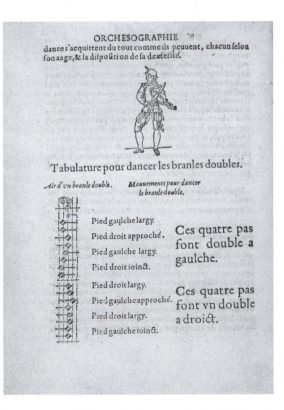

Figure 5.2 Arbeau, *Orchésographie*, 1589. Tabulation for dancing the double branle.

Praise of the Dance," Montagut emphasized the social and political purpose of dance: "It is the fact that in ceremonies and formalities, or among the most elevated in rank, one always notices some element of dance, whether it is a matter of carriage, or of joining grace to action, or of making a proper bow."[4]

By the mid seventeenth century, music theorists included descriptions of dance in their writings. Marin Mersenne (1588–1648) briefly described the *passemezzo, pavan, allemande, sarabande, volta, courante, galliard, gavotte*, and *bourrée* in *Harmonie universelle* (Universal Harmony, 1636). English composer, theorist, and viol player, Christopher Simpson, ranked dances according to social status in his popular *The Principles of Practical Musick* (1665). In Chapter 14, "On Instrumental Music," Simpson addresses repertory from the years around 1600, the heyday of English instrumental music. He gave top spot to consort music for viols, writing:

> Of this kind, the chief and most excellent for Art and Contrivance are Fancies, of 6, 5, 4, and 3 parts, intended commonly for Viols. In this sort of Musick the Composer (being not limited to words) doth employ all his Art and Invention solely about the bringing in and carrying on of these Fugues, according to the Order and Method formerly shown. (Document 1)

Simpson's hierarchy positions social dances with the slow pace and dignified character of the pavan at the top and the lighter country dances at the bottom, whose players "had not so much Skill in Musick as to Prick them down in Notes" (Document 1).

The influence of dance music extended beyond set dances for theatrical and social entertainment. The early decades of the seventeenth century witnessed a surge of both practical dance music and suites of stylized dances. Such suites comprised collections of pieces (often in the same key) that were clearly representative of particular dances, yet not intended as actual dance music. As a result, the phrase structure and contrapuntal treatment were often more complex and rhythmically pliable than one might expect in music composed specifically for dancing—they were aimed, in other words, at the instrumentalist and the listener. Dances arranged in either pairs or suites permeated the lute, keyboard, and string band repertory of France, England, Germany, and Italy from the early seventeenth century through Johann Sebastian Bach.

As the century progressed, the individual dances grew more distinct and standardized across Europe, although some dances always retained an association with a particular area or nationality. The main characteristics of the most common dances found in Baroque suites are summarized in Table 5.1. Building on the sixteenth-century practice of paired dances, Baroque composers expanded groupings of pavane-galliard to include up to eight different dances. The suite formed the backbone of both ensemble music and solo repertory for keyboard, lute, and viol. From roughly 1580 until 1630, most of the solo music was for the keyboard and lute families; the bulk of ensemble music, coming out of Italy, was for bowed strings.

Domestic Keyboard Music

Early Baroque solo keyboard music consisted largely of works for private study and performance in the home. Such pieces served as models of correct counterpoint and tasteful improvisation, and learning to play them was considered useful in teaching proper behavior. Indeed it may have been hoped that young women would see in the modest requirements of these pieces a metaphor for equally modest behavior. These attributes mark English keyboard music of the early seventeenth century, and the preferred keyboard instrument of the period was modest as well: the virginal, a small type of harpsichord with a single set of strings and keyboard. The virginal was marketed as especially suitable for female performers, for whom musical literacy was considered a fundamental social grace. In *The First Part of the Elementarie* (1582), London schoolmaster Richard Mulcaster recommended women study the virginals and lute "because of the full music which is uttered by them." The very name of the instrument speaks volumes: *virginal*, derived from *virgo* or *virginis*—a maiden.

There followed a repertory of virginal music designed for female consumption. The most noteworthy example is *Parthenia or the Maydenhead* (London, 1612/13), an anthology of twenty-one works by Orlando Gibbons (1583–1625), John Bull (1562/3?–1628), and William Byrd (*ca.* 1540–1623).

Table 5.1 Main features of Baroque dances. Prepared by Elissa Poole.

Dance	Back Story	Qualifiers	Description	Source quotation
Allemande, Alman, Almain	German, early 16th c.	Highly stylized in 17th and 18th c. instrumental suites	Duple meter, both fast and slow types, uncomplicated rhythms	"simple, rather sedate dance" (Thoinot Arbeau, 1589) "now only for instruments" (Friedrich Erhard Niedt, 1706)
Bourée, boree	French, early 16th c.	German composers favored it in instrumental suites	Moderate to quick duple meter with anacrusis	"relaxed, easy-going, comfortable and yet pleasing" (Johann Mattheson, 1739)
Branle, brando, brawl	French, beginning of 16th c. or earlier	Used to open court balls into the 18th c.	Variety of popular line or circle dances in mixed meters with sideways steps	"wherein many (men, and women) holding by the hands sometimes in a ring, and otherwise at length, move all together" (Randal Cotgrave, 1611)
Canary, canario,	Spain and Italy, mid-16th c.	Can be duple or triple in early sources	Unique stamping movements in all sources	"gay but nevertheless strange and fantastic with a strong barbaric flavour" (Arbeau, 1589)
Contredanse, country dance	English peasant dances related to branles, 16th c.	Transformed late 17th c. France into a slower, more elegant dance	Communal, informal, in duple or compound meter	"it is impossible not to follow almost any Country Dance" (Kellom Tomlinson, 1734)
Corrente, corranto	Italy, mid-16th c.	Becomes a virtuosic showpiece in 18th c. instrumental music	Moderate to fast triple meter; little rhythmic complexity	"Sprightliness and vigor, lively, brisk and cheerful" (Thomas Mace, 1676)
Courante, courente	French court dance evolving from corrente	Favored dance of Louis XIV	Slowest of the triple meter dances; rhythmic ambiguity	"noble and grand" (Pierre Rameau, 1725) "majestic" (Johann Joachim Quantz, 1752)
Galliard, galliarde, gagliarda, cinque passi	Italy, late 15th c.	Tempo varies; often follows a pavan as an "afterdance"	Vigorous couple dance in triple meter with hops and kicks	"one must be blithe and lively to dance it" (Arbeau, 1589)
Gavotte	French court dance; late 16th c., emerged from double branles	By end of 17th c. begins with an upbeat at middle of measure	Usually quick duple meter	"ordinarily graceful, often gay, and sometimes tender and slow" (Jean-Jacques Rousseau, 1768)
Gigue	French court dance, earliest choreographies from late 17th c.	Standard element of the instrumental suite	Moderately fast triple or compound duple meter; dotted, *sautillant* rhythms	"lively and spritely" (Antoine Furetière, 1690) with a "skipping quality" (Sebastien Brossard, 1703)

Menuet, minuet, minuetto	France, mid-17th c.	Popular into late 18th c. throughout Europe	Elegant dance in moderate to lively triple meter	"formerly very cheerful and fast, but now with an elegant and noble simplicity" (Rousseau, 1768)
Pavan, pavana, pavin	Italian or Spanish, early 16th c.	Falling out of fashion by early 17th c.	Slow duple meter	"used by kings, princes and great lords, to display themselves on some day of solemn festival" (Arbeau, 1589)
Sarabanda, zarabanda	Latin America, Spain, 16th c.	Faster sarabandas favored in Italy, Spain, England	Lascivious, exotic and fast; often performed with castanets	"Lively and licentious because it is done with disorderly wagging of the body" (Sebastián de Covarrubias, 1611)
Sarabande	French court dance, 17th c., evolved from sarabanda	J.S. Bach composed more sarabandes than any other type of dance	Slower triple meter, often with a lengthened second beat	"Soft passionate movement . . . apt to move the passions and to disturb the tranquility of the mind" (James Talbot, 1690)
Volte	French, mid-16th c.	Banned by Louis XII	A type of galliard in triple time in which the man lifts the lady into the air	"I leave it to you to consider if it be a proper thing for a young girl to make such large steps and separations of the legs . . ." (Arbeau, 1589)

Figure 5.3 Title page, *Parthenia or the Maydenhead*, 1612/13.

Parthenia is the most important early publication of English keyboard music. It was prepared as a wedding gift to Princess Elizabeth Stuart (1596–1662), daughter of King James I, and her betrothed, Elector Palatine Frederick V. The anthology served as both gift and tribute to Elizabeth, a talented musician whose royal education included dance and instruction on the virginal by John Bull. Not only was *Parthenia* "the first musicke that ever was printed for the virginalls," as the title page boasts, it was also the first engraved

Example 5.1 Gibbons, The Queen's Command, mm. 1–8.

book of English music. The collection exemplifies a new strategy by music publishers to create and exploit niche markets for specific instruments. The illustration on the title page could not be more obvious: The woman playing the virginal has her face turned demurely away from the viewer—a sign of chastity. The engraving, by William Hole, is based on a 1588 design of St. Cecilia, patron saint of music, by Henrick Goltzius.

The Queen's Command is one of six works by Gibbons found in *Parthenia*. It is a set of variations based on a ground bass (a repeated melodic pattern in the bass).

The first four bars over the ground are given a varied repeat, doubling the rate of melodic activity in the right hand from quarter notes to eighth notes: This forms the opening eight-measure unit (Ex. 5.1). The same treatment is given to the second part of the ground, also an eight-measure unit, which closes in the tonic C major. The last half of the piece is a variation of the first half, this time with rippling scales in sixteenth notes that alternate between hands. The frequent double oblique lines placed through the stems of the notes indicate that the note is to be ornamented, probably with some form of oscillation or rapid alteration of a note with the one immediately below or above it.

Gibbons composed The Queen's Command for the princess on the occasion of her marriage. The pitches *E* (for Elizabeth) and *F* (for Frederick) are prominent as the alternating starting pitches of the soprano part of almost every line. The printer labeled the pitches using capitalized initials to highlight the connection to Elizabeth and Frederick (Fig. 5.4).

Hole's dedication of *Parthenia* spoke of learning "to twine together . . . neighbor letters *E* and *F*, . . . that make so sweet a consonant . . . [and when] wedded together seem lively hierogliphicks [*sic*] of the harmony of marriage." Gibbons' musical tribute can be interpreted on a subtler level: The two lines intertwine in increasing excitement on the harmonic bed of a ground bass, ending in a shower of scalar passages across the virginal.

Lute Music

Lutes are members of the plucked-string family. Amateur and professional musicians played the lute in solo works and as part of the continuo in ensemble music of the early Baroque period. The lute family encompasses many types, sizes, and tunings, with much variation from region to region. The importance of the lute for church, domestic, court, theater, and leisure music was well established across Europe and England for the sixteenth and much of the seventeenth centuries.

In the sixteenth century, the lute served primarily as accompaniment to vocal music and as a medium for arrangements of French chansons, German Lieder, and Italian madrigals. Such arrangements of vocal repertoire were known as intabulations. Huge anthologies of lute music containing a transnational repertory of intabulated vocal music appeared in large print runs around 1600: *Florilegium* (1594) by Adrian Denss,

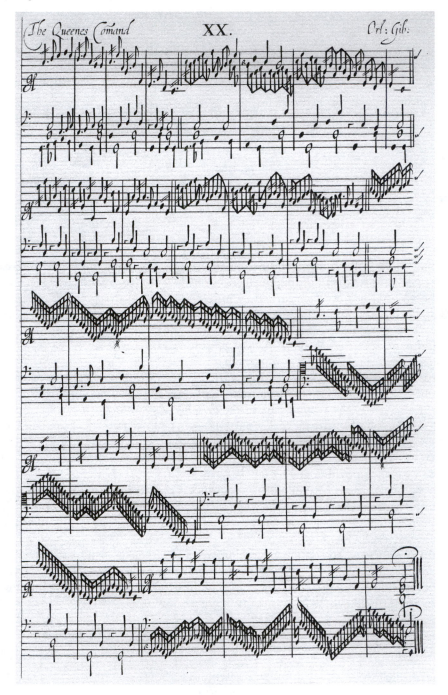

Figure 5.4 Gibbons, The Queen's Command.

Johann Rude's *Flores musicae* (1600), Besard's *Thesaurs harmonicus* (1603), and Johann Daniel Mylius's *Thesaurus gratiarum* (1622). From about 1550 onward, however, the popularity of intabulations declined and we begin to see a great deal of solo music composed specifically for the lute—indeed we see solo music composed specifically for all instruments. No longer tied to a pre-existing contrapuntal vocal format, composers invented new formats for instrumental music that exploited the resources of the instruments in new, idiomatic ways. Composers also seemed to delight in the freedom of writing for a single, and often virtuosic, player. This new repertoire includes toccatas, dances, variation sets, contrapuntal ricercars and fantasias, and pieces composed over ground bass patterns such as the *passamezzo antico*, the *passamezzo moderno*, and the *romanesca*.

The pairing of voice and lute was also extremely popular. In France the lute song, known as the *air de cour*, flourished at the court of Louis XIII (1610–43), and royal printers Le Roy and Ballard issued volumes of solo and polyphonic airs. Lute songs were perhaps even more popular across the Channel. Thirty song-books for voice and lute were published in England between John Dowland's *First Booke of Songes* in 1597 and John Attey's *First Booke of Ayres* in 1622.

The surge of repertory coincided with an extension of the lute's range, particularly in the bass register. In the sixteenth century, lutes had six pairs of strings, called "courses." The three lowest courses were tuned in octaves; an additional single string, known as the "chanterelle," was added to the top to project a clear tone. The number of courses increased to nine and ten courses by 1610.

Two new instruments also developed in the early Baroque period: the archlute and the theorbo (also known as the chitarrone). The archlute is a Renaissance-style lute with an extra octave of bass strings. It projected a clear treble line, which made it a popular choice well into the eighteenth century. The standard early seventeenth-century theorbo, which was larger than the archlute, had six courses on the fingerboard and an additional eight single bass strings. The extra resources in the bass register made the theorbo an especially effective accompaniment in Italian monody (solo song) and opera.

All countries adopted a form of notating lute music known as tablature. The basic tablature utilized a six-line staff in which each line represented a course, from lowest to highest. Letters or numbers were placed on the lines to indicate the fingers' positions on the frets. Symbols above the staff indicated durations of the notes. France, Italy, and Germany all had their own systems of tablature, but French tablatures became the

Figure 5.5 Cristoforo Choc, theorbo. Wood and ivory, Venice, 17th century.

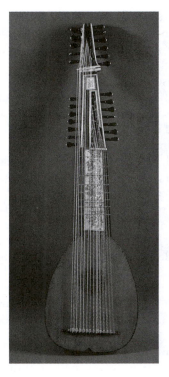

Figure 5.6 Matteo Sellas, archlute, 1638.

norm for much of Europe and England by the early seventeenth century. A representative example comes from the last printed lute book of the period, *Varietie of Lute-Lessons* (London, 1610), an anthology of forty-two works compiled by Robert Dowland (*ca.* 1591–1641), son of England's most famous lutenist, John Dowland (1563–1626).

The title page boldly advertised music "selected out of the best approved authors, as well beyond the seas as of our own country." The variety of composers, from Prince Moritz, Landgrave of Hessen, Germany, to Robert Dowland himself, is matched by the variety in dances and fantasies. Robert Dowland grouped the individual pieces into categories, with seven examples each of fantasias, pavans, galliards, almains, corantos, and voltes. Dowland adopted this structure from the Dutch and German anthologies of Emmanuel Adriaenssen, Adrian Denss, Johann Rude, and Jean-Baptiste Besard.

Robert Dowland included two prefatory essays that underscore the international breadth of the collection. First to appear is "Necessarie Observations Belonging to the Lute, and Lute Playing," a translation from Besard's *Thesaurus harmonicus* of 1603. Besard offers practical tips on right-hand technique and rules for left-hand fingering and stops. He addresses larger issues of how to learn the instrument and reminds the performer to be patient; he also gives advice on how to choose a lute and what lessons to begin with. Besard's remarks are followed by "Other Necessary Observations Belonging to the Lute" by John Dowland, who continues in the practical vein with advice on such matters as technique, choosing strings, and tuning.

John Dowland's "The Most High and Mighty Christianus the Fourth, King of Denmark, His Galliard" opens the settings of galliards in *Varietie of Lute-Lessons*, no doubt in honor of the dedicatee, the Danish king Christian IV (1577–1648).

In the 1590s Dowland left his native England to embark on an international career with posts at courts in Wolfenbüttel (1594), Kassel (1596), and Copenhagen (1598). Despite his status as one of the highest-paid servants at the Danish court, Dowland yearned to return to England; passed over for years, he finally received a court appointment in 1612. Dowland wrote music for solo lute, voice and lute, and mixed

Figure 5.7 French lute tablature. John Dowland, "The King of Denmark's Galliard," from Robert Dowland's *Varietie of Lute-Lessons*.

consort (an ensemble of instruments from different families) and many of his works survive in multiple versions for different performing groups. For instance, there is a version of "The King of Denmark's Galiard," for viol consort and lute in Dowland's *Lachrimae or Seaven Teares* collection.

France led the field in lute composition and technique for much of the seventeenth century. French influence was especially strong in England, whose court welcomed French musicians and musical style. Courtier and first duke of Buckingham, George Villiers, brought Parisian lutenist Jacques Gautier to the prince's household in 1619. Charles II's marriage to Henrietta Maria, the daughter of King Henry IV of France, strengthened musical and cultural bonds between England and France. Lutenist, author, and poet Charles

Figure 5.7 (continued)

de L'Espine traveled to England, Germany, and Italy between 1610 and 1627. Opportunities for cultural exchange also came from foreigners traveling to Paris, which was a recognized center for lute playing, construction, and teaching. Henry Lord Clifford, son of the fourth Earl of Cumberland, studied the lute at de Pluvinel's Academy in Paris and maintained a French lute tutor, a Monsieur Simon, on his return in 1611. Lutenists held prestigious appointments at the French royal court, most prominently during the reign of Louis XIII. Robert Ballard taught Louis XIII to play the lute, and Ennemond Gaultier (1575–1651) served as lutenist to Marie de Medici and lute teacher to Cardinal Richelieu.

The major contributors to French lute composition of the early Baroque period were Ennemond Gaultier and his younger cousin Denis Gaultier (*ca.* 1600–72). Denis Gaultier was among the first French composers to group his dances into suites, rather than placing all the dances of each type together in his anthologies. His most famous collection, *La rhétorique des dieux* (The Rhetoric of the Gods), compiled between 1648 and 1652, contains eleven suites designated by mode and given Latinized Greek titles that recall the humanist inclinations of the Renaissance period.

Ennemond Gaultier—who is usually referred to as "le Vieux" (the Elder) Gaultier to distinguish him from Denis—served as *valet de chambre* to Henri IV's queen from 1600 until her exile in 1631. He spent part of 1630–1 in England, where he played for Charles I, Queen Henrietta Maria, and the Duke of Buckingham. When he retired in 1631, none of his music had been published. Fortunately, Gaultier's reputation as a lutenist is chronicled in a manuscript tutor copied around 1670 by Mary Burwell, from an original belonging to her teacher, probably the lutenist John Rogers, who was in the employ of Charles II's Royal Music. In the book, which is known as the "Burwell Tutor," Burwell compares Ennemond to other lutenists, calling him "the sun among the stars," who "hath drawn the admiration and the praises of all the world."[5] In this broad-ranging tutor, Burwell addresses the origins of the lute, its basic technique, its various social and cultural contexts, and the instrument's expressive qualities. She then compares the lute with the virginal and viol, concluding that the lute is the ideal instrument:

> The shape of the lute is not so troublesome; and whereas other instruments constrain the body, the lute sets it in an advantageous posture. When one plays of the virginal he turns his back to the company. The viol entangleth one in spreading the arms, and openeth the legs (which doth not become man, much less woman). The beauty of the arm, of the hands and of the neck are advantageously displayed in playing of the lute; the eyes are used only in looking upon the company. (Document 2)

Ennemond "le Vieux" Gaultier composed the *Tombeau de Mesangeau* to commemorate his teacher, virtuoso lutenist René Mesangeau (d. 1638), active at the court of Louis XIII. Gaultier completed the *tombeau* shortly after his teacher's death. The word *tombeau* means tombstone in French, and it originally referred to a commemorative poem. Gaultier was the first to use the term *tombeau* to refer to a musical piece, although a French tradition of musical homage extends back at least to the Renaissance period. His *tombeau*—like many of the *tombeaux* written by French composers after him—is a sedate, stylized allemande. Although the allemandes were among the least likely of the stylized dances to retain a connection to actual dancing, it still adopts, like all dance movements, a binary form with a cadence on the dominant A major, to end the first section, and one on the tonic D major, to close.

Ennemond's elegant ornamentation is an integral part of his compositional process and typical of French style in the Baroque. In keeping with the somber tone of the *Tombeau*, Ennemond favors the middle and lower range of the lute.

Example 5.2 Ennemond Gaultier, *Tombeau de Mesangeau.*

Historically informed interpretations of the *Tombeau* acknowledge a performance tradition called *style brisé*, or "broken style," that modern performers who are not versed in historical style sometimes ignore. One of the best contemporary descriptions of the "broken style" comes from Burwell, who advised that "you may get that art by breaking the strokes; that is, dividing them up by stealing half a note from one note and bestowing of it upon the next note. That will make the playing of the lute more airy and skipping."[6] According to this convention, the notes of a chord are played one after another, from the bottom up, rather than at the same time as the notation indicates. The delays, irregular rhythms, and avoidance of obvious patterning in *style brisé* lend an improvisatory quality to French Baroque lute music. Of course, the arpeggiated harmonies associated with *style brisé* may also be written out, and then the performer must reverse the interpretive process, making sure that the notated rhythms are played with a certain amount of rhythmic freedom.

Lutenists were largely supplanted by harpsichordists and violists under Louis XIV. However, techniques associated with playing the lute, such as *style brisé*, were appropriated immediately by French harpsichordists like Louis Couperin and François Couperin. The practice of *style brisé* then spread from France across Europe and was imitated in the keyboard suites of Johann Jacob Froberger and Johann Sebastian Bach.

Ensemble Music

The development of ensemble music in the early Baroque era is characterized by regional variations, political and artistic networks, and the mobility of composers and performers. These features combined to create pockets of cultivation at different times and in different places.

Example 5.3 Schein, *Courente*, from *Suite no. 6.*

Example 5.3 (continued)

As we saw with solo music, dance movements and suites formed the cornerstone of the ensemble repertory. Beginning in the sixteenth century, there was a strong tradition of pairing single dance movements in English consort music, lute and keyboard repertory, and string bands. Pairs of allemande-tripla and pavan-galliards abound in sources from Germany, which reflects the strong influence of English instrumentalists such as John Dowland and Thomas Simpson (1582–1628). The Arundel part-books and *Pavans, Galliards, Almains* by Anthony Holborne (*ca.* 1545?–1602) are representative of Elizabethan sources of pavan-galliard pairs, a feature that increased in German sources after 1600 even as it declined in English ones.

It was a small step from dance pairs to full suites. That step culminates in the instrumental suites of Johann Hermann Schein, whose *Banchetto musicale* (Musical Banquet, Leipzig, 1617) is the first cyclic instrumental suite—that is, a collection of dances "arranged so that they correspond to one another in both mode and invention," as Schein himself describes. To the existing pairs of pavane-galliard and allemande-tripla, Schein inserted a *courante*. Schein's title page shows a preference for strings that is typical of German-speaking lands; it notes that the music can be played on all instruments, "bevoraus auff Violen" (violins above all else). Suite no. 6 is a typical example, progressing in four movements from the stately pavan to a lively galliard followed by a hybrid *courente*, and closing with a majestic allemand (see Table 1).

Schein's *courente* is an example of a dance in transition, for it exhibits aspects of both Italian and French traditions (Ex. 5.3). Many dances went through radical transformations over the course of their popularity, and this piece is a good example of such a development. Spelled halfway between the Italian *corrente* and the French *courante*—two distinctly different dances by the end of the seventeenth century—Schein's *courente* has elements of both. The late-sixteenth and early seventeenth-century *courante*, in its many and varied spellings, was a lively dance popular in both France and Italy and associated primarily with hop-step combinations. By the middle of the century, the French had slowed it down, notating it most often in 3/2, and providing it with elegant gliding steps. Its evolution into a stately French court dance is already evident in De Lauze's *Apologie de la Danse* of 1623, for De Lauze describes both sliding steps and the importance of arm movement. Arbeau, only a generation earlier, described a flirtatious and unruly dance with jumped steps in duple meter. Schein's *courente* is notated in 6/4, with only a few scattered hemiolas, and it is mostly homophonic, aligning it with the simpler, faster *corrente* rather than the dignified *courante*, with its typically ambiguous rhythms and phrases. On the other hand, Schein's dance lacks the rapid figuration in the upper voice that becomes common in later *correntes*.

This ambiguity in style and terminology for dances persisted throughout the Baroque period. Not even Johann Sebastian Bach gave the right names to many of his *courantes* and *correntes;* he likely assumed his readers and listeners would immediately know the difference.

The Sonata around 1600

The term *sonata* is a vague and all-encompassing word whose meaning has changed over time and context. It is broadly used to denote a piece of instrumental music in several movements written for either solo or small ensemble performance. We first see the term in the thirteenth century, where the word *sonnade* (to sound) can be found in literature to denote an instrumental piece. In his famous collection *El maestro* (1536), Spanish composer Luys Milan referred to *villancicos y sonadas* (popular songs and pieces), and included pavans and fantasias among the *sonadas*. *Sonata* continued to be used in the sixteenth century to refer to a variety of different techniques and pieces, but these are almost always instrumental works rather than vocal ones. The divisions into *sonata da chiesa* (church sonata, alternating slow and fast sections), *da camera* (chamber sonata, with dance movements), and trio sonata (for two or three melody instruments and continuo) happened primarily in the mid-Baroque and later.

The most important precursor of the early Baroque sonata is the instrumental *canzona*. The *canzona* (to sing) developed in Italy from instrumental arrangements of French chansons known as *canzone francese*. Hundreds of these instrumental transcriptions of chanson books were printed by Pierre Attaingnant in the sixteenth century. The terms *canzona* and *sonata* were used interchangeably by Giovanni Gabrieli and Tarquinio Merula for works such as Merula's *Canzoni overo sonate concertate per chiesa e camera* (1637). The sectional form and imitative textures of the canzona, as well as the return of the opening material, were all taken over in the sonata. Michael Praetorius cited the canzonas and sonatas of Gabrieli in his description of the sonata in the third volume of his treatise *Syntagma musicum* from 1618. Mantuan composer and string player Salamone Rossi (1570–ca. 1630) was the first to publish a significant number of sonatas with violin parts, which appeared alongside dances and other pieces in four collections issued from 1607 to 1622. Rossi's sonatas retain the multisectional form of the ensemble canzona, but look ahead in their scoring. Rossi's scoring of two violins and bass became standard for later Baroque trio sonatas.

Dario Castello (active 1600–50), a wind player and composer employed at the Basilica of St. Mark's in Venice, wrote a number of sonatas for various instrumental combinations that illustrate the transition from canzona to sonata. His *Sonata Sesta a 2* for treble instrument and trombone with basso continuo (from *Sonate concertate in stil modern*, Book 1, 1621) is performed here in the common pairing of cornett and trombone with organ continuo. Another option for the soprano part was the violin, since the two were often used interchangeably; Castello himself probably played cornett, dulcian (early bassoon), or both; his sonatas are not as idiomatic to the violin as those of some of his peers. The sonata opens with the familiar long-short-short rhythm and imitative entries typical of the canzona (Ex. 5.4).

The piece has both slow and fast sections in varying meters, including virtuosic solos for each of the two solo instruments. In Example 5.5, the solo line is modeled on the declamatory vocal style of Monteverdi.

It then becomes progressively more brilliant, and finishes with fleet passagework (Ex. 5.6).

The cornett (a wooden instrument with finger holes and a cupped mouthpiece) is unfamiliar to many listeners today: It was one of the instruments that declined during the Baroque era (preceding the viol family and the recorder families, which declined slightly later). However, in the decades around 1600, the cornett was highly prized for its ability to imitate the human voice, for its nimble technique—which was exploited in the brilliant passagework of improvised divisions—and for its nuanced articulation, executed using a sophisticated menu of articulation syllables that were described in a number of tutors, from Ganassi dal Fontego's *Opera intitulata Fontegara* (1535) to Bartolmeo Bismantova's *Compendio musicale* (1677). The art of the cornettist was especially cultivated in Venice—Giovanni Gabrieli was among those who included many virtuosic parts for cornetto in his concerted works—and Venice remained a center of cornett practice until about 1640 (the plague of 1630 may have precipitated its decline). The leading player at the turn of the century in Venice was Girolamo dalla Casa, who wrote a treatise on improvising divisions, *Il Vero Modo di diminuir* (The Correct Way of Playing Divisions, 2 vols., 1594), in which he tells the reader that "of all the wind instruments, the most excellent is the cornett for it imitates the human voice more than the others. This instrument is played piano and forte and in every sort of tonality, just like the voice."[7]

Imitating the human voice was not just a matter of timbre. Cornettists also modeled their articulation on singers, whose every syllable change was essentially an articulation and who used a glottal articulation

Example 5.4 Castello, *Sonata Sesta a 2*, mm. 1–4.

Example 5.5 Castello, *Sonata Sesta a* 2, mm. 34–38.

for the *passagi* and elaborate vocal embellishments known as *gorgie*. Cornettists, too, articulated almost everything (including cadential trills), often using complicated compound tonguing syllables that ensured a slight amount of rhythmic inequality in the notes. Single tonguing (*te te* or *de de*) was appropriate only for slower note values; an alteration of *te re* was used for diminutions of moderate speed; and the very fluid syllables *le-re-le-re*, *de-re-le-re*, or *te-re-le-re* were recommended for the fastest passages (Bismantova, in 1677, does present slurred notes). Ornamentation was also modeled on the singer's art. Vocal treatises such as Lodovici Zacconi's *Prattica di musica* (1592) and Giovanni Battista Bovicelli's *Regole, passagi di musica* (1594), and prefaces to vocal collections such as Caccini's *Nuove Musiche*, thus provide invaluable information for wind players as well as singers, especially since vocal repertoire in the *stilo moderno* of the early Baroque was moving away from virtuosic *passagi* and diminutions towards a variety of smaller ornaments known as *accenti* that were valuable for expressive purposes. These ornaments either fill in an interval or expand a descending interval by adding a note above or below it. *Accenti* were not rhythmically measured and were executed with an easy grace; and they were used wherever *passagi* were considered inappropriate or ineffective.

The sonata started to move away from the canzona to form a distinct identity in the hands of string virtuosos from Italy. Biagio Marini (1594–1663) was one of the first composers of violin sonatas with continuo. He began and ended his career in Venice, serving as violinist under his former teacher, Monteverdi, at the Basilica of St. Mark's from 1615 to 1618. After three years in his native Brescia and at the Farnese court at Parma, Marini left Italy for an extended period in northern Europe. He held positions as music director at the Wittelsbach court at Neuburg an die Donau (1623–49) and visited Brussels and Düsseldorf. Marini published his first volume of sonatas in Venice: *Affetti musicali* (Musical Affects, 1617). It contains sinfonias, canzonas, sonatas, and dances for one-to-three parts with basso continuo. During his 1624 trip to Brussels, Marini met the Archduchess Isabella, Regent of the Netherlands, to whom he dedicated his *Sonate, symphonie, canzoni, pass'emezzi, baletti, corenti, gagliarde, et ritornelli* (Opus 8, Venice, 1629). This varied collection contains sixty-two pieces advertised as "curious and modern inventions" for the violin.

Indeed these pieces were curious and modern, for Marini explores new sound effects and makes unusual technical demands on the player. For instance, his *Sonata in ecco*, for three violins and continuo, borrows

Example 5.6 Castello, *Sonata Sesta a* 2, mm. 43–44.

theatrical effects directly from the world of opera, and there are obvious similarities to "Possente spirto" from Monteverdi's *L'Orfeo* in the virtuosic first violin writing and in the imitative passagework—Monteverdi was also fond of echoes. Marini exploited these echo effects in a number of ways: by repeating a passage that gets progressively quieter (Example 5.7a); by overlapping triadic passages so that the full harmonies resonate (Example 5.7b); and by echoing a single repeated note at a close interval (Example 5.7c). Marini's first violin part is also challenging; in addition to some very quick passagework, there are double stops (Example 5.7d).

Marini took great care to instruct performers on how to play this piece, part of a growing trend among composers to make their intentions known to performers. His stage directions tell the first violin to "play

Example 5.7a Marini, *Sonata in ecco*, mm. 71–80.

Example 5.7b Marini, *Sonata in ecco*, mm. 94–98.

Example 5.7c Marini, *Sonata in ecco*, mm. 125–127.

Example 5.7d Marini, *Sonata in ecco*, mm. 64–67.

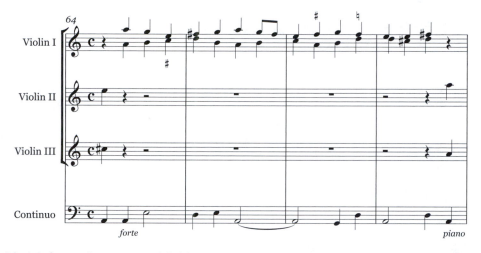

Example 5.8 Marini, *Sonata in ecco*, mm. 26–31.

Example 5.9 Caccini, preface, *Le nuove musiche*, 1602.

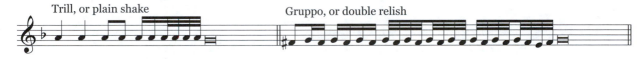

loudly and remain visible to the audience, whereas the second and third violins should be unseen throughout the work." Marini also illustrates such ornaments as the *groppo* and *trillo*. For example, he specifically labels the figure echoed in m. 28 as a *groppo* (Ex. 5.8).

As we know from Caccini (who called it a *gruppo*), this is a turned trill, and the performer could multiply the oscillations and gradually increase their speed (Ex. 5.9).

The scoring for from one to three instruments found in Marini's *Sonata in ecco* presented opportunities for idiomatic and soloistic writing, features found in the composer's later Opus 22 *diversi generi di sonate, da chiesa, e da camera* (Diverse Types of Sonatas, for Church, and for Chamber, 1655) for from two to four parts with basso continuo. Marini's early use of the terms *chiesa* and *camera* also forecast the two principal types of ensemble sonatas of the second half of the seventeenth century.

Organ Music

From Michael Praetorius's discussion of organs in *De Organographia* (1618) we get an impression of the variety, splendor, and huge potential for experimentation in organ building in the decades around 1600. And while organ design and the array of specific stops varied according to regional practices, churches all across Europe were installing and refurbishing organs. The magnificence of the instruments encouraged equal magnificence in the music in the form of free pieces such as fantasies and toccatas and more structured imitative works and variation sets. Virtuoso organ music for church services flourished from Catholic Italy to Lutheran Germany as shown by performer-composers such as Girolamo Frescobaldi (1583–1643), Dietrich Buxtehude (*ca.* 1637–1707), and Johann Sebastian Bach (1685–1750). Even the Calvinist churches of northern Europe valued organ music as a para-liturgical adornment to the service: Jan Pieterszoon Sweelinck (1562?–1621) was expected to provide music in the church twice a day as part of his duties in Amsterdam.

In the Lutheran service, the organist accompanied congregational singing and incorporated chorale melodies into preludes, transitional music, and extended choral fantasias, often improvising on the spot. Praetorius praises the organ and its players in part three of *De Organographia*, where he points out that a good organist plays hymns and psalms to ready listeners for the sermon that follows. And for that they should be better paid, he suggests:

> We might well wish that the organists who devote themselves to the noble art with all possible industry and zeal were furnished with better salary, and not treated as more contemptible and mean than the lowest of unskilled labourers.[8]

Samuel Scheidt's *Tabulatura nova* (New Tablature, 1624) is the principal collection of German organ music before 1650. Scheidt's title calls attention to the fact that his collection has been notated in open score, in which each polyphonic line is given a separate staff. This is the notation used by Frescobaldi in Italy, but previously unknown in German regions, where tablature with letters written on the staff was more common.

For the Catholic service, it was the *Caeremoniale episcoporum* (Ceremonial of Bishops, 1600) and local custom that defined the practical use of the organ. Convention allowed for the organ to provide music for the following occasions: preludes; interludes; versets in alternation with chanted verses of the psalms, canticles, or part of the Mass Ordinary; hymns; as substitute pieces for the Gradual and the Offertory; and as contemplation pieces at the Elevation. Two early Italian treatises on organ music are *Del sonare sopra*

Figure 5.8 Scheidt, *Tabulatura nova*, 1624.

il basso (On Playing upon the Thoroughbass, 1607) by Agostino Agazzari (1579/81?–1641/2); and *Conclusioni nel suono dell'organo* (Ideas about Playing the Organ, 1609) by Adriano Banchieri (1568–1634), organist, composer, theorist, and priest. Banchieri's principal objective was to guide young organists or organists employed in small churches in selecting the appropriate kinds and styles of music for various services or feasts. His treatise is also useful for its account of church history and for its comments on contemporary composers and organists.

Frescobaldi was the pre-eminent organ composer and virtuoso of early Baroque Italy. Active in Rome, Frescobaldi benefited from decades of service for Cardinals Antonio and Francesco Barberini, nephews of the reigning Pope Urban VIII. Frescobaldi joined Cardinal Francesco's payroll in 1634 and remained for the rest of his life. He apparently enjoyed privileged status at the Cardinal's court: Cardinal Francesco paid for the costs of moving the composer's household from Florence, raised his salary at the Cappella

Giulia, paid him regular sums for the rent of his house, showered him with gifts, and granted him a benefice for his talented son, Domenico. The Barberini family also subsidized all of Frescobaldi's late works. The papal family was surely impressed with Frescobaldi's skills as an organist. They must also have been aware that Frescobaldi's fame reflected back on them in a flattering way, since his performances inevitably attracted the attention of foreign dignitaries and travelers to Rome. Writing of his trip to Rome in 1637 or 1638, French bass viol virtuoso André Maugars praised Frescobaldi as follows: "This famous organist of St. Peter's well deserves his European reputation, for, although his printed works testify sufficiently to his ability, still, to judge properly of his deep science, he must be heard in his improvisations of toccades."[9]

Frescobaldi composed two collections of toccatas for keyboard, the *Primo libro di Toccate e partite d'intavolatura di cimbalo* (Rome, 1615, 1637) and a second book of toccatas in 1627. Together these two collections give us an idea of what Frescobaldi's "improvised *toccades*" might have sounded like. Since the notation of the toccatas does not specify the many nuances in rhythmic interpretation that Frescobaldi had in mind, the composer wrote a preface to Book I that explains how the pieces are to be played. Clearly Frescobaldi wanted to maintain some of the spontaneity that characterizes an improvisation. He began the preface by making a comparison with modern madrigals (by which he probably meant solo madrigals, as in those by Giulio Caccini, who also specified in his preface that they should be sung in a rhythmically free manner depending upon the words). According to Frescobaldi, the toccatas should be treated in similar fashion: "the manner of playing, just as in the performance of modern madrigals, should not be subjected to strict time. Although such madrigals are difficult, they are facilitated if one takes the beat now languidly, now lively, or holding back, according to the affection of the music or the meaning of the word" (Document 3).

After explaining that he has provided his pieces with a variety of passagework and expressive ornaments, and that the various sections of the piece may be played independently or mixed and matched and stopped at any time, Frescobaldi goes on to discuss precisely how the player ought to approach specific contexts within the piece. These guidelines are by no means obvious from the notation; nor are they the types of choices a performer today would intuitively make, so Frescobaldi's instructions are extremely important.

Figure 5.9 Frescobaldi, "Toccata Nono," first page.

They instruct the performer to arpeggiate harmonies written as block chords; stop briefly on the final note of a passage or a trill; slow down at cadences and hold the final note; precede a consonance or passagework in both hands with a slight preparatory silence; play trills rapidly and with as many oscillations as the time permits rather than reading the formulaic notation of a trill literally; give passages in equal sixteenth notes a dotted rhythm (short-long) in certain instances; and choose a moderate tempo for pieces with passagework, and a faster one for pieces without (Document 3).

The Toccata number 9 from Frescobaldi's *Toccate e partite d'intavolatura* is a good example of his flamboyant improvisational style. There are many opportunities for the performer to apply the points discussed in his preface (Fig. 5.9).

The first harmony (A), for instance, would be arpeggiated. The sixteenth note figure leading into the third (half note) beat is a typical formula indicating a trill (B): It might include as many oscillations, at as fast a speed, as the performer wishes; the same figure repeats many times and would be treated as a trill each time. The first significant cadence is the half cadence that occurs between mm. 11–12 (C); here the performer might slow down and hold the G major harmony before continuing with the next idea. Passagework in sixteenth notes throughout the piece could start slowly and then speed up. Some performers might exaggerate these details; others might be more subtle; but no historically informed performance would follow a strict, metronomic beat.

Conclusions

Many of the trends found in vocal music of the early Baroque period have parallels in instrumental music. Vocal monody had its counterpart in the new instrumental genres for one, two, or three solo instruments with continuo. This texture supplanted the consort music for groups of four or five instrumental parts popularized in England in the Renaissance period. The trend to soloistic vocal writing, with ornamental lines above the bass, found its parallel in the highly ornamented style of the English virginalists, French lutenists, and harpsichord players. Composers such as Samuel Scheidt, Biagio Marini, and Girolamo Frescobaldi prefaced their instrumental works with detailed advice on how to perform them, indicative of the growing shift from improvisation to composition, and from oral to written traditions.

The result was a truly instrumental soundscape, and for the first time instrumental repertoire can be considered idiomatic—specific to each instrument's timbre, range, dynamic possibilities, and mode of playing. Such idiomatic repertoire is in sharp contrast to the vast quantity of instrumental music from the sixteenth century that relied on vocal models, and to the practice of using whatever voices or instruments were at hand to play it: Many music books advertised that the music could be performed by instruments, voices, or combinations of the two. Different regions took the lead in developing idiomatic styles, distinct from vocal models, for specific instruments. France, under Louis XIII, cultivated solo lute music; northern Italian centers focused on repertoire for bowed strings; England favored the lute and the virginal. Technical improvements in the instruments also affected this emerging repertoire. Many instruments were improved, their ranges expanded, and new methods of tuning perfected; many other instruments, like the theorbo, were new. New developments in organ building, for instance, excited the imagination and technical prowess of performers like Girolamo Frescobaldi, who brought organ music to unprecedented levels of virtuosity in courtly, domestic, and religious settings.

Documents

Document 1. Christopher Simpson, *A Compendium of Practical Musick in Five Parts.* **2nd ed. London, 1667. pp. 141–5.**

Chapter 14. *Of Music designed for Instruments.*

We must now speak a little more of Musick made for Instruments, in which Points, Fugues, and all other Figures of Descant are in no less (if not in more) use than in Vocal Musick.

Of this kind, the chief and most excellent for Art and Contrivance are Fancies, of 6, 5, 4, and 3 parts, intended commonly for Viols. In this sort of Musick the Composer (being not limited to words) doth employ all his Art and Invention solely about the bringing in and carrying on of these Fugues, according to the Order and Method formerly shown.

When he has tried all the several ways which he thinks fit to be used therein, he takes some other point, and does the like with it, or else, for variety, introduces some Chromatic Notes, with Bindings and Intermixtures of Discords; or, falls into some lighter Humour like a Madrigal, or what else his own fancy shall lead him to, but still concluding with something which hath Art and excellency in it.

Of this sort you may see many Compositions made heretofore in England by Alfonso Ferabosco, Coperario, Lupo, White, Ward, Mico, Dr. Colman, and many more now deceased. Also by Mr. Jenkins, Mr. Locke, and divers other excellent men Doctors and Bachelors in Musick yet living.

This kind of Musick (the more is the pity) is now much neglected by reason of the scarcity of Auditors that understand it, their Ears being better acquainted and more delighted with light and airy Musick.

The next in dignity after a Fancy is a Pavan, which some derive from Padua in Italy, at first ordained for a grave and stately manner of Dancing (as most Instrumental Musicks were in their several kinds, Fancies and Symphonies excepted), but now grown up to a height of Composition made only to delight the Ear.

A Pavan (be it of 2, 3, 4, 5, or 6 Parts), doth commonly consist of three Strains, each Strain to be play'd twice over. Now, as to any piece of Musick that consists of Strains, take these following observations.

All Musick concludes in the Key of its Composition, which is known by the Bass, as hath been shown. This Key hath always other Keys proper to it for middle Closes (see page 45). If your Pavan (or what else) be of three Strains, the first Strain may end in the Key of the Composition, as the last doth, but the middle Strain must always end in the Key of a middle Close.

Sometimes the first Strain does end in a middle Close, and then the middle Strain must end in some other middle Close; for two Strains following immediately one another ought not to end in the same Key. Therefore when there are but two Strains, let the first end in a middle Close, that both Strains may not end alike.

I do confess I have been guilty myself of this particular fault (by the Example of others) in some things which I composed long since; but I willingly acknowledge my error, that others may avoid it.

Next in course after a Pavan follows a Galiard, consisting sometimes of two and sometimes of three Strains. Concerning their Endings, I refer you to what was last said of a Pavan. This (according to its name), is of a lofty and frolick movement: The measure of it, always a Tripla, of three Minims to a Time.

An Almane (so called from the Country whence it came, as the former from Gallia) is always set in Common Time like a Pavan, but of a quicker and more airy movement. It commonly hath but two Strains, and therefore the first ought to end in a middle Key.

In these, and other airy Musicks of Strains which now pass under the common name of Aires, you will often hear some touches of Points or Fugues, but not insisted upon or continued as in Fancy Musick.

I need not enlarge my discourse to things so common in each one's Ears, as Corants, Sarabands, Jiggs, Country-Dances, etc., of which sorts I have known some, who by a natural aptness and accustomed hearing of them would make suchlike (being untaught) though they had not so much Skill in Musick as to Prick them down in Notes.

Seeing this Compendium cannot contain Examples of all these which I give you account of, I would advise you to procure some, of such kinds as you most affect, and Prick them down in Score, one Part under another, as the Examples are set in this Book, that they may serve you as a Pattern to imitate.

But let them be of some of the best-esteemed Composers in that kind of Music.

You need not seek Outlandish Authors, especially for Instrumental Musick; no Nation (in my opinion) being equal to the English in that way, as well for their excellent as their various and numerous Consorts, of 3, 4, 5, and 6 Parts, made properly for Instruments, of which (as I said) Fancies are the Chief.

Document 2. Thurston Dart, "Miss Mary Burwell's Instruction Book for Lute." *Galpin Society Journal* 11 (1958), pp. 3–62. London: Royal Academy of Music, MS 604. pp. 48–9.

Chapter 13. *Of the Usefulness of the Lute and His Advantages*

For what concerneth the parts of the body the lute hath a great advantage over other instruments, and if it doth not improve them, at least it doth bring forth their beauty, and engage those that play upon the lute to give them all that art can add to nature. All the actions that one does in playing of the lute are handsome; the posture is modest, free and gallant, and do not hinder society. The shape of the lute is not so troublesome; and whereas other instruments constrain the body, the lute sets it in an advantageous posture. When one plays of the virginal he turns his back to the company. The viol entangleth one in spreading the arms, and openeth the legs (which doth not become man, much less woman). The beauty of the arm, of the hands and of the neck are advantageously displayed in playing of the lute; the eyes are used only in looking upon the company. One may walk and dance in playing; one may sing and talk; and chiefly one may entertain his thoughts very agreeably. The lute is a modest interpreter of our thoughts and passions to those that understand the language. One may tell another by the help of it what he hath in his heart. We may express upon it choler, pity, hatred, scorn, love, grief, joy; we may give hope and despair. And [for] those that have the grace to lift up their mind to the contemplation of heavenly things, this celestial harmony contributes much to raise our souls and make them melt in the love of God. Nothing represents so well the consort of angelical choirs and gives more foretastes of heavenly joys and of everlasting happiness. . . .

Document 3. Girolamo Frescobaldi, Preface to *Toccate e partite d'intavolatura*. In *Readings in the History of Music in Performance*. Ed. Carol McClintock. Bloomington: Indiana University Press, 1979. pp. 133–4. Copyright © 1979 Indiana University Press. Reprinted with permission of Indiana University Press.

1   The manner of playing, just as in the performance of modern madrigals, should not be subjected to strict time. Although such madrigals are difficult, they are facilitated if one takes the beat now languidly, now lively, or holding back, according to the affection of the music or the meaning of the word.

2   In the Toccatas I have attempted to offer not only a variety of passagework and expressive ornaments but also to make the various sections such that they can be played independently, so that the performer may stop wherever he wishes and not have to play the entire toccata.

3   The beginning of the toccatas should be played slowly and *arpeggiando*; similarly, syncopations and tied notes in the middle of the piece. Chordal harmonies should be broken with both hands so that the instrument may not sound hollow.

4   In trills and passages (either stepwise or by leaps) the last note should be held, even when these notes are eighths, sixteenths, or different from the following ones. This pause eliminates confusion of the different sections.

5   In the cadences, even though written in notes of small values, one must sustain them. As the performer approaches the end of a passage, he must slow the tempo.

6   A passage should be separated, and marked off from another one, when one encounters a consonance that is written for both hands in quarter notes.

   If there is a trill for the right or left hand, and the other plays a passage simultaneously, the trill must not be played note for note but rapidly, the accompanying passage being played less rapidly and expressively; otherwise there will be confusion.

7   If one finds passages in eighths and sixteenths in both hands together, one should not play them too fast. The hand that has sixteenths may play them somewhat dotted; of the two notes, no not the first but the second should be dotted and so on, the first not, the second dotted.

8   When playing passages in sixteenth notes in both hands, one should pause on the preceding note, even if it is black (short), then play the passage resolutely in order that the agility of the hands may appear.

9   In the Partitas, where runs and expressive passages occur, it will be advisable to play them broadly. The same applies to the Toccatas. On the other hand, in the Partitas without passagework one may play rather fast. It is left to the good taste and fine judgment of the performer to decide the tempo that best suits the spirit and perfection of the manner and style of interpretation.

   (The *Passacaglia* sections can be played separately *a piacere*. The tempo of one may be adapted to that of other sections. The same holds true for the Chaconnes.)

Notes

1   Henry Peacham, *The Compleat Gentleman* (London, 1622), p. 100.
2   Thinot Arbeau, *Orchesography*, trans. Mary Stewart Evans (New York: Dover, 1967), p. 67.
3   Thinor Arbeau, *Orchesography*, trans. Mary Stewart Evans (New York: Dover, 1967), p. 12.
4   B. de Montagut, *Louange de la danse: In Praise of Dance*, ed. Barbara Ravelhofer (Cambridge: Renaissance Texts from Manuscripts, 2000), p. 109.
5   Thurston Dart, "Miss Mary Burwell's Instruction Book for Lute," *Galpin Society Journal* 11 (1958), p. 13.
6   Thurston Dart, "Miss Mary Burwell's Instruction Book for Lute," *Galpin Society Journal* 11 (1958), p. 46.
7   Quoted in Bruce Dickey, "Why Did the Cornetto Die Out?" www.concertopalatino.com/Decline_of_Cornetto.html (accessed June 10, 2014).
8   Michael Praetorius, *Syntagma Musicum II. De Organographia Parts I and II*, trans. and ed. David Z. Crookes (Oxford: Clarendon Press, 1986), p. 12.
9   J.S. Shedlock, "André Maugars," in *Studies in Music by Various Authors: Reprinted from "The Musician,"* ed. Robin Igrey (London: Simpkin, Marshall, Hamilton, Kent, 1901), p. 223.

Part II

Baroque Ideals from the Mid-to-Late Seventeenth Century

6   Opera in Italy, 1637–1680

Opera for a Paying Public

While the courts of northern Italy provided the birthplace for opera subsidized by princes and royal rulers, it was the more democratic and free spirited city of Venice that offered the most suitable artistic environment for the first commercial operas. The first opera for a paying public premiered in Venice in 1637. *Andromeda*—with music by Francesco Manelli (after 1594–1667) and a libretto by Benedetto Ferrari (*ca.* 1603–81)—opened at the Teatro San Cassiano, staged by a traveling group of professional singers based in Rome and under Ferrari's direction. By the end of 1642, twenty-two operas had been produced in four separate theaters. From the 1640s until the opening of the Teatro San Giovanni Grisostomo in 1678, audiences enjoyed up to eight productions in a single season at six different venues. Among those operas were three new works by Claudio Monteverdi, who wrote his final masterpieces for Venetian theaters. However, it was Monteverdi's student, Francesco Cavalli (1602–76), who established the model of Venetian opera that was copied across Europe in the decades around 1700, composing twenty-eight operas over his thirty-year career in Venice.

The turn from court to public patronage had a significant impact on the content of opera and on what audiences expected that content to be. Opera did not evolve in a straight line: composers, librettists, patrons, and performers all pushed their own agendas as they vied for supremacy. All had a slightly different vision of what opera should be. But the crux of the debate had to do with the relative role of words to music: To what extent did music embellish the text? To what extent could a performer's virtuosity trump the text? And at what point does the music's dominance over the text compromise the drama?

As opera moved into the marketplace, its musical and financial infrastructure was reinvented. The single most important musical development associated with commercial opera after the mid-seventeenth century was the increased number of arias and their greater importance to the drama. The focal point of musical meaning and expression shifted from recitative to aria—from words to music—something we'll examine in operas by Monteverdi, Cavalli, and Antonio Cesti (1624–69). The highbrow, humanist environment of early Baroque courts could not compete with the flashy Venetian stage, and by the end of the century, opera had become a vehicle for ornamented arias and virtuosic display. Ludovico Antonio Muratori and Benedetto Marcello were among those who complained that singers had gone too far. Critics were soon clamouring for a return to higher literary standards.

The shift from court to commercial opera meant that operas had to be financed in a completely different way. In the past, wealthy princes and learned academies had sponsored operatic works for their own enjoyment, moral instruction, and status. But public opera had to turn a profit. In addition to music, drama, and poetry, entrepreneurial ingenuity and prudent planning became key ingredients for operatic success.

The Business of Opera

In his study *Music in the Seventeenth Century* (1987), Italian scholar Lorenzo Bianconi proposed a helpful model for understanding the complex world of opera finance. Bianconi identified three levels of operating costs and financiers at work in Venetian theaters: the theater owner, the impresario, and the creative team of artists and musicians.

An oligarchy, Venice was dominated by patrician families that had acquired their wealth through trade. Patrician families built, bought, or refurbished theaters to secure property and investment. In Venice, the Grimani family dominated the theater world. This noble family operated four separate theaters between 1639 and 1766: San Samuele, San Giovanni Grisostomo, SS. Giovanni e Paolo, and San Benedetto. Of these, the Teatro San Giovanni Grisostomo, built in 1677, surpassed its rivals in opulence and splendor.

The engraving highlights the many rows of boxes on the sides, the recessed stage, and the Grimani family name. Apart from a capital outlay, sponsors like the Grimani had little to do with the logistics of operatic production.

The second level of sponsorship was the impresario—or group of impresarios—who managed the theater for a given season. The season coincided with Carnival, which began the day after Christmas and lasted until Shrove Tuesday, forty days before Easter, which is also the beginning of Lent. Carnival in Venice was a time for partying and excess prior to the customary deprivations of Lent, when public performances were discouraged or banned. Forty days after Easter, during Ascension week (which was celebrated by all Christian churches to commemorate the bodily ascension of Jesus to heaven), there was essentially a second season; during this time it was common to revive popular operas. Feasts such as Carnival and Ascension attracted visitors from all over Europe. Foreigners were important ticket purchasers and ambassadors of the art form. English writer and diarist John Evelyn (1620–1706) toured Venice during Ascension week in 1645. Evelyn vividly described the sights of Venice: the Rialto bridge, the shops, the scents, the music. A highlight of his trip was going to Giovanni Rovetta's opera *Ercole in Lidia* at the Teatro Novissimo, where he heard famed soprano Anna Renzi. Writing for a European market, Evelyn drew in his readers with a multi-sensory account of the night's spectacle:

> This night, having with my Lord Bruce taken our places before we went to the Opera, where comedies and other plays are represented in recitative music, by the most excellent musicians, vocal and instrumental, with variety of scenes painted and contrived with no less art of perspective, and machines for flying in the air, and other wonderful notions; taken together, it is one of the most magnificent and expensive diversions the wit of man can invent. (Document 1)

Figure 6.1 The Teatro Grimani at San Giovanni Grisostomo in Venice, *ca.* 1750.

Remarkably, Evelyn was more impressed by the opera's castrato than by Renzi—a forecasting of the reign of the castrato singer on the Italian operatic stage (Document 1).

The impresario or manager of a company contracted with the owner of the theater to supply performances during the opera season. The impresario relied on box rentals as the largest and most secure source of income for the theaters. Venetian opera houses adapted the model of box rental from professional *commedia dell'arte* productions. The best seats in the house were commissioned and sold to wealthy patrons, who covered a flat-fee for construction costs and an annual user fee. Such boxes could be passed down from one generation to the next as a prime piece of family property. The less prestigious boxes and gallery seating were rented by the evening or leased for the season. Remaining seats were sold as open admission tickets. There were other sources of income, including loans, advances, guarantors, investors within the company, and ticket sales, but these were more precarious than box rentals. Cristoforo Ivanovich, who wrote the first history of Venetian opera, explained the box rental system to seventeenth-century readers in *Memorie teatrali di Venezia* (Memoirs of the Venetian Theaters, Venice, 1681):

> Theater proprietors have customarily practised two types of charges: first, a cash payment for each box (this serves largely to cover construction costs, . . .); second, an agreed annual rent, paid every year in which there is an opera season.[1]

These rentals were supplemented by nightly fees paid for less desirable boxes at ground and galley level.

Operatic success or failure rested with the impresario. It was his responsibility to secure a libretto; negotiate a new score; pay the composer; arrange for dancers, extras, costumes, an orchestra, and scenic effects; and recruit and retain singers. From two to four theaters were commonly active in a single season, and there was stiff competition for the best artistic personnel. In this marketplace, impresarios recruited talent from across Italy, often pleading for musicians to be released from other patrons.

In the early decades of public opera, the composer or librettist quite often doubled as impresario. Francesco Cavalli and librettists Benedetto Ferrari and Giovanni Faustini (1615–51) acted as their own impresarios. Librettist Maiolino Bisaccioni managed the Teatro Novissimo in 1645, when he produced *Ercole in Lidia* to great acclaim (Document 1). The role of impresario was an extremely complex and demanding job, however, and eventually it was filled by entrepreneurs who produced operas on a full-time basis.

Marco Faustini (1606–76), brother of Giovanni Faustini, was the first professional impresario; in other words, he did not double as a composer or librettist, but focused on successful operatic production. Trained as a lawyer, Marco served as legal counsel to the Salt Office, which managed Venice's lucrative salt monopoly. This background no doubt helped in contract negotiations with musicians. In partnership with Venetian noblemen and citizens, Faustini managed three public theaters in Venice: San Apollinare (1651–2 and 1654–7); San Cassiano (1657–60); and SS. Giovanni e Paolo (1660–8, probably with a gap, 1663–5). His first production was *Calisto*, with a libretto by his brother, Giovanni, and music by Francesco Cavalli. *Calisto* premiered at the Teatro San Apollinare in the 1651/2 season. Over the next thirteen years, Faustini produced twenty operas, ending his career at the Teatro SS. Giovanni e Paolo. During his final years as an impresario, Marco Faustini devoted himself to revivals of operas that set his brother's librettos. So good was he at his job that the Grimani family who owned the theater paid Marco to run it, rather than collecting rent from him.

Finally, we must acknowledge the role of the artists and musicians in commercial operatic production. The musicians themselves were especially important for the sponsorship of early operas in Venice. The singers of *Andromeda* performed without fee, for instance, hoping instead for ticket revenue, and a group of musicians had also pooled resources to rent the theater, the Teatro San Cassiano. We learn this from Ferrari's printed libretto, where he praised "the glory of the six musicians (collaborators with the author), who have performed the opera of *Andromeda* with great magnificence and refinement; this they have done entirely at their own expense, which was not inconspicuous."[2] Artistic experimentation and financial risk were integral parts of the earliest Venetian productions.

The system was so successful that by 1700 there were sixteen theaters, and 388 operas had been produced. Commercial opera even received its first history, along with a chronology of operatic productions to date, in Ivanovich's *Memorie teatrali di Venezia*. It is striking that this lengthy essay on opera makes no reference to courtly precursors to Venetian opera, although Ivanovich does note that palace opera is procured for "enjoyment" at the princes' expense, "while opera in Venice is a business." Ivanovich sees trouble ahead, however, and complains about the high fees paid to singers and the expense of lavish scenery: "Modern practice would require that every scene of the *dramma per musica* was replete with its own *mutazione*, and that the inventiveness of the machines was literally out of this world."[3] His warnings were timely: Librettists, composers, and performers had started to squabble over the aesthetic criteria of opera.

Operatic Conventions

Public opera tried to do what court opera did, but on a tighter budget. Without the backing of a wealthy prince, producers of Venetian opera had to make careful decisions about where the money was spent. Virtuoso singing was a top priority: Audiences demanded it. Singers dominated the stage and, as Ivanovich had protested, expected high earnings in return.

The impact of budgetary constraints can be felt in the documentation of public opera. Few music scores survive from the period, especially during the early phase of Venetian opera from 1637 until 1650. Only thirteen of about fifty operas produced before the mid-seventeenth century have survived. Manuscript scores, rather than lavish music publications, were the norm, and they often varied from one performance to another. Separated by more than thirty-five years, Monteverdi's *Orfeo* (1607) and *L'incoronazione di Poppea* (1643) are clear examples of this principle. The score for *Orfeo*, a court opera, was printed in 1609, and it is more than just a guide for future performances. This score is a commemorative account of the 1607 staging in Mantua and dedicated, accordingly, to Duke Francesco Gonzaga. On the other hand, the score for *Poppea*, a public opera, was never printed. The music survives in two different manuscripts, which served as performance scores for productions in Venice and Naples (1651), and there are five manuscripts and two publications of libretto (1651, 1656).

These sources, which vary greatly in the way they present the score, leave the modern performer with many questions about what to include and how to perform it. Italian scholar Nino Pirrotta summed up the situation in 1955 when he wrote that "opera scores . . . of the 17th century are only sketches or compendious drawings, the full realization of which was left open to the individual and collective creation of the performers."[4] Venetian librettos and short scenarios—which guided the audience through the plot—survive in much greater quantities and reveal details of productions such as the names of patrons, theaters, and musical and artistic personnel.

The competing demands of profit and artistry can be felt at all levels: on the libretto, the structure of the drama, the music, and the staging. Productions became more streamlined and formulaic, as one sees in the collaborations between Francesco Cavalli and librettist Giovanni Faustini, in the 1640s. By 1650, a series of operatic conventions emerged that remained in play for the rest of the century.

The main structural change in the libretto was the shift from five to three acts. While ancient dramas, according to Classical tradition, adhered to a five-act format, the *commedia dell'arte* and Spanish drama presented a compelling model for three-act divisions. Librettists liked it, so three acts became the norm for Venetian opera, although five acts remained in use for spoken dramas. The three-act format was predictable: Act 1 established the plot and subplots, Act 2 introduced complications and confusion, and Act 3 resolved conflicts, culminating in the reconciliation of the lovers. Librettists continued to base their texts on old stories, mythology, Ovid, Homer, and Virgil. But by 1650, they started to mix generic categories, adding comic characters to provide a little humor to tragic scenarios. Faustini's standard plot—two pairs of lovers surrounded by a variety of comic characters—served as a model until the end of the century.

Public operas were often forced to use fewer personnel than court operas; that, in turn, affected the type of music and how it was used. The role of the chorus is a prime example. In Monteverdi's *Orfeo*, the chorus is central and pervasive, providing commentary and framing the action. Forty years later, the composer's

Poppea uses the chorus only twice: as Seneca's followers react to his decision to die and when courtiers celebrate Poppea's coronation.

The impact of a bottom line can be seen in the first opera for Venice, Manelli's *Andromeda*. The librettist, Benedetto Ferrari, played in the orchestra; the composer and his wife sang; the production required only six singers in total; and the orchestra had only twelve instruments, including two harpsichords. Later Venetian operas reduced the instrumental group to a large continuo group and two violins. This offered flexible combinations for accompanying the voices as well as for playing ritornellos and the opening sinfonia. Cavalli expanded the string band by writing for five-part strings, although payment records from his late operas make it clear that only a single player was assigned to each instrumental part.

Recitative and aria were remarkably similar in style in the early years of Venetian opera. Speech-like *stile recitativo* alternated with settings that were only slightly more structured. These were occasioned in the libretto by rhymed lines or a special event in the plot, and sometimes required a change in meter. This is not so different from what occurs in the first operas from Florence and Mantua. Jacopo Peri and Claudio Monteverdi, for instance, used few completely closed forms; *stile recitativo* did most of the real dramatic work. Characters sang formal songs in response to an event or request: Orfeo sang the strophic aria "Vi ricorda o boschi ombrosi" (Do You Recall, O Shady Groves) in response to a call from his fellow shepherds to sing.

The aria only gradually emerged as a discrete musical form. Poet-librettists like Busenello and Faustini were more obvious in indicating closed forms. They created more occasions for "real" music in the plots; they provided more strophic texts and refrains; and they used meter and rhyme to differentiate aria from recitative.

Audiences paid to hear top singers, and arias were what they wanted to hear them sing. The popularity of individual singers created conditions for a disproportionate number of arias in opera. While early court opera averaged ten to fifteen arias, this figure more than doubled—and occasionally even tripled—by the end of the century. A main character might sing two or three arias in a row, virtually a mini concert within the drama at large.

Arias initially took a bipartite form with two sections (AB), although an exit aria often repeated the second section (ABB). By 1680 the dominant form of an aria was *da capo*: a three-part form with a return of the beginning material (ABA). In practice, this return was often ornamented profusely to display the singer's skill. Embellished repetitions served virtually no dramatic purpose, but they thrilled audiences.

Singers' salaries rose considerably in the 1660s, while fees paid to composers remained relatively constant. Cavalli's fee of 450 ducats was high for a composer, reflecting his status as the leading composer of opera in Venice. What level of lifestyle would his fee afford? Recognized as the first international currency, each Venetian ducat contained 3.5 grams of gold; Cavalli could live comfortably from his salary. But it would have been considered only an average fee for a singer. Most singers earned significantly more. The highly sought-after Giulia Masotti earned four times that in 1666 at the Teatro SS. Giovanni e Paolo and nearly six times as much in 1669 at the Teatro San Salvatore.

We can also see that singers were at the top of the hierarchy by observing the commonplace alterations composers made for them during rehearsals or for revivals. The composers' music was not sacrosanct: They readily adapted operas to suit new performers and new venues. In many cases, such changes were even made by someone other than the original composer. Multiple authors created a patchwork opera of old and new arias, cuts, and transpositions.

We know very little about the visual component of Venetian opera. Few engravings of stage sets survive and accounts give only passing or incomplete reference to scenery. Observers were most impressed by the magnificence of the sets and their general appeal. John Evelyn raved of the "variety of scenes" and "wonderful notions" (Document 1), although Cristoforo Ivanovich complained that they were too expensive. The most famous set designer of the period was Giacomo Torelli (1608–78). Trained as an architect and engineer, Torelli designed the Teatro Novissimo in 1641 and furnished sets for all of the operas staged there. His design included a novel system for speeding up scene changes: Sets were placed on tracks that ran on rails underneath the stage, and the whole set could be moved by a central roller. This also allowed for greater variety in the designs. Torelli's designs are among the few that survive from the period. They were

Figure 6.2 Torelli, set design with Venice in the background.

Figure 6.3 Burnacini, set design for Act 2 of Cesti, *Il pomo d'oro*.

made famous during his lifetime in a collection of set designs for the Teatro Novissimo. Included in this collection is Torelli's sets for *La venere gelosa* (Jealous Venus, 1643), which feature mythology associated with Venice and even a backdrop of the city with St. Mark's Basilica positioned in the center (Fig. 6.2).

Torelli's designs served as models for operatic sets for the rest of the Baroque period, both within Italy and across Europe. The court of Leopold I at Vienna showcased Italian opera for royal weddings, births, and celebrations. Here we have direct evidence that scenic display in commercial opera rivaled visual spectacle financed by courts. Ludovico Burnacini (1636–1707) designed twenty-three sets for Antonio Cesti's opera *Il pomo d'oro* (The Golden Apple, 1668), which was first performed at the Viennese court theater in 1668. Matthäus Küsel engraved the sets and published them with the libretto, thereby memorializing the performance and circulating the visual spectacle of Italian opera to readers across the Continent (Fig. 6.3). Burnacini's depiction of the Mouth of Hell for Act 2 must have evoked both terror and wonder in the audience. Such scenes remind us of Ivanovich's warnings of the expense of lavish design at the request of opera audiences, whether public or court patrons.

Claudio Monteverdi and the Venetian Stage

Monteverdi is the only major composer to play a critical role in both phases of early opera: court opera at the beginning of the century, and commercial opera in Venice. After almost two decades at the Mantuan court, the newly appointed Francesco Gonzaga, who was determined to trim the court's artistic budget, released Monteverdi. Monteverdi had previously attempted to get work in Rome—he had dedicated his 1610 *Vespro della Beata Vergine* (Marian Vespers) to the Pope—but to no avail. However, fortunes turned his way when he was appointed chapel master at St. Mark's Basilica in Venice on August 19, 1613. This was a prestigious post: Adrian Willaert and Gioseffo Zarlino were among his predecessors in the sixteenth century, and Francesco Cavalli and Giovanni Legrenzi were to succeed him later in the seventeenth century. Monteverdi remained in this appointment for the rest of his career.

Public opera—both the money and the challenge—lured Monteverdi from retirement. His first response was *Il ritorno d'Ulisse in patria* (The Return of Ulysses to his Homeland, 1640). Giacomo Badoaro (1602–54), in dedicating his libretto for *Il ritorno d'Ulisse* to Monteverdi, seems to allude to that challenge when he says in the dedication that he has written it "to stimulate the virtue of Your Excellence to make known to this city that in the warmth of the affections there is a great difference between a true sun and a painted one."[5]

Monteverdi went on to write two more operas for Venice: *Le nozze d'Enea e Lavina* (The Marriage of Aeneas and Lavina, 1641, lost), and *L'incoronazione di Poppea* (The Coronation of Poppea, 1643). The latter was Monteverdi's final opera—and probably his last composition as well—and it premiered at the Teatro SS. Giovanni e Paolo during the 1642–3 season. The libretto was by Gian Francesco Busenello (1598–1659), who drew on Cornelius Tacitus's *Annals of the Roman Empire* for the plot. Busenello was interested in more than recounting ancient Roman history in Venetian opera's standard three-act format, however. He belonged to the Accademia degli Incogniti (Academy of the Disguised), a Venetian society whose philosophical *raison d'être* was debating the age-old dynamics of body and soul. The Incogniti took the side of the body: For them sensual pleasure trumped conventional morality. Thus Busenello's focus on the ambitious Poppea, who successfully displaced Ottavia as wife of the Roman Emperor Nero, and who therefore makes an attractive metaphor for the Incogniti's advocacy of passion over reason (some have read this as a justification for the liberal politics, and libertine mores, of the republic of Venice). Busenello also has Nero reject the teachings of the Stoic philosopher, Seneca, a standard bearer for conventional morality, whose death therefore functions as a virtual declaration of faith in Incogniti precepts. The libretto is a masterful literary text, one that mixes dramatic intrigue, lust, humor, astute characterization, and abstract philosophical and political thought with a Shakespearean breadth. It is a worthy challenge to Monteverdi's musical imagination in every way.

Monteverdi met that challenge by engaging with Busenello's text on his own terms, fluidly weaving together recitative with arioso passages and occasional set pieces in a way that, interestingly enough, sometimes undercuts the Incogniti message. *Poppea*'s musical resources are modest, however, and illustrate the trend of commercial Baroque opera toward smaller performing ensembles. There are few choruses, little or no dancing, and the orchestra may have required no more than three- or four-part strings and continuo.

Monteverdi owes his reputation as a composer of opera to *Poppea* more than to any other work, and yet, remarkably, there is overwhelming evidence that Monteverdi did not work alone on the music. The sources of the surviving music and librettos for *Poppea* are multiple and varied. The score for the 1643 debut is lost. All that survives of this first performance is a published scenario and a manuscript libretto. For the only documented revival, which took place in Naples in 1651, two manuscripts of the music survive, along with a published libretto. A further five libretto manuscripts and one print appeared in a collection of Busenello's works from 1656. Inconsistencies in these sources, particularly in the music, show that it is unlikely that Monteverdi was the sole composer. It is now generally agreed that some sections were written by other, younger composers, such as Francesco Sacrati (1605–50), Benedetto Ferrari, and Francesco Cavalli. This was, however, a common practice throughout the Baroque: When an opera was revived, music was added or deleted to suit the new singers, and since the orchestral resources might change as well, instrumental parts might be freshly composed or arranged.

A comparison of Act 1, Scene 10, for Nero and Poppea, with the lovers' duet "Pur ti miro" that ends the opera illuminates the type of stylistic differences within the opera that alerted scholars to the probability that more than one composer worked on the score. In Scene 10, Nero and Poppea relive their night of voluptuous lovemaking and then—quite dispassionately—plan their future. The vocal style changes with the topic of conversation: an expressive arioso style in triple meter for the love-talk; and a more speech-like recitative ("What was that?") for the plotting. While most of the recitative proceeds in quite normal fashion over consonant chords, their erotic dialogue at the beginning slides between recitative and aria, and every nuance of the text is captured harmonically. Delicious semitone dissonances evoke, in a most explicit way, moments or memories of arousal—and, when the dissonances resolve, its satisfaction. Typical is the phrase in which Poppea asks Nero how he enjoyed "the mounds of her breasts" (di questo seno i pomi). Monteverdi breaks up her question with rests that make her seem breathless with desire and ends the phrase with a smoldering semitone (Ex. 6.1).

Poppea	*Poppea*
Come dolci, Signor, come soave riuscirono a te la note andata di questa bocca i baci?	Did I please you, my lord, and give you joy throughout the swift hours of night? How did you relish my mouth's endearments, my kisses?

Nerone	*Nero*
Più cari i più mordaci.	The most abandoned, the very fiercest brought most of blisses.
Poppea	*Poppea*
Di questo seno i pomi?	How like you the fruit which my bosom upraises?

By moving into the more lyrical style associated with an aria, Poppea signals that she is the one in control in this scene. Her triple meter melody to "My lord, your words are so sweet," for example, is easily the mistress of Nero's more prosaic response, "This imperial crown," (Ex. 6.2).

Poppea is so persuasive that Nero gradually adopts her aria-like style, and as a result of Poppea's seductive entreaties, he promises to make her empress. Poppea then exploits the security of her position to insinuate that Nero is Seneca's pansy. Nero calls for Seneca's death—a turning point in the opera's plot that also encapsulates the libretto's philosophical stance: the victory of love over reason, and of passion over conventional morality. Poppea's triumph echoes Cupid's message in the prologue ("you will admit that Love can change the world") and forecasts the end of the opera.

Example 6.1 Monteverdi, *Poppea*, Act 1, Scene 10, mm. 1–16.

Texts for Example 6.2

Poppea	*Poppea*
Signor, le tue parole son sì dolci	My lord, these words you utter are so sweet
ch'io nell'anima mia	That I to myself must repeat
le ridico a me stessa,	Them in a silent communion,
e l'interno ridirle	And when I do repeat them,
necessita al deliquio il cor amante.	My languid heart falls fainting with love and longing.
Come parole le odo,	As in your voice, I perceive them,
come baci io le godo;	As your kisses I do receive them.
son de'tuoi cari detti	So they restore all your loving speech to my senses
i sensi sì soave e sì vivaci,	Ah, so charming, so exciting
che, non contenti di blandir l'udito,	That not contented to beguile my hearing,
mi passano a stampar su 'l cor i baci.	They enter me and imprint my heart, with kisses,

Texts for Example 6.3

Nerone	Nero
Olà! Vada un di voi	Hola! go at once one of you there to Seneca this instant and straight inform him
a Seneca volando, e imponga a lui	His death has been decided.
che in questa sera ei mora.	Only in me, resides the act of judgment,
Vo'che da me l'arbitrio mio dipenda,	Not in his maxims,
non da concetti e da sofismi altrui!	Or in sophistic riddles.
Rinnegherei per poco	How low in estimation
la Potenza dell'alma s'io credessi	Were the powers of my spirit

Example 6.2 Monteverdi, *Poppe*a, Act 1, Scene 10, mm. 56–98.

che servilmente indegne
si movessero mai col moto d'altri.
Poppea, sta di buon core:
hoggi vedrai ciò che sa far Amore.

Were I ever so base and so unworthy
To allow it to yield with others' motion.
Poppea, smile, I entreat you,
Today by love's pow'r Rome shall as Empress greet you.

To the modern listener, the most disconcerting element in the music is probably Nero's high voice: The role was intended for a castrato and is now sung by a soprano, mezzo soprano, or occasionally a counter-tenor with a good high range. It is an early example of the male roles for castrati that were to dominate later baroque opera. In *Poppea*, it is not yet a convention, but the choice is psychologically acute: The contrast between Seneca's low bass and Nero's soprano reinforces the philosophical distance between the two characters.

The musical style of the final duet—like that of the entire finale—contrasts sharply with the main body of the opera. The luscious intertwining of the two solo voices, the fluid lines, and the triple meter clearly

Example 6.2 (continued)

point to music of the next generation, and indeed the duet is now believed to have been composed by Sacrati, Ferrari, or Cavalli. It is a clear departure from the musical style of the earlier scenes for Nero and Poppea in Act 1, Scene 10. The descending ostinato bass line of "Pur ti miro" is typically associated with love and pleasure, and it underlines the structure of the duet in a way that became almost a cliché in the generation after Monteverdi (Ex. 6.4).

The harmonic language of "Pur ti miro" ("I Gaze at You") expresses the complacent sensuality of the text in leisurely, drawn out dissonances. The greater lyricism in both vocal and ensemble writing are features more in keeping with the younger generation of Cavalli, Sacrati, and Ferrari than with the elderly Monteverdi.

Texts for Example 6.5

Nerone, Poppea
Pur ti miro, pur ti godo,
pur ti stringo, pur t'annodo.
Più non peno, più non moro,
o mia vita, o mio tesoro.

Poppea
Io son tua,

Nerone
Tuo son io,

Poppea, Nerone
Speme mia, dillo, dì.
Tu sei pur l'idol mio.
Sì, mio ben, sì, mio cor,
mia vita, sì.

Nero, Poppea
I adore you, I desire you,
I embrace you, I enchain you,
No more grieving, no more sorrow,
O my dearest, o my beloved.

Poppea
I am yours,

Nero
I am yours

Poppea, Nero
I am yours, tell me so.
You are mine, alone,
O my love, feel my heart,
My love, see.

Example 6.3 Monteverdi, *Poppea*, Act 1, Scene 10, mm. 178–208.

Example 6.4 Monteverdi, *Poppea,* descending bass pattern from "Pur ti miro."

Example 6.5 Monteverdi?, "Pur ti miro," mm. 344–376.

Example 6.5 (continued)

Poppea remains a work of compelling drama and purpose. The conflict between love and reason, passion and morality, reaches across generations. *Poppea* firmly stands as a mainstream operatic work that has been the subject of revival since the 1960s. Interpretation and staging decisions have varied widely, ranging from the classically inspired staging for an early revival of the opera at Versailles in 1962, to a medley of classic, contemporary, and burlesque for the 2009 revival at the Sydney Opera House under the direction of Barrie Kosky (Figs. 6.4–6.5).

Francesco Cavalli

Francesco Cavalli led operatic composition in Venice during the mid-seventeenth century. Born at Crema, in central northern Italy, he entered the choir at St. Mark's, Venice, in 1616. There he served under Monteverdi, who had arrived four years earlier. Apart from a brief stint in France (1660–2), Cavalli spent his entire

Figure 6.4 Teresa Berganza in *Il coronazione di Poppea*. Versailles, Gabriel Theater, May 1962.

Figure 6.5 Barbara Spitz (R) as Amor and Melita Jurisic (L) as Poppea in rehearsal. Sydney, Drama Theatre, August 6, 2009.

career in Venice, where he took the post of organist at St. Mark's in 1639. Even though he was employed as an instrumentalist, his surviving works are virtually all vocal, dominated by thirty-three operas. Many of these survive. Cavalli set himself apart from his contemporaries by arranging for his operas to be recopied during the 1670s; they now form part of the Contarini Collection, a group of 113 opera scores that covers the period to 1684.

More than any other composer, Cavalli shaped the key ingredients of Venetian opera. His first operas were largely experimental. In style, they are akin to Monteverdi's *Poppea*, dominated by recitative, yet mixed with occasional strophic or structured arias. Cavalli mastered the genre with operas like *Giasone* (1649) that perfectly balanced the demands of the text with those of the music. For many productions, Cavalli collaborated with librettist and impresario Giovanni Faustini. Together, they codified dramatic and formal conventions that were further developed by Faustini's successors, including Giacinto Andrea Cicognini (1606–*ca.* 1650), Nicolò Minato (*ca.* 1627–98), and Aurelio Aureli (*fl.* 1652–1708). Cavalli's final operas, from *Ercole Amante* (Hercules in Love, 1662) onwards, show a gradual decline in quality. In these later operas, the text is overpowered by elaborate, overworked arias that catered to singers and audiences more than dramatists.

Cavalli's *Giasone*

Giasone was first performed in 1649 at the Teatro San Cassiano. It became Cavalli's most famous work. It was revived at least twenty times by 1700 on stages all over Italy, including multiple revivals in Milan, Rome, Florence, Bologna, Naples, Ferrara, and smaller centers like Genoa and Lucca (featuring the composer and singer Antonio Cesti) between 1649 and 1681.

Example 6.6 Cavalli, *Giasone*, Act 1, Scene 14, Medea, "Dell'antro magico," mm. 4–22; Medea's part and general bass only.

Giasone's librettist, Giacino Andrea Cicognini, based the story on the Greek myth of Jason and the Golden Fleece. Jason and the Argonauts sail across the Aegean Sea to capture the Golden Fleece, which is protected by monsters near Medea's castle in Colchis. To the dismay of his wife, Queen Isifile, Medea becomes Jason's lover. Medea helps Jason retrieve the Golden Fleece and they live together happily. However, at the end of the opera, Isifile's poignant lament so moves Jason that he reunites with her. Cicognini designated *Giasone* a *dramma per musica* (drama in music), a term that signalled its serious nature. Nonetheless, Cicognini balanced the serious tone with comic elements, secondary characters, and subplots that appealed to audiences' desire for variety. While this was typical of the mid-seventeenth century, by the end of the century a lofty spirit of reform was in the air, and Cavalli's operas were criticized for inappropriately mixing the comic with the serious.

One of the most famous scenes is Medea's invocation of the spirits of the Underworld. Positioned at the end of Act 1, the scene is central to the plot, and it is here that Medea asks for help on Jason's behalf. Medea's rhetoric is the active agent throughout the opera: It secures the fleece for Jason, lets him return home with her, and then creates tension with his abandoned wife. Medea's invocation was the quintessential *ombra* scene, and served as the model for similar scenes in future operas. For its text, Cicognini used a special verse form borrowed from spoken theater: a twelve-line verse with an accent on the antepenultimate syllable of each line—on *luce* (light), for instance, in the final line (Ex. 6.6). Known as a *sdrucciolo* ending, this accent pattern was considered coarse by sixteenth-century standards, which favored an accent on the penultimate syllable. Metric verses signalled an opportunity for an aria, and Cavalli responded to Cicognini's cues with a closed aria whose stark instrumentation evokes the uncanny.

Example 6.7 Cavalli, *Giasone*, Act 1, Scene 14, Medea, "Dall'abbrucciate glebe," mm. 1–16; Medea's part and basso continuo only.

Medea	Medea[6]
Dell'antro magico	Of this magical cavern,
Stridenti cardini,	You creaking hinges,
Il varco apritemi.	Open wide for me.
E fra le tenebre	And into the darkness
Del negro ospizio	Of the black hospice
Lassate me.	Let me go.
Sull'ara orribile	On the horrible altar
Del lago stigio	Of the Stygian lake
I fochi splendino,	Let the flames rise,
E su ne mandino	And send forth
Fumi che turbine	Clouds of smoke to obscure
La luce al sol.	The light of the sun.

In the recitative that follows (Ex. 6.7), Medea calls upon the King of the Underworld to grant Jason the fleece. Medea's ambitious vocal and expressive range captures the urgency of her plea.

Medea	Medea[7]
Dall'abbruciate glebe,	From your fiery glebes,
Gran monarca dell'ombre, intent ascoltami!	Great monarch of the shades, listen carefully!
E se it dardi d'Amor giammai ti punsero,	And if Love's darts have ever struck you,

Example 6.8 Cavalli, *Giasone*, Act 1, Scene 14, Chorus, "Le mura si squarcino," mm. 1–32; Chorus only.

Example 6.8 (continued)

Adempi, o re dei sotterranei popoli,	Fulfill, O King of the Underworld,
L'amoroso desio che'l cor mi stimola,	The amorous desire that quickens my heart,
E tutto Averno alla bell'opra uniscasi!	And let all Hades join in the fair deed.

The chorus comments with dotted rhythms that convey the solemn nature of Medea's request (Ex. 6.8).

Chorus	Chorus[8]
Le mura si squarcino,	Let the walls collapse,
Le pietre si spezzino,	The rocks splinter,
Le moli si franghino,	The fortifications crack,
Vacillino, cadano,	Sway and fall,
E tosto si penetri	And soon we will enter
Ove Medea sis ta.	The place where Medea waits.

The scene ends with Medea's firm conviction that victory will be hers: "Yes, My king will conquer."

For the finale of Act 2, Cavalli exploits the operatic convention of the music scene, and the plot creates excuses for singing and ornamental lines. The scene is also an excellent example of Cicognini's mixing of characters. The comic servants Alinda and Besso are considered weighty enough to close the second act. Cavalli casts Cicognini's opening rhymed text, "Gradite tempeste" (Welcome Storms), as an energetic aria. A series of quick exchanges in recitative between Alinda and Besso ensue. The text is full of opportunities for jokes: Alinda inspects Besso's bumps and bruises and concludes that he

Example 6.8 (continued)

does not fit the part of soldier. Her "Allegrezza" (Rejoice) then makes reference to the *stile concitato* (agitated style), a way of generating excitement or tension with rapid repeated notes on a single harmony (Fig. 6.6). *Stile concitato* was cultivated by Cavalli's teacher, Monteverdi, and popularized in his dramatic scene, *Combattimento di Tracredi e Clorinda* (The Combat of Tancredi and Clorinda), from his eighth book of madrigals (1638). Cavalli's parody of the style here shows us that it was widespread and familiar to the audience.

Alinda	Alinda[9]
Allegrezza, allegrezza,	
o donne amanti!	Rejoice, rejoice, o amorous women!

Cavalli also pokes fun at the virtuosity of opera singers. When Alinda taunts Besso, saying "But how much more you'd charm my heart if you were a good musician and a singer," Besso responds, "Musician? My art is singing and harmony." His vocal line is, of course, ornamented (Fig. 6.7).

Besso	Besso[10]
Musico? L'arte mia	Musician? My art is
è'l canto e l'armonia!	Singing and harmony.

With Cavalli, the separation of recitative and aria was complete. His operas from *Giasone* onward concentrate on solo singing; there are fewer ensembles and less reliance on choruses and instrumental music. With the predominance of arias came new and distinct formal patterns and aria types. But Venetian operas

Figure 6.6 Cavalli, *Giasone*, Act 2, Scene 13.

Figure 6.7 Cavalli, *Giasone*, Act 2, Scene 13.

also grew more uniform in construction to accommodate the increased number of arias, and their presence began to compromise the dramatic integrity of the text.

Antonio Cesti and Italian Opera Exported

Venetian impresarios continued to produce opera to fit the tastes of ticket-paying audiences, and the competing artistic needs of singers, set designers, composers, and poets. The industry stabilized somewhat in the second half of the seventeenth century with a steady supply of new productions, with Francesco Cavalli at the lead, alongside revivals of earlier works. In the rest of Italy and across Europe, Venetian-style operas took hold at courts where patronage supported lavish sets, prized singers exported directly from Italy, and exquisite music by Italy's top composers.

Composer, organist, and tenor Antonio Cesti (1623–69) was the most important figure in the exportation of Venetian-style opera outside Italy. His best-known work, *Orontea*, sets a libretto by Antonio Cicognini that mixes comic and serious elements. Cicognini's story was so popular that it was set by five different composers, a rarity for the time. Cesti's version is by far the most famous with seventeen known revivals over thirty years after its 1656 performance in Innsbruck, where from 1652–7 Cesti led an elite group of Italian singers, mainly castrati, in operatic and theatrical performances as well as daily cantata and operatic excerpts for the court of Archduke Ferdinand Karl. From there, *Orontea*'s tour stops included Rome and Florence (1661), Lucca (1668), Bologna (1669), Naples (1674), Venice (1666, 1683), Wolfenbüttel (1686), and Hanover (1678). Seventeenth-century interest in the work is mirrored by its twentieth-century revival with full-scale productions beginning in 1961 in Milan, with Teresa Berganza in the title role, and the work's recording under Rene Jacobs in 1982.

Cesti's approach to words and music rested with a clear division of purpose and style for recitative and aria, a functional division that remained intact for Italian opera for the next fifty years. Recitative carried the dialogue, narration, and dramatic exchanges between characters, while arias became completely distinct, closed form set pieces for emotional expression or comic relief, in works that mixed serious and comic characters.

The formalization of the Baroque aria is evident in "Intorno all'idol mio." In this poignant solo scene, Queen Orontea—who at the start of Act 1 proclaimed herself unyielding to love—now succumbs to passion and confesses her love for the lowly painter, Alidoro, who lies asleep at her feet. It is a typical love versus duty conflict that shows the first signs of love's triumph in this scene. Cesti casts the aria in strophic form with accompaniment by two violins and continuo. Building on his own experience both as a singer and composer of stage, chamber cantatas, and church music, Cesti adopts a new vocal idiom of *bel canto* for Orontea's line. The *bel canto* style featured smooth, diatonic melodies, and easy rhythms set to 3/2 meter. Though he avoids the descending chromatic ostinato bass popularized by Monteverdi and Cavalli, Cesti achieves formal unity and a tight structure through the use of compact rhythmic and melodic motives.

Intorno all'idol mio	Around my idol
Spirate, pur, spirate,	Breathe, just breathe,
Aure, Aure soavi e grate,	Breezes sweet and pleasant,
E nelle guancie elette	And on the favored cheeks
Baciatelo per me,	Kiss him for me, gentle breezes!
Cortesi, cortesi aurette!	
Al mio ben, che riposa	To my darling, who sleeps
Su l'ali della quiete,	On the wings of calm,
Grati, grati sogni assistete	happy dreams induce;
E il mio racchiuso ardore	and my corert ardor
Svelate gli per me,	unveil to him,
O larve, o larve d'amore!	phantoms of love.

"Intorno all'idol mio" achieved immediate historical status, and was included by Charles Burney in his *General History of Music* (1789) as an example of early Baroque recitative and aria. In the nineteenth century, "Intorno" was transformed from a Baroque aria to a chamber piece in the hands of editors such as Henry Bishop, François-Auguste Gevaert, and Carl Banck, who subjected Cesti's music to translation, piano accompaniment, orchestration, phrasing, dynamics, and ornamentation.[11] Arguably, in its concise form and shape, Cesti's music provided perfect fodder for such manipulation, as Nino Pirrotta describes Orontea's scene:

Example 6.9 Cesti, *Orontea*, Act 1, "Intorna all'idol mio," mm. 1–17.

Example 6.10 Cesti, *Orontea*, Act 1, "Intorna all'idol mio," mm. 25–48.

Cesti's melody, which at times can have the pliable and enveloping tenacity of a branching vine, is here pure and concise as in few other instances. It is shaped with a chaste, slender grace, shaded by both a sweet, embracing ardor and cautious retreats from her sense of protective tenderness.[12]

Operatic Reform

The shift from recitative to aria-dominated opera came at the expense of dramatic cohesion and unity. The mixing of serious and comic elements, exemplified in Cavalli's *Giasone*, and the disregard for Classical unities of time, place, and action only exacerbated the problem. These abuses, as some called them, led to a period of reform in the decades around 1700. Critics called for a return to the literary models and standards of opera's roots.

Example 6.10 (continued)

Figures prominent in literary circles dominated debates on operatic aesthetics at the turn of the century. The focal point for Italian criticism and commentary was the Arcadian Academies. The first Arcadian Academy was founded in Rome in 1690 with poet and literary historian Giovanni Mario Crescimbeni as its leader. In his collection of dialogues, *La bellezza della volgar poesia* (The Beauty of Vernacular Poetry, 1700), Crescimbeni complained that Cicognini's mixing of comic and serious in works such as *Giasone* "brought about the total ruin of the rules of poetry." Taking an even stronger approach, Arcadian literary historian Lodovico Antonio Muratori addressed opera from the standpoint of spoken drama. In *Della perfetta poesia italiana* (On Perfect Italian Poetry, 1706), Muratori sympathizes with poets who are "placed in bondage" by composers and performers. "Good poetry," he says, is "condemned to be subservient to the demands of theater." Embellished singing, according to Muratori, had gotten so out of hand that "if the audience did not have before its eyes, in printed form, what is being sung, I am certain that they would understand nothing of the action or of the story" (Document 2). Muratori's was a two-pronged attack. He was a priest, and there is a certain amount of moral outrage in his diatribe. Still, by using Plato and the Roman rhetoricians to back up his criticism, he manages to question the very premise of opera. If it's sung, he seems to be saying, it's not drama.

Benedetto Marcello questioned some of the same things in a humorous style that suggests a wider target readership than Muratori's prose. A dilettante composer and writer, Marcello first tried to reform opera in the 1710s by introducing a style of singing that was more lyrical and less ornamented. But he probably made his point most effectively in his *Il teatro alla moda* (The Fashionable Theater, 1720), a satirical treatise in which he berated the decline in musical quality, the abuses of the libretto, and the demands of singers who insisted upon new arias and revisions. As Marcello saw it, the public's appetite for new operas had driven the quality down; virtuoso singers and fancy stage machinery had commandeered the spotlight. Mocking operatic convention, Marcello advises the librettist to "write the opera without any preconceived plan." Furthermore, the composer "must not reveal any of his dramatic intentions to the actors since he rightly assumes that they will do as they please anyway" (Document 3). Marcello's parody was widely read and inspired a number of *opera buffas* that satirized serious opera.

What followed in the eighteenth century was a series of libretto reforms aimed at reinstating the integrity of the drama. Separating the comic from the serious was part of that reform, and eventually led to the establishment of distinct genres for each—*opera buffa* on the one hand, *opera seria* on the other. One person in particular set the new standard for *dramma per musica*. That was Pietro Metastasio, the most renowned poet of the Arcadian movement in Rome, whose twenty-seven *opera seria* librettos returned opera to Classical ideals and to plots in which morality, logic, and an adherence to the Aristotelian unities took pride of place.

Documents

Document 1. John Evelyn, *The Diary of John Evelyn*. Ed. William Bray. New York: M. Walter Dunne, 1901. pp. 195–6 and pp. 201–2 (with omissions).

June, 1645.

The first public building I went to see was the Rialto, a bridge of one arch over the grand canal, so large as to admit a galley to row under it, built of good marble, and having on it, besides many pretty shops, three ample and stately passages for people without any inconvenience, the two outmost nobly balustered with the same stone; a piece of architecture much to be admired. It was evening, and the canal where the Noblesse go to take the air, as in our Hyde Park, was full of ladies and gentlemen. There are many times dangerous stops, by reason of the multitude of gondolas ready to sink one another. . . . Here they were singing, playing on harpsichords, and other music, and serenading their mistresses; in another place, racing, and other pastimes on the water, it being now exceeding hot.

Next day, I went to their Exchange [stock exchange], a place like ours, frequented by merchants, but nothing so magnificent; from thence, my guide led me to the Fondaco dei Tedeschi [headquarters for the city's German merchants], which is their magazine, and here many of the merchants, especially Germans, have their lodging and diet, as in a college. The outside of this stately fabric is painted by Giorgione da Castelfranco, and Titian himself.

Hence, I passed through the Mercera, one of the most delicious streets in the world for the sweetness of it, and is all the way on both sides tapestried as it were with cloth of gold, rich damasks and other silks, which the shops expose and hang before their houses from the first floor, and with that variety that for near half the year spent chiefly in this city, I hardly remember to have seen the same piece twice exposed; to this add the perfumes, apothecaries' shops, and the innumerable cages of nightingales which they keep, that entertain you with their melody from shop to shop, so that shutting your eyes, you would imagine yourself in the country, when indeed you are in the middle of the sea. It is almost as silent as the middle of a field, there being neither rattling of coaches nor trampling of horses. This street, paved with brick, and exceedingly clean, brought us through an arch to the famous piazza of St. Mark.

Over this porch stands that admirable clock, celebrated, next to that of Strasburg, for its many movements. . . . The buildings in this piazza are all arched, on pillars, paved within with black and white polished marble, even to the shops, the rest of the fabric as stately as any in Europe, being not only marble, but the architecture is of the famous Sansovini, who lies buried in St. Jacomo, at the end of the piazza. . . .

It was now Ascension week, and the great mart, or fair, of the whole year was kept, everybody at liberty and jolly; the noblemen stalking with their ladies on *choppines*. These are high-heeled shoes, particularly affected by these proud dames, or, as some say, invented to keep them at home, it being very difficult to walk in them. . . .

This night, having with my Lord Bruce taken our places before we went to the Opera, where comedies and other plays are represented in recitative music, by the most excellent musicians, vocal and instrumental, with variety of scenes painted and contrived with no less art of perspective, and machines for flying in the air, and other wonderful notions; taken together, it is one of the most magnificent and expensive diversions the wit of man can invent. The history was *Hercules in Lydia*; the scenes changed thirteen times. The famous voices, Anna Renzi, a Roman, and reputed the best treble of women; but there was an eunuch who, in my opinion, surpassed her; also a Genoese that sung an incomparable bass. This held us by the eyes and ears till two in the morning, when we went to the Chetto de san Felice, to see the noblemen and their ladies at basset, a game at cards which is much used; but they play not in public, and all that have inclination to it are in masquerade, without speaking one word, and so they come in, play, lose or gain, and go away as they please. This time of license is only in carnival and this Ascension-week; neither are their theaters open for that other magnificence, or for ordinary comedians, save on these solemnities, they being a frugal and wise people, and exact observers of all sumptuary laws [laws regulating consumption].

Document 2. Ludovico Antonio Muratori, *On Perfect Italian Poetry* [*Della perfetta poesia italiana*] Modena, 1706. Book 3, Chapter 5. In *Music and Culture in Eighteenth-Century Europe: A Source Book* by Enrico Fubini. Translated from the original sources by Wolfgang Freis, Lisa Gasbarrone, and Michael Louis Leone. Translation edited by Bonnie J. Blackburn. Chicago: University of Chicago Press, 1994. pp. 42–3. © 1994 by the University of Chicago. Reprinted with permission of the University of Chicago Press.

Let us then go on to consider other defects, focusing on the poetry that makes up the operas. It should not be thought that I wish to speak ill of poets. In fact, I sympathize with them, as the art they profess is today condemned to be subservient to the demands of theater. Nowadays this happens with such little integrity, indeed with such discredit to them, that I dare say poetry has been placed in bondage. Indeed, where once music was both a servant and minister to poetry, today poetry is a servant to music. If we were to attempt something of this nature, I do not know what fame or glory poets could hope to obtain by writing such harmonious operas. Today nothing is more obvious than the ancillary position that poetry occupies with respect to music. From the start, the number of characters and their vocal roles are imposed on the poet. In accordance with a composer's whim, a poet is asked to write, alter, add, or exclude ariettas and recitatives. Further, every performer claims the authority of telling the poet what to do, and of having him write verses according to the dictates of the performer's imagination. Also, it is necessary to distribute the roles in the opera suitably, and to divide the verses carefully among them, so that no singer will complain of having been assigned a part that is shorter or inferior to those given the other performers. Thus, poets are constrained to lay out and embellish their operas, not as art and the particular subject matter would demand, but in accordance with the dictates of music.

Let us add that, to comply with the wishes of the theater directors, it is at times necessary to suit the plot and the verses to some stage machine, or set design, which they of course wish to include and show to the audience. All this, however, could easily be tolerated. But, on stage, what utility or glory accrues to poetry? It is of course true that the verses are recited, but in such a way that either the melody or the ignorance of the performing musicians rarely allows the meaning to come through, and quite often not even the words themselves, as they alter and transform the vowels. Some composers consider this charming, and they speak of "diphthonged singing" [giving a syllable as many beats as the notes to which it is set], as if not only grammar, but also music had its diphthongs. If the audience did not have before its eyes, in printed form, what is being sung, I am certain that they would understand nothing of the action or of the story that is being staged. Should the people in the audience lack the *libricciuolo* [little book] (as it is called), they only see and listen to some performers who alternately go on and off stage, and in turn sing, without being able to make out what they are singing, nor what the story is all about. Thus music is what stands out in modern operas. As for poetry, today theaters demand only that it act as a means and an instrument for the music, whereas it used to be, as it should be, the main end. In fact, today's tastes have determined the music to be the very essence of these operas, and the selection of skillful singers to be the most important objective. This is the only reason why people flock to theaters. They certainly do not go to delight in the efforts of poets, whose verses, printed in the librettos, they deign hardly worth a glance. Furthermore, it may be said that the verses are not even recited, as they are uttered by those who do not understand them and who, moreover, I would almost say, are not capable of conveying their meaning to the audience precisely because of the modern manner of singing. In addition, it is well known that those dramas which have enjoyed particular fame are those whose music has been fortunate enough to delight audiences. It matters little whether the story itself and the poet's verses are excellent or if they merit derision. For this reason, many dramas written by the cleverest poets elicit no applause, while applause is offered to others that were horribly defective in terms of their poetry. In fact, composers are not fond of those librettos that are overwrought and contain excessively contrived sentiments, as it is not easy to set their verses and ariettas to music. Only sweet, sonorous words are desired; little does it matter—in fact the composer prefers it—if the ariettas lack strong emotions and profound reflections, as long as their words are harmonious and beautiful. In truth, however, I cannot blame these people for demanding such things, for if only, or at least mainly, musical delight is sought in operas, it follows logically that, when writing them, poets will follow the tastes and the demands of the music, and not their own talents and creativity. They will be in a position of subservience, not of command.

Document 3. Benedetto Marcello, *Il Teatro alla moda*. Trans. Reinhard G. Pauly, "*Il Teatro Alla Moda—Part I.*" *The Musical Quarterly* 34/3 (July, 1948), pp. 371–403 and pp. 372, 373, 377, 378, 379, 380.

A writer of operatic librettos, if he wants to be modern, must never have read the Greek and Latin classic authors, nor should he do so in the future. After all, the old Greeks and Romans never read the modern writers.

Nor should he have the slightest knowledge of Italian meter and verse. . . .

Before the librettist begins writing he should ask the impresario for a detailed list giving the number and kind of stage sets and decorations he wishes to see employed. He will then incorporate all these into his drama. He should always be on the lookout for elaborate scenes such as sacrifices, sumptuous banquets, apparitions, or other spectacles. When those are to occur in the opera the librettist will consult with the theater engineer [machinist] in order to find out how many dialogues, monologues, and arias will be needed to stretch each scene of that type, so that all technical problems can be worked out without hurrying. The disintegration of the drama as an entity and the intense boredom of the audience are of no importance in connection with all this.

He should write the whole opera without any preconceived plan but rather proceed verse by verse. For if the audience never understands the plot their attentiveness to the very end of the opera will be insured. One thing any able modern librettist must strive for is frequently to have all characters of the piece on the stage at the same time, though nobody knows why. . . .

The aria must in no way be related to the preceding recitative but it should be full of such things as sweet little butterflies, bouquets, nightingales, quails, little boats, little huts, jasmine, violets, copper basins, little pots, tigers, lions, whales, crabs, turkeys, cold capon, etc.

Notes

1 Cristoforo Ivanovich, *Memorie teatrali di Venezia* (1681), in Lorenzo Bianconi, *Music in the Seventeenth Century*, trans. David Bryant (Cambridge: Cambridge University Press, 1987), p. 308.
2 Lorenzo Bianconi, *Music in the Seventeenth Century*, trans. David Bryant (Cambridge: Cambridge University Press, 1987), p. 181.
3 Cristoforo Ivanovich, *Memorie teatrali di Venezia* (1681), in Lorenzo Bianconi, *Music in the Seventeenth Century*, trans. David Bryant (Cambridge: Cambridge University Press, 1987), p. 309.
4 Nino Pirrotta, "Commedia dell'arte and Opera," *The Musical Quarterly* 41/3 (July, 1955), p. 323.
5 Ellen Rosand, *Opera in Seventeenth-Century Venice: The Creation of a Genre* (Berkeley: University of California Press, 1991), p. 17.
6 Francesco Cavalli, *Giasone*, Concerto Vocale, cond. René Jacobs (Harmonia Mundi, HMX2901282.84), trans. Derek Yeld, pp. 109, 111.
7 Francesco Cavalli, *Giasone*, Concerto Vocale, cond. René Jacobs (Harmonia Mundi, HMX2901282.84), trans. Derek Yeld, p. 111.
8 Francesco Cavalli, *Giasone*, Concerto Vocale, cond. René Jacobs (Harmonia Mundi, HMX2901282.84), trans. Derek Yeld, p. 113.
9 Francesco Cavalli, *Giasone*, Concerto Vocale, cond. René Jacobs (Harmonia Mundi, HMX2901282.84), trans. Derek Yeld, p. 177.

10 Francesco Cavalli, *Giasone*, Concerto Vocale, cond. René Jacobs (Harmonia Mundi, HMX2901282.84), trans. Derek Yeld, p. 181.

11 See Margaret Murata, "Four Airs for Orontea," *Recercare* 10 (1998), pp. 249–62.

12 Nino Pirrotta, "Tre capitol su Cesti," in Antonio Bruers, Nino Pirrotta et al., *La scuola romana: G. Carissimi, A. Cesti, M. Marazzoli*, Accademia Musicale Chigiana (Siena, 1953), p. 55, quoted in translation in Murata, "Four Airs for Orontea," *Recercare* 10 (1998), p. 259.

7 Church, State, and Spectacle in France: Music under Louis XIV

Louis XIV assumed sole power in 1661 and ruled until 1715, making his reign the longest in European history. During that time, Louis XIV reformed the military, further centralized the administration, and supported and enjoyed lavish culture at court. The court of Louis XIV was one of the most opulent in European history. The architectural refinements of the king's palaces, the fine portraits of the king, and the elegant statues of him that dot the city of Paris are hallmarks of the cultural display that reached a highpoint during his realm. Music also peaked under Louis XIV, for the king both supported and enjoyed the many types of musical performances available to him—intimate chamber music concerts in the privacy of his apartments, sumptuous dance and theatrical productions in his court theatres, and elaborate motets in his chapel. This chapter connects the cultivation of music under Louis XIV to the political and religious goals of the king's reign. We will see that music was an extraordinarily effective means of enhancing Louis XIV's reputation, and by extension, that of his court and country.

Louis XIV: The Boy King

Louis IV's birth in 1638 was celebrated all over France with bonfires, fireworks, bell-ringing, cannon fire, and the solemn chanting of the *Te Deum*. Sermons, speeches, and poems further commemorated the event. Louis XIV's first taste of power came at the age of four, when the death of his father in 1643 cast the boy king on the world stage (a position he occupied until his own death in 1715). The ritual coronation and anointing of Louis in 1654 at the cathedral of Rheims and the royal processions of his early reign immediately established the young ruler's majesty. Even his personal activities contributed to this impression. Louis indulged his love of dancing by participating in nine court ballets between 1651 and 1659. His role as the rising sun in *Le ballet de la nuit* (1653), for which he wore a magnificent golden wig, was to become emblematic of his reign at large and to give him the sobriquet by which he is best known today: the Sun King.

Having taken the throne at such a young age, the young king was at an initial disadvantage. He first held joint rule with his Spanish mother, Anne of Austria, and the chief minister, the Italian Cardinal Mazarin, during a phase known as the Regency. These early years were rife with dissension: The nobility vied for power with the king, and a series of civil wars, known as the *Fronde*, erupted between 1648 and 1653 as factions of the upper classes reacted against royal encroachments on their traditional authority. Not until 1661 did Louis XIV rule independently without regent; nor did he appoint a prime minister. The political result was a form of absolutism, and an extreme personalization of power.

There were ongoing political campaigns as well, both military and diplomatic, with Spain, the Netherlands, and their allies, and these external conflicts were particularly troublesome in the second half of Louis's reign. The Dutch War, in which France had opposed Spain and the Dutch Republic (now the Netherlands) did not end until the treaties of Nijmegen of 1678–9. A series of treaties between France and the Netherlands, Spain, Holy Roman Emperor Leopold I, Denmark, and Brandenburg made Louis XIV the most powerful of Europe's monarchs, and gave him some respite from following his armies. The final decades of Louis XIV's reign were marked by decline, due to the high costs of court expenditures, military defeats, two famines (1693–4 and 1709–10), and domestic tensions. Chief among the latter was the fierce opposition between Jansenists, a subset within the Catholic Church that drew inspiration from Saint Augustine, and powerful Jesuit factions, which accused the Jansenists of Calvinist leanings.

The court of Louis XIV was known for its splendor and lavish festivities, and the ostentatious display of wealth and art helped position Louis XIV as a major European leader in the face of these internal and external conflicts. From the start, Louis needed to project the image, real or not, of a strong, capable, Catholic ruler, and he exploited the visual arts, dance, theatre and music to that end, and to further his social, religious, and political goals. For the French king, culture was a form of image-management akin to modern-day public relations. Its central strategy was to glorify the king. Indeed *gloire*, or glory, was a keyword of the time, and glory, as Furetière wrote in the *Dictionnaire universel* (1690), is bestowed by the world in general, not by individuals. Glory personified appeared in plays, in ballets and operas, and on public monuments such as the Fountain of Glory in the gardens at Versailles. Then as now, glory was best bestowed through brilliance, spectacle, and lasting tributes.

Writing in 1709, political theorist Jacques-Bénigne Bossuet (1627–1704) remarked that the court of a king was "dazzling and magnificent" in order "to make the peoples respect him." His contemporary, social theorist Charles-Louis Montesquieu, made a similar point: "The magnificence and splendor which surround kings form part of their power." Louis XIV embraced the strategy unequivocally. The series of grandiose projects Louis undertook in the 1680s were part of this systematic program of glorification. During this period Louis doubled expenditures on the palace and gardens of Versailles, where he took official residence in 1682. The statue campaign of 1685–6 resulted in a series of nearly twenty statues of the king, usually on horseback, placed in public squares in Paris and in provincial towns. The number of surviving images of the king is staggering: 287 datable finished portraits, 770 engravings, numerous tapestries, and 318 official medals struck during his lifetime.[1]

Royal portraits glorified the king and disguised his faults. The famous state portrait by Hyacinthe Rigaud (1659–1743) masks the king's short stature (he stood only 5'3" tall) by augmenting Louis's height with high heels and wigs, and by positioning his body strategically (Fig. 7.1). The classical column (with an allegorical figure of Justice at the base) and the velvet curtain are reminiscent of sixteenth-century portraiture. The head of the king, allowed to show the wisdom of his age, is portrayed on a young body with elegant legs. The feet are in a ballet pose, reminiscent of the king's dancing days. It is known that Louis particularly liked Rigaud's portrait and ordered copies of it.

The portrait was carefully constructed to highlight attributes of leadership and royalty. These same qualities are emphasized in a lengthy account from the *Memoirs of the Reign of Louis XIV* by Louis de Rouvroy (1675–1755), known as Saint-Simon. A soldier, diplomat, and courtier, Saint-Simon had a strong interest in Versailles politics and received secret information from a network of spies and confidantes. His description reveals his own pettiness, yet sheds light on the king's vanity and character:

> Louis XIV's vanity was without limit or restraint; it colored everything and convinced him that no one even approached him in military talents, in plans and enterprises, in government. Hence those pictures and inscriptions in the gallery at Versailles which disgust every foreigner; those opera prologues that he himself tried to sing; that flood of prose and verse in his praise for which his appetite was insatiable. (Document 1)

Cultural Institutions

A highly centralized musical establishment was the cultural counterpart to the political absolutism of the Sun King's reign. Louis XIV had inherited a system of musical organization and patronage that dated back to his father's reign. The royal household comprised three departments of musicians: the Chapelle, the Chambre, and the Ecurie. The *Vingt-quatre Violons du Roi* (Twenty-Four Violins) and the *Petits Violons du Roi* (or *Petite Bande*), although technically under the administration of the Chamber, were virtually autonomous because of their great prestige. Known as the *Grande Bande*, the *Vingt-quatre Violons* featured not

Figure 7.1 Rigaud, portrait of Louis XIV, 1701.

only the Italian norm of four string parts but five: six first violins, four each of the middle parts, and six basses. When more sound was required, twelve wind instruments, the *Grande Hautbois*, joined them. Louis XIV reduced the size of the group to sixteen string players when he became king, but this did not weaken its efficacy as a metaphor of state control. With rhythmic accuracy, crisp articulation, and uniform bow strokes—every down bow in unison on every downbeat—the King's instrumental groups earned a reputation for discipline and precision.

To maintain quality and lend stability to the pool of available musicians, Louis XIV developed a highly refined system for training and mentoring composers and performers. By the end of his reign, Louis XIV employed between 150 and 200 musicians. The positions of *officier* were usually inherited, which explains the number of musical dynasties in Paris, such as the Philidor and Boesset families; however, these positions could also be bought and sold. Court musicians who could not qualify for *officier* were divided into three categories: *musiciens ordinaires* (musicians regularly employed by the court); *musiciens extraordinaires* (those not regularly employed at court but used for special occasions—town musicians or foreigners, for instance); and *musiciens suivant la court* (minor artists or apprentices). *Musiciens ordinaires* were recruited from the lower-middle class Parisian families of musicians,

Figure 7.2 Garnier, allegory of Louis XIV. Protector of the arts and sciences, 1672.

and their salaries depended upon rank, tenure, and in some cases the instrument they played; those affiliated with the chamber were paid the most. Despite these administrative divisions, members passed freely from one group to another and performances by combined groups were common for major events such as royal births, deaths, and marriages.

The musical establishment was part of a centralized plan to promote the image of the king as a generous patron of the arts. Cultural patronage was not a haphazard affair but a highly sophisticated and integrated program. Louis XIV surrounded himself with a plethora of cultural advisors. Among the most effective was Jean-Baptiste Colbert (1619–83), who gradually assumed the posts of minister of finances, secretary of state for the navy, and superintendent of construction. Colbert successfully restored French finances in the decades between 1661 and 1671, doubling state revenues. Under Colbert, arts and sciences served the needs of the state. He established the king's dominance as a patron through an integrated plan for music, literature, poetry, history, panegyric, medals, tapestries, frescoes, engravings, and monuments. Following a 1662 report by Jean Chapelain on the uses of the arts "for preserving the splendor of the king's enterprises," Colbert organized cultural affairs into a series of academies that mobilized artists, writers, musicians, and scholars. Taking the great academies of Antiquity and Renaissance Italy as his models, Colbert oversaw the founding of the Academy of Dance (1661), the Royal Academy of Painting and Sculpture (founded in 1648 and restructured in 1663), the Academy of Sciences (1666), the Academy of Architecture (1671), and the short-lived Academy of Opera (1671), which was replaced by the Royal Academy of Music in 1672. Louis XIV's support for the artistic system is captured in a painting by Jean Garnier (1632–1705) (Fig. 7.2).

Jean-Baptiste Lully, *Surintendant de la musique*

In 1672 Louis XIV charged Jean-Baptiste Lully (1599–1667) with establishing the Royal Academy of Music. The king gave Lully free artistic reign of the academy. The development and longevity of a national style of French music are the result of the royal patronage of Louis XIV and the vision and talents of his *surintendant de la musique* (head of music), Jean-Baptiste Lully.

Born in Florence in 1632, Lully arrived in Paris in 1646 as *garçon de chambre* to the king's cousin, Grande Mademoiselle Anne-Marie-Louise d'Orléans. By 1653 Lully had entered the young king's service as a composer of court ballets, which were often vehicles for showcasing Louis's skill as a dancer. The two danced together in the 1653 *Ballet de la nuit*. A key point in Lully's career was his appointment as *surintendant de la musique de la chambre du roi* in May 1661.

As *surintendant*, Lully commanded a world of singers and instrumentalists, dancers and makers of stage machinery, scene painters and costume designers, all of whom drew their salaries from the funds of the "king's revels," the *menusplaisirs*.

Lully distinguished himself as an administrator and businessman. When Louis XIV made Lully head of the Royal Academy of Music in 1672, the patent specified that the position gave Lully a monopoly over theatrical productions in France:

> We hereby grant him permission to give public performances of all his compositions, including those represented in Our presence, save that he shall not be permitted to make use of those musicians in Our personal employ for performances of the said dramas. (Document 2)

Figure 7.3 Portrait of Jean-Baptiste Lully.

No work that was sung throughout could be performed without Lully's written permission, under penalty of a ten thousand-*livre* fine and confiscation of the theater, machines, decorations, and costumes. An ordinance of April 30, 1673, restricted the number of musicians who could appear in any production independent of the Royal Academy of Music to two voices and six instrumentalists, and limited these to musicians and dancers not in the employ of the Royal Academy of Music. The patent dramatically curtailed competition and gave Lully an immense strategic advantage in developing his compositional and theatrical crafts.

With control of the Royal Academy of Music, Lully embarked on the creation of a new genre of French music drama. In collaboration with librettist Philippe Quinault (1635–88), Lully founded the *tragédie en musique* (tragedy in music), modeling it on the five-act, spoken tragedy of French classical theatre, revered for its dramatic intensity and literary quality. Beginning with *Cadmus et Hermione* in 1673, Lully and Quinault produced eleven *tragedies*, establishing an influential model for French opera for more than a century. Quinault was contracted by Lully to write one *tragédie* per year at a fee of four thousand *livres*. Lully exerted considerable control over the process, however, and there is much evidence that Quinault made extensive revisions at his request. Lully's monopoly of the French stage gave his works a high degree of exposure at the Paris Opéra and at court.

What did a *tragédie en musique* sound like? Quinault used a flexible approach to verse length in his libretti, mixing clearly audible, classical alexandrine lines of twelve syllables—the standard verse length in the spoken tragedies of Racine and Corneille—with shorter lines that lacked a regular rhyme scheme. Flexibility in poetic organization was reinforced with repetitions, refrains, and choral interjections that added structure to the text and presented the composer with more options for rhythmic variety. (Had Lully set only alexandrine lines, the repetitive phrase lengths would soon have become monotonous.) Heroic plots drawn from ancient mythology and medieval chivalry offered opportunities for amorous intrigue among heroes and heroines, for fight scenes, celebrations, heroic quests, sleep scenes, journeys to the underworld, and, tellingly, for clear metaphorical references in praise of Louis XIV. These features come together in Lully's *Phaëton*.

Lully and Quinault's *Phaëton*

Phaëton premiered in 1683 at the height of Lully's career as Superintendent of the King's music and Director of the Royal Academy of Music. Quinault based his libretto on the myth of Phaëton as it is told in Ovid's *Metamorphoses*. The title character is young and inexperienced; prompted by a rival, he makes a foolish effort to drive the chariot of the Sun and dies as a result. Most interpretations of the opera see his death as Louis XIV's cautionary warning. Certainly, the libretto offered many occasions for references to the king: The title character is the son of Clymene and the Sun.

Phaëton was first performed on January 6, 1683, at Versailles, where Louis XIV had made his principal residence the year before. Operas were still performed on a temporary stage set up in the riding school of the royal stables. There was neither machinery nor multiple sets, but the luxurious costumes by royal designer Jean Berain, which appeared in a series of etchings enhanced by watercolors, provided ample enticement for the eye. On April 27, 1683, *Phaëton* received its first public performance at the Paris Opéra, now with the full stage sets and machinery by Berain. The opera was extremely successful. Lecerf de La Viéville de Fresneuse reported that it was called "the Opera of the People," an accolade that probably refers to the spectacular scenery and stage effects.

The printed score contains Lully's dedication to Louis XIV. In it, Lully trumpets the opera's success at court. The dedication reveals that Lully assumed a "larger share" of artistic responsibilities, which extended to supervising the costumes, "one of the principal elements in this kind of spectacle." Lully thanks the king for permission to create an Academy of performers befitting Paris and the king's court. Lully's words remind us of his position at court and his arrogance; but they also show how crucial Louis XIV's favour was in fostering Lully's career and reputation.

Lully opened his tragedies and theatrical works, whether opera, ballet or suite, with a substantial instrumental movement now referred to as a "French overture." *Phaëton* is no exception. These overtures were more than mere orchestral introductions; because they signalled the entrance of Louis XIV to the theater, they were designed to create an impression of majesty and pomp. As it was standardized by Lully, the French overture paired a slow section in duple meter in stately dotted rhythms (usually marked *grave* or *lento*), which was generally repeated, with a quicker, imitative section that was complementary in key and texture (this section was also repeated, and was more frequently in triple meter). The form originated with Lully's ballet overtures of the 1650s and quickly became the sole blueprint for French opera and ballet overtures. So imposing was the French overture, and so closely associated was it with the magnificence of Louis XIV's court, that it was soon imitated across Europe, inspiring copies and adaptations by Purcell, Handel, Bach, and Telemann in both orchestral and chamber music. Even Beethoven recalled the French overture in the introduction to his "Pathètique" piano sonata (Opus 13), thus stretching the influence of the French overture to the early 1820s.

The primary features of the French overture are easy to hear. The slow tempo and pervasive dotted rhythms that give the first section its characteristic majesty are unmistakable in performance (Ex. 7.1). Note that i has been orchestrated in five parts, which was standard for Lully, and clearly differentiates French orchestral style from Italian four-voice practice. Overtures were played by the full orchestra, which comprised up to forty string players and a continuo section: The top part would have been taken by the violin, the middle three parts by different sizes of viola (*hautes-contre, tailles,* and *quintes*), and the bottom voice by the bass violins (the orchestration was weighted considerably towards the top and bottom voices). Since Lully's orchestra often included up to eight oboes and bassoons, pairs of recorders and/or flutes, and sometimes trumpets and timpani as well, some doubling—not indicated in the score, although it is often possible to reconstruct more detailed orchestration by looking at the individual parts—is also likely.

On the page however, the French overture's signature is less obvious. How the notation is realized is crucial, and we know from a number of contemporary treatises of the time that the performers exaggerated the effect of the dotted rhythms by lengthening the time allotted to the dotted note (usually treating much of the dot as a rest—Baroque style is in general quite detached) and shortening the corresponding anacrusis into the next beat. This over-dotting, as it is called, was not notated; the style was simply understood. It has become a common performance practice today amongst period instrument ensembles, although contemporary performers, musicologists, and critics do not always agree on its relevance to music outside of France or from later in the eighteenth century. (In fact, some form of over-dotting was a common practice well into the twentieth century, even in nineteenth-century piano repertoire; mathematically precise interpretations of dotted rhythms in general are arguably a manifestation of a modernist aesthetic.) Regardless, it was this particular aspect of the French overture—and the dotted rhythms may have been associated with the halting

Example 7.1 Lully, French overture from *Phaëton*, mm. 1–9.

footsteps employed in ceremonial processions—that gave rise to the descriptive adjectives inevitably linked to the style: majestic, heroic, festive, and pompous.

The faster note values and rapid imitative entries in the second section of the French overture provide obvious contrast to the first part (and perhaps generate excitement for the spectacle to come) (Ex. 7.2). Often in triple meter, this quicker section brings the overture to a tonal close, although occasionally material related to the opening rounds off the overture in a sort of coda.

The French overture remains a distinct and recognizable entity because its most basic features of tempo, rhythm, form, and texture are so obvious. Its unequivocal profile also made the French overture ideal for image-making. Like a musical counterpart to the gold coins and engravings that bore the king's image and gave him credit for the realm's wealth, the music's majesty advertised the glory of the king.

Phaëton is a good example of Lully's mature style of *tragédie lyrique*. Lully combined speech-like material, whose rhythms were governed by the long and short syllable lengths of the French language, with more structured airs, choruses, and refrains. The three examples below were chosen to showcase the emotional effectiveness of Lully's settings: the end of Act 1 when Proteus reveals Phaëton's fate, the start of Act 2, and the spectacular finale in which Jupiter strikes down the arrogant Phaëton as he rides recklessly across the sky in his father's chariot.

In the final scene of Act 1, Proteus reveals to Clymene the terrible destiny reserved for her son, Phaëton. The passage is an accompanied recitative with strings and continuo. The strings provide melodic and rhythmic support—a foretaste of the increasing role of the orchestra in Lully's last operas. The jagged dotted rhythms of the string introduction are noteworthy for their association with the French overture; they aptly reflect Proteus's godly standing and are juxtaposed with the speech-like rhythms of the vocal line when the singer enters. Meter changes, a characteristic of French recitative, ensure that the important syllables of the text, particularly at the end of a line, fall on downbeats (mm. 20–39) (Fig. 7.4).

Lully intensified Proteus's speech by repeating sections of the text and employing melodic sequences that push the music forward. Proteus's imprecation to Phaëton ("Tu vas tomber!" You shall fall) occurs multiple times, the first time in sequence: mm. 57–60 and subsequently at the head of longer phrases, where it maintains the same melodic shape (mm. 64–70) (Ex. 7.3). Lully also repeated a direct reference to the role Clymene's ambition played in inciting Phaëton to embark on his fateful ride. The line "Tremblez, tremblez pour vostre Fils, ambitieuse Mere" (Tremble for your son, ambitious mother) first occurs towards the middle of Proteus's speech (mm. 36–39) and again at the end, almost like a refrain (mm. 74–77). Positioning it as Proteus's last word points an unmistakable finger of blame at Clymene.

Example 7.2 Lully, French overture from *Phaëton*, mm. 18–21.

Figure 7.4 Lully, *Phaëton,* Act 1, Scene 8, mm. 16–45.

je fremis!   Que voy-je!   O   Dieux!   Tremblez .ij.   pour Voftre Fils ambitieufe

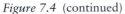
BASSE-CONTINUE.

Mere.   Où vas-tu .ij.   Jeune Teme- raire?   Tu dois trouver la mort dans la

BASSE-CONTINUE,

Figure 7.4 (continued)

Example 7.3 Lully, *Phaëton*, Act 1, Scene 8, mm. 57–77.

Texts for Figure 7.4.

Proteus
Le sort de Phaëton se découvre à mes yeux.
Dieux! je fremis: Que voy-je! O Dieux!
Tremblez, pour vostre Fils, ambitieuse Mere.
Où vas-tu, jeune Temeraire?
Tu dois trouver la mort dans la gloire où tu cours.

Proteus[2]
Phaëton's fate is revealed to my eyes.
Gods! I shudder: What do I see? O Gods!
Tremble for your son, ambitious mother!
Where are you going, you rash young man?
You'll meet nothing but death in your race to-
wards glory.

The second example from the beginning of Act 2 shows Lully moving smoothly from sparse recitative to a more structured aria form (Fig. 7.5). Clymene's opening *recit* follows the rhythms of the text—mostly

Example 7.3 (continued)

a mix of twelve- and eight-syllable lines—and is accompanied by light strings and continuo. As Phaëton questions Proteus's power in the passage beginning with "Protée a-t'il le droit suprême" (Has Proteus the supreme right?), the scene moves into a more structured arioso with regular rhythms and cadence points, a nice match with the text, which speaks of rights and the control of one's destiny. The meter changes to triple just at the end of Phaëton's line, as he urges his mother to believe in his courage, and the arioso makes way for quicker note values and more natural, speech-like rhythms. Clymene responds, first with recitative, and then with her own air on life's pleasures ("Live, and limit your desires"). The latter is fittingly cast in triple-time; as Clymene sings of pleasure and the sweetness of power, several short ornaments decorate her vocal line.

Texts for Figure 7.5.

Phaëton	**Phaëton**[3]
A l'himen de sa Fille, il me veut engager	He wants to commit me to marrying his daughter,
Son interest a dicté sa réponse.	His interests have determined his response.

Clymene	**Clymene**
Je voy que j'ay trop entrepris.	I see that I have undertaken too much.

Phaëton
Quoy? ma grandeur, n'est pas vostre plus   What? My greatness, isn't that your dearest wish?
chere envie?

Clymene	**Clymene**
Il vous en cousteroit la vie,	It will cost you your life,
Je ne veux point pour vous de grandeur	I don't want greatness for you
at *this* price.	
à ce prix.	

Phaëton	**Phaëton**
Protée a-t'il le droit supreme	Has Proteus the ultimate right
De donner des Arrests ou de vie, ou	To pronounce sentences of life or death?
de mort?	
Est-ce à luy de regler mon Sort?	Is it up to him to settle my fate?
Un Coeur comme le mien fait son destin	A heart such as mine makes its own destiny.
luy-mesme.	
Croyez-en mon courage, il doit vous	Believe in my courage, it is bound to reassure you.
rasseurer.	

Clymene	
Vous estes digne de l'Empire,	You are worthy of sovereignty,
Mais si vostre grand Coeur me force à	But however much your mighty spirit compels me to
l'admirer,	admire it,
C'est en tremblant que je l'admire.	I tremble as I do so.

Vivez, & bornez vos desirs	Live, and limit your desires,
Aux tranquilles plaisirs	To the tranquil pleasures
D'une amour mutuelle:	Of mutual love:
Aimez, contentez-vous	Love, and content yourself
De regner sur un coeur fidelle,	With reigning over a faithful heart,
Il n'est point d'empire plus doux.	There is no power more sweet.

Performers knowledgeable in French Baroque performance practice apply a performance convention known as *notes inégales* (unequal notes) to the eighth notes in the bass line that accompanies Clymene's air, above, dividing the quarter note beat into long and short values, even though they are notated equally (Exs. 7.4a–c). This rhythmic practice is similar in effect to the way jazz musicians "swing" their eighth

Figure 7.5 Lully, *Phaëton*, Act 2, Scene 1, Clymene and Phaëton, mm. 13–51.

luy de regler mon Sort? Un Cœur comme le miē fait son destin luy-mes- me. Croyez-en mõ cou-

BASSE-CONTINUE.

Vous estes digne de l'Empire, Mais, si vostre grand

rage, Il doit vous rasseurer.

BASSE-CONTINUE.

Cœur me force à l'admi- rer, C'est en tremblât que je l'ad- mire. Vi-

BASSE-CONTINUE.

vez, & bornez vos desirs Aux tranquiles plaisirs D'une amour mutu- elle: elle: Ai-

BASSE-CONTINUE. H ij

Figure 7.5 (continued)

Example 7.4a–c Lully, *Phaëton*, Act 2, Scene 1, Clymene and Phaëton, mm. 49–50, bass.

notes, although the degree of inequality can vary from strict dotted rhythms to an extremely subtle lilt. It existed in France from the mid-sixteenth century to the late eighteenth. It was considered appropriate for passages moving in generally stepwise motion below the level of the beat, and some instrumental techniques aided in making inequality almost automatic. These include the fingering for keyboard players (a string of 2–3 fingerings, for example) and the tonguing syllables for wind players, in which lengthened notes would receive a different type of tongue stroke than the shorter notes. Therefore the eighth notes in the bass line in the air above at the approach to the double bar would not be played as notated but subjected to some amount of inequality.

Phaëton answers Clymene with a song in praise of glory. A series of exchanges between mother and son in recitative on the dire implications of Phaëton's decision complete the scene.

In the final act, Epaphus, son of Isis, calls upon Jupiter and Isis to avenge him: His rival, Phaëton, has robbed him of the hand of Libye, heir to the throne of Egypt. The crisis escalates as Phaëton loses control as he drives the Chariot of the Sun. Isis, goddess of Earth, pleads with Jupiter to strike Phaëton down when the chariot nearly sets the earth on fire. Frantic, the people urge Jupiter to hurry in a loud, brisk chorus in 3/8 meter supported by the full orchestra (tempos were linked to meter signatures, and 3/8 would have been immediately understood as indicating a faster speed than 3/4) (Fig. 7.6).

O Dieu qui lancez le Tonnerre   O God who launches thunder[4]

Proclaiming Phaëton's fate an example for all those brazen enough to challenge authority, Jupiter strikes the chariot with his thunderbolt and Phaëton plunges to his death. Aghast, the chorus responds in a six-measure outburst that is cut off as abruptly as Phaëton's short life, and the opera, too, comes to an end (Fig. 7.7).

Merops, Libye, & le Choeur   Merops, Libye, and Chorus[5]
O chûte affreuse!   O frightful descent!
O temerité malheureuse!   O unfortunate rashness!

Phaëton remained popular well into the eighteenth century. It received multiple performances at the Paris Opera, running for three months after it opened on July 30, 1683, and it was revived in 1692, 1702, 1710, 1721, 1730, and 1742. Its longevity speaks to both its quality and to Lully's fame. Evrard Titon du Tillet (1677–1762) praised Lully in *Le parnasse françois* (The French Parnassus, 1732), which depicted an imaginary Parnassus of poetry and music, ruled by the divine Louis XIV. *Le parnasse françois* is a biographical chronicle comprised of 259 brief *vite* of poets and musicians. Titon summarized Lully's accomplishments as follows: "In short, Lully well deserves the title 'Prince of French Musicians.' He is considered the inventor of our great and beautiful French music, whether of Opera or the large ensembles of vocal and symphonic music, and he has brought it to the peak of perfection. Lauded by the greatest artists and regarded as a model *par excellence*, he has been the father of our most illustrious musicians."

Instrumental Music at the French Court

Instrumental music also played a role in Louis XIV's image-making and early cultural education. As a boy, the future King Louis XIV learned to play the lute from Germain Pinel, the guitar from Bernard Jourdan de La Salle and Robert de Visée, and the keyboard from Etienne Richard. The finest musicians of the day, Michel-Richard de

Figure 7.6 Lully, *Phaëton*, Act 5, Scene 7, Chorus, mm. 1–16.

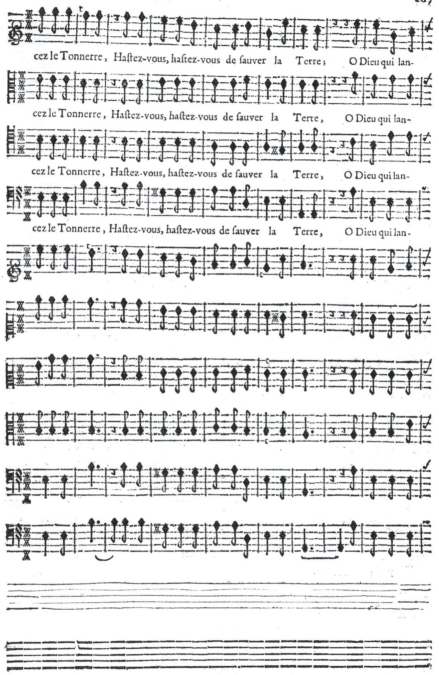

cez le Tonnerre, Haftez-vous, haftez-vous de sauver la Terre; O Dieu qui lan-

cez le Tonnerre, Haftez-vous, haftez-vous de sauver la Terre, O Dieu qui lan-

cez le Tonnerre, Haftez-vous, haftez-vous de sauver la Terre, O Dieu qui lan-

cez le Tonnerre, Haftez-vous, haftez-vous de sauver la Terre, O Dieu qui lan-

Figure 7.6 (continued)

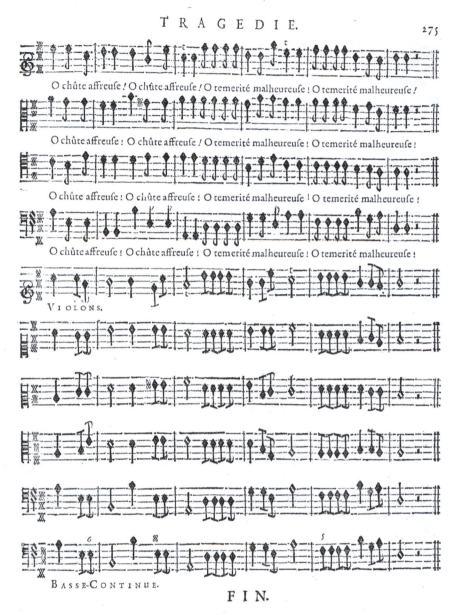

O chûte affreuse! O chûte affreuse! O temerité malheureuse! O temerité malheureuse!

O chûte affreuse! O chûte affreuse! O temerité malheureuse! O temerité malheureuse!

O chûte affreuse! O chûte affreuse! O temerité malheureuse! O temerité malheureuse!

O chûte affreuse! O chûte affreuse! O temerité malheureuse! O temerité malheureuse!

VIOLONS.

BASSE-CONTINUE.

FIN.

Figure 7.7 Lully, *Phaëton,* Act 5, Scene 8, mm. 9–14.

Lalande and François Couperin, later taught music to the king's children. Louis XIV sponsored virtuoso instrumentalists in both daily concerts and more formal performances, for his own enjoyment and that of his guests.

The instrument with the most prestige in the second half of the seventeenth century was the viola da gamba, an instrument played between the legs (da gamba) and similar in size to a cello. Prized for its plangent, voice-like quality, it was used for ensemble and solo works and for the accompaniment of voices. In 1687 Le Sieur Danoville and Jean Rousseau each published a manual on how to play the instrument. The books focused on hand positions and ornamentation, and included elaborate fingering charts. The instrument's popularity encouraged a tradition of viol virtuosos in France, including André Maugars, Nicolas Hotman, Jean de Sainte-Colombe, Marin Marais, and Danoville. The viol maintained a position of supremacy in France far longer than in other parts of Europe, where it was superseded by the violin. Writing a final *Défense de la basse de viole* (Defense of the Bass Viol, 1740), Hubert Le Blanc called the violoncello a "miserable canker" and assured his reader that "the heightened Tone and explosive Sound of the Violin does not agree at all with persons of quality or of noble education."

The most important of all Sainte-Colombe's students was Marin Marais (1656–1728), who was appointed *ordinaire* of the king's chamber music in 1679. Marais wrote the major portion of his works for the small bass of the viol family, which in the seventeenth and early eighteenth centuries included as many as nine different sizes of instruments, all called by the generic name viola da gamba. Marais's instrument—whether called the viola da gamba, bass viol, *basse de viole*, or, simply, "gamba"—was somewhat smaller than the modern cello and had frets and seven strings.

Much of what we know about Marais comes from the word of his close contemporary, Titon du Tillet, whose *Le parnasse françois* painted a vivid picture of the relationship between Marais and his teacher, Sainte-Colombe, and of the quality of domestic music making. According to Titon, "Marais brought the viol to the pinnacle of perfection." Marais's reputation extended far beyond the French realm. Johann Gottfried Walther, in his *Musikalisches Lexicon* (Musical Lexicon, 1732), described Marais as an "incomparable Parisian violist whose works are known all over Europe." Marais's visage circulated widely in a portrait by André Bouys from 1704.

Marais's crowning achievement was his *Pièces de viole*, which totaled 596 pieces for one, two, or three viols and continuo, distributed in five separate volumes published between 1686 and 1725. Each book contains a mix of over a hundred titled dances and descriptive pieces arranged in suites. The suites were probably not meant to be performed as a unit, but to be browsed for individual movements chosen on the basis of taste or technical difficulty. Marais provided precise information on how he wanted his pieces performed in extensive prefaces. Marais's lengthy prefaces to his five volumes of *Pièces de viole* form a composite guide on basic technique, ornaments, fingering, bowing, and accompaniment. A savvy salesman, Marais sanctioned performances on organ, harpsichord, lute, theorbo, violin, treble viol, transverse flute, recorder, guitar, and oboe (see prefaces to Books 2 and 3). He referred discreetly to the policy of mixing the difficult with the easy in his preface to Book 1: "And because simple melodies meet the taste of a lot of people, I have composed some pieces with this in mind, where chords scarcely enter; one will find others where I have used them more, and several which are entirely filled with them for those who love harmony and who are more advanced."[6]

Marais continued the tradition of French dance suites and *tombeaux* that was cultivated by the French lutenists and harpsichordists of the mid-seventeenth century—among them Jacques Gallot (d. *ca.* 1690), Charles Mouton (1617–before 1699), and Denis Gaultier the Younger (1597 or 1603–1672). Gaultier's *La rhétorique des dieux* (The Rhetoric of the Gods, composed between 1648 and 1652) contains fifty-six lute pieces grouped by key into eleven suites. Gaultier's title reflects the way in which composers of instrumental music of the period took impassioned speech as their model, hoping to share in vocal music's potent impact on the listener's emotions. The collection concludes with three works that form a sort of program suite: "Tombeau du Sieur Lenclos," "Consolation des amis de Sieur Lenclos," and "Résolution sur sa mort." Marais used these memorial works as models for his own *tombeau* for "Mons.[ieur] de Lully" from Book 2 (1701), a stylized lament that exploits affective gestures and harmonies to extraordinary effect.

Marais captured the speech-like intensity admirably in his *tombeau* for Lully, his teacher and collaborator at court.

Marais's *tombeau* for Lully was neither gentle farewell nor formal memorial. It is both more intense and more intimate, and its affect is clearly defined from the first measures. Marais opened the *Tombeau pour Monsieur Lully* with a brief continuo introduction (Ex. 7.5), which recurs three more times in the course of the piece like a small refrain. When the solo viol enters an octave higher in measure five, it restates the continuo's initial phrase. Note that these opening phrases, with their affective melodic intervals (the falling fourth, followed by a falling diminished fifth that rebounds on a diminished fourth) suggest passionate declamation. In fact it would be easy to imagine the first few lines as settings of alexandrine verse—the twelve-syllable lines of classical tragedy that Quinault frequently utilized in his opera librettos for Lully. Marais was precise about the ornaments that he wanted and notated them carefully. Many of these were specific to viol playing, and include two different types of vibrato, selectively applied to an individual note to make it more expressive. The vibrato most like modern string vibrato, called a *plainte*, was marked with a vertical wavy line, as in the solo viol's first note; a second type of vibrato, called *flattement*, and notated with a horizontal wavy line, was played by placing two fingers very close together on the string, one producing a slightly lower pitch (m. 9).

The piece's affect is further defined by extremes in range. For instance, in mm. 17–21, the solo line rises dramatically over three octaves in just two measures, and then drops down again (Ex. 7.6).

Emotional urgency is reinforced through harmonies rich in sevenths and ninths and by forceful modulations. In mm. 34–39, precisely midway in the piece, Marais is in the key of F-sharp minor, a tonality associated with extreme grief (Ex. 7.7). The first part of the phrase, supported by an F-sharp pedal in the bass, is especially speech-like. The lines grow in intensity, with both sevenths and ninths in the harmonies, as they approach a cadence in A major (m. 39). Marais also notates ornaments: A comma after the A in the fourth beat of m. 35 indicates a trill; and the small *x* on the downbeat of m. 36 indicates a mordent.

Even more crucial to defining the piece's affect is the way in which the phrases, often irregular in length, mimic impassioned speech. The rests after the chords (mm. 45–49) are a powerful rhetorical marker and make these gestures seem like gasps, while the expressive arpeggiated chords recall the intimate lute music of the early French Baroque by Denis Gaultier and his cousin, Ennemond Gaultier (1575–1651).

Example 7.5 Marais, *Tombeau pour Monsieur Lully*, mm. 1–11.

Example 7.6 Marais, *Tombeau pour Monsieur Lully*, mm. 17–21.

Example 7.7 Marais, *Tombeau pour Monsieur Lully*, mm. 34–39.

Marais's bowings, which he notated with a small *p* for *pousser* (push) and a *t* for *tirer* (pull), are carefully notated to reinforce the affect by ensuring that the performer does not choose an alternate bowing that would delete the expressiveness of a gesture. Since the viola da gamba is bowed underhand, the *pousser* stroke is the stronger one, and will provide the light stress suitable for strong beats of the measure. The *pousser* stroke can be thought of as an infusion of breath, light, or energy; the *tirer* as more of an expulsion, or as a gesture of resignation rather than affirmation. Thus the long sweeps of thirty-second and sixty-fourth notes under one *tirer* bow in mm. 40–42 suggest the expulsion of air so connected to a sighing gesture and to the desperation, oblivion, or exhaustion of grief (Ex. 7.9).

In mm. 47–48 of Example 7.8 Marais specifically asks for two successive *tirer* bowings on notes separated by a rest. The gesture suggests a breath caught in a sob, and Marais's bowing has more gravitas than an alternate bowing of *pousser*–rest–*tirer*; indeed the passage would seem inconsequential, even glib, in the latter bowing. The incredible detail in Marais's indications, supported by the instructions he provides in his prefaces, paint Marais as a generous teacher.

Harpsichord music was equally cherished at the court of Louis XIV and in Parisian musical circles. Jacques Champion de Chambonnières (1601/2–72) and Louis Couperin (ca. 1626–61) established what has become known as the French classical school of harpsichord playing and composition. Together they transferred the improvisatory lute style of Ennemond Gaultier and his contemporaries (referred to as *style brisé* in reference to the many broken, or arpeggiated, chords) to the harpsichord. Another key figure in the development of harpsichord music was Johann Jacob Froberger (1616–67), who visited Paris in 1652 and who was remembered by Louis Couperin in his A minor prelude "a l'imitation de Mr Froberger." Froberger, as a student of Frescobaldi, was important in introducing French composers to his teacher's improvisatory preludes, and to their rhythmically free manner of performance in particular; these certainly had some influence on the unmeasured preludes of the French *claveçinistes*.

Example 7.8 Marais, *Tombeau pour Monsieur Lully*, mm. 45–49.

Example 7.9 Marais, *Tombeau pour Monsieur Lully*, mm. 40–42.

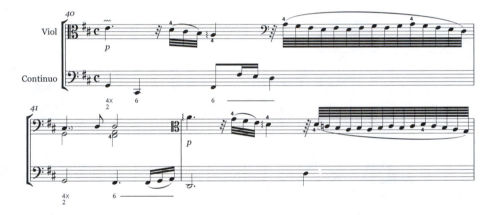

Jean Henry D'Anglebert (1629–91), Elisabeth-Claude Jacquet de La Guerre (1665–1729), and François Couperin (1668–1733) dominated harpsichord playing and composition for the rest of the Baroque period. D'Anglebert's *Pieces de clavecin* (Paris, 1689) is a summary of his life's work, a lavish engraved volume which he dedicated to the Princesse de Conti, legitimated daughter of Louis XIV and Mlle de la Vallière. D'Anglebert's influential table of ornaments that prefaces the volume served as a model not only for French composers such as Jean-Philippe Rameau, but also for Johann Sebastian Bach, whose ornament table from the *Clavier-Büchlein vor Wilhelm Friedemann Bach* (1720) bears a strong resemblance to that of D'Anglebert (Fig. 7.9).

An accomplished harpsichordist, child prodigy, and composer, Elisabeth-Claude Jacquet de La Guerre is one of the most important woman composers of the Baroque period. A prodigy, her performance career began at the age of five when she played the harpsichord and sang at the French court. She left the court in 1684 to marry the organist Marin de La Guerre. Her activities in Paris centered on teaching and giving the concerts that brought her such great fame in the city. As a composer, she contributed to the central genres of the period: opera, Italian cantata, trio sonatas, and harpsichord music. La Guerre was the first woman in France to write an opera tragedy in music: *Cephale et Procris* was produced at the Royal Academy of Music in 1694.

Born into a family of master instrument builders and organists, La Guerre came to her musical talent naturally. Her first keyboard teacher was her father, Claude Jacquet (d. 1702), organist at the church of

Saint-Louis on the île Notre-Dame from about 1661 until his death. Her mother's side had links to the French court. La Guerre harnessed her musical background, talent, and entrepreneurship to actively pursue the publication of her music. She published a total of six books, at first privately and then with the firm of Christopher Ballard.

La Guerre's first publication, *Les pièces de clavessin . . . premier livre*, dates from 1687. La Guerre self-published the volume: She paid for plates to be engraved by Henri de Baussen, for the paper, and for the printing costs. Self-publishing gave the composer greater control of production and profit, but it also brought greater financial risk. La Guerre used the same method for her double volume of *pièces de clavecin* and *sonates* for violin and continuo (1707), and for her collection of secular cantatas (1715).

La Guerre offset the financial risk of self-publication with royal patronage, dedicating the 1687 collection to Louis XIV, the first of four publications dedicated to the French king. La Guerre praised Louis for recognizing and fostering her talent from such a young age:

> I am mindful that, finding in me at the age of five some talent for playing the harpsichord, You ordered that care should be taken to nurture it in me. Who could understand how responsive I was—young child that I was—to the joy that such a compelling command instilled in my soul, and how much it inspired passion for the work. (Document 3)

An astute businesswoman, La Guerre leveraged Louis XIV's early support for her career to prompt him to continue to support her work. La Guerre carefully crafted the dedication to highlight her productivity as a composer, emphasizing the positive reception of her works and her contribution to the reputation of the French court abroad—the more remarkable for her age and gender.

La Guerre's first book consisted of suites: groups of dances united by key. Each suite begins with an unmeasured prelude, which translates the improvisatory style of the lutenists to the harpsichord. The opening prelude from the *Suite no. 1 in D minor* has three sections: two unmeasured sections—mostly notated in whole notes without any indication of the rhythm—bookend a measured section in the middle (Fig. 7.8). The line that separates composer from performer is hard to pinpoint, for the score assumes the performer's understanding of much that is not written out: choice of tempo, flexibility of rhythm, arpeggiation, observance of repeats, and application of ornaments.

The unmeasured sections are the most problematic to interpret, although La Guerre's notation provides more concrete direction than one finds in the unmeasured preludes by Louis Couperin that were notated exclusively in whole notes (white notation). La Guerre used whole notes in the unmeasured sections mainly to indicate harmonic structure, while quarter and eighth notes (stemmed and flagged black notes) designate melodic or non-harmonic tones. Slurs (curved lines) are used in three different ways: (1) to indicate that a note should be sustained; (2) to indicate that several notes should be grouped to a single harmony; and (3) to group a stemmed black note with a whole note.

The profusion of ornaments in the repertory of the French harpsichord school led to the development of an efficient system of notation for ornaments. This abbreviated notation generally indicates the shape of the ornament, while leaving the speed of execution, the number of repercussions in a trill or mordent, and more subtle rhythmic and dynamic nuances up to the performer. Chambonnières, D'Anglebert, François Couperin, Rameau, and others included detailed tables of ornaments as prefaces to their works. Though there is considerable variation among writers and composers, a series of common practices can be considered convention for the French Baroque. Arguably the most influential table was that of D'Anglebert, who listed twenty-nine ornaments *(agréments)* in his *Pièces de clavecin* of 1689 (Fig. 7.9). In contrast to the earlier practice of diminution signs, which applied to the entire melodic line, *agréments* applied only to single notes or chords.

La Guerre did not provide an ornament table of her own in either of her books of keyboard music, so performers today generally interpret her signs based on the ornament table left by D'Anglebert (1689) and an earlier one by Chambonnières (1670) (Fig. 7.10), who was D'Anglebert's teacher.

These tables are not the same: Some of the symbols refer to different ornaments, and some ornaments are interpreted in slightly different ways. La Guerre's symbols look more like those of Chambonnières, so it is

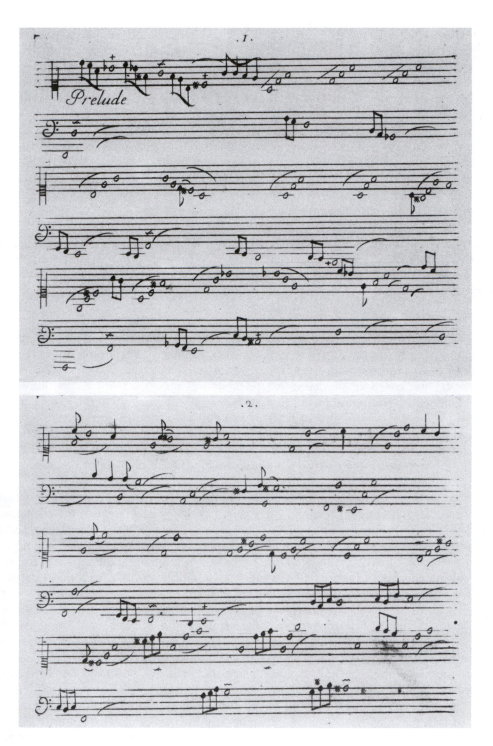

Figure 7.8 La Guerre, *Prelude in D, Pièces de clavecin*, 1687.

Figure 7.8 (continued)

Figure 7.9 Lebert, Ornament Table, *Pièces de clavecin*, 1689.

Figure 7.10 Chambonnières, Ornament Table, *Les pieces de clauessin*, 1670.

useful to refer to his table in order to determine which ornament each shorthand sign indicates. However, since La Guerre was of D'Anglebert's generation, the actual interpretation of that ornament probably followed D'Anglebert's practice. For instance, the cross (+) on the fourth note in the treble indicates a *port de voix*, an appoggiatura approached from below. (D'Anglebert would have notated this *port de voix* with a small backwards comma placed before the note.) Chambonnières realized the *port de voix* as an unaccented appoggiatura, placed before the beat; D'Anglebert, however, realized the *port de voix* as an accented appoggiatura, placed on the beat. La Guerre probably would have considered it an accented appoggiatura, as well.

La Guerre uses only a few additional ornament signs in the prelude: a horizontal wavy line for a trill; a horizontal wavy line with a diagonal slash for a *pincé* (mordent); a curved (concave) line hooked to a note like a tail to indicate that the chord is arpeggiated; and the standard double-curve sign for a turn.

La Guerre, described in 1678 by the *Mercure galant*, the journal of the French court, as "the marvel of our century," achieved considerable fame during her lifetime. Titon du Tillet positioned her in the seventh rank with André Campra (1660–1744), Michel-Richard de Lalande (1657–1726), and Marais. Only Lully surpassed her. Titon included as an illustration an engraving based on Simon Curé's memorial medallion struck in La Guerre's honor in 1729 (Fig. 7.11). The motto reads, "I contended for the prize with the great musicians."

With François Couperin's four harpsichord books (Paris, 1713–30) and his *L'Art de toucher le clavecin* (The Art of Playing the Harpsichord, 1716) we reach the peak of French harpsichord music of the Baroque period. Called *ordres*, Couperin's twenty-seven suites are a mix of stylized dance movements and descriptive character pieces of extreme subtlety and ingenuity. Building on the tradition of Chambonnières, Couperin adopted fanciful titles for many of the pieces; these are generally either descriptive musical portraits of friends and patrons or works that imitate nature, ideas, or events. In the preface to the first book (1713), Couperin notes that "the pieces that carry these titles are kinds of portraits which have sometimes been found to be quite a good likeness under my fingers, and that most of these flattering titles belong rather to the charming originals that I wanted to portray than to the copies of them which I have drawn."[7] A good example is Couperin's depiction of virtuoso viol player Antoine Forqueray (1672–1745), who entertained Louis XIV and his guests at mealtimes and became *ordinaire de la chambre du roi* in 1689. Couperin casts his musical portrait, *La superbe, ou La Forqueray* (Book 3, 1722), as an Allemande with brilliant sixteenth-note passagework above a steady-moving bass line in eighth notes. Some of Couperin's pieces have an

Figure 7.11 Jacquet de la Guerre, Titon du Tillet, *Le Parnasse François*, 1732.

emotional intensity unique in French keyboard music of the period, and it is no exaggeration to say that the refinement and variety of expression in Couperin's chamber music makes him one of the Baroque era's greatest composers.

"L'âme en peine" (The Soul in Pain) is the final movement of the thirteenth *ordre* (or suite) in B minor from Couperin's third publication of keyboard music (1722). "L'âme en peine" ends a series of twelve chaconne variations in a variety of moods entitled "Les Folies Francaises, ou les Dominos" (The French Follies, or the Costumes) (Fig. 7.12). Couperin's ground bass (a recurring harmonic and melodic pattern) shares an affinity with the *folia* chaconne, which had been set by D'Anglebert, Marais, Frescobaldi, and, most famously, Corelli (Opus 5, no. 12; see Chapter 10). Couperin assigns each variation a title that refers to a particular carnival character, in costume, each of whom represents an emotional state or human type

Figure 7.12 Couperin, "L'âme en peine," *Troisième livre de pièces de clavecin*, 1722.

ranging from "L'Esperance" and "La Langueur" (hope and languor) to "La Frénésie, ou le Désepoir" (frenzy or desperation). The characters are further delineated by the color of their costumes—in this case, green, purple, and black, respectively. Each variation defines its emotional terrain within a very small scope, using all the means at a Baroque composer's disposal for defining affect: a minuet in simple harmonies to characterize virginity; intense chromatic complexity for jealousy; mercurial meter and tempo changes for flirtatiousness. Coming at the end of the suite, "L'âme en peine" seems to sum up the parade of human foibles and passions. The movement, which is provided with the additional performing instruction "languissament" (in a languishing manner), is full of drooping gestures, choked sighs, suspended dissonances, and affective augmented intervals. Couperin notated the ornaments he wanted, even placing commas at the ends of phrases to ensure that the player would take time to "breathe." As he explains in his preface, "Generally it is almost imperceptible, although when this little silence is not observed people of taste feel that something is missing from the performance; in a word, it is the difference between those who read through without a break and those who stop at full stops and commas. In observing these the tempo must not change."[8]

The quantity and quality of Louis XIV's chamber music added to the luster of the court, and the virtuosic performances and compositions of La Guerre, Marais, and their colleagues could be seen as yet another conspicuous example of the king's taste and cultural largesse. Thus even chamber music was a pawn of the political agenda, enhancing the king's reputation both at home and abroad.

The Ecurie

Historically, the most overlooked wing of Louis XIV's musical establishment has been the Ecurie, or stables. This department, which came under the Master of the Horse, comprised the Petit Ecurie, containing riding and carriage horses for the king's use, and the Grand Ecurie, made up of warhorses, riding-school horses, and the staff who cared for them. The Musique de l'Ecurie belonged administratively to the Grand Ecurie. The musicians were divided into five categories: twelve trumpeters; twelve players of violins, oboes, sackbuts and cornets; six oboists and players of the bagpipes; eight players of the fife and drum; and six players of crumhorns and *trumpet marina*—a single-stringed instrument, about two meters in length, played with a bow to produce a buzzing sound closer to a brass instrument than a stringed one, hence the name. (The instrument enjoyed a brief revival in the early eighteenth century.) This parade body performed on official occasions, most often out of doors: at proclamations of peace, pageants, parades, the reception of foreign legations, processions for royal baptisms, weddings and funerals, tournaments and carousels, celebrations on the water, and as the hunt set out. The livery of the Ecurie was made from rich fabrics, laced with gold and silver, enhanced by large hats and buff leather belts and by trumpet slings.

Since the performances took place outdoors, much of the music for the Ecurie does not survive. Yet engravings show us a great deal about the role of the Ecurie played in the king's aggrandizement. Elaborate books of engravings were printed and distributed across Europe to promote the French court and king, an especially important venture during the years of the king's personal rule after 1661. In 1662, the twenty-four-year-old king organized a major public spectacle, the *carrousel*, in a square opposite the Tuileries palace in Paris. A *carrousel* was a competition for horsemen that involved various feats of skill popular in the medieval period, but in the late Renaissance it had been transformed into a kind of equestrian ballet. For Louis XIV's *carrousel*, five teams of nobles were dressed in fantastic costumes, supposedly Roman, Persian, Turkish, Indian, and American, and each competitor had his own device on his shield. Louis's appearance on horseback as "emperor of the Romans" paralleled his appearances on stage as a dancer. The device on his own shield was a sun inscribed with the words, "as I saw I conquered" (UT VIDI VICI).

The competition was commemorated in 1670 in a magnificent book of engravings with an explanatory text by Charles Perrault (Fig. 7.13). Louis XIV's costume emulated the supposed apparel of a Roman emperor, and it was also designed to make an important statement of royal magnificence by the very richness of its materials, as is evident from Perrault's description. The attire of members of Louis's squadron complemented that of Louis himself.

Premiere Quadrille

F. Chauveau delin. et sculp

TIMBALIERS ROMAINS.

LA Coiffure étoit un Casque d'or couvert de plumes couleur de feu.
  Le Corps de l'habit étoit de toille d'argent rebrodée d'or, bandée de satin couleur de feu brodé d'argent.

Le tonnelet & les manches étoient de même que le corps, & les lambrequins étoient de couleur de feu brodé d'argent.

Les bas de soye étoient de gris de perle, & les botines d'argent chamarées d'or en brodequins. Cette chaussure étoit semblable en tous ceux de la Quadrille.

Le manteau étoit de même satin couleur de feu brodé d'or, & doublé de toille d'argent.

Le caparaçon & le harnois étoient aussi de satin couleur de feu brodé d'or & d'argent, garny de pieces d'Orféverie.

Les Banderoles des Timballes étoient de couleur de feu brodées d'or & d'argent, avec des Aigles d'or.

O

Figure 7.13 "Trompettes romains" (Roman Trumpeters) from Perrault, *Courses de testes et de bague* (Head and Ring Races), 1670.

TROMPETTES ROMAINS.

LA Coiffure étoit en forme d'un mufle de Lion d'or, couvert de plumes couleur de feu. Le corps de l'habit étoit de toille d'argent, bordé d'une bande de broderie d'or à écailles.

Le Tonnelet étoit de même toille d'argent, couvert de dix grandes bandes de broderie d'or.

Les manches tenant au corps, & les manches pendantes & les lambrequins étoient de satin couleur de feu, brodé d'or & d'argent, & doublées de toille d'argent.

Le caparaçon & le harnois étoient de satin couleur de feu, chargé d'une bande d'or brodée d'argent, terminez par leurs campanes & lambrequins.

Le poitrail & la croupiere étoient enrichies de masques d'Orféveries, & les crinieres des chevaux liées d'Echarpes de toille d'argent.

P

Figure 7.13 (continued)

Catholicism under Louis XIV

Louis XIV's chapel music embellished the liturgy, and, by extension, the king himself. Court preacher and political theorist Jacques-Bénigne Bossuet argued that rulers were *images vivantes* (living images) of God and "representatives of God's majesty." It is clear that Louis XIV took this, and his religion, seriously. In 1682 the Gallican Church declared its independence from Rome, an act that paved the way for Louis's revocation of the Edict of Nantes in 1685. This initiated an exodus of Protestants from France and increased the hostility of Protestant nations bordering France. Bossuet drafted the Gallican Declaration, known also as the Four Gallican Articles, in an effort to sanction the French crown's control of the Church within its borders. Inherent in Gallicanism was the autonomous organization of the French Church and the subordination of the Papacy to the General Councils of the Church; the power of the king was greater than the power of the Pope. Not surprisingly, the Papacy opposed the Declaration, and in 1690 Pope Alexander VIII professed its articles null and void by the Bull *Inter multiplices*. Louis XIV reached a compromise in 1693 under Pope Innocent XII, but the independent spirit of Gallicanism remained vital to the French Church throughout the eighteenth century.

The invigoration of Louis XIV as an independent, Catholic sovereign was accompanied by a more lavish chapel, in both the physical and the musical sense. Louis XIV took up permanent residence at Versailles in 1682. After a series of temporary chapels, a final chapel dates from 1710 as the aging Louis approached the final years of his long reign. Illustrations of the lavish Versailles chapel, the focal point of Louis XIV's last building campaign from 1699 to 1710, confirm the role of the visual arts in portraying the image of Louis XIV. It was dedicated to Saint Louis, patron saint of the Bourbons, and features sculptural and painted decoration of Old and New Testament themes and, at the foot of the steps leading to the altar, a crowned monograph of an interlaced double "L" alluding to Saint Louis and Louis XIV.

Louis XIV's residency at Versailles coincides with his stronger and more public expressions of Catholicism. The 1683 retirement of Henry Du Mont and Pierre Robert left the post of *sous-maîtres* free. Eager to dramatize his personal interest in the music of his chapel, Louis XIV established a competition for the position of the four *sous-maîtres*. Thirty-five musicians from all over France competed. Each had a motet of his own composition performed, after which the king eliminated twenty from the contest. Those that remained were kept in isolation for several days while each composed a motet to the text of Psalm 31, *Beati quorum remissiae sunt*. From this final competition, four *sous-maîtres* were chosen: three relatively unknown composers Coupillet, Collasse, and Minoret, and the more established Michel de Lalande (1657–1726), for whom Louis XIV made a special appeal. As *sous-maître* Lalande chose works suitable for the liturgy of the day, supervised rehearsals, and conducted performances.

Louis XIV's chapel musicians were an illustrious group comprised of lay and ecclesiastical singers, organists, a string band, and a cornettist; for special services their number was augmented by the voices of women (most often wives and daughters of the *ordinaires*) and, notably, Italian castratos, as well as further instruments from the chamber and Ecurie. Over the next thirty years Lalande bought out the quarters of his colleagues to become the undisputed master of the king's church music. He did the same for chamber music, starting as one of the *sous-maîtres* in 1685 and buying up all of the titles. In 1689 he was appointed *Surintendant*.

The *Grand motet* and the Versailles Style

Michel-Richard de Lalande provided arguably the most distinctive French religious music ever written in the form of the *grand motet*—a sacred counterpart of spectacle that used a Latin liturgical text, vocal soloists, a chorus, and an orchestra. Lalande composed a total of seventy-one grand motets (plus seven lost) for a combined choir and orchestra of close to ninety members.

Grand motets were occasioned by celebrations of military and naval victories, royal births, marriages, and deaths; or simply at the express order of the king for use during the low Mass in his chapel. According to Pierre Perrin's collection of motet texts, *Cantica pro Capella Regis* (1665), "For the King's Mass, there are ordinarily three [motets] sung: a *grand*, a *petit* for the Elevation, and a *Domine salvum fac Regem*"

(Grand Victory to the King, O Lord), a salutation to the king that traditionally closed both high and low Mass. Louis's preferred form of worship was the low Mass, a format that gave him a chance to hear at least one *grand* and perhaps two *petits motets*, which he favoured over settings of the Mass Ordinary. Fifty *grand motets* by Henry Du Mont, Pierre Robert, and Lully were printed "by the express order of His Majesty" by Christopher Ballard in a sumptuous collection of 1684–6. Many bore texts by French poet, librettist, and cofounder of the Academy of Music, Pierre Perrin. Their splendor was amplified by the magnificence of the four-manual organ with thirty-six stops at the Versailles chapel. Designed as much to glorify the King of France as the King of Heaven, these motets became the officially sanctioned models for works that formed the basic repertory of the Royal Chapel, the provincial music academies, and the Parisian Concert Spirituels—the first public concert series in Europe, which ran from 1725 to 1790.

Michel-Richard de Lalande's *De profundis*

Lalande's *De profundis* best captures what musicologist James Anthony dubs the "Versailles style," music whose texture and scope mirrors the physical beauty of its surroundings. Lalande wrote the work for a performance in 1688 that coincided with the death of the king's niece, Marie-Louise, queen of Spain. This would explain the added introit "Requiem aeternam" from the Roman Catholic Mass for the Dead to a text otherwise drawn from the Book of Psalms.

Lalande continually revised his motets and *De profundis* is a good example of his musical updates. Lalande transformed *De profundis* from the 1689 manuscript copy into a ten-movement version in 1720; the first published version appeared in Alexandre Tannevot's engraved edition of forty motets from 1729; a manuscript copy made after 1741 now survives at the municipal library in Versailles. Lalande revised his motets to create autonomous movements of chorus, solo, and ensemble; he transformed simple *récits* with five-part homophonic accompaniment into independent, elaborate concert arias with *obbligato* accompaniment. Polyphonic textures outweigh homophonic ones; and rather than doubling vocal lines, the orchestra is more independent.

Marked *gravement*, the instrumental introduction to the opening chorus, establishes an affect appropriate to the weighty subjects of despair and redemption. The bass *recit* (m. 18) takes up themes introduced by the orchestra and builds to a climax just before the quasi-imitative entries of the choir (m. 44) on the pivotal text "De profundis," (Fig. 7.14). The syllabic text setting, slow dotted rhythms, and predominately homorhythmic declamation contribute to the somber mood, as does the downward shape of the opening gesture and the grating dissonance in the second measure.

De profundis clamavit te Domine	From the depths I cried to you, Lord:
Domine exaudi vocem meam.	Lord, hear my voice.

Lalande gives precise indications of performing forces: chorus, four-part strings, soprano (sung by boys or *castrati*), high tenor *(haute-contre)*, tenor, bass baritone, bass, and figured basso continuo. He divided both the instruments and singers into large and small groups to maximize contrast and dramatic effect.

A turn to the Italian side can be seen in "Sustinuit anima me" for soprano and oboe with organ continuo. The voice and oboe adopt a call and respond style for the first line of text (Fig. 7.15).

Sustinuit anima mea in verbo ejus:	I look for the Lord; my soul doth wait for him:
speravit anima mea in Domino.	In his word is my trust.

For "speravit," however, there is three-part counterpoint between oboe, soprano, and bass, and attention is drawn equally to both accompanying parts, especially when the soprano is holding long tones (Fig. 7.16).

The material for "Sustinuit anima mea" then returns, resulting in a three-part form. However, unlike the Italian da capo form, in which the opening material returns unchanged, Lalande's return explores new tonal areas and builds upon previous material. Continuous development of this type is more characteristic of French style.

Figure 7.14 De Lalande, *De Profundis*, 1741, mm. 15–60.

Figure 7.14 (continued)

Figure 7.14 (continued)

The revisions Lalande made to the "Requiem aeternam" movement in particular illustrate some of the ways in which the composer transformed the original manuscript version of *De Profundus* before it was published in the early eighteenth century. The 1689 manuscript copy begins this movement with a *symphonie* of fourteen measures that introduces a solo *récit* of eight measures; both introduction and the *récit* are declamatory in style and function as a link. This first section is followed by a second *symphonie* of six measures that also serves as an introduction, this time to a chorus of thirty-one measures that continues to the "Et lux perpetua." This chorus is basically homophonic with clear separation of textual elements.

The 1741 version dispenses with the solo *récit* and its instrumental introduction. Instead, a *symphonie* of nine measures, in duple meter and marked "lentement," follows concisely upon the previous section in triple meter and immediately establishes an air of gravity and solemnity (Ex. 7.10). This *symphonie* introduces the imitative subject that forms the basis of the choral entry that follows, merging fluidly with a hefty chorus of fifty-three measures—considerably longer than the original chorus—that leads up to "Et lux perpetua." Unlike the homophonic choral writing in the earlier version (Fig. 7.17), the later version features dense, five-part polyphony in which both voices and instruments participate. Some instruments double the choral lines; others weave an independent counterpoint. The mood is intensified by spacing imitative entries close together.

Requiem eternam, Domine	Grant them eternal rest, Lord

Lalande's motets were immediately recognized as symbols of French nationalism and Catholicism. Jean-Jacques Rousseau considered Lalande's motets "masterpieces of the genre" and noted their performances in far off Italy.[9] The *grand motets* reflected the importance of religious music to the king's image and reputation. The cult of Louis XIV was first revived in the highly nationalist writings of Michel Brenet, who was eager to carve out the high points of French cultural history. Writing in 1899 Brenet penned this tribute to the king, his music, and his chapel:

Figure 7.15 De Lalande, *De Profundis*, "Sustinuit anima me," 1741, mm. 1–15.

Figure 7.16 De Lalande, *De Profundis*, "Sustinuit anima me," 1741, mm. 29–42.

Figure 7.17 De Lalande, *De Profundis*, "Requiem aeternam," 1689, mm. 1–9.

The old sovereign crosses by foot the galleries of Versailles to come to his recently finished chapel, brilliant with gold and light; one hundred Swiss guards line the way of his passage . . . he passes, noble, handsome, always the king; . . . the celebrant begins the Office, and Lalande lifts his baton; the music, indifferent to any liturgical chronology, is a motet for large chorus. . . . At first there is a *symphonie* played by all the musicians of the chamber; there are the *gracieux*, the *tendrement*, the *legers*, and the *loure* [gracious, tender, light and heavy movements] . . . set off by the overwhelming effect of the choruses . . . that follow the instruments and prepare for the end of the ceremony and the departure of the King.[10]

Here we have a compact summary of French Baroque music, with its ornaments, instrumental virtuosos, choruses, and soloists, cast with Louis XIV as the central figure.

Conclusions

For modern audiences, music is intrinsically linked to the image of Louis XIV, the Sun King, for whom music served both politics and pleasure. Music gave Louis XIV *éclat*, a seventeenth-century term used figuratively to refer to a brilliance equivalent to a flash of lightening or a clap of thunder—a brilliance that was, by extension, both unexpected and impressive. Magnificence and glory manifested themselves in music of the court in ways that created a distinctive French style that was recognized and imitated for decades to come. Taken together, the key features of this style—the majestic rhythms of the French overture, the instrumental virtuosity of Marin Marais and Elisabeth Jacquet de La Guerre, and the religious solemnity of Lalande's motets—form a grand style, a musical counterpart to the manner of narrative painting, state portraits, literary odes, and engravings.

Example 7.10 De Lalande, *De Profundis*, "Requiem aeternum," 1741, mm. 1–24.

Example 7.10 (continued)

What made the French style such a success was the fact that Louis XIV's personal taste was well informed and well defined. The king did not blindly promote a propagandistic musical agenda, and, of course, music also functioned in France, as it did elsewhere, as art pure and simple, and as popular entertainment. But the king was an educated patron with a highly developed notion of elegance in music. Under his patronage composers such as François Couperin and Marais pushed French style to an expressive apogee, writing music that was nonetheless underlined by its grace and a certain emotional containment. Although French music was not necessarily virtuosic from a technical standpoint, a nuanced performance demanded great skill and sophistication, and in the hands of the best composers French music was extraordinarily sensuous. Its harmonic palette was rich in added sevenths and ninths, and its sinuous melodies, pervasive dance rhythms and sometimes ambivalent tonal attitude distinguished French style from both the goal-oriented harmonic progressions and dramatic dissonance treatment of the Italians, and the contrapuntal complexity of the Germans.

Elements of the French style entered into the common vocabulary of composers as geographically distinct as Vivaldi, Handel, and Bach, long after the King was dead, and yet it would still have been immediately identified as "French." The central organization of the king's musical establishment demonstrates the care and attention he gave to cultural expenditures, and a direct parallel can be drawn between strategies of French absolutism in the political arena and efforts to centralize cultural affairs.

Documents

Document 1. "Saint-Simon's Portrait of Louis XIV." In *Readings in European History*, 2 vols. Ed. J. H. Robinson. Boston: Ginn, 1906. Vol. 2, pp. 285–6.

Louis XIV's vanity was without limit or restraint; it colored everything and convinced him that no one even approached him in military talents, in plans and enterprises, in government. Hence those pictures and inscriptions in the gallery at Versailles which disgust every foreigner; those opera prologues that he himself tried to sing; that flood of prose and verse in his praise for which his appetite was insatiable; those dedications of statues copied from pagan sculpture, and the insipid and sickening compliments that were continually offered to him in person and which he swallowed with unfailing relish; hence his distaste for all merit, intelligence, education, and, most of all, for all independence of character and sentiment in others; his mistakes of judgment in matters of importance; his familiarity and favor reserved entirely for those to whom he felt himself superior in acquirements and ability; and, above everything else, a jealousy of his own authority which determined and took precedence of every other sort of justice, reason, and consideration whatever. . . .

The king's great qualities shone more brilliantly by reason of an exterior so unique and incomparable as to lend infinite distinction to his slightest actions; the very figure of a hero, so impregnated with a natural but most imposing majesty that it appeared even in his most insignificant gestures and movements, without arrogance but with simple gravity; proportions such as a sculptor would choose to model; a perfect countenance and the grandest air and mien ever vouchsafed to man; all these advantages enhanced by a natural grace which enveloped all his actions with a singular charm which has never perhaps been equaled. He was as dignified and majestic in his dressing gown as when dressed in robes of state, or on horseback at the head of his troops.

He excelled in all sorts of exercise and liked to have every facility for it. No fatigue nor stress of weather made any impression on that heroic figure and bearing; drenched with rain or snow, pierced with cold, bathed in sweat or covered with dust, he was always the same. I have often observed with admiration that except in the most extreme and exceptional weather nothing prevented his spending considerable time out of doors every day.

A voice whose tones corresponded with the rest of his person; the ability to speak well and to listen with quick comprehension; much reserve of manner adjusted with exactness to the quality of different persons; a courtesy always grave, always dignified, always distinguished, and suited to the age, rank, and sex of each individual, and, for the ladies, always an air of natural gallantry. So much for his exterior, which has never been equaled nor even approached.

In whatever did not concern what he believed to be his rightful authority and prerogative, he showed a natural kindness of heart and a sense of justice which made one regret the education, the flatteries, the artifice which resulted in preventing him from being his real self except on the rare occasions when he gave way to some natural impulse and showed that,—prerogative aside, which choked and stifled everything,—he loved truth, justice, order, reason,—that he loved even to let himself be vanquished.

Nothing could be regulated with greater exactitude than were his days and hours. In spite of all his variety of places, affairs, and amusements, with an almanac and a watch one might tell, three hundred leagues away, exactly what he was doing. . . . Any man could have an opportunity to speak to him five or six times during the day; he listened, and almost always replied, "I will see," in order not to accord or decide anything lightly. Never a reply or a speech that would give pain; patient to the last degree in business and in matters of personal service; completely master of his face, manner, and bearing; never giving way to impatience or anger. If he administered reproof, it was rarely, in few words, and never hastily. He did not lose control of himself ten times in his whole life, and then only with inferior persons, and not more than four or five times seriously.

Document 2. Patent to Jean-Baptiste Lully, 1672. In Lorenzo Bianconi, *Music in the Seventeenth Century*. Trans. David Bryant. Cambridge: Cambridge University Press, 1987. pp. 240–1. Copyright © 1987 Cambridge University Press. Reprinted with the permission of Cambridge University Press.

In so far as the most beautiful ornaments of any State are the sciences and arts, no other type of amusement has been more to Our pleasure—having secured peace for Our peoples—than their revival, calling to Our service all those who are reputed to excel in their respective fields, not only within the confines of Our kingdom, but also from abroad. As inducement to further improvement, We have honoured them with tokens of Our goodwill and esteem. And, since music occupies one of the foremost positions among the liberal arts, with the aim of encouraging its favourable development We had granted permission (with patent letter of 28 June 1669) to M. Perrin for the establishment of musical academies in Our city of Paris and other cities of Our kingdom with a view to the public performance of theatrical dramas in the manner of Italy, Germany and England. This patent was to have the duration of twelve years. Having subsequently been informed, however, that the abundant efforts and care of M. Perrin in this venture were nevertheless insufficient in respect of Our intentions to raise the art of music to the levels desired, We have believed it appropriate to appoint a person of known experience and ability, capable of training future experts in singing and scenic action and establishing ensembles of violins, flutes and other instruments.

To this end, well aware of the intelligence and great musical knowledge of Our dear and much-beloved Jean-Baptiste Lully (who, since entering Our service, has given, and continues to give, daily—and pleasurable—proof of his abilities, for which reason he has already been honoured with the post of *Surintendant et compositeur de la Musique de Notre Chambre*), We hereby grant and permit the said Lully (with the present letter, signed by Our hand) to establish a Royal persons which he shall retain most appropriate and whom We ourselves shall select and register on the basis of his references and recommendations for the performance in Our presence (when We so desire) of *pieces de musique* in French verse and foreign tongues, in the manner of the Italian academies. And M. Lully shall be granted this privilege for life—as, after him, whichever of his sons shall inherit the aforesaid office of *Surintendant de la Musique de Notre Chambre*—with power to associate with whomsoever he deems most appropriate for the establishment of the aforesaid Academy.

And as compensation for the notable expenses which M. Lully shall inevitably be required to sustain in connection with aforesaid representations (with regard to the scenes, costumes, machines, theatre and all other necessities), We hereby grant him permission to give public performances of all his compositions, including those represented in Our presence, save that he shall not be permitted to make use of those musicians in Our personal employ for performances of the said dramas; he shall also be authorized to request such sums as he shall retain necessary and to station guards or other officials at the entrances of the venues where the aforesaid performances shall be given. At the same time, all persons of whatsoever quality or condition (including Our own court officials) are expressly forbidden to enter the venues in question without having paid; likewise, no person whatever may organize the performance of any wholly musical drama (in French or any other language) without the written consent of M. Lully, upon pain of a fine of ten thousand *livres* and confiscation of theatres, scenes, machines, costumes, and other things—a third for Our own direct benefit, a third for the *hôpital-général*, and a third for M. Lully, who shall also be empowered to establish private schools of music in Our city of Paris and wherever else he deems necessary for the good and well-being of the aforesaid *Académie royale*. And since the said Academy shall be modelled upon those already in existence in Italy, where gentlemen may sing in public without contravening aristocratic decorum, We desire and hereby command that all gentlemen and *Mademoiselles* be permitted to sing in the aforesaid dramas and other entertainments in Our Royal Academy without prejudice to their titles of nobility, privileges, offices, rights and immunities.

Document 3. Jacquet de La Guerre, Dedication of *Les Pièces de Clavecin, Premier Livre*. Paris, 1687. Madrigal and Epigram to La Guerre by Her Cousin by Marriage, René Trépagne, Sieur de Menerville (1654?–1734). In Elisabeth-Claude Jacquet de La Guerre, *The Collected Works. Volume 1: Harpsichord Works*. Ed. Arthur Lawrence with biographical essay by Mary Cyr. New York: The Broude Trust, 2008. pp. xxxvi–xxxvii. © The Broude Trust for the Publication of Musicological Editions 2008. Reprinted with permission of The Broude Trust.

To the King.

Sire,

Here is the first work that I dare to make public, and I take the liberty of dedicating it to Your Majesty, because I am indebted to You for all that my genius has produced up to the present. Indeed, Sire, I am mindful that, finding in me at the age of five some talent for playing the harpsichord, You ordered that care should be taken to nurture it in me. Who could understand how responsive I was—young child that I was—to the joy that such a compelling command instilled in my soul, and how much it inspired passion for the work. I saw my youngest years pass in continual study, and from time to time being presented before Your Majesty, I was filled with pleasure to see You favorably attentive to my feeble chords. The happiness of pleasing You made me go further. I imposed on myself a long period of seclusion with my father, where I was always accustomed, Sire, to consecrate all my waking hours to You. It was there that, putting new plans into practice, I tried to become even more deserving, one day, of Your Majesty's precious esteem. By the grace of heaven my pains were rewarded. Your Majesty, having learned that I had set a pastorale to music, had the interest to listen to it as something that a person of my sex had not previously attempted. Five consecutive performances with scenery and dances (created by the princesses of the court themselves), so much applause as Your Majesty gave me, the gratification that I received from it, the honor that Madame the Dauphine [Marie-Anne Christine Victoire of Bavaria (1660–90)] paid me in asking for a performance of this work at her home—I recognized it (and I believe I cannot be blamed for taking pride in such a glorious reception): All these rewards were the indisputable signs of the unexpected success of my first effort. Your confirmation, Sire, was in being so satisfied that You then deigned to commission me to write a divertissement for the wedding of Mademoiselle de Nantes [Louise-Françoise de Bourbon (1673–1743)]. Fate did not see fit to have it serve to celebrate this august festivity, although it was ready in plenty of time. But this impediment did not interrupt the usual exercise of my muse, which continually blesses the peace of this glorious reign, so appropriate for cultivating the fine arts which one see flowering throughout the entire empire because of the efforts of the grandest monarch in the universe. I would be so happy if, in order to blend my melodies with the cries of joy that the return of Your health—on which the safety of Europe depends—causes to arise everywhere, Sire, I could come to have Your Majesty hear three new works, all of which I have ready. In the meantime, Sire, please accept this book as a very respectful homage of my complete gratitude, of my untiring zeal, and of the profound veneration, with which I am,

Sire,

Of Your Majesty

The very humble, very obedient,
very loyal and very grateful servant
and subject,
Elizabeth Jacquet.

Notes

1 See Appendices 1–2 of Peter Burke, *The Fabrication of Louis XIV* (New Haven, CT: Yale University Press, 1994).
2 Translated by Elissa Poole. Used with permission.
3 Translated by Elissa Poole. Used with permission.
4 Translated by Elissa Poole. Used with permission.
5 Translated by Elissa Poole. Used with permission.
6 Trans. in James R. Anthony, *French Baroque Music from Beaujoyeulx to Rameau*, rev. ed. (Portland, OR: Amadeus Press, 1997), p. 401.
7 Trans. in David Tunley, *François Couperin and "The Perfection of Music"* (Aldershot, UK: Ashgate, 2004), p. 130.
8 Trans. in David Tunley, *François Couperin and "The Perfection of Music,"* (Aldershot, UK: Ashgate, 2004), p. 141.
9 Trans. in James R. Anthony, *French Baroque Music from Beaujoyeulx to Rameau*, rev. ed. (Portland, OR: Amadeus Press, 1997), p. 228.
10 Michel Brenet, *La musique sacrée sous Louis XIV* (Paris, 1899), pp. 12–13, quoted and trans. in James R. Anthony, *French Baroque Music from Beaujoyeulx to Rameau*, rev. ed. (Portland, OR: Amadeus Press, 1997), p. 246.

8   Restoration England

England underwent tumultuous changes in politics and religion in the seventeenth century that had a profound impact on music in both the secular and sacred realms. During the first half of the century, religious tension grew between supporters of the Church of England, who favored traditional Anglican ritual and ceremony, and Puritans, a conservative religious group within the Church of England, who fought to align the church with Calvinist Europe. Puritans openly criticized King James's efforts to find a Spanish Habsburg wife for Prince Charles, a union that would surely have increased Catholic influence in England. Charles's eventual marriage to French princess, Henrietta Maria, also a Roman Catholic, affirmed Puritan concern. A more pressing threat was the growing influence of anti-Calvinists and so-called ceremonialists, who argued that the ritual of the sacraments played a more crucial role in worship than the rhetoric of the sermon. Unrest culminated in all-out Civil War in 1642. Charles was tried for treason and executed on January 30, 1649, and the monarchy was replaced with the Commonwealth under military commander Oliver Cromwell (1599–1658) as Lord Protector.

The Civil War (1642–49) had tremendous cultural and social repercussions, including some 80,000 deaths in combat and another 100,000 from disease and other war-related causes, out of an English population of around five million.[1] Puritan influence led to the closure of theaters as early as 1642, and all cathedral chapels were abolished, with immense fallout for musicians and the artistic community in general. Theological and political arguments between the two factions fuelled intense debate about the role of music within worship and its stylistic prerogatives. While the Church of England continued to support a rich musical presence in the Church, Puritans, ever uneasy with music's seductive powers of distraction, advocated a lesser role for music and a simpler style as well.

When Cromwell's son, Richard, proved to be an ineffective leader, he lost the confidence of the army and a parliament was reinstated on May 6, 1659. Royalist forces united around the restoration of the Stuart monarchy in the figure of the deposed king's son, Charles II, who had escaped to France in 1646. In May 1660 Charles sailed across the Strait of Dover on board the H.M.S. Naseby as the restored monarch (ruled 1660–86). His return saw an immediate revival of culture and arts, much of it influenced by Charles II's long tenure in France. This period is known as the Restoration, a reference both to the return of the Stuart monarchy and a restored period of economic, political, religious, and cultural stability.

Sacred Music

The restoration of the monarchy in 1660 also restored the Church of England, and with it, after fifteen years of repression under Puritan influence, church music. Singers were once again hired for choirs, organists filled posts at parish and cathedral churches, and, with Louis XIV as his model, Charles II recreated the Chapel Royal as an instrument of both church and state, designed to glorify God and king alike. This was an illustrious phase for the Chapel Royal, whose payrolls—graced at the turn of the previous century by the names Orlando Gibbons (1583–1625), John Bull (1562/3?–1628), and William Byrd (*ca.* 1540–1623)—now boasted the second great school of English composers: Pelham Humfrey (1647/8–74), Matthew Locke (1621/3–1677), John Blow (1648/9–1708), and Henry Purcell (1659–95).

Music for a cathedral church—the seat of a bishopric—was fittingly grand and elaborate, but the protocol was in need of revision after its long dormancy. Once musical ritual was reinstated, guidelines such as organist Edward Lowe's *A Short Direction for the Performance of Cathedrall Service* (1661) became extremely useful. Lowe set out the various roles for priest and choir in both the Ordinary and Extraordinary (the recurring and special) parts of the Anglican service. This service remained rooted in Catholic tradition, celebrating Holy Communion on Sundays and Holy Days, and its ties to the Roman rite only increased during the reign of Charles's brother and heir, the Catholic James II (reigned 1685–8). James's open support of Catholicism was expressed in his preference for ritual and Italianate music (London naval administrator and politician, Samuel Pepys, who chronicled the Catholicization of London in his diary, objected to both). The daily celebration of Morning and Evening Prayer was specifically Anglican, however. Psalms, using traditional psalm-tones or harmonized versions distinct to Anglican practice, were sung antiphonally (with the choir divided into groups that perform in alternation), while traditional chants were retained for responses (refrains sung after each psalm verse).

The English anthem became the high-status, musical showpiece of the Restoration period. The genre was cultivated by England's most respected composers, including Blow, Humfrey, Locke, and Purcell. The 1662 Prayer Book officially provided for the singing of an anthem after the third collect of Morning and Evening Prayer. Anthems were particularly flexible, since they could be used for multiple services throughout the year. This allowed for a range of compositional choices, including the full anthem (and full plus verse anthem), which alternated soloists and chorus, with a basso seguente (a basso continuo part that duplicated the bass line); and the verse anthem and symphony anthem, which used one or more soloists and chorus, and had an independent basso continuo part.

Charles II, who attended services on Sundays and Holy Days, preferred the symphony anthem, which was a verse anthem with orchestral accompaniment. It was, for all intents and purposes, sacred entertainment for the royal class. The primary composer of this genre was Henry Purcell.

Henry Purcell: The English Orpheus

Henry Purcell (1659–95) is Restoration England's undisputed master of music (Fig. 8.1). His father, also Henry, was a singer in the choirs of Westminster Abbey and the Chapel Royal, and young Henry followed in his father's footsteps, entering the Choir of the Chapel Royal as a boy. He remained on the court payroll for the rest of his life. The Chapel Royal under Charles II was a vibrant place for a musician, since the king had developed a taste for French culture during his exile and was keen to duplicate it at his court. Charles II modeled his own Twenty-Four Violins directly on Louis XIII's group, which played both chamber and chapel music. From 1677, Purcell was the official composer for the Twenty-Four Violins (replacing Locke), and two years later he also took over as organist of Westminster Abbey, succeeding John Blow. Purcell's sacred, dramatic, and domestic music is infused with the spirit of optimism and stability that characterizes this era.

Purcell's "O Sing unto the Lord" (Z.44, 1688) sets Psalm 96, verses 1–6, 9, and 10, a text of praise and jubilation that literally calls out for music. Purcell casts the text in a large-scale formal structure of contrasting sections for instruments, soloists, and full choir. The long-range planning, harmonic continuity, and virtuosic writing for the solo voices and upper strings point to Italian style, which Purcell encountered at the Chapel Royal during the short tenure of the Catholic James II. The opening strings are an extended "Symphony" that introduces the principal motive (Ex. 8.1).

The initial, fanfare-like motive is instantly recognizable and captures the joyous energy of the text. All four voices share aspects of the motive in the opening Symphony (mm. 1–45), although its contours are cleverly adjusted in the bottom voice to create an effective continuo bass line. This shifts to pure accompaniment, with the half notes in mm. 14–18. In m. 19, the first violin initiates a more formal fugal passage, its subject loosely derived from the opening motive (Ex. 8.2). This subject is briefly inverted (m. 26), and then returns to its original ascending form in preparation for the vocal entry with the first verse (m. 45).

The bass solo enters with the principal motive set to "O sing unto the Lord" (m. 45) and alternates with homophonic choral exclamations of "Alleluia" that contrast in range, rhythm, meter, mass, and texture (Ex. 8.3).

Figure 8.1 Henry Purcell. Painting by of after John Closterman, 1695.

A connective ritornello (m. 90) carries over the lilting triple meter of the Alleluia and closes in F major. A shift to minor mode and imitative contrapuntal texture and the return from triple to duple meter when the soloists enter with "Sing unto the Lord" (m. 118) provide even more contrast (Ex. 8.4).

Purcell's artful text expression comes to the fore in the bass solo "Declare his honour" (m. 135). The stately dotted rhythms (Ex. 8.5), the homophonic punctuation in the strings, and the virtuosic leap to a high note followed by running sixteenths that tumble down an entire octave and a half on the word "wonders" are prime examples of word painting (we will see similar word painting later in Handel's English oratorios).

Such word painting can be quite subtle: note, for example, the way the forward motion slows down until the music stops in its tracks in the chorus's plea, "Let the whole earth stand in awe of him," (Ex. 8.6). The penultimate chorus with bass solo, "The Lord is King," looks forward to Handel's choruses in its rhythmic drive, harmonic clarity, and expressive text ("he who hath made the round world").

There are relatively few English sources on singing from the seventeenth century to guide modern performers of Purcell's music. Even the matter of pitch is murky, for there was multiple pitch standards used in seventeenth-century Europe. It is now thought that Purcell's church music was likely performed at Quire Pitch, which sits one-to-two semitones above modern pitch.[2] Contemporary sources offer more general advice on such matters as presentation and expression. Charles Butler is among the first to address how to sing in *Principles of Musick* (1636), where he points out the value of good posture, clear pronunciation, and textual articulation whereby the rhetorical structure of the words dictate that of the music. These attributes are repeated in John Playford's "Brief Discourse of the Italian Manner of Singing," included in editions of 1664 and later of *An Introduction to the Skill of Musick*. Drawing heavily on Giulio Caccini's *Le nuove*

Example 8.1 Purcell, "O Sing unto the Lord," mm. 1–8.

Example 8.2 Purcell, "O Sing unto the Lord," mm. 19–27.

Example 8.3 Purcell, "O Sing unto the Lord," mm. 45–65.

musiche (The New Music, 1602), Playford calls for the expression of the text as the basis for dynamic contrast, phrasing, articulation, and embellishment. Rooted in speech and rhetoric, these principles remain important factors for performing English choral music today.

Preserving England's Musical Traditions

Purcell's "O Sing unto the Lord" captures at once the tradition of England's choral past, even as it looks forward to the extroverted public face of Handel's expansive choral movements in the eighteenth century. The contribution of the Restoration Chapel Royal to the English choral tradition was almost immediately recognized and efforts made to preserve it abound. Purcell's anthem survives in the Gostling Manuscript, an anthology of sixty-four anthems by Purcell, Blow, Humfrey, Clarke, Locke, and others, compiled around 1706 by John Gostling (1650–1733), a cathedral singer, music copyist, and Gentleman of the Chapel Royal. Most of the anthems had previously appeared in music books; Gostling's purpose seems to have been to collect and preserve some of the finest models of the genre.

Example 8.3 (continued)

Example 8.4 Purcell, "O Sing unto the Lord," mm. 118–121.

Example 8.5 Purcell, "O Sing unto the Lord," mm. 135–138.

Example 8.6 Purcell, "O Sing unto the Lord," mm. 258–267.

Example 8.6 (continued)

Gostling's efforts reflect a broader musical phenomenon, that of collecting music for its own sake, independent of performance or educational objectives. Starting in the late sixteenth century, patrons and elites from across Europe assembled libraries of music books and manuscripts, in parallel with similar collections of books, portraits, and even coins. In the eighteenth century this collecting spirit fused with national efforts to preserve and promote a given country's musical heritage.

Thomas Tudway (*ca.* 1650–1726) was even more ambitious in his efforts to preserve the English choral tradition. Between 1715 and 1720 Tudway compiled the six-volume *Services and Anthems*, a collection of 244 anthems by eighty-five composers for a total of seventy services—a virtual memorial to the English anthem. Adopting a historical stance in the preface to the final volume, Tudway reviews the genre of anthem writing, acknowledging major contributors from the time of Elizabeth I, James I, Charles I, and Charles II. The massive collection (London, British Library, Harleian MSS 7337–42) was commissioned by Robert, Lord Harley, future Earl of Oxford. Tudway praised his patron for his "piety and zeal, for the Honour of Cathedral Service," which inspired this "Everlasting Memorial" in the face of "discouragements & disregards," a probable reference to declining arts patronage after the death of Charles II.[3]

Psalm Singing

Psalm singing was an important component of music for church services and for informal worship in the homes of rich and poor alike. Psalm texts addressed both the individual and communal aspects of spirituality, and their simple melodies and familiar texts—friendly to all religious stripes—made them attractive to composers and performers. Psalms remained popular under the Puritans and continued to be performed in a variety of settings in the decades around 1700.

Psalms offered a range of performance options: solo song, unison group singing, and in metrical versions for multiple parts, with or without instrumental accompaniment. Samuel Pepys, whose diary from 1660–9 is a vital source of information on Restoration England, captures an occasion of psalm singing in an entry for Sunday, November 27, 1664:

> (Lord's day). To church in the morning, then dined at home, and to my office, and there all the afternoon. . . . In the evening come Mr. Andrews and Hill, and we sung, with my boy, Ravenscroft's 4-part psalms, most admirable music. Then (Andrews not staying) we to supper, and after supper fell into the rarest discourse with Mr. Hill about Rome and Italy; but most pleasant that I ever had in my life. At it very late and then to bed.[4]

By the mid-seventeenth century, a series of four-line melodies in stepwise motion became the standard canvas for singing psalms. London printers Thomas East (*ca.* 1540–1608) and John Playford named the common melodies after historic towns, such as Oxford, Winchester, and Cambridge. The words to specific psalms could be applied to one of these melodies as long as the tune suited the meaning of the text and the occasion for singing the psalm. In the 1672 edition of his popular *An Introduction to the Skill of Musick*, John Playford (1623–1686/7) gave directions on how to sing psalms, noting the common tunes used in parish churches and their names (Fig. 8.2). He matched the melodies to particular situations, depending upon whether the psalm texts were for funerals, prayer, consolation, or confession, thereby giving a substantial nod towards the Baroque principle of *Affektenlehre*.

Psalms books occupied a prominent place in the commercial world of the English book industry. Between 1652 and 1677, John Playford issued books of psalms, psalm paraphrases, and hymns, including many editions of the metrical psalms for one, two, three, and four voices, and for keyboard, cittern, and gittern. Playford's marketing targeted a range of audiences, including parish churches, choirs, and students. His advertising highlighted the importance of practising psalm singing and the possibility of multiple performance options. In the preface to *The Whole Book of Psalms* (1677), Playford gushes, "I cannot but commend the Parish Clerks in London, who for the Improvement of Musick have set up an Organ in their Common-Hall, where they meet once a fortnight [every two weeks], and have an Organist to attend them,

Figure 8.2 Playford, *An Introduction to the Skill of Musick*, 1672.

to practise the singing of Psalms." Playford goes on to recommend the psalms to university students who "shall practise Song, to sing to a Lute or Viol" and notes that "All Three Parts may as properly be sung by Men as by Boys or Women." So popular were these psalms that the Playford family continued to publish them well into the eighteenth century.

Instrumental Music

Instrumental music was another pocket of specialization for London music printers. John Playford capitalized on the market for virginal music, forged earlier in the century with *Parthenia*, by issuing a sequel, *Musicks Hand-Maid: New Lessons and Instructions for the Virginals or Harpsichord* (London, 1678) (Fig. 8.3). The title page shows a woman playing the virginal, a male violinist playing the treble part along with the virginal, and another woman holding a music book.

In the preface, Playford answered requests from "such who dwelt in the Country remote from an able Master" for "rules and directions" for playing the pieces. His response was a short primer on the principles of notation, rhythm, and meter. The music that follows is simple fare, suitable for the growing market of amateur domestic music-making. A typical example is the *Corant* in G major (Fig. 8.4).

The English market for instrumental music reflects the growing interest in the harpsichord in the decades around 1700. We can see this in Playford's *Musicks Hand-Maid*—whose title page recommends it for virginals or harpsichord—and even more clearly in *The Ladys Banquet* or *The Lady's Entertainment*. This was a widely popular series of six anthologies of keyboard music, published by John Walsh between 1704 and 1735, which capitalized on the current frenzy in London for opera (see Chapter 9). Geared to the amateur domestic market, the bulk of *The Ladys Banquet* comprises transcriptions of opera arias and overtures for home consumption, rather like the anthologies of pop songs with guitar tablature and keyboard parts do today.

Dance remained an important social facet of instrumental music-making in England during the Restoration period. Dance continued to be an important marker of good etiquette and social mobility; there was a constant demand for dance music in flexible forms that could accommodate different abilities and tastes. A good example is Playford's *The English Dancing Master*, first printed in 1651, and reprinted as *The Dancing Master* until its final edition in 1728. Playford includes tunes and directions for dancers and their instructors. "Greensleaves" appears in all ten editions of *The Dancing Master* that were published before 1700, thus making it a verifiable hit of the late seventeenth century (Fig. 8.5). Playford's compositional

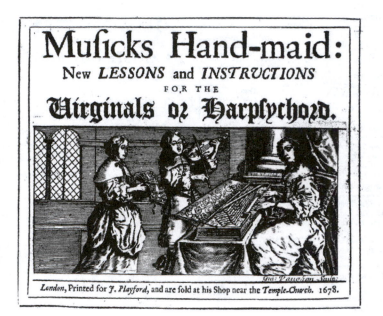

Figure 8.3 Title page, *Musicks Hand-Maid: New Lessons and Instructions*, 1678.

Figure 8.4 Playford, *Musicks Hand-Maid: New Lessons and Instructions*, no. 4, *Corant*.

interventions across successive versions of the tune demonstrate shifts from modal to tonal language and from a free to a more prescriptive approach to melodic accidentals, whereby performers of later versions of "Greensleaves" are expected to play the notes as written.[5]

Restoration music for strings continued the tradition of English consort music with suites of variations on grounds, dance movements, and free fantasies. The viol remained a popular choice for whole consorts (comprised of a single instrument type), while the broken consort (implying a group of different types of instruments) offered greater opportunities for contrasts in timbre. There is also evidence of a greater degree of coherence and unity across the repertory. In the *Consort of Four Parts*, Matthew Locke paired suites by key and began each odd-numbered fantasia with a homophonic slow introduction. Like Purcell's consorts, Locke composed for viols, but—following the royal lead—the violin family was gradually replacing the viol family as the principal string instrument for music-making at home and at court.

Evidence of an Italianate turn in violin music and at the royal court more broadly can be seen in the adoption of the trio sonata, generally scored for two melody instruments (often violins, paired in imitative fashion) and continuo, in the 1680s. As Italian composers experimented with the trio sonata, two basic stylistic types had emerged according to the different performance contexts for small ensemble music: the *sonata da chiesa* (church sonata) comprised several sections in alternating slow-fast tempos; the *sonata da camera* (chamber sonata) was essentially a suite of stylized, bi-partite dances. With the publication of *Sonnata's of III Parts* (1683), Purcell was the first English composer to engage with the trio sonata at an early period in the genre's development. For this, Purcell's first publication of instrumental music, Purcell claimed to compose in "just imitation of the most fam'd Italian masters." Rather than Arcangelo Corelli, who captivated English audiences of the early eighteenth century, it is likely that Purcell had in mind the previous generation of Italian instrumentalists as models, among them Giovanni Legrenzi (1626–90) and Giovanni Battista Vitali (1632–92).

Purcell dedicated his *Sonnata's of III Parts* (1683) to his patron, King Charles II. On the title page, the phrase "Printed for the author" suggests that Purcell may have financed the book himself, especially since he included an engraved portrait of himself in the publication (Fig. 8.6). Vanity prints, then as now, were aimed at boosting the composer's image in the print marketplace. Certainly the volume shows all the signs of a commercial enterprise: It was advertised at a special subscription rate in the *London Gazette* on

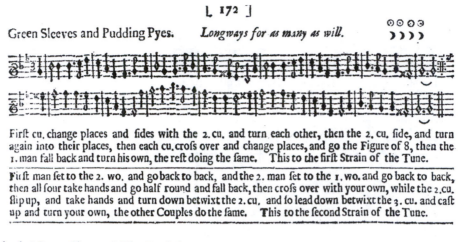

[172]

Green Sleeves and Pudding Pyes.   *Longways for as many as will.*

First cu. change places and sides with the 2. cu. and turn each other, then the 2. cu. side, and turn again into their places, then each cu. cross over and change places, and go the Figure of 8, then the 1. man fall back and turn his own, the rest doing the same.   This to the first Strain of the Tune.

First man set to the 2. wo. and go back to back, and the 2. man set to the 1. wo. and go back to back, then all four take hands and go half round and fall back, then cross over with your own, while the 2. cu. slip up, and take hands and turn down betwixt the 2. cu. and so lead down betwixt the 3. cu. and cast up and turn your own, the other Couples do the same.   This to the second Strain of the Tune.

Figure 8.5 Playford, "Green Sleeves," *The English Dancing Master,* 1690.

Figure 8.6 Title page, Purcell, *Sonnata's of III Parts,* 1683.

May 28, 1683, and subscribers were directed to pick up copies from the composer's house in St. Anne's Lane, beyond Westminster Abbey (*LG,* June 11).

Since Purcell was directly involved with the book's publication, its preface demands special attention. Of particular interest are the instructions to English musicians for interpreting Italian musical terms: "It remains only that the English Practitioner be enform'd, that he will find a few terms of Art perhaps unusual to him; the chief of which are these following: *Adagio* and *Grave,* which import nothing but a very slow movement: *Presto Largo, Poco Largo,* or *Largo* by itself, a middle movement: *Allegro,* and *Vivace,* a very brisk, swift, or fast movement: *Piano,* soft."

Such a tutorial on Italian tempo markings would have been extremely relevant for negotiating the alternating slow and fast tempos of the *sonata da chiesa.* A representative example is Purcell's *Trio Sonata in A Minor* (Z. 794), whose multiple sections are differentiated by tempo designations: [Allegro], *Adagio, Largo, Grave, Canzona Tempo primo,* and an *Adagio* close. The first movement features a fugue, but one whose subject is harmonically ambiguous with the presence of both G-natural and G-sharp (Ex. 8.7).

The tonal ambiguity climaxes in the final *Canzona* with a series of entries over the bass line Bb-C-C#-D (mm. 121–122) (Ex. 8.8). The passage generates excitement for the return of the main theme, a unifying device not normally found in Purcell's instrumental music.[6]

Example 8.7 Purcell, *Trio Sonata in A Minor*, mm. 1–7.

Example 8.8. Purcell, *Trio Sonata in A Minor*, mm. 121–126.

The outright virtuosity of all three parts in this closing *Canzona* section is also noteworthy, and suggests that the level of playing amongst professionals and amateurs was fairly high.

The reception of Purcell's trio sonatas in the late seventeenth and eighteenth centuries was mixed, and they were not as revered as his choral or dramatic music. Amateur musician and author Roger North, who performed the sonatas with Purcell at the harpsichord, observed that the sonatas were "unworthily despised" for being "clog'd with somewhat of an English vein." Indeed the scoring, in which the bass viol is often independent of the continuo bass line and occasionally participates on an equal footing with the two violins, is more typical of earlier mid-seventeenth-century trio sonatas by such composers as Giovanni Legrenzi and G.B. Vitali. Corelli's more contemporary trio writing tends to make a clear separation between the bass part and the virtuosic duo violins. Moreover, Corelli's sonatas realize the full implications of functional tonal harmony to an extent that Purcell's do not, although since Corelli's first trio sonatas were not published until 1681, Purcell probably did not know them. Another factor lending to their particular "English vein" is the marked way in which they retain elements of the English fancy, the contrapuntal fantasies for viol consort so popular from the early sixteenth to mid-seventeenth century in England. This was a genre to which Purcell provided some fifteen examples in 1680. Tellingly, he did not publish his fantasies, which were out of fashion and far outside Charles II's taste by this time, but Purcell did not entirely abandon their style in his trio sonatas, and it contributes to their somewhat archaic flavor.

Dramatic Music

The Restoration paved the way for an unprecedented surge of creative energy for drama, which was repressed during the eighteen years of civil war and the Commonwealth. Soon after his coronation in 1661, Charles II issued licenses to playwrights Thomas Killigrew (1612–83) and William Davenant (1606–68) for theater companies. Killigrew's patent (Document 2) granted him and his heirs the right to build a theater in London or Westminster, to manage a company of actors, and to collect money from theater-goers. Significantly, Charles II granted Killigrew the right to act "peaceably and quietly without the impeachment or impediment of any person or persons whatsoever"; the patent suppressed all other playhouses with the exception of Davenant's (who was granted his own patent on January 15, 1663). The Killigrew and Davenant patents thus formed a vital and lucrative element of the London theater world that lasted until the Theatre Regulation Act of 1843, which ended the dual monopoly.

The principal theatrical genre, especially during the first twenty years of the Restoration, was the spoken play, into which songs, choruses, dances, processions, special effects, and incidental music were interspersed. Music had been an important part of English spoken dramas for at least a century. Shakespeare's plays abound in references to music and occasions for songs: "O mistress mine" and "If music be the food of love," from *Twelfth Night*, and "Take, O, Take those lips away" from *Measure for Measure* are well-known examples.

Restoration drama typically included two sets of instrumental music (the First and Second Music), the Prologue (which often included singing and dancing), an Overture, and additional short instrumental numbers or songs called "act-tunes," which were performed between the acts. The act-tunes often took up action from the preceding scene or prepared the audience for the next one. Songs sung within an act, however, were occasioned by a specific request for music, whether for entertainment, celebration, magic scenes, or characterization, since English authors and audiences believed there needed to be a dramatic reason to sing.

Because the English aesthetic insisted upon a just cause for singing, the development of music in English theater followed a markedly different path than that of Italian opera (and the aria in particular) in the second half of the seventeenth century. At the close of the century, Italian arias were at their most excessive, with elaborate and virtuosic repeats that not only detracted from the meaning of the text but compromised dramatic unity. As some commentators quipped, Italian opera was no more than a string of da capo arias held together by a flimsy narrative thread (see Chapter 6). In England, however, the text remained the primary vehicle for emotion and passion, owing to the country's strong tradition of plays and its considerable contemporary dramaturgical talent—playwright John Dryden, for example. This is not to say that most playwrights did not accommodate plenty of singing in their works, but protagonists were expected to conduct the main business of the drama in spoken dialogue.

Restoration drama continued to expand the length and number of entirely sung, masque-like episodes within the play and the size of ensembles. *Psyche* (1675), with music by Matthew Locke on a libretto by Thomas Shadwell (*ca.* 1642–92), is still essentially a play, despite the addition of a great deal of music. Though Locke called *Psyche* "an English opera," contemporaries referred to such works as "dramatick operas." The term "semi-opera" is now used for such plays that include multiple and distinct episodes or masques with elaborate staging, spoken dialogue, dancing, and extensive music.

The first all-sung, full-length opera was Dryden's *Albion and Albanius* (1685), originally conceived not as an autonomous work but as a prologue to the musical play *King Arthur* (1684), and only later enlarged to stand on its own. But even in a work that qualifies as a true opera, with words sung throughout, the way Dryden uses the music signals that its status is lower than the text's. The main characters do not sing arias; they sing only in recitative, a style of singing closer to speech than song and dominated by the words. "The songish part" Dryden reserved for characters of lower rank. As he claims in the preface to *Albion and Albanius*, characters must act according to their particular traits:

> The recitative Part of the *Opera* requires a more Masculine Beauty of Expression and Sound: The other, which (for want of proper English Word) I must call *The Songish Part*, must abound in the Softness and Variety of Numbers; its principal Intention, being to please the Hearing, rather than to gratifie the Understanding. (fol. 2v)

Note that Dryden's distinction between recitative and aria reflects a common view that spoken text was rational and thus associated at the time with masculine traits. By the same token, he implies that music, which was merely pleasurable and appealed to the senses, was a feminine attribute. Such dualities reflect thinking of the time and are ripe for scholarly scrutiny.

Dryden's experiment in opera was just that—an experiment. It, too, was essentially an extension of current English practice—a play with music—for it did not provide a new and workable model for uniting music and poetry in the service of a narrative.

However, the music of the semi-opera was not necessarily of secondary quality. At the close of the seventeenth century, the master of the "semi-operatic" genre was Henry Purcell, who produced four opera scores—*Dioclesian, King Arthur, The Fairy-Queen,* and *The Indian Queen*—as well as incidental music for forty plays and many revivals.

The Fairy-Queen

Purcell's most lavish semi-opera from this decade was *The Fairy Queen* (1692), an anonymous adaptation of Shakespeare's *A Midsummer Night's Dream.* The *Fairy-Queen* typifies the heroic dramas and semi-operas of the Restoration period in the way that it combines spoken text, dance, instrumental music, and self-contained masques with solo singing, choruses, and stage spectacle. Purcell's *The Fairy Queen* premiered at London's Queen's Theatre, Dorset Garden, on May 2, 1692 (Fig. 8.7). *The Fairy Queen* was expensive, costing £3000 to stage, and although it was revived in February 1693, *The Fairy-Queen* is generally seen as a financial failure.[7]

Shakespeare's works were held in high esteem after his death, and his dramas provided worthy originals that were altered, imitated, and updated by playwrights and librettists for centuries to come. All but about two hundred lines of the spoken parts for *The Fairy-Queen* are taken directly from Shakespeare, appearing there in a modified form to suit Restoration taste and to create a frame for the large music scenes. A representative example of the process of modification is the opening of Act 2, presented here in Shakespeare's original and in the anonymous adaptation as set by Purcell.

> Puck. How now, spirit! whither wander you?[8]
> Fairy, Over hill, over dale,
>
> Thorough bush, thorough brier,
> Over park, over pale,

PLAYHOUSE.   Plate II

The Dukes Theatre in Dorset Gardens.

Figure 8.7 The Dorset Garden Theater, London. Engraving, *ca.* 1820.

'Thorough flood, thorough fire,
I do wander every where,
Swifter than the moon's sphere;
And I serve the fairy queen.
To dew her orbs upon the green.
The cowslips tall her pensioners be: lo

In their gold coats spots you see;
Those be rubies, fairy favours.
In those freckles live their savours:
I must go seek some dewdrops here,
And hang a pearl in every cowslip's ear.
Farewell, thou lob of spirits; I'll be gone:
Our queen and all her elves come here anon.

Anon., *The Fairy Queen*, 1692. Act 2, Scene 1[9]
Fairy. Over Hill, over Dale, thro' Bush, thro' Bryer,
Over Park, over Pale, thro' Flood, thro' Fire,
I wander swifter than the Moon's bright Sphere.
I serve the Mighty Fairy-Queen,
Sprinkle her Circles on the Green.
The Cowslips tall, her Pentioners be;
Spots in their Gold Coats you see.
Those be Rubies, Fairy-Favours,
In those freckles live their favours;
I must gather Dew-drops here,
And hang a Pearl in every Cowslips Ear.

Example 8.9 Purcell, *The Fairy-Queen,* Act 1, no. 14. Night, "See, See, See Even Night Is Here," mm. 1–24.

Farewell Lob-Spirit, I'll be gone,
The Queen and all her Elves come here anon.

Shakespeare's play offered opportunities for realistic music-making, including fairy scenes, enchanted gardens, royal dancing, and a sleep scene. All of the music scenes set newly written text, however, probably by Thomas Betterton (the actor-manager of the United Company, which oversaw the production of all semi-operas until 1694). The masques are placed toward the end of each act and reflect on the action, rather than move it forward.

Purcell adhered to the practice of differentiating between professional singers and singer-actors: Incidental songs were given to the non-speaking, professional singers. The marketing of *The Fairy-Queen* acknowledged the separation between drama and music, and care was taken to position the work clearly

Example 8.10 Purcell, *The Fairy-Queen*, Act 1, no. 14. *Night*, "See, See, See Even Night Is Here," mm. 58–68.

Example 8.11 Purcell, *The Fairy-Queen*, Act 1, no. 14, "Hush, No More, Be Silent," mm. 1–7.

in the semi-opera tradition. The advertising for *The Fairy-Queen* in Peter Motteux's *Gentleman's Journal* reiterates the customary dichotomies of mind and the senses, spoken word and music (February 12, 1692):

> Other nations bestow the name of opera only on such plays whereof every word is sung. . . . But our English gentleman, when their ear is satisfied, are desirous to have their mind pleased, and music and dancing industriously intermixed with [spoken] comedy or tragedy.[10]

One of the most irresistible musical episodes is the Masque of Sleep in Act 2, in which Night, Secrecy, and Sleep take turns lulling Titania to sleep in a series of short arias in closed forms. There is both harmonic and motivic unity across the masque, which starts with Night's "See, Even Night Herself" and ends with Sleep's bass aria, "Hush, No More, Be Silent All."

Night's "See, Even Night Herself Is Here" opens with muted strings playing a slow, gentle theme in steady half notes in the home key of C minor (Ex. 8.9). Textual and musical repetition and word painting set the tranquil mood. The word painting on "murmuring" comes from the rich tradition of madrigal writing (Ex. 8.10).

Example 8.12 Purcell, *The Fairy-Queen*, Act 1, no. 14, "Hush, No More, Be Silent," mm. 23–29.

The mood intensifies for Sleep's aria, "Hush, No More, Be Silent (Ex. 8.11)." Here Titania's slumber is depicted by a growing number of rests that draw out the breath until the line, "no noise disturb her sleeping sense." A chorus repeats Sleep's words and music to close the scene (Ex. 8.12).

Writing for a cast of professional singers, Purcell offered more elaborate music than was customary for actor-singers. This may have whetted an English appetite for solo virtuoso singing, which was to become the mainstay in Handel's Italian operas in London twenty years later (Chapter 9).

The Fairy-Queen also extended the English tradition of plays with music. There is nothing particularly operatic about it, and it did not bring English drama closer to opera. Nor was the genre of semi-opera universally appreciated. Reflecting on the theater scene of the late seventeenth century, musical commentator Roger North wrote, "For some that would come to the play, hated the musick, and others that were very desirous of the musick, would not bear the interruption, that so much rehearsall [spoken text] gave."[11] In 1698, English bishop and theater critic, Jeremy Collier, complained that theater music "warms the Passions and unlocks the Fancy and makes it open to Pleasure like a Flower to the Sun."[12] "Musick," he warned, "is almost as dangerous as Gunpowder; And it may be requires looking after no less than the Press, or the Mint."[13] There's even a nationalist tone to some of these aesthetic arguments: In the anonymous *A Comparison Between the Two Stages* (1702), Italians are ridiculed as "Idolators of Musick, an effeminate Nation," in contrast to England, "where our Passions are more manly."

The decades around 1700 were a turbulent time for London theaters, as the many aesthetic debates in journals, pamphlets, and newspapers from the period reveal. A profound change can be seen in the audience for English theater after Purcell's death. The reign of William III brought with it the War of Spanish

Example 8.12 (continued)

Succession and increased instability, as well as greater commercialization of the theater industry. London was one of the few centers where theater sponsorship lay entirely in the hands of the public—and that public was not only larger and more heterogeneous than it had been during the reign of Charles II, it was less sophisticated, as we read in the complaints of critic and playwright John Dennis (Document 2). This was partly a question of class, partly a question of the increasing internationalization of England in the early eighteenth century, as Dennis writes in 1702:

> But a 3d sort of People, who may be said to have had no education at all in relation to us and our Plays, is that considerable number of Foreigners, which within these last twenty years have been introduced among us. (Document 2)

Henry Purcell and the Creation of an English School

Later writers singled out the Restoration period for having produced a distinct English school of composition, and eighteenth-century commentators crowned Purcell as the undisputed head of that school. He was named the English Orpheus, a direct reference to the mythological Orpheus, whose music charmed the gods. Oliver Goldsmith, in *The British Magazine* for February 1760, asserted that "the English school was first planned by Purcell: he attempted to unite the Italian manner that prevailed in his time with the ancient Celtic carol and the Scotch ballad, which probably had also its origin in Italy . . . his manner was something peculiar to the English; and he might have continued as head of the English school, had not his merits been entirely eclipsed by Handel."[14] In his monumental *A General History of Music*—the country's first history of music—Charles Burney praised Purcell's "latent power and force in his expression of English words" and drew attention to the composer's "indigenous expressions of passion."[15]

As is apparent in the way that Purcell oversaw the publication of his *Sonnadas*, the composer consciously managed his public image. Aided by the Playford family, who made vast quantities of his music available in print, Purcell became a commercial phenomenon in the 1690s, and the timing could not have been more opportune: Purcell's success in the marketplace occurred just as court prestige and opportunity declined after the death of Charles II (Charles's successors, James II and William and Mary, were less active patrons of the arts), and just as the city of London, rather than the royal court, became the focal point of cultural production.

By the 1690s Purcell was indeed a truly public figure, celebrated in his own lifetime in engravings, music books, and the popular press. His death on November 21, 1695, was publicly mourned and inspired tributes from composers, authors, and printers (Document 3). Henry Playford's two-volume series *Orpheus Britannicus* (1698, 1702), part commemoration and part anthology of songs by Purcell, further solidified his posthumous reputation:

> Next to the Man who so Divinely Sung,
> Our Praise, kind *Playford*, does to thee belong,
> For what you gave us of the Bard's before,
> Vast Thanks were due, and now you merit more.
> Tho' *Purcell* living, had our utmost Praise,
> And dead, almost does Adoration raise,
> Yet He, even He, had scarce preserv'd a Name,
> Did not your Press perpetuat his Fame. (Document 3)

By the end of the eighteenth century, his status as an emblem of the nation's heritage was unassailable, as Burney affirmed: "HENRY PURCELL, who is as much the pride of an Englishman in Music, as Shakespeare in productions for the stage, Milton in epic poetry, Locke in metaphysics or Sir Isaac Newton in philosophy and mathematics."[16]

Conclusions

Nowhere in the Baroque world was music the subject of more controversy than seventeenth-century England. Rocked by religious conflict and ambivalent in their relationships with Continental fashions, English composers, commentators, patrons, and church figures debated the merits of new and old, English and French, more music or less, on their own terms and often at odds with Continental norms. Many historical accounts of English music paint a picture of a culture separated from Continental developments, and to an extent, it is true. The revival of the English anthem is a case in point, for essentially it picked up where Gibbons left off, despite changes to accommodate Restoration preferences for orchestral and choral textures. Similarly, the belated English interest in all-sung opera may be explained as a result of England's having had a viable alternative to opera in its long-established practice of integrating music into spoken theater.

Certainly England seems to have had a desire to project an insular artistic identity: The very act of crowning Purcell head of an English school proclaims this. Nonetheless, the notion of a national school is problematic, for it assumes that English music developed in isolation and it undermines the strong evidence of intercultural exchange and the influence of the many foreigners active in England, not the least of whom was Handel. Ultimately the representation of English music as "unique" may be more of a cherished illusion than a historical reality, even if the idea retains a certain attraction today.

Documents

Document 1. Theater License for Thomas Killigrew, April 25, 1662. Original in possession of The Theatre Museum. Copy at PRO c/66/3013. Percy Fitzgerald, *A New History of the English Stage*. London, 1882. Vol. 1, pp. 77–80.

Charles the Second, by the Grace of God, King of England, Scotland, France, and Ireland, Defender of the Faith, etc. . . . do give and grant to the said Thomas Killigrew, his heirs and assigns, full power, license, and authority, that he, they, and every of them . . . shall and may lawfully, quietly and peaceably frame, erect, new build, and set up in any place within our cities of London and Westminster, or the suburbs thereof, . . . one theater or playhouse . . . wherein tragedies, comedies, plays, operas, musick, scenes, and all other entertainment of the stage whatsoever may be shown and presented: And we do hereby . . . grant unto the said Thomas Killigrew, his heirs and assigns, full power, license, and authority, from time to time to gather together, entertain, govern, privilege, and keep such and so many players and persons to exercise and act tragedies, comedies, plays, operas, and other performances of the stage within the house to be built as aforesaid, or within any other house where he or they can be best fitted for that purpose . . . said company shall be the servant of us and our dear consort, and shall consist of such number as the said Thomas Killigrew, his heirs or assigns, shall from time to time think meet; and such persons to permit . . . to act plays and entertainment of the stage of all sort peaceably and quietly without the impeachment or impediment of any person or persons whatsoever, for the honest recreation of such as shall desire to see the same: and that it shall and may be lawful to and for the said Thomas Killigrew, his heirs and assigns, to take and receive of such our subjects as shall resort to see or hear any such plays, scenes, and entertainment whatsoever, such sum or sums of money as either have accustomably been given or taken in the like kind, or as shall be thought reasonable by him or them in regard of the great expenses of scenes, music, and such new decorations . . . we do hereby give and grant . . . Thomas Killigrew . . . full power to make such allowances out of that which he shall so receive by the acting of plays and entertainment of the stage as aforesaid to the actors and other persons employed in acting, representing or in any qualities whatsoever about the said theater, as he or they shall think fit; . . . we . . . will and grant that only the said company to be erected and set up by the said Thomas Killigrew . . . and one other company to be erected and set up by Sir William Davenant . . . shall from henceforth act or represent comedies, tragedies, plays, or entertainment of the stage within our cities of London and Westminster and the suburbs thereof . . . we do by this present declare all other company and companies before mentioned to be silenced and suppressed, and for as much as many plays formerly acted do contain several profane, obscene, and scurrilous passages, and the women's parts therein have been acted by men in the habit of women, at which some have taken offence, for the preventing of these abuses for the future, we do hereby strictly command and enjoin, that from henceforth no new play shall be acted by either of the said companies containing any passages offensive to piety and good manners, nor any old or revived play containing any such offensive passages as aforesaid, until the same shall be corrected and purged by the said masters or governors of the said respective companies from all such offensive and scandalous passages as aforesaid; And we do likewise permit and give leave that all the women's part to be acted in either of the said two companies for the time to come may be performed by women. . . .

Document 2. Adapted from John Dennis, A *Large Account of the Taste in Poetry, and the Causes of the Degeneracy of It*. London, 1702. In A.M. Nagler, *A Source Book in Theatrical History*. Mineola, NY: Dover, 1952. pp. 252–253.

Besides, there are three sorts of people now in our audiences, who have had no education at all; and who were unheard of in the reign of King Charles the Second. A great many younger brothers, gentlemen born, who have been kept at home, by reason of the pressure of the taxes. Several people, who made their Fortunes in the late War [the war with France, 1689–97], and who from a state of obscurity, and perhaps of misery, have risen to a condition of distinction and plenty. I believe that no man will wonder, if these people, who in their original obscurity, could never attain to any higher entertainment than tumbling and vaulting and ladder dancing, and the delightful diversions of Jack Pudding [a comic character in stage and street performances], should still be in love with their old sports, and encourage these noble pastimes still upon the Stage. But a 3d sort of People, who may be said to have had no education at all in relation to us and our plays, is that considerable number of foreigners, which within these last twenty years have been introduced among us; some of whom not being acquainted with our language, and consequently with the sense of our plays, and others disgusted with our extravagant, exorbitant rambles, have been instrumental in introducing sound and show, where the business of the theater does not require it, and particularly a sort of a soft and wanton music, which has used the people to a delight which is independent of reason, a delight that has gone a very great way towards the enervating and dissolving their minds.

Document 3. Henry Playford, "To Mr. Henry Playford, on His Publishing the Second Part of *Orpheus Britannicus*." In *Orpheus Britannicus: A collection of all the choicest songs for one, two, and three voices.* London, 1698. Volume 2, p. ii. With permission of the University of Victoria Libraries.

Next to the Man who so Divinely Sung,
Our Praise, kind *Playford*, does to thee belong,
For what you gave us of the Bard's before,
Vast Thanks were due, and now you merit more.
Tho' *Purcell* living, had our utmost Praise,
And dead, almost does Adoration raise,
Yet He, even He, had scarce preserv'd a Name,
Did not your Press perpetuate his Fame,
And shew'd the coming Age as in a Glass,
What our all-pleasing *Britain's Orpheus* was.
Go on my Friend, nor spare no Pains nor Cost,
Let not the least Motett of his be lost;
Whose meanest Labours your Collections show,
Excells our very best Performance now.

Duly each day, our young Composers Bait us,
With most insipid Songs, and sad Sonato's.
Well were it, if the World woul'd lay Embargo's
On such *Allegro*'s and such *Poco Largo*'s:
And would Enact it, There presume not any,
To Teize *Correlli*, or Burlesque *Bassani*;
Nor with Division, and ungainly Graces,
Eclipse good Sense, as weighty Wiggs do Faces.
Then honest *Cross* might Copper cut in vain,
And half our Sonnet-sellers Starve again:

Thus while they Print their Prick'd-Lampoons to live,
Do you the World some piece of *Purcell*'s give,
Such as the nicest Critick must Commend,

For none dare Censure that which none can Mend.
By this my Friend, you'll get immortal Fame,
When still with *Purcell* we read *Playford*'s Name.

H. Hall, Organist of *Hereford*

Notes

1 Jeremy Black, "England," in *Europe, 1450 to 1789: Encyclopedia of the Early Modern World*, ed. Jonathan Dewald (New York: Charles Scribner's Sons, 2004), vol. 2, pp. 271, 275.

2 Bruce Haynes, *A History of Performing Pitch: The Story of "A"* (Lanham, MD: Scarecrow Press, 2002), pp. 86–92 and 129–32, quoted in Stephen Rose, "Performance Practices," in *The Ashgate Research Companion to Henry Purcell*, ed. Rebecca Herissone (Farnham, UK: Ashgate, 2012), p. 126.

3 The complete preface to the final volume (1720) is transcribed in Ian Spink, *Restoration Cathedral Music, 1660–1714* (Oxford: Clarendon Press, 1995), pp. 443–9.

4 Samuel Pepys, *The Diary of Samuel Pepys*, ed. Henry B. Wheatley (London, 1893), www.pepysdiary.com/diary/1664/11/27/ (accessed April 9, 2014).

5 The most detailed account of this tradition is found in Christopher Marsh's " 'The Skipping Art': Dance and Society," chapter 7 of *Music and Society in Early Modern England* (Cambridge: Cambridge University Press, 2010), pp. 328–90.

6 Martin Adams, *Henry Purcell: The Origins and Development of His Musical Style* (Cambridge: Cambridge University Press, 1995), pp. 110–11.

7 Curtis Price, "Fairy-Queen, The," in The New Grove Dictionary of Opera. Grove Music Online. Oxford Music Online. Oxford University Press. www.oxfordmusiconline.com.ezproxy.library.uvic.ca/subscriber/article/grove/music/O009948 (accessed July 3, 2014).

8 William Shakespeare, *A Midsummer Night's Dream*, ed. O.J. Stevenson (Toronto: Copp Clark, 1918), p. 13.

9 Anonymous, *The Fairy Queen an Opera* (London, 1692), p. 9.

10 Michael Burden, ed., *The Purcell Companion* (Portland, OR: Amadeus Press, 1995), pp. 69–70.

11 Roger North, *Memoirs of Musick*, ed. Edward Rimbault (London: G. Bell, 1846), p. 117.

12 Jeremy Collier, *A Short View of the Immorality, and Profaneness of the English Stage* (London, 1698), p. 278.

13 Jeremy Collier, *A Short View of the Immorality, and Profaneness of the English Stage* (London, 1698), p. 279.

14 Oliver Goldsmith, *The Bee and Other Essays* (Oxford 1914), pp. 256–7, in Richard Luckett, " 'Or Rather Our Musical Shakespeare': Charles Burney's Purcell," in *Music in Eighteenth-Century England: Essays in Memory of Charles Cudworth*, ed. Christopher Hogwood and Richard Luckett (Cambridge: Cambridge University Press, 1983), p. 61.

15 Charles Burney, *A General History of Music* (London, 1789), vol. 3, p. 509.

16 Charles Burney, *A General History of Music* (London, 1789), vol. 2, p. 380, quoted in Richard Luckett, " 'Or Rather Our Musical Shakespeare': Charles Burney's Purcell," in *Music in Eighteenth-Century England: Essays in Memory of Charles Cudworth*, ed. Christopher Hogwood and Richard Luckett (Cambridge: Cambridge University Press, 1983), p. 72.

Part III

The First Half of the Eighteenth Century

9 Music for the Stage in Europe's Big Cities

Across Europe and England, cities and large towns presented musicians with new job opportunities in the eighteenth century. Urban areas were home to universities, print shops, businesses, churches, courts, and a growing middle and upper class, and the confluence of money and cultured clienteles fostered the growth of musical institutions, including opera, concert series, orchestras, and music schools. Courts, churches, and wealthy aristocrats continued to provide traditional forms of employment, but the rise in public concert-going also opened up new jobs—the marketing of those concerts, for instance, in magazines, newspapers, and journals.

Eighteenth-century London was typical of this new musical environment (Fig. 9.1). Its population grew dramatically during the Baroque era, from about 200,000 inhabitants in 1600 to 575,000 by 1700. By the end of the seventeenth century, it had overtaken rival cities Naples and Paris as Europe's largest city, and by 1800 its population had burgeoned to 900,000. London welcomed foreigners, whose talents were vital for commerce, politics, trades, and the arts. Lawyers, politicians, and bankers congregated there; and even members of elite classes whose principal domiciles were outside the city considered a London residence essential for maintaining status and reputation. Such demographics created a high demand for luxury commodities—not just sugar and silks—but leisure activities as well. Playhouses, theaters, and commercial concerts rose to meet the demand. These cultural institutions were not new, *per se*: They date back to the seventeenth century. But it was not until the early decades of the eighteenth century that the artistic scene became a truly public one, fostered by magazines such as *The Tattler* and *The Spectator*.

Opera and music for the theater were arguably the genres of music with the greatest artistic and financial impact on urban centers. Whereas early opera had been largely a court phenomenon, commercial opera (beginning in Venice in 1637) shifted the center of production to urban centers, where the public largely drove innovation and change in the art form. English taste finally embraced Italian trends at the start of the eighteenth century, initiating a period of intense cultivation of Italian opera in London's theaters and a massive influx of Italian artists. Over three hundred Italian instrumentalists, composers, librettists, singers, dancers, and scene designers dominated London's musical life in the first half of the eighteenth century. Writing in 1713, German theorist Johann Mattheson exclaimed, "In these times, whoever wishes to be eminent in music goes to England. In Italy and France there is something to be heard and learned; in England something to be earned."[1]

Ironically, the dominant figure in Italian opera for the first half of the eighteenth century was not an Italian himself. George Frideric Handel (1685–1759), who settled in London in 1710, achieved his greatest fame as a composer of Italian operas and English oratorios, and it was he who introduced London audiences to Italian opera of the highest caliber.

George Frideric Handel

Along with Johann Sebastian Bach, George Frideric Handel is seen as the culminating figure of the Baroque period. The painting of the composer by Balthasar Denner (1685–1749) (Figure 9.2) is typical of the era in its portrayal of reverence and status. Born in the north-German town of Halle in 1685, Handel's career was

Figure 9.1 A new map of London, 1720.

a cosmopolitan one. In Hamburg (1703–6), he played second violin and harpsichord and wrote his own works for the city's opera house, and it was there that he met the influential composer and theorist Johann Mattheson. Handel spent an extended period in Italy, with stops in Florence, Rome, Naples, and Venice (1706–10); and he served as chapel master to the Elector of Hanover in 1710. By the end of 1710 Handel had arrived in London, and there he remained for the rest of his career.

Handel composed operas, but he also produced them, and between 1711 and 1717 he worked for a series of impresarios in the highly competitive London opera market. Opera in London was performed for ticket-paying audiences in public theaters. These were built and maintained as private or jointly-owned enterprises, although royal patents and grants did provide some funding. The two theaters under royal patent, Drury Lane and the Queen's Theatre in the Haymarket, offered operas on Tuesdays and Saturdays. They were in direct competition with the other theaters, however, who were free to stage musical entertainments—ranging from pantomime and masques to full-scale English operas—six nights a week, including Tuesdays and Saturdays. For obvious reasons, this schedule was not financially viable. To remedy it, opera lover King George I granted a royal charter for the Royal Academy of Music in 1719, personally subsidizing this joint-stock company at the lavish rate of £1,000 per year. Handel worked for the Royal Academy from 1719 until 1728. This period, which includes the productions of both *Giulio Cesare* (1724) and *Rodelinda* (1725), marks the highpoint of Italian opera in London.

Despite the king's patronage, the Royal Academy of Music went out of business in 1728. When this happened, Handel and his partner, John Jacob Heidegger, put their inherited stock of scenery and costumes to good use in a second academy, which they operated between 1729 and 1734. In 1734 Handel entered into yet another new partnership, this time with John Rich at Covent Garden, where they sponsored Italian opera and oratorios. They were in direct competition with another company, however, also devoted to Italian opera, which had opened in 1733. It was more than the market could accommodate: Neither Handel's Covent Garden opera company nor the rival Opera of the Nobility survived after their 1737 seasons. Handel's final performance of Italian opera in London came shortly thereafter, in 1741.

Figure 9.2 Balthasar Denner, portrait of George Frideric Handel, *ca.* 1726.

Rinaldo

Handel's *Rinaldo*, which opened at London's Haymarket Theatre on February 24, 1711, was the first Italian opera designed specifically for the London stage. Its libretto was coauthored by Aaron Hill, director of the Haymarket Theatre, and Giacomo Rossi, an Italian. Hill supplied the outline for the opera, based on Torquato Tasso's *Gerusalemme liberata* (Jerusalem Delivered, 1581), an epic tale of the First Crusade (1096–9). Hill adapted and expanded Tasso's original to suit English taste. Rossi then translated Hill's English prose into Italian verse, and probably provided texts for many of the arias. In his preface, Hill commended Rossi's adaptation:

> It was a very particular happiness, that I met with a gentleman so excellently qualified as Signor Rossi, to fill up the model I had drawn, with words so sounding and so rich in sense, that if my translation is in many places led to deviate, it's for want of power to reach the force of his original. (Document 1)

In his prefatory remarks, Hill criticized the earlier Italian operas that had been performed in London for their lack of machines and scenic effects. He further complained that the music did not match the English taste and singers:

> The deficiencies I found, or thought I found, in such Italian operas as have hitherto been introduced among us, were: first; That they had been composed for tastes and voices, different from those who were to sing and hear them on the English stage; And secondly, that wanting the machines and decorations, which bestow so great a beauty on their appearance, they have been heard and seen to very considerable disadvantage. (Document 1)

Rinaldo, however, had been specifically composed for London audiences and the particular milieu of English theater. Its novelty would have been immediately apparent from the moment one entered the theater, where translated librettos were made available. Concessions to English taste went far beyond this, however. The abundance of machines and scenic effects in *Rinaldo*, long a tradition in the English masque and semi-opera, were clear attempts to cater to English audiences.

Musically, the most significant way in which *Rinaldo* was molded to accommodate English taste was in the ratio of recitative to aria. Recognizing that lengthy discourse in a foreign language could easily bore or annoy audiences—and that recitative would not therefore be as effective in moving the action forward or informing the audience of nuanced plot details—Hill simply reduced it, drastically. The proportion of overall time devoted to the aria—ever the focal point, and a style in which Handel excelled—was thus significantly higher in *Rinaldo*.

Over his career, Handel composed more than 2,000 arias in operas, oratorios, and cantatas. Most of them are in *da capo* form, a tripartite structure (frequently designated *ABA*) in which the opening section returns after an intervening contrasting one. The form is problematic in dramatic terms. In a typical *da capo* aria, for instance, a character who vows revenge in the A section will find momentary calm in the B section. However, when the A section repeats, the return to vengeance is likely to seem unconvincing. But if such a form disrupted dramatic unity and occasionally affronted common sense, there were compensations. The singers usually improvised extravagant ornamentation on the repeats of the A sections, and these

Example 9.1 Handel, "Ah! crudel, il pianto mio" from Act 2 of *Rinaldo*. Bassoon and continuo, mm. 1–12.

Example 9.1 (continued)

embellished repeats especially delighted audiences; indeed, they were, to many, the aria's purpose. The loss of dramatic continuity may have seemed a small sacrifice in exchange for the greater musical thrill.

Italian singer and teacher Pierfrancesco Tosi (*ca.* 1653–1732) offered the following advice in his influential *Observations on the Florid Song* (London, 1743):

> Let a student therefore accustom himself to repeat them always differently, for, if I mistake not, one that abounds in invention, though a moderate singer, deserves much more esteem, than a better who is barren of it; for this last pleases the connoisseurs but for once, whereas the other, if he does not surprise by the rareness of his productions, will at least gratify your attention with variety.[2]

According to Tosi, skilled attention to the Baroque aesthetic for variety can compensate for a singer's talent.

Armida's "Ah! Crudel il pianto mio" (Ah! Cruel Man for Pity's Sake) from Act 2 of *Rinaldo* is an example of the Baroque *da capo* aria in its full glory. Armida is a prototypical Handelian sorceress. Rejected by the Christian knight, Rinaldo, she expresses her anguish in a pivotal lament in *da capo* form. The initial ritornello, in a stately *largo* tempo, is richly scored for strings and solo oboe, bassoon, and double bass. Its opening gesture, a long sustained note that drops down a minor seventh in a sigh of despair, immediately establishes the *affect*.

Heard first in the bassoon and echoed in the oboe, this gesture forms the basis of Armida's opening exclamation, "Ah! Crudel, il pianto mio" (Ex. 9.1). The accompanying texture is animated by a matrix of short two- and three-note motives that recur obsessively in all of the voices. Some of these motives are clearly related to the descending sighing motive; others, reversed in contour and sometimes reaching upwards as

Example 9.1 (continued)

far as an octave, seem to plead or question. Armida's grief is further portrayed in the way she fragments and repeats sections of the text: Her emotion is so intense she can barely get the words out.

In the B section, sixteenth note passages in pairs of repeated notes recall Monteverdi's *stile concitato* and unmistakably signal a change of mood from grief to anger. As Armida plots revenge, furious sixteenth note passagework shows at once her virtuosity and her rage (Ex. 9.2). The contrast between the two sections could not be greater. Nonetheless, Handel manages to maintain a semblance of dramatic integrity—without denying the audience's desire for vocal display—by seamlessly joining the end of the B section and the return of "Ah! crudel" with a clever pivot on the pitch D.

Armida	Armida[3]
Ah! crudel,	Ah! cruel man,
il pianto mio,	For pity's sake,
deh! ti mova per pietà.	Be moved by my tears.
O infedel	Or you will feel my cruelty
al mio desio	For having spurned
proverai la crudeltà.	My desire.

The *da capo* form leaves modern singers with a challenge. What is the best approach to interpreting the return of the A section? Should it be a controlled and modest ornamental version of the original or a more flamboyant and highly ornamented return? The recording history of *Rinaldo* shows evidence of both approaches.

Example 9.2 Handel, "Ah! crudel! il piano mio" from Act 2 of *Rinaldo*. Continuo and Armida, mm. 27–36.

Rinaldo's triumph as Christian hero is cause for celebration in Act 3 as the military win precipitates Rinaldo's reunion with Almirena, who was abducted by the sorceress Armida at the start of the opera. Rinaldo's "Or la tromba" (Now the Trumpet) celebrates the victory in a triumphant trumpet aria, Handel's only aria scored for four trumpets (Ex. 9.4). Here, Handel brings to English audiences a convention of *opera seria* popularized by Alessandro Scarlatti (1660–1725), whose *Il prigioniero fortunato* (The Fortunate Prisoner, 1698) contains the famous trumpet aria "Ondeggiante agitato" (Fluctuating, Agitated (Ex. 9.3)).

Doricle	Doricle
Ondeggiante, agitato il pensiero,	Fluctuating, agitated thoughts,
gran battaglia m'accende nel cor.	A great battle breaks out in my heart.

In fact, Italian castrato Nicolo Nicolini (1673–1732) débuted the aria in Scarlatti's opera for the Teatro di S Bartolomeo in Naples, moved to London in 1708, and sang the title role in Handel's *Rinaldo*. Written for the same singer, there are obvious similarities between the ornamental lines of both "Ondeggiante agitato" and "Or la tromba." The trumpet's symbolic import as an instrument associated with battle is clear in Handel's *Rinaldo*. Handel (like Scarlatti) exploits the opportunity for vocal virtuosity by having the singer imitate the trumpet's triadic calls, scalar passages, and florid ornaments.

Example 9.2 (continued)

Rinaldo	Rinaldo[4]
Or la tromba in suon festante	The jubilant sound of the trumpet
mi richiama a trionfar.	Summons me to triumph.

Rinaldo was a tremendous popular success in Handel's time, receiving fifteen performances before the close of the 1710–11 season. Among its major attractions were its many scenic delights, so touted by Hill (including stage fountains, dragons, and waterfalls); Handel's performance on the harpsichord, which "was thought as extraordinary as his Music," according to John Mainwaring's *Memoirs* of Handel;[5] and the performance of *castrato* Nicolini, in the title role. Revived in 1712, 1713, 1714, 1717, and again in 1731 (with substantial revisions to reflect cast changes and a downsizing of scenic effects), *Rinaldo* was performed a total of fifty-three times during Handel's lifetime, more than any of his other operas.

Rinaldo's public success contrasts with barbed criticism of the opera by Joseph Addison and Richard Steele. Would-be opera librettists themselves, Addison and Steele founded *The Spectator* in 1711 as a satirical commentary on contemporary events and culture. On March 6, 1711, Addison quipped:

An Opera may be allowed to be extravagantly lavish in its Decorations, as its only Design is to gratify the Senses, and keep up an indolent Attention in the Audience. Common Sense however requires, that there should be nothing in the Scenes and Machines which may appear Childish and Absurd. How

Example 9.2. (continued)

would the Wits of King *Charles*'s Time have laughed to have seen *Nicolini* [famous castrato Nicolo Nicolini in the title role] exposed to a Tempest in Robes and Ermine, and sailing in an open Boat upon a Sea of Paste-Board?[6]

Addison and Steele aimed their satire at what they considered literary and scenic weaknesses in *Rinaldo*. William Hogarth's engraving, *The Bad Taste of the Town* (Fig. 9.3), self-published in 1724, picks up on a more general negative attitude towards Italian opera, one rooted in England's suspicion of Roman Catholicism and its uneasiness with Italy's cultural domination. In satirizing England's voracious appetite for foreign culture, Hogarth specifically targets lavish Italian opera, pantomime, and the masquerade dances staged by Heidegger. At the center of the engraving he positions the English dramatists William Congreve, John Dryden, Thomas Otway, and William Shakespeare—sold as waste paper.

The Spectator and similar rival publications kept the opera wars raging until the early 1740s. The reaction against Italian opera contributed to the genesis of a new genre called ballad opera, which avoided the virtuosity and literary pretense of foreign opera and featured spoken dialogue and popular songs in English instead.

Example 9.3 Scarlatti, "Ondeggiante agitato," from Act 3 of *Il prigioniero fortunate*, mm. 1–17.

John Gay, *The Beggar's Opera*

The most famous ballad opera of the eighteenth century was *The Beggar's Opera*, based on a libretto by John Gay that used the texts of existing popular songs that Gay had chosen himself. The songs were then arranged by Johann Christoph Pepusch. Much of Pepusch's musical arrangement is formulaic: Instrumental introductions and codas were generated from the opening and closing measures of each song, and he scored the entire work for unison violins and continuo. He did update the songs, however, providing new bass lines and harmonizations.

The Beggar's Opera opened at Lincoln's Inn Fields on January 29, 1728, and its novelty was noted from the outset. The *Daily Journal* reported on February 1, 1728, that "Mr. Gay's new English Opera, written in a Manner wholly new, and very entertaining, there being introduced, instead of Italian Airs, above 60 of

Example 9.3 (continued)

the most celebrated old English and Scotch tunes. . . . [N]o Theatrical Performance for these many Years has met with so much Applause."[7]

Set in and around London's Newgate Prison, *The Beggar's Opera* is one of the first truly urban works: It is unimaginable without the grit, politics, and personalities of eighteenth-century London. *The Beggar's Opera* unfolds around a love triangle, as Polly Peacham and her rival, Lucy Lockit, vie for the love of the unscrupulous highwayman, Captain Macheath. Gay's is a bold social critique. Only a thin line separates criminals, prostitutes, and thieves from respectable society, and its satire of the economic, social, and political corruption of the city was sweeping. Not even British statesman Robert Walpole, who governed effectively as England's first prime minister from the 1720s until 1742, was spared. Criticism of the play's controversial sexual, political, and social overtones led to a suppression of Gay's sequel, *Polly*, which was not performed until 1777. The backlash made Gay rich, though, since the stage ban created a market for the book: *Polly* was a bestseller, with ten thousand copies and pirated editions.

Example 9.3 (continued)

Example 9.4a Handel, "Or la tromba," from Act 3 of *Rinaldo,* mm. 1–6.

Example 9.4a (continued)

The mixing of genres is fundamental to *The Beggar's Opera*, which is a blend of satiric poetry, comedy, country tunes, broadside ballads, and criminal plots. The very title suggests the juxtaposition of incompatible elements: What, after all, does an impoverished beggar have to do with the elite genre of opera? Musically, these contradictions are underscored by mixing spoken dialogue with popular song—hallmarks of the English tradition of stage plays with incidental music—and by using actor-singers rather than the *castrati* and *prima donna* of *opera seria*. Gay was well versed in the components of Italian *opera seria*, knowledge gleaned from his position as secretary to Aaron Hill, whom he may have assisted in the production of *Rinaldo*. Yet despite his collaborations with Hill and Handel, Gay considered the English obsession with Italian opera unnatural. Writing to Jonathan Swift in 1723, he noted:

> People have now forgot Homer, and Virgil and Caesar, or at least they have lost their ranks, for in London and Westminster in all polite conversations Senesino [celebrated castrato singer, Francesco Bernardi Senesino] is daily voted to be the greatest man that ever lived.[8]

Gay's solution was a more natural style of singing that could be realized by actor-singers. Swift's review claimed that *The Beggar's Opera* "exposeth with Great Justice that unnatural Taste for Italian Musick among us, which is wholly unsuitable to our Northern Climate, and the Genius of the People, whereby we are overrun with Italian-Effeminacy, and Italian Nonsense."[9]

Example 9.4b Handel, "Or la tromba," from Act 3 of *Rinaldo*, mm. 11–23.

A representative example of this new approach to singing as it occurs in *The Beggar's Opera* is Mr. Peacham's "Through All the Employments of Life." A member of the bourgeois class, Mr. Peacham is a shopkeeper and an informant (the term "to peach" had been in ordinary English usage for a long time), and his character functions as a connection between the criminal underworld and the world of town, court, and city. As the opening air, Mr. Peacham holds his ledger as he sings the text "Through All the Employments of Life" to the tune "An Old Woman Clothed in Gray" (Fig. 9.4). The link between criminality and respectability is reinforced by Peacham's monologue: "A Lawyer is an honest Employment, so is mine. Like me too he acts in a double Capacity, both against Rogues and for 'em; for 'tis but fitting that we should protect and encourage Cheats, since we live by them." The simple melody moves in sinewy, stepwise motion. Pepusch's bass notes indicate the underlying harmonic structure, with G minor as the primary tonal area.

The second air, Filch's "The Bonny Gray-ey'd Morn," parodies a conventional aria type in Italian opera, the love aria in praise of female virtue (Fig. 9.5). Here, though, it is women's "wheedling Arts," tricks, and bribery that are praised. Cast in B-flat major with a melody of steady, lilting eighth notes, the short phrases are free of ornamentation. Such stepwise, unadorned melodies and simple rhythms speak to the intended performers—actors, not professional singers—and an aesthetic of natural expression.

The Beggar's Opera was an immediate crowd pleaser, with sixty-two performances its first year. Writing to Dean Swift on February 15, 1728, John Gay outlined a plan for the work that brought him much financial success:

Example 9.4b. (continued)

Tonight is the fifteenth time of acting, and it is thought it will run a fortnight longer. I have ordered Motte [Benjamin Motte, the bookseller] to send the play to you the first opportunity. I have made no interest, neither for approbation or money: nor has anybody been pressed to take tickets for my benefit: notwithstanding which, I think I shall make an addition to my fortune of between six and seven hundred pounds. I know this account will give you pleasure, as I have pushed through this precarious affair without servility or flattery. (Document 2)

Gay bragged about its success, joking that the popularity of Italian *opera seria* was now so thin that *it* was called The Beggar's Opera.

The work remained popular throughout the eighteenth century and received major revivals in the first half of the twentieth century. In 1920, Nigel Playfair revived the work at the Lyric Theatre, Hammersmith, in an arrangement by Frederic Austin. It, too, was a tremendous hit, with 1,468 performances in three years. Bertolt Brecht's adaptation as *Die Dreigröschenoper* (The Threepenny Opera, 1928), with music by Kurt Weill, reached international audiences and was filmed in 1931. *The Beggar's Opera* remains part of the standard repertory today, and its dynamic plot and social critique continue to speak to audiences.

Example 9.4b. (continued)

Comic *Intermezzi* in European Cities

At the same time that urban taste in London was creating a craze for the realism of ballad opera, cities across Europe were embracing the comic *intermezzo* as a relief from serious opera. The idea of the *intermezzo* was not new: The *intermezzo* or *intermedio* dates back at least to the Renaissance period, when musical *intermedi* were inserted at the end of the acts of a play. The six *intermedi* performed at the Florentine wedding celebrations of 1589 represent the culmination of the sixteenth-century genre (Chapter 3), and ballets and choral dances found in early Baroque opera are a carryover of this tradition. The novelty of the later manifestation of the *intermezzo* was its focus on comedy, manifest in characters drawn from real life and satirizing of various social classes, a clear inheritance from the improvised, populist theater of the *commedia dell'arte*.

Roman composers were the first to introduce comic episodes into serious opera. The drinking song for Charon, ferryman of the underworld, from Stefano Landi's *La morte d'Orfeo* (The Death of Orpheus, 1619), is a prime example. Comic servants and sub-plots drawn from the *commedia dell'arte* tradition abound in the Roman opera *Chi soffre speri* (Who Suffers May Hope, 1637), which critics regard as an important forerunner of opera buffa. Comic elements soon became a regular feature of public opera in

Example 9.4b. (continued)

Venice. Claudio Monteverdi drew from the stock character types of *commedia dell'arte* for the comic servant Iro in *Il ritorno d'Ulisse in patria* (1640). Similarly, Francesco Cavalli mixed comic and serious elements—to the audience's delight and the literary critic's disdain—in *Giasone* (Chapter 6).

Comic episodes and full-fledged comic *intermezzos* were a staple of serious opera in Naples from the 1670s until approximately 1725, at which point the *intermezzi* separated from their parent *seria* operas to become a completely independent genre. Steeped in both Italian and Spanish literary traditions and in two centuries of *commedia dell'arte* plays and characters, the city of Naples offered the ideal cultural, historical, and literary backdrop for the cultivation of the comic interlude. It was among Europe's largest cities, with 350,000 inhabitants before the devastating plague of 1656, 215,000 in 1707, and 315,000 in 1742.[10] Naples had a long history of being tossed back and forth between Spanish, Austrian, Italian, and even French rule, but the extensive period between 1503 and 1707, when it was a viceroyalty of Spain, was of particular importance culturally, given Spain's rich and varied theatrical tradition. (Naples became a viceroyalty of Austria in 1707, only resuming its status as the capital of a kingdom in 1734.)

Out of this cultural and theatrical diversity, Naples developed its own special brand of comic opera, which was legitimized by the quality of the composers who practiced it. In 1683, Alessandro Scarlatti—probably the most important and prolific of the Italian *opera seria* composers of this period—became director of the Teatro di S Bartolomeo and led operatic production in Naples until 1702 and again from 1708 until his

Figure 9.3 William Hogarth, *The Bad Taste of the Town* ("Masquerades and Operas"), 1724.

death in 1725. In addition to his many contributions to serious opera, Scarlatti and his colleagues Leonardo Vinci, Leonardo Leo, and Giovanni Pergolesi also cultivated the various comic genres of Neapolitan opera, including *commedia per museca* (in Neapolitan dialect), comic *intermezzos*, and *opera buffa*.

We know very little about the staging and performance of specific comic *intermezzos* from the decades around 1700. These were largely ephemeral performances designed to divert the audience's attention rather than to memorialize an event or person. A general guide to the performance of comic plays and, by extension, comic *intermezzos* and operas, is *Dell'arte rappresentiva* (The Art of Staging Plays, Premeditated and Improvised, 1699) by Andrea Perrucci (1651–1704). As artistic director of the Teatro di S Bartolomeo, Perrucci had firsthand experience in the multiple genres and styles staged at the theater each season. In a chapter on "The Choosing of Costumes," Perrucci offers advice that was applicable to plays and operas, whether comic or tragic:

> Costumes are also a necessary component part of decorum in the theater, because they cause a man to be respected and considered as something more than what he is. . . . Costumes make a person seem to be a character he is not.[11]

In the absence of colored engravings and written descriptions, Perrucci's advice offers modern producers insight into what the original singers and actors might have worn.

The *intermezzo* became an international phenomenon in the first half of the eighteenth century. We find *intermezzi* texts in serious opera libretti from the period; we also see instructions—such as "segue

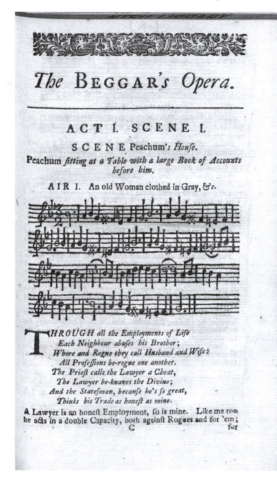

Figure 9.4 Pepusch/Gay, Act 1, Air no. 1, "An Old Woman Clothed in Gray."

l'intermezzo" (intermezzo follows)—noted at the end of the acts of serious operas that indicate that an *intermezzo* was to have been performed. Naples and Venice were the major exporters of *intermezzi* to European opera centers. Singers and traveling troupes spread the flourishing *intermezzo* repertory to London, Copenhagen, Dresden, Linz, Prague, and—most famously—to Paris, where the 1752 performance of Pergolesi's *La serva padrona* (The Maid as Mistress) created one of the Baroque period's most heated artistic debates.

The comic *intermezzo* was popular in the north German city of Hamburg, where the *Zwischenspiel* (literally "between the play"), as it was known, featured stock *buffo* characters and scenarios. As a Hanseatic city-state, Hamburg had a long history of economic stability and governance by a city council and attracted a clientele that supported a rich, urban, artistic culture. Situated at the head of the Elbe River, Hamburg connected northern ports to southern Europe, and was known for sugar refinery, tobacco preparations, textiles, and commerce. The city enjoyed an active amateur and professional music scene, with virtuoso organ concerts and talented musical leaders. Hamburg attracted one of Germany's top musicians of the later Baroque period, Georg Philipp Telemann (1681–1767), who became the Church Music Director for the city in 1721, and, in the following year, director of the city's opera (Fig. 9.6). Telemann's duties as music director for the city's five main churches paralleled those taken up by Johann Sebastian Bach in Leipzig in the same decade. These included satisfying the ongoing demand for cantatas for church services and civic events and instructing the choirboys in singing, theory, and music history (Chapter 11 and Document 1).

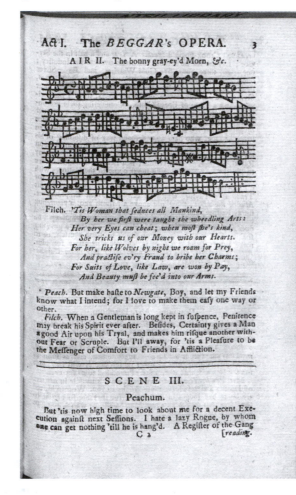

Figure 9.5 Pepusch/Gay, Act 1, Air no. 2, "The Bonny Gray-ed'd Morn."

As director for the opera, Telemann composed five comic works in German and a polyglot, Italianate *intermezzo* with German and Italian texts, *Pimpinione* (1725). Telemann's only *Zwischenspiel* to survive complete in full manuscript, *Pimpinione* was first performed between the acts of Handel's serious opera *Tamerlano* at the Theater am Gänsemarkt. The libretto, by Johann Philipp Praetorius (after Pietro Pariati), is a prime example of the Germanization of the Italian comic *intermezzo*. Praetorius's libretto included arias in both Italian and German; recitative, which carried the conversation and advanced the plot, was in German. The libretto was printed in advance and made available to the audience to follow during the performances. Its compact three scenes required only two singers, both drawn from *commedia dell'arte* stock character types: the wealthy bachelor, Pimpinione, cast as a comic bass; and his clever chambermaid, Vespetta.

A typical German aria in *Pimpinione* is "Hoflich redden" (Polite Speech) from the first *intermezzo*, in which Vespetta charms her master, Pimpinione. As in serious opera, comic arias offered a chance for emotional outpouring (either real or comic), self-reflection, and commentary. Like their counterparts in *opera seria*, they are usually in *da capo* form. The comic version is more compressed than its serious counterpart, with only a short instrumental ritornello (Ex. 9.5); the scoring is reduced to string orchestra; and harmonies and cadential patterns are simple.

Figure 9.6 Georg Philipp Telemann, *ca.* 1754.

Vespetta's "Höflich reden" is a typical *buffo* style aria with repeated notes, disjunct vocal lines over a wide range, repetitive rhythmic motives, and bits of coloratura that embellish the text (Ex. 9.6).

Vespetta	Vespetta
Höflich reden, lieblich singen,	Courtly speech, pleasant singing,
Künstlich spielen, fertig springen,	Clever play, able dancing,
Sind schooner Damen Zeitvertreib.	Are the pastimes of charming ladies.

The main duet for Vespetta and Pimpinione comes in the second *intermezzo* with "Reich die Hand mir, o welche Freude!" (Give Me your Hand, Oh What Delight). Like its counterparts in serious opera, it is constructed from a series of motives, only here they are more compact and come in close succession (Exs. 9.7–9.8).

Pimpinone	Pimpinone
Reich' die Hand mir,	Give me your hand,
o welche Freude!	O what delight!
Süß Gesichtchen,	Sweet faces,
Tu was Liebes!	Aren't you sweet!
Unbezahlbar!	Priceless!
Vespetta	Vespetta
Drück' mich an dich,	Squeeze me against you,
o welch ein Glükke!	O what happiness!
Rechter Thor du.	You're a real God.

Example 9.5 Telemann, Intermezzo 1, "Höflich redden," mm. 1–8.

| Mein Cupido! | My cupid! |
| Er ist köstlich! | He is crazy! |

The juxtaposition of *opera seria* with comic *intermezzi*, whose plots and characters generally bear no relation to the serious opera they accompany, may seem curious to us today, but it still fits comfortably within the general Baroque aesthetic of variety and display. The class conflicts explored in the Neapolitan comic *intermezzi* (and in Pergolesi's iconic *La serva padrona*, first performed in Naples in 1733) are particular to urban life, however. In that respect, *Pimpinione*'s portrayal of the bold aspirations of the lower social orders is a manifestation of the commercial and socio-economic realities of early eighteenth-century Hamburg.

Going to the Opera in Eighteenth-Century Paris

The most important shift of focus for French music and arts of the first half of the eighteenth century was the move from the French court to the city of Paris. With the death of Louis XIV in 1715, Versailles court culture diminished in significance under his successor, the Dauphin. Indeed, Paris—a cosmopolitan city of European stature—already rivalled the royal court as the true cultural capital of France by 1700. With its churches, the Sorbonne, and the Opera, Paris attracted visitors and diplomats from all corners of Europe. The population of the city in the first half of the eighteenth century (which grew from 250,000 inhabitants in the mid-sixteenth century to well over 600,000 by the Revolution in 1789) was second in size only to that of London. Artisans, tradesmen, printers, and instrument builders flocked to Paris to cater to the growing consumer class. Salons, coffeehouses, art galleries, and theaters became public meeting places

Example 9.6 Telemann, Intermezzo 1, "Höflich redden," mm. 9–20.

for intellectual and artistic exchanges. And as the city grew in size and complexity, so did the Paris Opera. As German traveler Joachim Christoph Nemeitz remarked on his sojourn in Paris in 1727:

> Opéra employees form a little republic made up of about two hundred people, some of whom sing, some dance, and others play various instruments. The lowliest among them are those who collect the tickets at the doors and *loges*, those who handle the money, and those who operate the machines.[12]

At the same time, the royal academies founded during the reign of Louis XIV became the domain of such influential thinkers as Voltaire, Denis Diderot, and Jean-Jacques Rousseau. The population of Paris itself was highly literate, as suggested by the 100,000 plus book titles printed in the city in the eighteenth century.

The eighteenth century saw many improvements in creature comforts in Paris: gas lanterns in the city streets, and cemeteries outside the city walls—a more sanitary solution that reduced the spread of disease and improved the foul smell typical of an early modern city. Many of the boulevards and cityscapes familiar in today's Paris date from the eighteenth century, including the Place de la Concorde and the rue Royale. Royal geographer N. de Fer captured the growth of the city in a series of chronological maps produced for the *Traité de la police* (Treatise on the Police, 1720, Fig. 9.7).

Example 9.6 (continued)

Example 9.7a Telemann, Intermezzo 2, "Reich die Hand mir, o welche Freude!" mm. 1–2.

Example 9.7b–d Telemann, Intermezzo 2, "Reich die Hand, mir, o welche Freude!" m. 5; m. 7; m. 9.

Example 9.7b

Example 9.7c

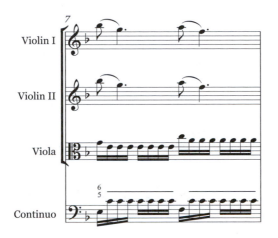

Example 9.7d

Example 9.8 Telemann, Intermezzo 2, "Reich die Hand mir, o welche Freude!" mm. 11–20.

The most important French composer of the first half of the eighteenth century was Jean-Philippe Rameau (1683–1764). Rameau spent the early part of his career as an organist in Avignon and Dijon, where he took over his father's post of cathedral organist, before settling for good in Paris in 1722. With its vibrant and musically discerning public, Paris proved the ideal ground for Rameau to launch his ideas, first in a series of treatises on music theory, then in the composition of harpsichord music, opera, and ballet.

At the age of fifty, Rameau made his debut with *Hippolyte et Aricie* (1733) at the premier venue for opera, the Académie Royale de Musique (the Opéra). Despite public enthusiasm for the lighter styles of *opéra comique* and *opéra-ballet*, for his first opera Rameau returned to the serious tone of *tragèdie lyrique*,

Example 9.8 (continued)

a genre still dominated by the spectre (and still-performed works) of Jean-Baptiste Lully. Rameau's complex and adventurous approach to harmony in *Hippolyte et Aricie* caused an immediate stir. Public response was divided between Ramistes, who appreciated the direct emotional appeal of Rameau's music and saw it as a path forward; and Lullistes, who preferred the grandiose overtures, allegorical prologues, simple airs, and unassuming harmonies of Lully's style.

Rameau was central in the dispute over the future of French theater, much of which was carried out in the cultural presses, where music theorists and critics weighed the merits of French music against those of the Italian style. Indeed the debate was not entirely new: Italian music had long been viewed as the "other," first as the style against which the French would differentiate its own music, then as an ongoing threat to the integrity of that style. Louis XIV had actively suppressed change, but by the end of his reign, the invasion of Italian music was essentially a *fait accompli*—the freedom of its modulations, the bold, affective treatment of dissonance, the harmonic sequences and thrilling motor rhythms of concerto style had, indeed, been discreetly absorbed into French music for years, whether in cantatas, chamber music, comedy ballets, or keyboard music. Nonetheless, because Lully's operas still dominated the stage, the official bastion of French music remained relatively intact. Writing in 1725 and already somewhat behind the times, Lecerf de la Vieville epitomized the point of view that saw this as a necessary good, praising Lully's French overtures for containing "beauties that will be new and admirable in all centuries."[13] Thirty-three years later that view was impossible to rationalize, and Jean le Rond D'Alembert complained that "the [overtures] of Lully,

Figure 9.7 N. de Fer, eighth plan of Paris, 1720.

completely insipid and all fashioned from the same mold, have been the unchanging model for over sixty years for those who have followed; during this time, there has been only one overture at the Opera."[14] This stark shift in the reception of Lully—once inconceivable, and held off for as long as possible—demonstrates an irreversible change in French cultural taste in the second quarter of the eighteenth century. We might also view this change as an acceptance of reality: The stasis of French style had functioned as a metaphor of national stability, which the realm no longer had; the dynamic energy of the Italian style was a more potent, and a more honest metaphor for progress and the current age.

The change in the reception of Rameau's *Castor et Pollux* from its premiere in 1737 to its revival almost two decades later reflects this cultural shift. When *Castor et Pollux* debuted in 1737, the response was lukewarm and there were only twenty-one performances (compared to forty for *Hipployte* and sixty-four for *Les Indes*). When it was revived in June of 1754, however, the production was enthusiastically received, with thirty performances that year and a further ten in 1755. The title page of the published score acknowledges both the work's premiere of October 24, 1737, and its revival of 1754 (Fig. 9.8). It also reveals that Rameau distributed the score himself, with copies also available "at the normal places" and at the door of the *Opéra*.

Jean-Philippe Rameau, *Castor et Pollux*

We cannot blame Pierre-Joseph Bernard's libretto for the opera's modest reception in 1737, although it was certainly tightened for the 1754 revival. The original plot contained all the requisite ingredients for

Figure 9.8 Title page, Rameau, *Castor et Pollux*, 1754.

success: an ancient Greek setting, opportunities for spectacle (including the popular underworld scene), love triangles, and themes of brotherly love and family loyalty. But Rameau's progressive musical style was more adventurous than anything French audiences of the time were accustomed to in Lully. His harmonies were bolder and his modulations were more frequent and forceful. Rameau considered such an expanded harmonic palette an essential dramatic tool. What sounds logical and dramatically effective to our ears today apparently disconcerted French opera audiences in 1737.

Telaïre's celebrated aria, "Tristes apprêts," positioned in Act 1 of the 1737 version, is representative of the way in which Rameau's theories on modulation informed his music, and it also illustrates a number of ways in which Rameau's musical style departed from Lully's (Fig. 9.9).

Tristes apprêts, pâles flambeaux,	Mournful plans, pallid torches,
Jour plus affreux que les ténèbres	Day more horrible than darkness,
Astres lugubres des tombeaux,	Miserable stars of the dead,
Non, je ne verrai plus que vos	No! I will never see more than your glow of death.
clartés funèbres.	
Toi, qui vois mon cœur éperdu,	You, who sees my lost heart
Père du jour, ô soleil, ô mon pére !	Father of the day, O Sun, O my father!
Je ne veux plus d'un bien que Castor	I don't want to gain at Castor's loss,
Et je renonce à la lumière.	And so I renounce your light.

In this poignant lament—a combination of air and something closer to accompanied recitative, Telaïre sings of her distress at the death of her beloved Castor, King of Sparta. Demure strings and the striking use of the bassoon's plaintive high range, a particularly artful example of Rameau's imaginative exploitation of orchestral color, create an unusual and distinctly anguished mood. The melody respects the stresses of the French language (note the several meter changes, especially in the declamatory sections, mm. 26–33) and its light ornamentation does not compete with what appears at first to be a rather simple melody. Rameau's careful declamation immediately suggests this melody as French. Yet its strained and disjunct contour is not French at all. Rising from the fifth scale degree up a fourth, then down a fifth, up a third, then down another fourth, this melody is highly artificial, what Jean-Jacques Rousseau would have called "unnatural" or "Baroque," and it makes little sense without its accompanying harmonies. The air also illustrates several points crucial to Rameau's theory of expressive "modulation": His tonic, E-flat major, is firmly established with a four-measure tonic pedal (which gives rise to some rather pungent dissonances that reinforce a standard cadential progression in E-flat); but he quickly makes a number of what he would call "sensed modulations"—cadential articulations on diatonic scale degrees that are strongly directional but transient. These momentary cadential actions generate the chromaticism in the melody; in other words, the harmony drives the melody, not the other way around. This procedure was atypical of French music. Thus a great deal would have struck Rameau's 1737 listeners as unusual: the angularity of the melody and its awkward descent to an E-flat in the fourth measure, which gives the opening gesture a full octave range; the strong gravitational pull of the dissonant harmonies over the pedal in mm. 2 and 3; the clearly directed motion towards each transient cadence (subdominant harmonies with added seventh or sixths followed by dominant seventh chords, often in inversion); and how quickly and forcefully Rameau touches down on his transitory "sensed" tonics—A-flat major in m. 19; B-flat major in m. 22; C minor in m. 25; B-flat major again in m. 28; A-flat major again in m. 32.

Rameau completely restructured the opera for its 1754 revival, jettisoning the by now outdated prologue, which had celebrated the 1736 Peace of Vienna. Whereas the 1737 original opened with a chorus in mourning (Castor is already dead), the 1754 version begins earlier, with a newly written act that introduces the

Figure 9.9 Rameau, "Tristes apprêts," from Act 1 of *Castor et Pollux*, 1737.

Figure 9.9 (continued)

lovers, Telaïre and Castor, and their separation, which is the central theme of the opera. The 1737 version is thus pushed forward by one act: The original Acts 1 and 2 are now Acts 2 and 3; and the original Acts 3–4, condensed and combined in order to maintain the conventional five-act structure of French *tragédie lyrique*, become Act 5. Telaïre's lament, now more centrally positioned in Act 2, is the more potent for coming after the lovers have been separated in the first act, and it is a worthy French counterpart to the famous Italian laments of Orfeo and Arianna by Monteverdi (Chapter 3). Its status was no doubt due in part to legendary soprano Marie Fel (1713–94), who assumed all the principal female roles at the Opéra from 1745 until her retirement in 1758, and who was known for her dramatic intensity. Fel studied, incidentally, with Italian singer Mme Van Loo, which suggests a path for the subtle absorption of Italianate elements in Rameau's vocal writing.

The intervening seventeen years between the original production of *Castor et Pollux* and its revision in 1754 were turbulent ones in French operatic discourse. In 1752 a small troupe of Italian musicians were invited to the Paris Opera to stage *La serva padrona*, a comic *intermezzo* by Pergolesi first heard in Naples twenty years prior. The performance sparked a pamphlet war known as the Querelle des Bouffons, literally the "Wars of the Clowns," between camps of pro-Italian and pro-French supporters. Philosopher and composer Jean-Jacques Rousseau sided with the Italians in a scathing *Lettre sur la musique française* (Letter on French Music, 1753), which proffered Italian melody, harmony, and accompaniment as the model for true expression. Rameau weighed in on the other side of the debate, not only with his 1754 revival of *Castor et Pollux*, but also in a commentary on Lully's "Enfin il est en ma puissance" (At Last, He Is in My Power) from *Armide*, also written in 1754. These established Rameau as the leading proponent of the French operatic tradition—albeit one in transition—as opposed to the Italian tradition. The sentiment is summarized by Nicolas Bricaire de La Dixmérie in *Les Deux âges du gout*, 1769 (Document 3). After the greatness of Lully, "eventually Rameau appeared," as Dixmérie continues:

> He [Rameau] introduced a degree of energy worthy of Michaelangelo's brush and borrowed in turn those of Rubens and Albano. We know the moving and awesome effect produced by that fine piece 'Tristes apprêts' in *Castor*. In *Zoroastre* we know that sublime act set in hell and the one in the Elysian Fields in this same *Castor*. No contrast could be more striking. And what loftiness in the *entrée* 'Les Incas'. . . . What charm, what provocative and delightful simplicity in the *entrée* 'Les Sauvages'! [both from *Les Indes galantes*] (Document 3)

There is a certain amount of irony here, for the favorable reception of Rameau in the 1750s also reflected a broader narrative of cultural and artistic progress in which anti-Lully, pro-Rameau factions assumed the upper hand.

Conclusions

Opera in its various forms flourished in European cities during the first half of the eighteenth century. Italian *opera seria* swept most of the Continent for the entire eighteenth century, but from the middle of the century, the comic *intermezzo*, exported from Venice and Naples, became hugely popular and influential as well. Italian *opera seria* flourished in the hands of Alessandro Scarlatti. England came to Italian opera late: Under George Frideric Handel in the early decades of the century, *opera seria* dominated the London stages and English taste gained an appreciation for the genre's castrato voices and virtuosic singing. England's unique contribution to opera during this period was John Gay's *The Beggar's Opera*, a highly innovative, one-off commentary on urban life and a take-off on *opera seria* that continues to be of interest today for its social and artistic satire. Working in Hamburg, a city whose commercial, social, and artistic base made opera a viable musical product, Telemann conducted and composed Italian and German-texted operas in both serious and comic genres. France, however, remained largely insular to

Continental developments until the presentation of Pergolesi's *La serva padrona* by an Italian troupe of performers in 1752. A flurry of pamphlets and discourse ensued, setting the tone for the revival and appreciation of Rameau's *Castor et Pollux* as a path forward for French opera. The coming decades saw a greater division of operatic categories, with distinct *seria* and *buffa* styles firmly established and demarcated.

Documents

Document 1. Aaron Hill, Preface to Giacomo Rossi, *Rinaldo,* An Opera as It Is Perform'd at the Queen's Theatre in London. London: Thomas Howlatt, 1711. In Otto Deutsch, *Handel: A Documentary Biography.* London: A. and C. Black, 1955. pp. 32–3.

The deficiencies I found, or thought I found, in such Italian operas as have hitherto been introduced among us, were: first; That they had been composed for tastes and voices, different from those who were to sing and hear them on the English stage; And secondly, that wanting the machines and decorations, which bestow so great a beauty on their appearance, they have been heard and seen to very considerable disadvantage.

At once to remedy both these misfortunes, I resolved to frame some drama, that, by different incidents and passions, might afford the Musick scope to vary and display its excellence, and fill the eye with more delightful prospects, so at once to give two senses equal pleasure.

I could not choose a finer subject than the celebrated story of *Rinaldo* and *Armida,* which has furnished operas for every stage and tongue in Europe. I have, however, used a poet's privilege, and varied from the scheme of Tasso, as was necessary for the better forming a theatrical representation.

It was a very particular happiness, that I met with a gentleman so excellently qualified as Signor Rossi, to fill up the model I had drawn, with words so sounding and so rich in sense, that if my translation is in many places led to deviate, it's for want of power to reach the force of his original.

Mr. Handel . . . has made his Musick speak so finely for itself, that I am purposely silent on that subject; . . . as when I undertook this affair, I had no gain in view, but that of the acknowledgement and approbation of the gentlemen of my country; so no loss, the loss of that excepted, shall discourage me from a pursuit of all improvements, which can possibly be introduced upon our English theatre.

Document 2. John Gay to Dean Swift, Whitehall, February 15, 1728. In *Life and Letters of John Gay (1685–1732).* Ed. Lewis Melville. London: Daniel O'Connor, 1921. p. 87.

I have deferred writing to you from time to time, till I could give you an account of 'The Beggar's Opera.' It is acted at the playhouse in Lincoln's Inn Fields with such success that the playhouse has been crowded every night. Tonight is the fifteenth time of acting, and it is thought it will run a fortnight longer. I have ordered Motte [Benjamin Motte, the bookseller] to send the play to you the first opportunity. I have made no interest, neither for approbation or money: nor has anybody been pressed to take tickets for my benefit: notwithstanding which, I think I shall make an addition to my fortune of between six and seven hundred pounds. I know this account will give you pleasure, as I have pushed through this precarious affair without servility or flattery.

As to any favours from great men, I am in the same state you left me, but I am a great deal happier, as I have no expectations. The Duchess of Queensbury has signalised her friendship to me upon this occasion in such a conspicuous manner, that I hope (for her sake) you will take care to put your fork to all its proper uses, and suffer nobody for the future to put their knives in their mouths. Lord Cobham says, I should have printed it in Italian over against the English, that the ladies might have understood what they read. The outlandish (as they now call it) Opera has been so thin of late, that some have called it the Beggar's Opera, and if the run continues, I fear I shall have remonstrances drawn up against me by the Royal Academy of Music.

Document 3. La Dixmérie, *Les Deux ages du gout,* 1769. pp. 252–61. In *French Baroque Opera: A Reader.* Ed. Caroline Wood and Graham Sadler. Ashgate, UK: Aldershot, 2000. pp. 56–7.

Eventually Rameau appeared and, guided by his genius, he branched out along a hitherto unknown route. Prejudice did not stop him, though it dogged him. . . . Rameau himself had too much taste to cling to old practices that were monotonous, restricted and stale. . . . Almost all [opportunities for] great tone-paintings had been missed by his predecessors. He introduced a degree of energy worthy of Michaelangelo's brush and borrowed in turn those of Rubens and Albano. We know the moving and awesome effect produced by that fine piece 'Tristes apprêts' in *Castor*. In *Zoroastre* we know that sublime act set in hell and the one in the Elysian Fields in this same *Castor*. No contrast could be more striking. And what loftiness in the *entrée* 'Les Incas'. . . . What charm, what provocative and delightful simplicity in the *entrée* 'Les Sauvages'! [both from *Les Indes galantes*] . . . .

Thus all the signs reveal that a happy revolution has come about in our vocal music. Nothing restricts progress in the arts more than an exaggerated respect for the practices of the past. Nature reaches its goals only by slow degrees, and art itself is subject to this progress. Lully will always have the advantage of having first shaped our music, and Rameau of having perfected harmony and its dramatic effects. It remained to give more liveliness to our melodic style. We have made this last and most risky breakthrough. We have too long imitated Ephorus of Sparta [Greek historian, ca. 405–330 BC], who forbade [criticized] Terpander to add a seventh string to his lyre.[15]

Notes

1 Johann Mattheson, *Das neu-eröffnete Orchestre* (Hamburg, 1713), p. 211, quoted in Lowell Lindgren, "Handel's London—Italian Musicians and Librettists," in *The Cambridge Companion to Handel*, ed. Donald Burrows (Cambridge: Cambridge University Press, 1997), p. 78.

2 Pierfrancesco Tosi, *Observations on the Florid Song* (London, 1743), p. 94.

3 George Frideric Handel, *Rinaldo*, original 1711 version, The Academy of Ancient Music, cond. Christopher Hogwood, trans. Kenneth Chalmers (DECCA 289 467 087-2. 2000), p. 64.

4 George Frideric Handel, *Rinaldo*, original 1711 version, The Academy of Ancient Music, cond. Christopher Hogwood, trans. Kenneth Chalmers (DECCA 289 467 087-2. 2000), p. 84.

5 Quoted in Winton Dean and John Merrill Knapp, *Handel's Operas, 1704–1726* (New York: Clarendon Press, 1987), p. 181.

6 Joseph Addison and Richard Steele, *Spectator* (1711), in Otto Erich Deutsch, *Handel: A Documentary Biography* (London: A. & C. Black, 1955), p. 35.

7 Quoted in Calhoun Winton, *John Gay and the London Theatre* (Lexington: The University Press of Kentucky, 1993), p. 99.

8 John Gay, *The Letters of John Gay*, ed. Chester Francis Burgess (Oxford: Clarendon Press, 1966), p. 43.

9 Jonathan Swift, *The Intelligencer* 3 (1728), in *The Works of Jonathan Swift* (London: G. Faulkner, 1742), p. 284.

10 John A. Marino, "Naples, Kingdom of," in *Europe, 1450 to 1789: Encyclopedia of the Early Modern World*, ed. Jonathan Dewald (New York: Charles Scribner's Sons, 2004), vol. 4, p. 238.

11 Andrea Perrucci, "The Choosing of Costumes: On the Costumes in Tragedy, Satyric Drama, Etc.," from *Dell'arte rappresentiva*, quoted in *Baroque Naples: A Documentary History, 1600–1800*, ed. Jeanne Chenault Porter (New York: Italica Press, 2000), pp. 102–3.

12 Caroline Wood and Graham Sadler, *French Baroque Opera: A Reader* (Ashgate, UK: Aldershot, 2000), p. 27, from Joachim Christoph Nemeitz, *Le Séjour de Paris* (Leiden, 1727), vol. 1, pp. 99–100.

13 Jean-Laurent Lecerf de la Vieville, *Comparaison de la musique italienne et de la musique françoise* (Amsterdam, 1725; repr. Graz: Akademische Druck- u. Verlagsanstalt, 1966), vol. 2, p. 62, quoted in James R. Anthony, *French Baroque Music from Beaujoyeulx to Rameau* (Portland, OR: Amadeus Press, 1997), p. 130.

14 Jean le Rond D'Alembert, *De la liberté de la musique* (Amsterdam, 1758; 1821–1822) in *Oeuvres* 1, pp. 544–5, quoted in James Anthony, *French Baroque Music from Beaujoyeulx to Rameau* (Portland, OR: Amadeus Press, 1997), p. 130.

15 The Spartan Terpander famously sang to the accompaniment of the stringed kithara, an instrument he may have invented. Example 3.1 Cavalieri, "Dalle più alte sfere," mm. 1–14.

10 The Concerto

The concerto gave instrumental ensemble music new tools to stir the emotions, making it more expressive, more dramatic. It pulled instrumental music off the dance floor; freed it from the academic workings of *stile antico* counterpoint; and gave it the means to generate excitement independent of text or narrative.

The concerto also gave instrumental music a public voice and a forceful metaphorical presence. Rhetoric, long a model for vocal music, became one for instrumental ensemble music as well. This is not to say that instrumental music had not had rhetorical qualities before or that it had not made use of vocal idioms: There are many instances in which an instrumental melodic line in a sonata duplicates the same affective gestures that a singer might use. German theorist Johann Mattheson put it succinctly in *Der vollkommene Capellmeister* (The Complete Music Director, 1739), where he explains that "instrumental melody differs from vocal mainly in the fact that the former, without the aid of words and voices, attempts to express just as much as the latter does with words."[1] Significantly, the concerto does not ask the listener to imagine a textual counterpart. Its drama is autonomous; since by definition a concerto is about contrasting different bodies of sound, its drama is created through the interactions of those bodies. Thus, if the orchestra interrupts the soloist, it can be interpreted in a number of ways, depending upon the musical context. If the solo line is tender, and the interruption is sudden and aggressive, the interpretation is one thing; if the solo line is tentative, and the orchestra interruption helps the solo line seem more assertive, then the interpretation will be something else. Neither of these interpretations requires any reference to a text, though. The metaphorical equivalent is constructed entirely by musical means, by the various qualities in the music and by their interaction.

In providing an infinite variety of possibilities for contrast and dialogue between the soloist(s) and a larger ensemble, the concerto emerged as a natural medium for rhetorical expression of a dramatic nature. The type of musical engagement epitomized by the concerto came to be seen as a metaphor of social discourse. The many faces of that discourse—intimate, conversational, communal, political, rational, impetuous, violent, humorous, shocking, surprising, whimsical—gave the concerto extraordinary metaphorical reach.

The Baroque concerto was an extremely varied phenomenon. We are most familiar with the solo concerto, which pits a virtuoso soloist against an orchestral tutti, and this became a standard type of Baroque concerto—one that maximized its inherent dramatic potential. However, it was not the concerto's earliest manifestation, although tracing the concerto's development is far from straightforward. Terminology was extremely varied. The word *concerto* was applied to a wide range of musical styles and scorings from the sixteenth to eighteenth centuries, but its use was not consistent; nor does it automatically signal the presence of a valid concerto when it *is* used. The term itself probably derived from the root verb *consero*, which means to join or bind together, and as a result, it was often applied to works that do not fit the modern conception of a concerto at all. Andrea and Giovanni Gabrieli titled their polychoral works *Concerti* (Venice, 1587), and the title tells us *prima facie* that the pieces combine instruments with voices. However the title also imparts something else (as its bold advertisement makes clear): the idea that the pieces will exploit the contrast, and even the rivalry, of parts. Indeed, these very qualities were codified, in 1594, as specific attributes of the concerto by Italian theorist Ercole Bottrigari, who described the concerto as a work that exploits "contention or contrast" (see Figure 4.3).

It follows, then, that since contrast may also take place on a modest level, the term *concerto* could be applied not only to large-scale works and instrumentation, but to smaller scorings as well. Lodovico Viadana's *Cento concerti ecclesiastici* (One Hundred Sacred Concertos, 1602) were scored for only one to four voices with organ continuo. As in the Gabrieli polychoral works, *concerto* as it is used here implies a joining together of singer(s) and instrument(s).

To make the issue more confusing, some early examples of actual concertos are called something else. Scholars have isolated a number of pieces from Giovanni Gabrieli's *Sacrae Symphoniae* (Sacred Symphonies, 1597) that fit the criteria for concertos, but Gabrieli labelled them *canzonas*. Neither publishers, musicians, nor composers were consistent with nomenclature, and throughout the seventeenth century they often used the terms *concerto* and *sonata* interchangeably. Giuseppe Torelli himself was careful to distinguish his own *concerti* from his *sinfonie*: the latter were consistently more conservative and contrapuntal in style, but interestingly, the concerti did not exploit contrast. Even Arcangelo Corelli's famous Opus 6 concerti, when issued by London publisher John Walsh in 1715, were entitled *Great Concertos or Sonatas* (although as we shall see, Walsh was in fact making the point that the concertos could be performed as either chamber or orchestral works).

The development of the Baroque concerto is thus characterized by tremendous diversity. Not only are the boundaries circumscribed by the genre in its early days somewhat amorphous, but the digressions taken by various composers as the genre matures, the differing ways in which concertos were performed, and the geographic dispersion of the style and the ways in which it influenced composers across the continent present multiple scenarios. Certainly discrete styles coexisted, but there was also much cross-fertilization. Nonetheless, we can isolate two strands of development for the Baroque concerto that will serve as a useful means of surveying the genre at large. Both strands emerged in Italy in the closing decades of the seventeenth century. Both contrast a small solo force or single soloist—known as the *concertino* group—against a larger force—referred to as the *concerto grosso* or *ripieno*. The principal difference in the strands is in the relative weight they afford to the two opposing bodies.

Rome, a city with a strong orchestral tradition and a wealthy patronage network that supported it, was a center of concerto production. The Roman concerto model, with Arcangelo Corelli (1653–1713) as its lead proponent, featured a typical trio sonata formation of two violins and continuo at the core of the orchestra as its *concertino*. The larger group, or *ripieno*, comprised the same instruments, but with optional doublings and additional contrabasses and violas. The element of contrast, so central to the concerto genre, is achieved primarily through oppositions of large and small sonorities. The concertos were notated on a seven-stave score: three staves for the *concertino* and four for the *ripieno*. There were several performance options, but in all, the *concertino* played continuously. The *concertino* might be separated spatially from the *ripieno* players. The *ripieno* part could be left out altogether; or it could be added to the *concertino* where indicated with as little as one instrument to a part. The *ripieno* parts could also be doubled at will. Roman orchestras might be quite large: Corelli himself directed a performance by an orchestra of more than eighty players—including two trumpets.

The second stylistic model is associated with the northern cities of Bologna, Milan, and Venice, where a greater distinction between the soloist(s) and the orchestra led to the growth of the solo concerto. The earliest concertos by Tomaso Albinoni (1671–1750/1) and Giuseppe Torelli (1658–1709) were conceived as sonatas for four-part orchestra (two violins, viola, and cello) with solo violin(s) drawn from the *ripieno* parts. The continuo might be independent; or it might match the cello part. Antonio Vivaldi's 350 solo concertos, justly famous for their virtuosic writing, tonal clarity, motivic vitality, and formal organization, fall into this category.

These two models formed the basis for concerto writing for the rest of Europe and can be heard in the works of Georg Muffat, Francesco Geminiani, Georg Frederic Handel, and Johann Sebastian Bach.

Figure 10.1 Portrait of Arcangelo Corelli. Engraving, 18th century.

Arcangelo Corelli

Arcangelo Corelli (Fig. 10.1), credited by the eighteenth-century English historian Charles Burney as the originator of the form, is the main figure of the Roman style of concerto writing. Born in Fusignano in 1653, Corelli likely spent time in nearby Bologna, a city known for its vibrant instrumental music scene. By 1675 he had settled in Rome, where he remained for the rest of his life. Music and culture in Rome was dominated by a dense network of powerful patrons who sponsored performances of the highest quality; Corelli worked for Queen Christina, Cardinal Benedetto Pamphili, and Cardinal Pietro Ottoboni, grand-nephew of Pope Alexander VIII and vice-chancellor of the Church. The patronage of Cardinal Ottoboni gave Corelli the leisure to devote himself to composing and revising his six life works: four sets of twelve trio sonatas (Opp. 1–4, 1681–94), one set of twelve solo violin sonatas (Op. 5, 1700), and one collection of twelve concertos for string orchestra (Op. 6, 1714). While the size of Corelli's output might appear small compared to European standards of his time, Roman virtuosi had little need to publish and many were discouraged from the commercial venture by their private patrons.

Musically, Corelli's distinguished reputation rests with his place in creating a link between the sonata and concerto genres. It is in his final collection, Opus 6, that we best see the overlap between the sonata and concerto. We are not sure when Corelli actually composed the set, which makes it difficult to situate Corelli's Opus 6 in the history of the concerto. Corelli's *Concerti grossi . . . Opera sesta* (Amsterdam, 1714) was published by the northern firm of Estienne Roger (1665/6–1722) one year after the composer's death. However, evidence for an earlier date of composition comes from one of Corelli's followers, the well-traveled Georg Muffat (1653–1704), who left the court of the Archbishop of Salzburg for Rome in the early 1680s "to learn the Italian musical style." Muffat reflected on his Italian training in the preface to his own collection of chamber sonatas and concertos, *Auslesene Instrumentalmusik* (1701), where he writes:

> The first thoughts of this ingenious mixture came to me some time ago in Rome, where I was learning the Italian style on the keyboard under the world-famous Bernardo Pasquini, when I heard with great excitement and amazement some concertos of the talented Arcangelo Corelli performed most beautifully and with great precision by a large number of instrumentalists. As I noticed the many contrasts in those pieces, I composed some of these present concertos, and I tried them out in the home of the above-mentioned Arcangelo Corelli (to whom I feel greatly obliged for generously conveying to me many useful observations concerning this style); and with his approval, I was the first to bring some samples of this hitherto unknown harmony to Germany. (Document 1)

From Muffat's eloquent testimony, we learn that Corelli used solo/tutti orchestration in the early 1680s, though it is uncertain whether these refer to his Opus 6 or to other, lost concerti.

Corelli's Opus 6 is a cross between the sonata and concerto idioms. This hybrid style originated in the 1660s and 1670s in the works of Roman-based composer Alessandro Stradella (1639–82), whose music pitted a trio scoring of two violins and continuo against four-part strings, with optional doublings, and a separate continuo. The larger group provided intermittent reinforcement of the *concertino;* the term *di rinforzo* (reinforcement), used in works such as Giuseppe Torelli's Opus 8 (1709) and as late as Giuseppe Sammartini's Opus 2 (1738), refers to this characteristic.[2] Stradella's *Sonata di viole* features a *concertino* of two violins and lute alternating with a *concerto gross di viole*. Stradella's *Sonata* may have been a direct model for Corelli's Opus 6: The two composers possibly met in Rome, where they dominated the city's musical scene of the 1670s.

As Corelli adjusted his compositional approach in the transition from the trio sonata texture of Opuses 1–5 to the *concerti grossi* of Opus 6, it is fair to ask if Corelli envisioned Opus 6 as concertos from the start, or if he viewed them as enhanced trio sonatas with (optional) tutti reinforcement. The latter is the most likely scenario. The twelve concertos of Opus 6 are scored for two violins and violoncello in the *concertino* group, and four-part strings, comprised of two violins, viola, and basso (all with optional doublings) in the *concerto grosso* group. Corelli provides each group with its own basso continuo part, which suggests that the *concertino* was conceived as an independent, self-sufficient ensemble. The title page of the 1714 Roger edition presents the *concertino* parts as *obligati* (necessary) and the *ripieno* as *ad arbitrio* or "arbitrary," (Fig. 10.2). This suggests that the pieces could be performed in a number of different ways.

Multiple performance options enabled publishers and composers to reach both the sonata and the concerto markets. Muffat's preface to *Auserlesene Instrumentalmusik* (1701) might be applicable to Corelli's set, for Muffat advised: "If you have few violinists, or if you would prefer to try these concertos with only a few, then you will form a complete, indispensable trio from the following three parts: *Violino 1. Concertino, Violino2. Concertino* and *Basso*.[3]" Muffat continued:

> If, however, you have an even greater number of musicians at your disposal, you can increase the number of players per part for not only the first and second violins of the large choir (*Concerto grosso*), but also, with discretion, both the middle violas and the bass, and to adorn these with the accompaniment of harpsichords, theorbos, harps, and similar instruments. However, the small choir or trio which is always indicated by the word *Concertino* should ideally be played with only one per part by your three best players, with the accompaniment of an organist or theorbist, each part being played by the most

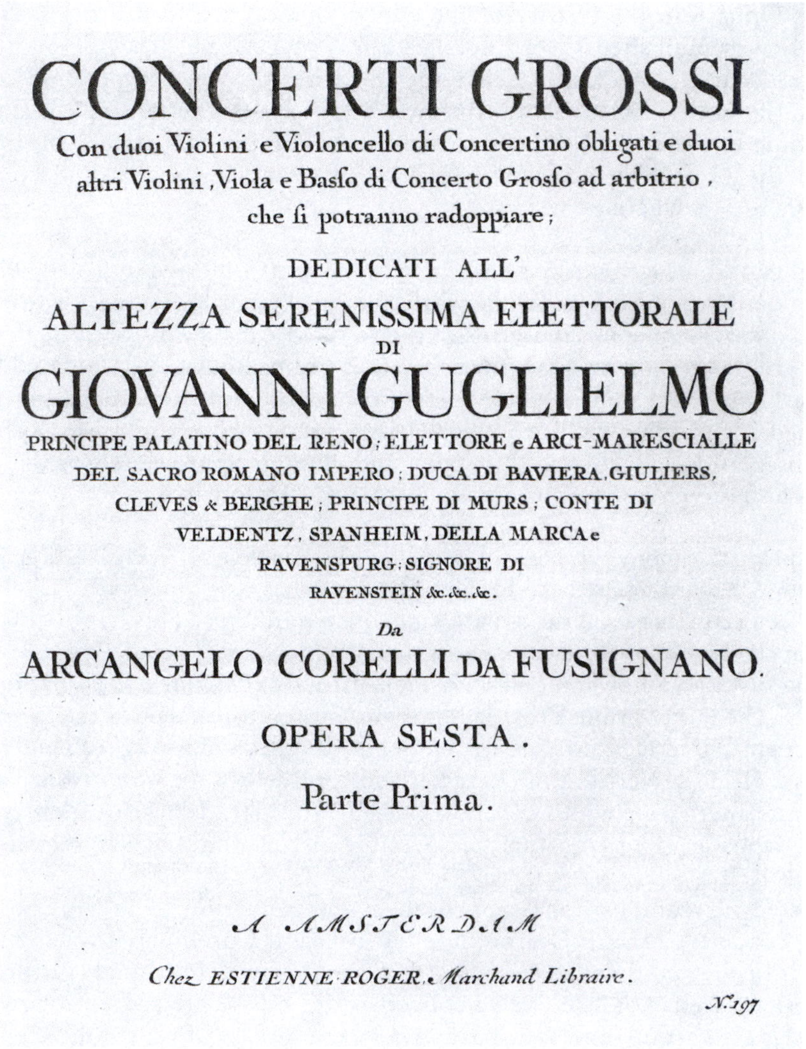

CONCERTI GROSSI

Con duoi Violini e Violoncello di Concertino obligati e duoi
altri Violini, Viola e Baſſo di Concerto Groſſo ad arbitrio,
che ſi potranno radoppiare;

DEDICATI ALL'

ALTEZZA SERENISSIMA ELETTORALE
DI

GIOVANNI GUGLIELMO

PRINCIPE PALATINO DEL RENO; ELETTORE e ARCI-MARESCIALLE
DEL SACRO ROMANO IMPERO; DUCA DI BAVIERA, GIULIERS,
CLEVES & BERGHE; PRINCIPE DI MURS; CONTE DI
VELDENTZ, SPANHEIM, DELLA MARCA e
RAVENSPURG; SIGNORE DI
RAVENSTEIN &c.&c.&c.

Da

ARCANGELO CORELLI DA FUSIGNANO.

OPERA SESTA.

Parte Prima.

A AMSTERDAM

Chez ESTIENNE ROGER, Marchand Libraire.

Nº 197

Figure 10.2 Corelli, title page, Opus 6, *Concerti grossi*, published by Roger, 1714.

accomplished musician, and never with more, except in very expansive halls where the larger choir is generally bigger, where they should be played with at most two per part.[4]

Composers and their publishers envisioned concerti as malleable forms that could be enlarged or contracted according to the quantity and quality of available resources.

Corelli's title page does little to clarify the issue of scoring. The gorgeous engraving of a painting by Roman Francesco Trevisani depicts a female muse playing the lute; she sits by a harpsichord; a stringed instrument leans against a corner of the harpsichord, and a stack of books sits on top of the keyboard. An open partbook on the music stand shows the beginning of the first violin part of Opus 6, no. 1. The scene is set in a courtyard: The coat of arms of the dedicatee, the Elector Palatine, hangs against the wall.

The image conveys that the music was of a high enough status to attract the support of an important patron.

Opus 6 no. 1 in D Major is typical of the set for its combination of relatively short, slow, and fast movements and the presence of a fugue, a feature found in eight of the concertos. In the opening *Largo*, Corelli establishes a stately affect through the use of short motives and rests (Ex. 10.1). A short sequential motive, heard first in m. 3, moves quickly through a circle of fifths progression, a series of compact dominant-tonic relationships from D to G, E to A, and F-sharp to B minor and back again (E to A, D to G), before an extended pause on the dominant harmony on A major. This is a good example of Corelli's clear understanding of functional harmony: His concise exploitation of the gravitational forces within harmonic progressions and between individual keys is one of the main reasons his concerti were so influential. Strongly melodic bass lines, sequences (with a variable and usually unpredictable number of repetitions), circle of fifths progressions, and any number of formulas that reinforced the listener's sense of key were mixed and matched, waylaid and redirected. The miniature dramas that took place as one key succumbed to another paralleled the drama acted out between contrasting bodies of sound.

The opening is typical in the way that the *concertino* and *ripieno* groups share their material, with little distinction between the two. After the pause, the sequential motive from the opening movement returns in the *concertino* in quick imitation between first and second violin, now energized in an *Allegro* tempo. Corelli repeats the same circle of fifths sequence, which gives the impression of urgent forward motion while merely circumscribing the key. The salient difference here with the opening *Largo* is in the distinct sound of the *concertino* group: With its active bass line and close interaction, this movement is a miniature trio sonata.

Short *Adagio* incursions (Ex. 10.2) for full ensemble prevent the solo-dominated *Allegro* from gaining sufficient momentum to really take off. These *Adagio* interruptions pull away from the tonic (pausing on F-sharp minor and A major, respectively); each of the *Allegro* sections, scored only for the *concertino* group,

Example 10.1 Corelli, Opus 6, no. 1, first movement, mm. 1–7.

Example 10.1 (continued)

attempts to pull the music back to the tonic, using a variety of dynamic sequential progressions. This miniature tonal drama amplifies and further differentiates the contrast between the two groups. They not only sound different, they have different functions.

The final movement offers significant separation of solo and tutti roles. It is preceded by an *Allegro* fugue that features a whole-note subject heard first across the *concertino* instruments and then across the *ripieno* (Ex. 10.3).

This movement, mostly scored for tutti ensemble except where the *concertino* enters alone with the fugue subject, has an archaic quality that is enhanced by having the full orchestra play. The viola part of the *ripieno* is doubled by the *concertino* cello when it initially enters with the fugue subject, but elsewhere the viola adds an independent, extra line of counterpoint. Often this line is even peripheral, and does not partake in the imitation. In mm. 33–39 (Ex. 10.4), for instance, the other voices are engaged in stretto imitation of the subject, while the viola moves independently.

The rich sonorities and dignified affect of the sixth movement contrast with the gigue-like vitality of the finale (10.5), where the lighter texture of the *concertino* makes the contrast in rhythm and affect all the keener. The two *concertino* violins flourish here, with independent and virtuosic music that the *ripieno* never shares. This is exemplary of the early phase of the concerto ritornello, in which the *ripieno* was used to reinforce the impact of cadences and modulations, and to enrich the sound of an otherwise independent trio sonata texture. The *ripieno* here provides contrast and formal punctuation, a role the full-fledged ritornello will eventually fill with more definition.

This is accessible music that many students can perform. A useful starting place for guidance on performing this set is Muffat's preface of 1701, which (in addition to advice on scoring, discussed above) offers tips on dynamics and tempo. Muffat advises performers to draw out points of contrast in the music: to exaggerate the difference between *piano* and *forte* and to take the slow movements more slowly, "sometimes to such an extent that one can hardly believe it" and those marked *Allegro, Vivace, Presto, Più Presto* and

Example 10.2 Corelli, Opus 6, no. 1, second movement, mm. 1–4.

Prestissimo "much livelier and faster." The goal, for Muffat and perhaps modern performers as well, was as follows:

> Through the rigorous observation of the opposition or contrast between slow and fast, loud and soft, the fullness of the large choir and the tenderness of the trio, the ear will be transported by the contrast of light and shadow.[5]

Corelli himself insisted on high standards for performances of his works. His student, Francesco Geminiani claimed that "Corelli regarded it as essential to the *ensemble* of a band, that their bows should all move exactly together, all up, or all down; so that at his rehearsals, which constantly preceded every public performance of his concertos, he would immediately stop the band if he discovered an irregular bow" (as reported by Charles Burney, Document 2).

Corelli attracted a dedicated following of imitators, patrons, listeners, and printers, both during his lifetime and throughout the eighteenth century. His own career as a virtuoso violinist surely furthered his international reputation. In *A General History of the Science and Practice of Music*, English historian John Hawkins (1719–89) writes:

> The proficiency of Corelli on his favourite instrument, the violin, was so great, that the fame of it reached throughout Europe; and Mattheson has not scrupled to say that he was the first performer on it in the world; and Gasparini styles him 'Virtuosissimo di violino, e vero Orfeo de nostril tempi' [virtuoso of the violin, and true Orpheus of our time]. . . . The style of his performance was learned, elegant, and pathetic, and his tone firm and even: Mr. Geminiani, who was well acquainted with and had studied it, was used to resemble it to a sweet trumpet. A person who had heard him perform says that whilst he was playing on the violin, it was usual for his countenance to be distorted, his eyes to become as red as fire, and his eyeballs to roll as in an agony.[6]

Example 10.3 Corelli, Opus 6, no. 1, sixth movement, mm. 1–9.

Example 10.4 Corelli, Opus 6, no. 1, sixth movement, mm. 33–39.

Example 10.5 Corelli, Opus 6, no. 1, seventh movement, mm. 1–6.

Hawkins's account of Corelli, rapt in performance, foreshadows the descriptions of nineteenth-century virtuosi such as Paganini and Franz Liszt, whose bodies became part of the performance.

The trans-European reception of Corelli's concertos is another example of a musical repertory that transcended geographic and linguistic borders, much like Italian opera in the vocal realm. The tradition of seven parts was retained by Roman-based composers Pietro Locatelli (1694–1764), Giuseppe Valentini (1681–1753), and Giovanni Mossi (1680–1742), though in other respects Corelli's music was more closely emulated outside Italy, particularly in England, where Corelli's reputation was firmly established. English fascination with Italian music and culture took hold in the seventeenth century, first with the cultivation of madrigals and later with Purcell's trio sonatas. English gentlemen and noblemen embarked on Grand Tours, which took them as far south as Venice and Rome. Italian singers and instrumentalists held top posts and operatic roles in London, and the firm of John Walsh supplied a steady stream of Italian and Italianate music to English audiences. Corelli's Opus 6 appeared from Walsh's firm in 1715. It is likely that English musical taste and ability favored Corelli's less demanding and harmonically straightforward concerti to the more soloistic writing found in the works of Vivaldi. As John Hawkins remarked, "it may be observed of the compositions of Corelli, not only that they are equally intelligible to the learned and unlearned, but that the impressions made by them have been found to be as durable as general."[7]

Two examples illustrate the types of Corelli-inspired emulation at work in the first half of the eighteenth century. The first is virtuoso violinist and composer Francesco Geminiani (1687–1762), a former student of Corelli's, who achieved lasting fame as a writer of the influential treatises *The Art of Playing on the Violin* (1751) and *A Treatise of Good Taste in the Art of Musick* (1749). Geminiani left Italy for London in 1714 and immediately capitalized on his affiliation with Corelli. In addition to composing a set of original concertos, Geminiani reworked the solo violin sonatas of his teacher's Opus 5, transforming them into two sets of six *Concerti grossi* (1726, 1729). In 1735 he followed these with additional sets of *concerti grossi* based on Corelli's Opuses 1 and 3. Reworkings and transcriptions were considered a normal part of the compositional process, although commentators often dismiss such works for their supposed lack of originality. Virtuoso violinist Francesco Maria Veracini (1690–1768) may have had his rival Geminiani in mind when he complained of "reheaters" *(rifriggitori)*—new works that simply "reheated" older ones.[8]

Geminiani reconfigured Corelli's sonatas, notated for solo violin and basso continuo, by distributing the material between a *concertino* of two violins and cello and a *ripieno* of two violins, viola, and basso. He added rests to the *ripieno* to indicate solo/tutti contrasts, and a new viola part either doubled or filled in harmonies. The opening of Geminiani's *concerto grosso* "La Follia," an amplification of Corelli's Opus 5, no. 12, demonstrates the process of orchestral expansion. Corelli set a late version of the traditional *folia* melody and harmonic progression as the basis for a set of variations. The stressed second beat, key of D minor, and the slow tempo and solemn affect are typical of later treatments of this very popular tune and its typical bass line contour of i-V-i-VII-III-VII-i-(VI)-V-i. Corelli's original two voices of solo violin and

Example 10.6 Corelli, Violin Sonata, Opus 5, no. 12, first movement, mm. 1–8, and Geminiani, *concerto grosso*, "La Follia," first movement, mm. 1–8.

bass are provided in large font (Ex. 10.6), in the example below; Geminiani's additions are in smaller, cue-sized font.

Expanding trio sonatas was one way of serving the growing market for concertos and concerto-like music. There was great appetite for such works among the English nobility, with whom Geminiani cultivated close relations as cofounder in 1725 of the city's Philo-Musicae et Architecturae Societas, a musical society established by and for freemasons. The group commissioned Geminiani to rework Corelli's Opus 5 sonatas into concertos, which its members could purchase by subscription.

George Frideric Handel's *Grand Concertos*

The most famous emulation of Corelli came from the hands of Handel, who acknowledged his debt by assigning the opus number "six" to his twelve *Grand Concertos* (HWV 319–330). The title, *Grand Concertos*, is an English translation of *Concerto grosso*, a unique appellation that deliberately calls attention to the link between Handel and Corelli. Handel was immersed in the Corellian world of string writing, probably having first come into direct contact with Italian style in 1702 on a trip to Berlin, where Italian instrumentalists Attilio Ariosti and Giovanni Bononcini resided at the Prussian court. He also traveled to Italy in 1706–10, and it was during this period that he met and performed with Corelli in Rome.

Almost thirty years later, Handel, having adopted England as his host country, paid tribute to Corelli with the *Grand Concertos*. By this point, Corelli's music had already achieved the status of a classic: When Corelli's Opus 6 appeared in London in 1740, it marked the first publication of orchestral music in score. The fact that it was published in full score, rather than as partbooks, gives every indication that the set was valued for its historical significance. Handel composed the twelve concertos of his Opus 6 in a remarkably concentrated span of about one month, between September 29 and October 30, 1739. Working quickly, and probably hoping to capitalize on the rage for Corelli by coming out with his own concerti as soon as possible, he used the most attractive themes at hand, some of them not his own. Scholars have identified themes from Domenico Scarlatti's *Essercizi* (London, 1738) and Gottlieb Muffat's *Componimenti Musicali* (Augsburg, *ca.* 1739) in the Opus 6; there are also instances of self-borrowing, such as the first and last movements of no. 5, which draw on Handel's *Ode for St. Cecilia's Day*. This was not an uncommon practice with Handel, and does not carry the pejorative associations it does today. Indeed these borrowed themes may have given Handel's listeners special pleasure, and Handel recycled and recomposed this borrowed material with special care. Handel also took a direct hand in the work's publication. A notice in the *London Daily Post* (October 29, 1739) directs that "subscriptions are taken by the Author, at his Home in Brook's-street, Hanover-square; and John Walsh in Catherine-street in the Strand."[9] Handel's attention to the composition and publication of Opus 6 lends weight to Donald Burrows's assertion that "This conscious production of masterpieces—for indeed the concertos are one of the peaks in Baroque instrumental music—suggests that Handel's motives in composing his own 'Op. 6' included an intention to match Corelli's famous Op. 6 Concerti Grossi with works of equal quality."[10]

Handel's close supervision of the Opus 6 may be linked to his intention to perform the concertos as interlude music for his oratorios, though it is difficult to match the concertos with specific oratorios from the 1739–40 season. The wide market of interest is affirmed by the list of subscribers. John Walsh published the set by subscription and included with the volume a list of 100 subscribers, among them aristocrats, composers, concert promoters, and music societies. The range suggests that the concertos were seen as appropriate for a diversity of performance venues, from concert halls to clubs and private gatherings. While modern practice positions orchestral music in free-standing concert performances, in Handel's age such music was performed as part of a larger musical event, such as an opera or oratorio.

Handel adopted an outwardly Corellian model for all twelve *Grand Concertos*: They are cast in multi-movement form of four to six movements each that alternate slow and fast tempos; all include a fugue except no. 5; and all follow the Corellian seven-part scoring, with a *concertino* of two violins, and basso continuo, and a *ripieno* that often doubles and amplifies the *concertino*. The optional oboe parts that survive in manuscript sources for nos. 1, 2, 5, and 6 may have been used in the theater for concerto performances that coincided with operas or oratorios, which typically featured a large orchestra that included oboes and bassoons. The absence of the oboe parts from Walsh's printed edition of Opus 6 suggests that the typical Corellian string groupings were still standard.

Handel expanded upon Corelli's model, adding binary and da capo forms, dance-like movements, and a French overture. Opus 6, no. 5, for example, exhibits both its Corellian roots and Handel's innovations on that model. The first movement is a French overture, an important genre for Handel (but not for Corelli). Handel's orchestral introductions to his operas and oratorios are almost exclusively in French overture style, and feature a slow section with dotted rhythms followed by a faster section with imitative writing (see Chapter 7). Handel recasts Lully's model of the French overture, however, playing with expectations: He heads off the overture with a short violin solo, perhaps a bow to Vivaldi, who used a similar gesture at the start of the first concerto of *L'estro armonico* (Ex. 10.7–10.8).

Example 10.7a Handel, Op. 6, no. 5, first movement, mm. 1–3.

Example 10.7b Handel, Op. 6, no. 5, first movement, mm. 3–8.

Example 10.7b (continued)

Example 10.8 Handel, Op. 6, no. 5, first movement, mm. 1–4.

Charles Burney praised the opening of Opus 6, no. 5 as "the most spirited and characteristic of all the movements that were written by Handel, or any other composer, on Lully's model of the Opera Overture."[11]

The slow movement has a touching simplicity: A yearning bass line ascends by step and then gently retreats, almost dominating a plaintive descending gesture that is passed imitatively between the two violins (Ex. 10.9). The chromatic inflection on the C-natural in the third measure (in second violin) is an especially subtle harmonic touch. Sequences and suspended dissonances darken the affect somewhat, but the oft-repeated anacrusis in all three voices confers a weightless quality, and the frequent and leisurely cadences keep despair at bay.

The jocular fourth movement, with its burring, offbeat trills and light-hearted play between ascending eighth-note and sixteenth-note motives, immediately breaks the spell of the slow movement. The long passages of motoric repeated notes are usually associated with excitement, but they are almost theatrically comic in this context against one of Handel's classic walking basses (Ex. 10.10).

Example 10.9 Handel, Op. 6, no. 5, second movement, mm. 1–11.

The final movement—another calculated contrast—ushers the music into a communal, social sphere. An unassuming, binary-form minuet with each half repeated is extended with the addition of two variations: The first variation increases activity in the lower voices, the second features a more active treble part (Ex. 10.11–10.12). When performed with multiple players per part, as was likely the practice in England in the late 1730s, one can imagine a fairly direct line of development from this piece to an orchestral movement in a symphony from later in the eighteenth century.

Example 10.10 Handel, Op. 6, no. 5, fourth movement, mm. 1–12.

Example 10.11 Handel, Op. 6, no. 5, fifth movement, Menuet, mm. 1–8.

Example 10.12 Handel, Op. 6, no. 5, fifth movement, Menuet, mm. 41–45.

Towards the Solo Concerto

The notion of the concerto as a vehicle for solo display—as opposed to the Roman model where sound rather than technical facility provides most of the contrast—formed the principle for concerto composition in northern Italy. An early center for the solo concerto was the collegiate church of San Petronio in Bologna, a city under papal control but with strong ties to the northern cities of Lombardy and Venice. The San Petronio maintained a large permanent orchestra featuring such talented players as Giuseppe Torelli (1658–1709), and led by high caliber chapel masters, Maurizio Cazzata (1616–78) and Gian Paolo Colonna (1637–95). All were prominent cultivators of the trumpet sonata, an important precursor to the violin concerto. The sonata for one or more trumpets with string orchestra introduced, ended, or punctuated solemn services. It was but a small step for the violin to imitate the trumpet's triadic figures and rapid-note repetitions, known as the *stile tromba*. We hear examples of this in Alessandro Scarlatti's *Il prigioniero fortunato* (Naples, 1698) and Handel's *Rinaldo* (London, 1711), where it is the voice that takes on the easily recognized *stile tromba*. Attention to soloistic playing fed the desire for full-fledged concertos or *Concerti a cinque*: concertos for four-part strings and continuo, and solo violin. Torelli's Opus 6, *Concerti musicali* (Augsburg, 1698), is a landmark publication for his inclusion of passages marked "solo" to be played by the principal violin with continuo (Ex. 10.13).

Torelli published the set in Germany, where from 1698 until 1699 he served as *maestro di concerto* for the Margrave Georg Friedrich of Brandenburg at Ansbach. He dedicated the concertos to Sofia Charlotte, wife of the Elector Frederick III of Brandenburg, for whom he performed in Berlin in May of 1697. As such, the *Concerti musicali* played a critical role in introducing the concerto to German-speaking lands.

After 1700, the key figure in the cultivation of the concerto was Antonio Vivaldi, who many credit as the "creator" of the three-movement solo concerto (although others note that Torelli standardized it earlier). Of a total of more than five hundred concertos of all types, Vivaldi wrote about 350 solo concertos, for a variety of instruments (violin, bassoon, cello, oboe, flute, recorder), a tally that varies according to whether one includes the fifty double concertos (including twenty-five for two violins) as solo concertos. Vivaldi's concertos provided a regular diet for the talented girls at the Pio Ospedale della Pietà in Venice, where he served as violin master from 1703 until 1717. The position gave Vivaldi a regular income and employment, as well as musical resources. The Ospedale, literally *hospital*, was one of the city's four orphanages, this one for girls only. Its choir and orchestra gained a Europe-wide reputation for its high performance standards.

Example 10.13 Torelli, Concerto no. 6 in C minor, mm. 1–15.

Example 10.13 (continued)

Like Corelli, Vivaldi established a relationship with the firm of Estienne Roger in Amsterdam to publish his collections. These tended to bear fancy titles, such as *L'estro armonico* (Music Mania), Opus 3 (Amsterdam, 1711); *La stravaganza, La cetra,* and *Il cimento dell'armonia e dell'inventione* (The Trial of Musical Skill and Contrivance); and *Le Quattro stagioni* (The Four Seasons, Op. 8, 1725). While *The Four Seasons* are descriptive pieces, most of the other titles appear to be more whimsical, and were probably used to attract attention in the marketplace.

Vivaldi's violin concertos were recognized immediately for their virtuosity and for the manner in which they displayed the soloist's skill. The solo concerto was aptly suited for public performance, yet also appropriate for princely chambers and such private settings as the Ospedale. Vivaldi's activity in Venice, a city that attracted tourists and culture lovers from all over Europe, must have helped establish Vivaldi's hold on the genre. That hold has remained for centuries. Scholar Karl Heller singles out the 1710s as an especially significant decade, where "innovations of the Vivaldi instrumental style changed the musical language and the musical thinking of an entire generation."[12]

Antonio Vivaldi's L'estro armonico

Vivaldi's earliest set of concertos, the highly influential *L'estro armonico*, contains four solo concertos for violin, four double concertos, and four concertos for four violins. In effect, eight of the concertos are *concerti grossi* (nos. 1, 4, 7, 10 for four violins and nos. 2, 5, 8, 11 for two violins), since they have two or more soloists. The remaining four violin concertos (nos. 3, 6, 9, 12) are solo concertos. This collection offered consumers tremendous variety, and demonstrates not only Vivaldi's versatility but the interplay among concerto styles. Vivaldi openly appealed to a European market. He dedicated the set to Prince Ferdinand III of Tuscany, a patron of European stature who was firmly outside the Venetian orbit. He also selected the cosmopolitan firm of Estienne Roger as publisher (Amsterdam, 1711); at least fourteen more editions followed, by Roger himself, by John Walsh of London, and by Le Clerc de Cadet of Paris.

Opus 3, no. 3

The underlying formal principle for Vivaldi's fast movements is ritornello form, a structural plan based on the alternation of a ritornello, played by the string ripieno, with more virtuosic solo sections (Table 10.1). The timbral contrast between solo and tutti was heightened through embedded oppositions of key and thematic material. The ritornello, usually with an easily recognized musical profile, typically opened and closed the movement in the tonic key, and its thematic material recurred throughout the movement. One (or more) intermediary ritornellos, generally articulating modulations to new keys, were positioned between the intervening solo episodes, which generally explored new tonal and thematic areas. Identifying the opening and closing ritornello is usually straightforward; what happens in between can be more challenging to label. Flexibility and play were the norm: Ritornello motives pop up in solo material, for example, and sometimes only portions of the ritornellos return at the expected spots.

The solo passages are less stable than the ritornellos, in terms of harmonic language and thematic content, though there are cases of ritornello theme incursions in solo material.

The opening ritornello of Opus 3, no. 3, fulfills the necessary functions of introducing motives and establishing the tonic key of G major (Ex. 10.14). The head motive (m. 1) is an easily recognized opening gesture; it highlights formal contours and flags recurrences of the ritornello throughout the movement. After establishing the tonic with a combination of G major scales and triads, it leads directly to two phrases constructed on a sixteenth-note motive (m. 3), the second repeated as an echo in m. 4. This passage serves as an antecedent phrase, and it reinterprets the tonic as the subdominant of D major; the consequent, a little sequential passage that follows (mm. 5–6) confirms this with a cadence on the dominant, D major. The ritornello ends with a third idea, an ascending scale passage (m. 7) used in a sequence that gravitates strongly back to the tonic.

The end of the ritornello merges directly with the first entry of the solo violin, a short, four-measure solo (m. 12) in G major that is immediately eclipsed by the reappearance of the ritornello (m. 16). This time, however, the ritornello leaves out the third of its components. It makes a definitive modulation to the dominant, D major, where the second solo episode begins (beat 3 of m. 22, (Ex. 10.15)). The soloist continues in steady sixteenth notes that are lightly punctuated by three-note motives in second violin, while the accompaniment continues in the steady eighth notes that have been present for most of the movement.

The third ritornello (mm. 30–37) appears in D major as the soloist again joins the *ripieno* strings. The ritornello motives reappear in sequence and move towards a cadence in the relative B minor. Another solo episode begins at this point, and furthers the sixteenth-note idea, moving through a circle of fifths progression that confirms the key of B minor. The head motive of the ritornello appears in that key (m. 45) and reinforces the modulation, but is bluntly repeated a third above, in D major, and fourth above that, in G major, which initiates the return of the final ritornello (mm. 49 onward). This statement of the ritornello is almost identical to its first appearance, except for a substitution of solo figuration for the second idea of original tutti (mm. 51–54).

One of the earliest descriptions of concerto technique is Johann Joachim Quantz's *Versuch einer Anweisung die Flöte zu spielen* (On Playing the Flute, 1752), a treatise whose worth extends well beyond tips on playing the flute. Quantz describes concerto form wherein "The best ideas of the ritornello must be dismembered, and intermingled during or between the solo passages."[13] The advice aptly applies to Vivaldi's approach to this first movement.

Slow movements of concertos appear in a wide range of forms. Vivaldi builds this movement from the opening gesture of three hammer strokes, in quarter notes, on a single harmony, followed by a measure in which the soloist presents the same harmony in linear form (Ex. 10.16). The simplicity of this figurative gesture, which generally outlines a triad on the first note of each beat, allows for easy modulation to different keys as the movement unfolds.

In Quantz's description of the concerto genre, he reserves a special place for the listener when he describes slow movements, writing that "The Adagio furnishes more opportunities than the Allegro to excite the passions and to still them again . . . In general the *Adagio* must be distinguished from the first Allegro by its rhythmic structure, metre, and tonality."[14] Vivaldi's Opus 3 changes tempo, key, and rhythmic contour. Yet Vivaldi's movement also falls into what Quantz would describe as an older style: "In former times

Table 10.1 Ritornello form

R1	R2	R3	R4
I	V	(vi)	I
S	S	S	

Example 10.14 Vivaldi, Opus 3, no. 3, first movement, mm. 1–8.

the Adagio was usually set in a very dry and plain fashion that was more harmonic than melodic. The composers relinquished to the performers that which they should have done themselves, that is, make the melody sing."[15] Vivaldi's slow movement is more of a harmonic elaboration than a melodic one (Ex. 10.17).

The finale, an energetic *Allegro* in ritornello form, brings a brilliant return of G major. Vivaldi immediately foregrounds the idea of contrast by repeating the head motive, now *piano*, as an echo (Ex. 10.17).

Solo episodes feature vigorous gestures that plummet down the scale, zigzag up again, and finish with a bounce back down a broken triad, a gesture that is then repeated in a rising sequence (mm. 111–124). After a short ritornello in E minor (begins m. 139), Vivaldi seizes the opportunity for a solo violin display in an extended solo episode that sounds more difficult than it is (mm. 152–184, (Ex. 10.18)). This is not a cadenza (nor is there an obvious place for a cadenza in this movement), as it is accompanied by the

Example 10.15 Vivaldi, Opus 3, no. 3, first movement, mm. 22–24.

Example 10.16 Vivaldi, Opus 3, no. 3, second movement, mm. 65–70.

orchestra, albeit lightly; nor is it rhythmically free (or improvised) as a cadenza would normally be. However, the type of figuration is similar to what one might see in a cadenza, which is often positioned before the final tutti or after a fermata.

None of Vivaldi's cadenzas appeared in print (they would have been out of place in editions geared to the wider public), although a few survive in manuscripts and it is known that cadenzas circulated among top performers (Fig. 10.3). Vivaldi himself became known for his ravishing performances of cadenzas. German

Example 10.17 Vivaldi, Opus 3, no. 3, third movement, mm. 97–104.

law student, traveler, and patron of the arts, J.F.A. Uffenbach, felt frightened upon hearing Vivaldi improvise a cadenza at the end of an aria at an opera performance in Venice on February 4, 1715:

> I doubt anything like it was ever done before, or ever will be again: he came to within a hairsbreadth of the bridge, leaving no room for the bow, and this on all four strings, with imitations and at an incredible speed.[16]

The final ritornello begins in B minor (m. 215) and works its way back to G major through the dominant. Another solo episode seems to emerge, but ritornello material (some of it new) interrupts and dominates the solo violin's attempts to take off, and the movement ends in a series of quick, breathless phrases.

Vivaldi's prototypical concerto was a highly malleable form with application across genres, instruments, and locales. His music and reputation spread across Europe through the circulation of his music in print and manuscript, through accounts of his virtuosity and performances by traveling virtuosi (in addition to Uffenbach, Charles Burney recognized Vivaldi's prowess as composer and violin virtuoso; see Document 2), and through the composers he inspired, including German Baroque master Johann Sebastian Bach.

J.S. Bach and the Concerto

Bach's engagement with the Italian concerto began during his tenure as organist and later *Konzertmaster* at the court of Duke Wilhelm Ernst at Weimar, 1708–17. An Italophile and amateur instrumentalist, his younger brother, Johann Ernst, supplied the court musicians with copies of the latest Italian concertos, which he had collected during a trip to the Netherlands. Vivaldi's *L'estro armonico* may have been one of those scores. Concertos also reached Bach through a dense network of manuscript circulation. Between 1713 and 1714 in Weimar, Bach arranged sixteen concertos for solo clavier (BWV 972–987) and five concertos for organ (BWV 592–596), probably for the personal use of his patron, Johann Ernst, although Bach may have performed the works himself on the chapel organ. Of this group, nine were arrangements of concertos by Antonio Vivaldi, the single most important influence on Bach's concerto writing.

Example 10.18 Vivaldi, Opus 3, no. 3, third movement, mm. 166–177.

Bach would have been twenty-three years old at the time: a practiced composer to be sure, but a young man eager to expand his musical world. It is no exaggeration to say that Vivaldi's concertos hit him like a thunderclap. According to Bach scholar Christoph Wolff, Bach's confrontation with Vivaldi provoked "the strongest single developmental step toward the formation of a genuinely personal style."[17]

Transcription was a recognized training ground for composition and Johann Nicolaus Forkel, in his famous biography of Bach from 1802, specifically informed the reader that Bach taught himself composition by studying and transcribing these violin concertos. We might compare Bach to a translator who first adhered to the model while addressing the idioms of this new language, but soon learned to speak it on his own. It was a two-part process: One involved the act of transferring an ensemble idiom to the keyboard; the

Figure 10.3 Cadenza to the last movement of Violin Concerto RV 340 in Vivaldi's hand.

Example 10.19 Bach, Concerto no. 7 in F major, BWV 978, first movement, mm. 1–10.

Example 10.20 Bach, Concerto no. 7 in F major, BWV 978, second movement, mm. 1–4.

other, and more important part of what Bach learned in working with Vivaldi's scores, involved understanding and absorbing the revelatory, nitty-gritty of Vivaldi's compositional method.

The actual transcribing process required Bach to make changes to the string original so that the material would be more idiomatic for the keyboard. The types of changes Bach made can be seen in Bach's transcription of Vivaldi's Opus 3, no. 3 (BWV 978). To begin, Bach transposed the work down a whole step to F major to accommodate material from the upper range of the violin part that would have been too high for his keyboard (Ex. 10.19). He also created a much more active role for the left hand, especially in the ritornellos where it compensates for the absence of the denser sound and texture of an orchestra. Idiomatic keyboard figuration in sixteenth notes fills in the harmonies without impeding the forward motion with individual chords. The left hand also engages in some (invented) imitation with the solo part (m. 2).

In the *Largo* slow movement, both the chords played by the strings and the figurative solo passages transfer to the keyboard with relative ease (Ex. 10.20).

We can assume that the process of transcribing Italian concertos honed Bach's skills (and perhaps whetted his appetite) for transferring orchestral writing to the keyboard. However, the encounter with Vivaldi was much more fundamental than this. According to Forkel, who would have received the information from one of Bach's sons (who in turn would have heard if from Bach himself), the confrontation with Vivaldi's concertos inspired no less than a complete reconfiguration of the way Bach approached the art of composition. Vivaldi taught Bach a new way of "thinking musically"—a way of thinking that took into account the ordering of ideas, their connections to one another, the continuity of his material, the relationship of one part to another, and the proportions of the various constituent parts. The tonal coherence and pregnant thematic integrity of Vivaldi's ritornellos embody many of the principles that Bach absorbed into his compositional style, including the spinning-out of thematic material, the development and integration of various motives and their balanced arrangement. Yes, these ideas were initially encountered and nurtured in Bach's study of the concerti; however, they were not tied to the concerto form *per se*. They could be applied, and were from this point on, to Bach's composition in general. That is why we find elements of concerto-style thinking in pieces that have nothing to do with the concerto: in the Kyrie from Bach's *Mass in B Minor*, which is a concerto fugue for example; or in the fugue from the *Well-Tempered Clavier*, discussed in Chapter 11, where the key plan, the motivic connections, the periodicity and long-range symmetries, and the alternation of fugal sections and episodes reflects his new compositional world view. It is why Bach's actual concertos often expand so dramatically upon the Vivaldi model, for everything that was part of Bach's style prior to his encounter with Vivaldi remained relevant—the counterpoint, the harmonic density, the melodic complexity, all of which allowed Bach to work on a broader, more ambitious palette than Vivaldi.

Bach exercised his newly forged skills in a number of concerto works composed during his appointment as chapel master to Prince-Leopold of Anhalt-Cöthen, 1717–23. He explored soloistic treatment for a diverse range of instruments in *The Brandenburg Concertos*, six concertos, each of which approaches the concerto in a different way, scored for various combinations of woodwinds, strings, harpsichord, and brass, and dedicated to Christian Ludwig, Margrave of Brandenburg. (There is some question as to whether *Brandenburg Concerto no. 1* predates Bach's introduction to Vivaldi.) Two solo violin concertos and a double concerto also date from this period.

During his tenure at Leipzig, Bach focused on the keyboard concerto in multiple forms: seven concertos for solo clavier and orchestra (BWV 1052–1058), the 'Italian' concerto for clavier alone (BWV 971), three concertos for two claviers and orchestra (BWV 1060–1062), two concertos for three claviers and orchestra (BWV 1063–1064), and a concerto for four claviers and orchestra, which was an arrangement of Vivaldi's concerto for four violins, Opus 3, no. 10. Some of these concertos may have been transcriptions of earlier concertos for solo instrument (solo violin or wind instrument) and orchestra that Bach would have written during his Cöthen period, and have been lost.

Composed in 1734 and published in Nuremberg the following year, the *Concerto nach Italienischen Gusto* (Concerto after the Italian Style, BWV 971) was part of the second volume of the *Clavier-Übung*, a volume devoted half to French style (*Overture in French Style*, BWV 831), half to Italian (Fig. 10.4).

The basic tenets of concerto form as Vivaldi standardized it are found in the *Italian Concerto*: the macro-structure of a three-movement form, the tempo pattern of fast-slow-fast, and ritornello principles and formal organization (Table 10.2). The ritornello of the first movement, which adheres to Vivaldi's model of a concerto movement closely, features three main thematic ideas (a, b, c), although we can also divide b into two sub-ideas, and the last four measures of c is essentially a variation of the first six measures of c. The head motive (a) ushers in the first ritornello and subsequent ritornellos; it is immediately repeated on the dominant, which reinforces its thematic content and establishes the key (Ex. 10.21).

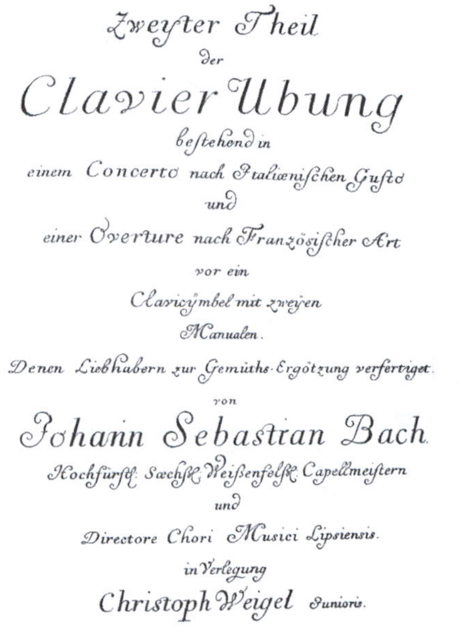

Zweyter Theil
der

Clavier Übung

bestehend in

einem Concerto nach Italienischen Gusto
und

einer Overture nach Französischer Art

vor ein

Clavicymbel mit zweyen
Manualen.

Denen Liebhabern zur Gemüths-Ergötzung verfertiget.

von

Johann Sebastian Bach.

Hochfürstl. Sæchsl. Weißenfelsl. Capellmeistern
und

Directore Chori Musici Lipsiensis.

in Verlegung

Christoph Weigel *Junioris.*

Figure 10.4 Bach, title page, *Clavier-Übung II*, 1735.

Table 10.2 Ritornello form in J.S. Bach, *Italian Concerto*, BWV 971, first movement

R1	S1	R2	S2	(R1 returns)	R3
mm. 1–30 FM	mm. 30–53 FM	mm. 53–90 CM-dm	mm. 90–139 dm	mm. 103–106 B♭M R3? "false recap" mm. 139–146	mm. 163–192 FM

Ritornello motives b (pickup to m. 9–downbeat 11) and c (pickup to m. 15–21 with extension) show Bach's penchant for motives that spin out—in other words, they can easily be repeated in sequence or turned into varied repetitions (Ex. 10.22). At the same time, they flow logically from one to the next and impart structural coherence on both the micro and macro levels. There are also smaller motives that emerge from the ritornello that are used later in the piece, including the ornamental thirty-second notes in the melody in m. 13, and the pattern of two pickup sixteenth notes plus eighth note in the bass in m. 16.

Bach's long-range tonal planning imparts structural coherence to the movement, as ritornellos appear in the logical sequence of tonic; dominant (V), which modulates to relative minor (vi); head motif only in the subdominant (IV); then full ritornello again, in its entirety, in the tonic at the end of the movement. Bach alternates between tutti and soloistic treatments, which are implied by the type of harmonic activity (stable or modulatory), the thematic material, the texture, and level of virtuosity. He provided dynamic markings in the score: The ritornellos are often marked *forte* for both hands, and solo episodes often have the right hand *forte* and left hand *piano*. The harpsichordist could use different manuals for different dynamics. For instance the bottom manual could be coupled, which would activate two sets of strings, making it louder. The top manual would then be softer than the bottom one. Surprisingly, though, the dynamic markings are not a foolproof way of determining whether a passage would have been played by the orchestra or by the solo instrument had the piece been an actual violin concerto. However, the *Italian Concerto* is not a transcription of an actual concerto, even though it imitates such a transcription. An earlier (keyboard) version of this movement, discovered in 1995, has no dynamic markings, and yet the distinctions between tutti and solo are actually more obvious than they are in Bach's final version.[18] Bach was thus not attempting to alert the performer to tutti/solo contrasts with his dynamic markings; instead, he deliberately chose to blur the orchestra/episode, perhaps to show off the effects of using different manuals, perhaps because he simply found it more interesting.

The slow movement is reflective and intimate, with the solo treble floating an expressive, highly ornamented melody over a simple, quasi-ostinato accompaniment. The spare accompaniment has no obvious orchestral counterpart; it seems to have been conceived with the keyboard in mind (Ex. 10.23).

The ostinato proves highly malleable as it modulates to F major for the second section, which features a variant of the opening melody on top (Ex. 10.24).

The elaborate embellishment continues atop the bass until the end of the movement. It was this type of written-out ornamentation, probably meant to sound as if it were being improvised, that sparked Johann Adolf Scheibe's complaint that Bach's music was laden with excess artifice, when he wrote that ". . . every little embellishment, and everything that involves playing 'by the method,' as it is called, he writes out in actual notes; this deprives his pieces not only of the beauty of harmony, but it also renders the melody imperceptible." (See Chapter 12, Document 3.)

The finale shifts to a lighter mood in jaunty cut-time meter, with syncopated gestures and periodic phrasing (Ex. 10.25).

Following Vivaldi, Bach immediately repeats the opening gesture (Ex. 10.26), this time varying it slightly to spend more time in the subdominant (B-flat major) during the spinning-out of the theme, but returning again to the tonic at the end.

A new triadic motive is introduced in the bass m. 25 that will prove significant for generating subsequent material in new keys and in other voices (Ex. 10.27). The tutti-solo distinctions are especially obscured in this movement, which often proceeds in two-part counterpoint. Bass and treble lines even alternate *piano* and *forte* markings, suggesting a concerto movement for, perhaps, cello and violin.

The remainder of the movement spins out these initial motives, extending and varying them as they explore new tonal areas.

Bach's *Italian Concerto* has remained part of a keyboard player's standard repertory from his day until present. Even Bach's critics, including Scheibe, were impressed. In a review of 1739, Scheibe wrote:

> Pre-eminent among works known through published prints is a clavier concerto of which the author is the famous Bach in Leipzig and which is in the key of F major. It is arranged in the best fashion

Figure 10.5 Bach, *Italian Concerto*, BWV 971, first movement, 1735.

which is applicable alone in these pieces. This clavier concerto is to be regarded as a perfect model of a well-designed solo concerto.[19]

Conclusions

The Baroque concerto, as a genre, as a set of techniques, and as a way of thinking about composition in general, permeated instrumental and vocal music of the first half of the eighteenth century. Bach is a good

Figure 10.5 (continued)

Figure 10.5 (continued)

Figure 10.5 (continued)

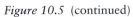

Figure 10.5 (continued)

Example 10.21 Bach, *Italian Concerto*, BWV 971, first movement, mm. 1–8.

Example 10.22 Bach, *Italian Concerto*, BWV 971, first movement, mm. 9–30.

Example 10.23 Bach, *Italian Concerto*, BWV 971, second movement, mm. 1–8.

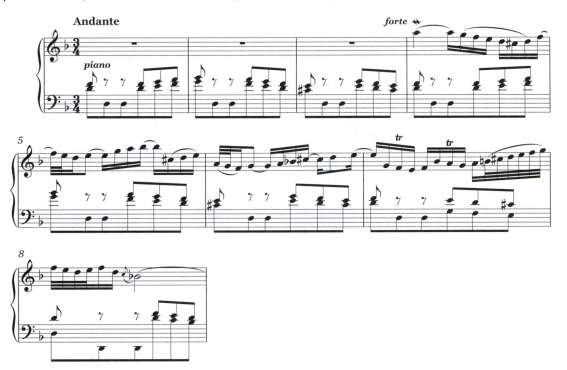

Example 10.24. Bach, *Italian Concerto,* BWV 971, second movement, mm. 27–32.

Example 10.25 Bach, *Italian Concerto*, BWV 971, third movement, mm. 1–13.

Example 10.26 Bach, *Italian Concerto*, BWV 971, third movement, mm. 13–24.

Example 10.27 Bach, *Italian Concerto,* BWV 971, third movement, mm. 25–35.

example of a composer who contributed a comparatively small number of concertos, yet employed principles gleaned from his immersion in concerto style across many genres and works. The concerto engaged with prevailing performance trends, including ornamentation, scoring, and musical taste in soloistic writing. The genre's geographic scope stretched from Italy to England, to Germany, and to France in the works of Joseph Bodin de Boismoitier (1689–1755), the first to write and publish solo music under the title 'concerto,' and Jean Marie Leclair (1697–1764), who spent time in Turin in 1722 and again in 1726–7, when he met Quantz and studied with Corelli's student, Giovanni Battista Somis.

The other side of the rage for the concerto was the notion that the genre was a suspect, degenerate art form that merely showcased the pyrotechnics of the soloist. The reception of the solo concerto was mixed among journalists and commentators. Uffenbach's account of Vivaldi's performance of a concerto cadenza hints at this when he writes that the performer induced fear in him. Musical historian John Hawkins blamed Vivaldi for the downfall of good taste:

> Corelli, who lived a few years before him, had introduced a style which all the composers of Italy affected to imitate: as Corelli formed it, it was chaste, sober, and elegant, but with his imitators it degenerated into dullness; this Vivaldi seemed to be aware of, and for the sake of variety, gave into a style which had little but novelty to recommend it.[20]

Hawkins suggests here that the tension was a question of musical taste: that of the masses versus that of the *cognoscenti*, a tension that the flamboyance of the solo concerto brought to the fore. We remember, however, that England—and Handel—adopted the Corellian model long before Hawkins made his complaint.

For modern scholars, the concerto has inspired much new analysis in recent years. Some have picked up on the idea of the concerto as a metaphor for social discourse, and see the concerto as embedding the new spirit of individualism that typified the age of the Enlightenment. Susan McClary has applied a narrative reading to Bach's *Brandenburg Concerto no. 5*, in which the harpsichord "overthrows the other forces in a kind of hijacking of the piece."[21] Michael Marissen has done much the same with Bach's *Brandenburg Concerto no. 1*, in speculating that the three separate groups of instruments, horns, strings and oboes, refer to different social strata—aristocrat, court musician, and town musician, respectively. Marissen believes that Bach neutralized the differences in status by treating the instruments as equals within the piece.[22] Whether the notion that solo-tutti relationships signify social and political hierarchies was present in the original composers' minds would be impossible to prove. Without a doubt, the solo concerto makes opposition its subject: public and private, chamber and concert, concert hall and salon are obvious correlatives. Expanding its metaphorical realm to include patron and employee is, if nothing else, a way of saying that the Baroque concerto is still relevant in the twenty-first century.

Documents

Document 1. Georg Muffat, Forward to *Auserlesene Instrumentalmusik*. Passau, 1701. In *Georg Muffat on Performance Practice: The Texts from* Florilegium Primum, Florilegium Secundum, *and* Auserlesene Instrumentalmusik. *A New Translation with Commentary.* Ed. and trans. David K. Wilson. Bloomington: University of Indiana Press, 2001. pp. 71–2. Copyright © 2001, Indiana University Press. Reprinted with permission of Indiana University Press.

Foreword

After the publication of my Bouquets or *Florilegia* of lovely ballet pieces, the first in August in 1695 and the second in Passau in 1698, I now present to you, well-meaning Reader, this first collection of my instrumental concertos of choicest harmony, both serious and light-hearted; so named because it not only contains intact the brisk liveliness of the ballet arias which spring from the Lullian fountain, but also contains certain melancholy, exquisite affects of the Italian manner, assorted humorous artistic ideas, and various sorts of carefully arranged alternations of the large choir and the solo trio. These concertos, since they were composed only for the particular delight of the ear, can be most fittingly performed for (above all) the amusement of great Princes and Lords, and for the entertainment of prominent guests, grand meals, serenades, and gatherings of music-lovers and virtuosi; they are suitable for neither the Church, because of the ballets and other arias which they contain, nor for dancing, because of the alternation of slow and tragic passages with lively and nimble ones.

The first thoughts of this ingenious mixture came to me some time ago in Rome, where I was learning the Italian style on the keyboard under the world-famous Bernardo Pasquini, when I heard with great excitement and amazement some concertos of the talented Archangelo Corelli performed most beautifully and with great precision by a large number of instrumentalists.

As I noticed the many contrasts in those pieces, I composed some of these present concertos, and I tried them out in the home of the above-mentioned Arcangelo Corelli (to whom I feel greatly obliged for generously conveying to me many useful observations concerning this style); and with his approval, I was the first to bring some samples of this hitherto unknown harmony to Germany, just as previously, upon my return from France, I was the first to introduce the Lullian Ballet style. I have increased the number of these pieces to twelve concertos, which were favorably performed on the most dignified occasions at various times and are explained by the mysterious titles placed before each concerto. These meager compositions of mine were granted hearings by His Most Gracious Imperial and Royal Majesty and by certain gracious Electors and other Princes, in Vienna, in Augsburg at the royal Coronation, and also in Munich, Salzburg, and Passau; the great favor (of which I am unworthy) freely conferred to them by these persons, as well as the approval of the most famous masters of exquisite discrimination and the acclaim of listeners (which is spreading also in distant lands), will easily comfort me when critics and jealous people come out against this work, people whose wicked efforts have always preceded a fortunate outcome for me. May you then, understanding Reader, sample this First Collection with a benevolent soul, and observe the following remarks, so that you might achieve my desired goal and achieve the full effect of these compositions in performance.

Document 2. Charles Burney on Corelli and Vivaldi. In Charles Burney, *A General History of Music*. London, 1789. Vol. 2, pp. 441, 442, 443, 445.

[vol. 2, p. 441] To attempt to give a character here of Corelli's compositions, which have been so long heard and universally admired, may to many of my readers appear wholly useless; yet as they are thrown aside as antiquated lumber by some, and regarded as models of perfection by others, my wish to rank each musician in his true place, with equity and fairness, inclines me to make a few reflections on the genius and works of this master, before I quit the subject.

[vol. 2, p. 442] The *Concertos* of Corelli seem to have withstood all the attacks of time and fashion with more firmness than any of his other works. The harmony is so pure, so rich, and so grateful; the parts are so clearly, judiciously, and ingeniously disposed; and the effect of the whole, from a large band, so majestic, solemn, and sublime, that they preclude all criticism, and make us forget that there is any other Music of the same kind existing. . . .

[Francesco] Geminiani's character of Corelli, upon the whole, seems very just: he said, that "his merit was not depth of learning, like that of Alessandro Scarlatti; nor great fancy, or rich invention in melody or harmony; but a nice ear and most delicate taste, which led him to select the most pleasing harmonies and melodies, and to construct the parts so as to produce the most delightful effect upon the ear." At the time of Corelli's greatest reputation, Geminiani asked Scarlatti what he thought of him; who answered, that "he found nothing greatly to admire in his composition, but was [vol. 2, p. 443] extremely struck with the manner in which he played his concertos, and his nice management of his band, the uncommon accuracy of whose performance, gave the concertos an amazing effect; and that, even to the eye as well as the ear:" for, continued Geminiani, "Corelli regarded it as essential to the *ensemble* of a band, that their bows should all move exactly together, all up, or all down; so that at his rehearsals, which constantly preceded every public performance of his concertos, he would immediately stop the band if he discovered an irregular bow."

There seems some justice in Geminiani's opinion, that Corelli's continual recourse to certain favorite passages betrays a want of *resource*. They were so many *bar rests* for his invention. All the varieties of Corelli's harmony, modulation, and melody, might perhaps be comprised in a narrow compass. The musical index to his works would not be long.

Indeed, Corelli was not the inventor of his own favorite style, though it was greatly polished and perfected by him.

[vol. 2, p. 445] But this most popular composer for the violin, as well as player on that instrument, during these times, was Don Antonio Vivaldi [d. 1743], maestro di capella of the Conservatorio della Pietà, at Venice [1713]; who, besides sixteen operas which he set for the Venetian theaters, and several others for different parts of Italy, between the year 1714 and 1737, published eleven different works for instruments, of which a list is given in Walther, without including his pieces called *Stravaganze*, which among flashy players, whose chief merit was rapid execution, occupied the highest place of favor. . . .

Albinoni, Alberti, Tessarini, and Vivaldi are, however, classed among the light and irregular troops; the Roman school, formed by Corelli, having produced the greatest performers and composers for the violin which Italy could boast during the first fifty years of the present century.

Document 3. Johann Joachim Quantz, *On Playing the Flute. A Complete Translation with an Introduction and Notes by Edward R. Reilly*. New York: The Free Press (A Division of The Macmillan Company), 1966. p. 314.

---

37. Since, however, the Adagio ordinarily finds fewer admirers than the Allegro among those who are not well versed in music, the composer must seek in every possible way to make it pleasing to inexperienced listeners such as these. To this end he should observe the following rules in particular. (1) In both the ritornellos and the solo sections he must strive for the greatest possible brevity. (2) The ritornello must be melodious, harmonious, and expressive. (3) The principal part must have a melody that permits some addition of graces, yet can also please without them. (4) The melody of the principal part must alternate with the interspersed tutti sections. (5) This melody must be just as moving and expressive as one with accompanying words. (6) From time to time some portions of the ritornello must be introduced. (7) The composer must not move through too many tonalities, since this is most detrimental to brevity. (8) The accompaniment during the solo passages must be plain rather than figured, so that the principal part is not hindered in making some embellishments, and retains complete freedom to introduce many or only a few graces judiciously and in a reasonable manner. (9) Finally, so that the required tempo may be easily divined,

the composer must seek to characterize the Adagio with an epithet that clearly expresses the sentiment contained in it.

Notes

1   Johann Mattheson, "The Difference between Vocal and Instrumental Melody," in *The Complete Music Director* (1739), part II, chapter 12, excerpted in *Strunk's Source Readings in Music History*, rev. ed., gen. ed. Leo Treitler (New York: W.W. Norton, 1998), part IV, ed. Margaret Murata, pp. 699–700.

2   Peter Walls, "Geminiani and the Role of the Viola in the Concerto Grosso," in *Liber Amicorum John Steele: A Musicological Tribute*, ed. Warren Drake (Stuyvesant, NY: Pendragon Press, 1997), p. 381.

3   Georg Muffat, Preface to *Auserlesene Instrumentalmusik* (Passau, 1701), in *Georg Muffat on Performance Practice: The Texts from* Florilegium Primum, Florilegium Secundum, *and* Auserlesene Instrumentalmusik. *A New Translation with Commentary*, ed. and trans. David K. Wilson (Bloomington: University of Indiana Press, 2001), p. 72.

4   Georg Muffat, Preface to *Auserlesene Instrumentalmusik* (Passau, 1701), in *Georg Muffat on Performance Practice: The Texts from* Florilegium Primum, Florilegium Secundum, *and* Auserlesene Instrumentalmusik. *A New Translation with Commentary*, ed. and trans. David K. Wilson (Bloomington: University of Indiana Press, 2001), pp. 73–4.

5   Georg Muffat, Foreword to *Auserlesene Instrumentalmusik* (Passau, 1701), in *Georg Muffat on Performance Practice: The Texts from* Florilegium Primum, Florilegium Secundum, *and* Auserlesene Instrumentalmusik. *A New Translation with Commentary*, ed. and trans. David K. Wilson (Bloomington: University of Indiana Press, 2001), p. 76.

6   John Hawkins, *A General History of the Science and Practice of Music* (New York: Dover, 1963), vol. 2, pp. 674–5.

7   John Hawkins, *A General History of the Science and Practice of Music* (New York: Dover, 1963), vol. 2, p. 677.

8   Enrico Careri, *Francesco Geminiani (1687–1762)* (Oxford: Clarendon Press, 1993), p. 136.

9   Otto Erich Deutsch, *Handel: A Documentary Biography* (London: A. & C. Black, 1955), p. 488.

10   Donald Burrows, ed., *The Cambridge Companion to Handel* (Cambridge: Cambridge University Press, 1997), p. 205.

11   Quoted in Alfred Mann, *Handel: The Orchestral Music: Orchestral Concertos, Organ Concertos, Water Music, Music for the Royal Fireworks* (New York: Schirmer Books, 1996), p. 64.

12   Karl Heller, *Antonio Vivaldi: The Red Priest of Venice*, trans. David Marinelli (Portland, OR: Amadeus Press, 1997), p. 277.

13   Johann Joachim Quantz, *On Playing the Flute*, 2nd ed., trans. Edward R. Reilly (London: Faber and Faber, 2001), p. 311.

14   Johann Joachim Quantz, *On Playing the Flute*. A Complete Translation with an Introduction and Notes by Edward R. Reilly (New York: The Free Press [A Division of The Macmillan Company], 1966), p. 313.

15   Johann Joachim Quantz, *On Playing the Flute*. A Complete Translation with an Introduction and Notes by Edward R. Reilly (New York: The Free Press [A Division of The Macmillan Company], 1966), p. 313.

16   Eberhard Preussner, *Die musikalischen Reisen des Herrn von Uffenbach* (Kassel: Bärenreiter, 1949), p. 67, trans. Pierro Weiss and quoted in *Music in the Western World: A History in Documents*, ed. Pierro Weiss and Richard Taruskin, 2nd ed. (Belmont, CA: Thomson Schirmer, 2008), p. 200.

17   Christoph Wolff, *Bach: Essays on His Life and Music* (Cambridge, MA: Harvard University Press, 1991), p. 74.

18   See Kirsten Beißwenger, "An Early Version of the First Movement of the *Italian Concerto* BWV 971 from the Scholz Collection?" in *Bach Studies 2*, ed. Daniel R. Melamed (Cambridge, UK: Cambridge University Press, 1995), pp. 1–19.

19   Quoted in Christoph Wolff, *Bach: Essays on His Life and Music* (Cambridge, MA: Harvard University Press, 1991), p. 201.

20   John Hawkins, *A General History of Music of the Science and Practice of Music* (New York: Dover, 1963), vol. 2, p. 837.

21   Susan McClary, "The Blasphemy of Talking Politics during Bach Year," in *Music and Society: The Politics of Composition, Performance, and Reception*, ed. Richard Leppert and Susan McClary (Cambridge: Cambridge University Press, 1987), p. 28.

22   Michael Marissen, "Concerto Styles and Signification in Bach's First Brandenburg Concerto," in *Bach Perspectives*, ed. Russell Stinson (Lincoln: University of Nebraska Press, 1995), vol. 1, pp. 79–101.

11 Johann Sebastian Bach in His Time and Ours

Johann Sebastian Bach has long been regarded as the consummate Baroque composer (Fig. 11.1). His is the music performers and listeners return to time and again, knowing there is always some other way of interpreting it or some detail that was missed in a previous performance. For scholars, Bach remains a cornerstone of Baroque research, and his music has been examined from all angles: editing, biography, source studies, archival work, gender, symbolism, tonal theory, and formal analysis. Some scholars consider Bach's music the pinnacle of the Baroque period, the natural culmination of decades of contrapuntal practice and Lutheran musical values. His contrapuntal skills, which can be seen not only in fugues and partitas, but across his instrumental and vocal works, were unparalleled among his peers.

Partly this is a function of the music's density. Bach's music is known for the amount of contrapuntal activity at a single moment, the complexity and purposeful force of the harmonic progressions, the ever-shifting, but skillfully managed dissonance, and, in the sacred music, the degree to which he invested his music with symbolism designed to intensify its spiritual import. Bach used a variety of techniques to convey symbolic import. He used number symbolism, such as matching the number of phrases to a number with theological associations. He used harmonic modulation to a sharp key, for instance, to signal the crucifixion. In large-scale works, he used symbolism as an organizational principle to group movements by key or genre into symmetrical, so-called "chiastic" structures—signifying the cross. These principles are evident as early as *Cantata no. 4*, "Christ Lag in Todesbanden," and are especially prominent in the *St. John Passion* and central portions of the *B Minor Mass*. Even Bach's melodies seem dense—loaded with affective intervals and ornamental figuration, spun out into long phrases, often unpredictable yet supremely logical. A prime example is the melody from the slow movement of Bach's *Brandenburg Concerto no. 1*, in which the serpentine melody heard first in the solo oboe seems an extremely unlikely candidate for the canonical treatment it receives when it is taken up in the violin (Ex. 11.1).

The association of Bach's music with contrapuntal complexity was firmly established in the composer's lifetime, and spread across Europe through the circulation of paintings and engravings. Elias Haussmann's classic painting of the composer from 1746, poised with a copy of his six-part *Canon triplex* (BWV 1076), still serves as a model for images of the composer.

We also sense that Bach considered and exploited the potential inherent in his material with more rigor than other composers of the Baroque. Rarely did Bach leave textures bare: Melodies seemed to have been born in his mind with countermelodies already in place. He was fluent in Italian and French idioms, from Vivaldi's concertos to D'Anglebert's elegant keyboard suites, yet as these were absorbed into his Germanic style, they were inevitably transformed, enriched in counterpoint, and informed with greater rhetorical urgency.

Bach composed no operas, yet his Passions and church cantatas, no less than his flamboyant improvisatory organ fantasies, attest to a finely tuned dramatic impulse. In vocal music, Bach exploited every means in the Baroque composer's toolkit to wrest the full expressive potential out of his texts and to make his meaning audible to the listener. These include defining the affect in his opening bars, painting individual words with descriptive gestures, using affective intervals in the melodic line to draw attention to a significant word or a change in emotional intensity, and, perhaps most importantly, manipulating the harmony

Example 11.1 Bach, *Brandenburg Concerto no.* 1, BWV 1046, Adagio, mm. 1–4.

for dramatic purposes, both on individual chords and in long term progressions. We have only to look at the remarkable twenty-four measure bridge at the end of the F-sharp minor "Confiteor" movement from the *Mass in B minor*, where Bach's masterful voice leading, the subtle escalation of harmonic tension, and its delayed resolution so vividly depict the long wait for the resurrection of the dead (Ex. 11.2).

(Confiteor unum baptisma)	(I acknowledge one baptism)
in remissionem peccatorum	For the remission of sins
Et expecto resurrectionem mortuorum	And I await the resurrection of the dead

The voices glide in slow motion through a series of suspended dissonances, secondary dominants, and diminished seventh harmonies, touching upon a number of unrelated keys in quick succession. These range from the rarely used E-flat minor—a key associated with profound distress—to B-flat major and C-sharp major, and lead to the eventual arrival of the augmented sixth harmony in m. 145. Traditionally used by Bach as a metaphor for the soul's transformation through Christ's death, this mystical German sixth harmony then eases into an A major dominant seventh that resolves in triumphant D major with the entry of the whole orchestra: Music springs to life in ebullient upward-rising gestures.

Indeed Bach enriched almost every genre he touched. The large works that he produced in his later years sum up his life's work and expertise on an unprecedented scale. These include the *Clavier-Übung* (1726–41), a four-part anthology of harpsichord and organ music in an encyclopaedic variety of styles and genres; the *Mass in B Minor*, which features movements ranging from *stile antico* choruses to *galant* arias and duets (these are for the most part revisions of earlier cantata movements); *The Art of the Fugue*, a magisterial set of complex fugal works based on a single subject; and the virtuosic *Goldberg Variations* for two-manual harpsichord. To be sure, there were precedents for similar types of works, but the scope, variety, and the exhaustiveness of musical invention set them apart.

Figure 11.1 Elias Gottlob Haussmann (1695–1774), painting, Johann Sebastian Bach, 1764.

Bach's achievement transpired within the traditional bounds of patronage and the modest career options available to musicians of his generation living in German-speaking lands. Unlike the career of the cosmopolitan Handel, Bach's orbit during his lifetime circumscribed only a small area in central Germany. Bach's music, however, is arguably more cosmopolitan than Handel's in the way that it fused the multifarious national styles. That this was possible also says much about the world in which Bach lived, a smaller world indeed from that of a century earlier, and one in which knowledge of the music and performing styles of the courts and urban centers of Europe was accessible to an untraveled composer in a provincial corner of Germany.

Bach's fusion of national styles can be seen nicely in the opening chorus of the cantata *Jesu, der du meine Seele* (Jesus, by Whom My Soul, BWV 78). The orchestral introduction announces itself immediately as a chaconne in the French style, with four bar phrases that are heard twice, thereby signalling its dance affinity. It is also a lament: The affect is established with the descending chromatic bass (Ex. 11.3).

The chaconne has much in common with the long chaconne from Lully's *Armide* that comes at the end of the second act: Bach and Lully feature sections, all continuous, some choral, some vocal solos and duets, and some purely instrumental. In BWV 78, Bach superimposes a German Lutheran chorale motet on top of the chaconne (Ex. 11.14).

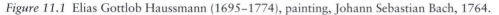

Jesu, der du meine Seele   Jesus, by whom my soul

The whole piece is also organized according to a ritornello structure that connects it to the Italian concerto tradition. The mix of sacred and secular associations gives the whole movement a worldly grandeur: One imagines a whirl of nationalities, social classes, and eras caught up in the dance of time.

Example 11.2 Bach, "Confiteor," *Mass in B Minor*, BWV 232, mm. 119–147.

Bach's Career Path

Johann Sebastian Bach was born on March 21, 1685, in the small town of Eisenach in central Germany, one of some seventy professional musicians from the sixteenth to the end of the eighteenth centuries to hold the name Bach. Johann Sebastian came from a long line of town musicians, organists, and cantors dating back to the early years of the sixteenth century. Many of Bach's ancestors were also fine composers, especially his uncle, Johann Christoph Bach, whom Sebastian referred to as "the profound composer." To be born into so prodigious a musical dynasty would have provided Bach with an advantage in his musical education and in his exposure to appropriate career opportunities. Indeed his future must have seemed ordained, for Bach's career as an organist and composer was traditional in most respects.

Example 11.2 (continued)

As a student, Bach absorbed humanistic and Lutheran influences during his early years at the local Latin School and his two years in Lüneburg (1700–2). In the summer of 1703, Bach was given the opportunity to inspect the organ at the New Church in Arnstadt, which led to his employment as organist there until 1707. Arnstadt had approximately 3,800 residents and was of regional significance as a commercial and industrial town. It was from Arnstadt that Bach made his now famous 250-mile journey on foot to the north-German town of Lübeck in 1705, presumably to hear Dietrich Buxtehude (1637–1707) play the organ. Bach transcribed organ works by both Buxtehude and Hamburg organist Johann Adam Reinken (1643–1722), which are the earliest sources in Bach's hand (Fig. 11.2). These composers were important influences on his organ music, and he heard both composers perform.

Example 11.3 Bach, *Jesu, der du meine Seele*, BWV 78, opening chorus, mm. 1–9.

Bach's next organ post (1707–8) was for the city of Mühlhausen, where he was employed by the town council. He wrote his first published work, Cantata 71, for that city; it was performed for the changing of the town council on February 4, 1708.

Bach stayed only a year in Mühlhausen. His last three posts were to be at more prominent cultural centers in central Germany, where he would assume progressively more musical and administrative responsibilities. From Mühlhausen, Bach accepted a job, again as organist (1708–17), in Weimar, which was the seat of a small duchy led by music-loving rulers under Duke Wilhelm Ernst. When Bach was promoted in 1714 to the post of concert master, he was required to compose his first series of church cantatas. In 1717, Bach left Weimar to take a position as chapel master at the court of Cöthen, another small princely town. His *Brandenburg Concertos* and much of his secular chamber music—composed to suit the taste of Margrave Christian Ludwig—dates from his tenure in Cöthen.

Example 11.4 Bach, *Jesu, der du meine Seele*, BWV 78, opening chorus, mm. 21–25.

Bach spent the final phase of his career in Leipzig, a bustling town of 30,000 inhabitants in the region of Saxony. A commercial hub with a university, Leipzig boasted many more cultural offerings than Bach's prior residences. Bach entered into a protracted set of auditions and negotiations for the position of cantor at St. Thomas Church and civic director of music, in February 1723, and finally signed a contract on May 5 of that year. On that date, Bach set down for the town council a list, in fourteen points, of his principle duties (Document 1). The contract establishes Bach's dual position to serve St. Thomas School and train its choirboys and to organize music for Leipzig's principal churches, while obeying the wishes of the town council. Bach remained affiliated with the prestigious school for the rest of his life; a monument of the composer now stands in the church courtyard (Fig. 11.3).

In addition to his school duties, Bach was expected to compose, copy, rehearse, and perform music for the city's four churches each Sunday. His contract confirms that Lutheranism in Leipzig was conservative

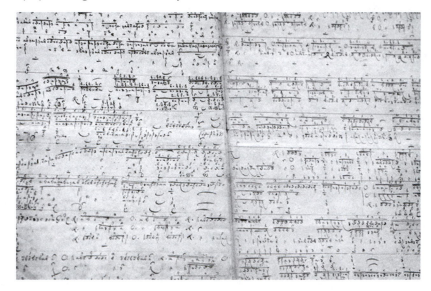

Figure 11.2 Bach, transcriptions of organ works by Buxtehude and Reinken.

Figure 11.3 Leipzig, courtyard of St. Thomas Church with statue of Johann Sebastian Bach.

in its commitment to devotional music, and an admonition against operatic style in the church was a clear manifestation of this. Nonetheless, Bach often defied this provision: The six cycles of sacred cantatas—one for every Sunday and feast day of the church year—that he composed (or revised) during his tenure as music director for the city contain many instances of operatic style.

Bach's written complaints to the town council show his frustration at the lack of influence he felt in matters of artistic decision-making and his resentment at his superiors' apparent lack of appreciation for him. On August 23, 1730, he sent a pointed letter, known as the *Entwurff*, to the Leipzig town council protesting the lack of financial support for musicians. In this "Brief but highly necessary draft for a well-appointed church music," Bach outlined the minimum vocal forces he considered necessary for providing music, presumably in all four churches, on a given Sunday. The document sheds light on the size and quality of Bach's performing resources and on the practicalities of the day:

> Every musical choir should contain at least 3 sopranos, 3 altos, 3 tenors, and as many basses, so that even if one happens to fall ill (as very often happens, particularly at this time of year, as prescriptions written by the school physician for the apothecary must show) at least a double-chorus motet may be sung. N.B. Though it would be still better if the classes were such that one could have 4 singers on each part and thus could perform every chorus with 16 persons.[1]

The situation did not improve. On October 28, Bach sent a letter to Georg Erdmann, an old school friend, in Danzig, Poland (then Germany), advertising (in vain) his musical accomplishments and his availability for employment elsewhere. Disputes continued throughout the 1730s and Bach was even forced to cancel a Passion performance in March 1739. Bach had gradually redirected his creative energy towards more personally satisfying projects—the Collegium Musicum for example, and the great abstract works of his later years—but he was fortunate to have been able to do so. In other respects, Bach's career as organist, church musician, and chapel master was indistinguishable from that of most of his predecessors and contemporaries in German-speaking lands, and his disputes with the Leipzig town council and church authorities underscore how much an artist's autonomy was at the mercy of his employers.

Instrumental Music

Bach worked within the confines of a typical patron-client relationship. Much of what he wrote was determined by where and for whom he worked. A good example is the profusion of cantatas that Bach composed

Table 11.1 Instrumental music, Cöthen period

BWV Number	Title	Genre/Contents	Date
691, 753, 772–801, 824, 836–7, 841–3, 846a, 847/1, 848/1, 849/1, 850/1, 851/1, 853/1, 854/1, 855a, 856/1, 857/1, 924–32, 953, 994	*Clavier Book for Wilhelm Friedemann*	Keyboard Music: 15 praeambula and 15 fantasias, 9 preludes, 11 preludes	1720
1001–6	*6 Partitas and Sonatas for Violin Solo*		1720
573, 728, 812–16 (French suites), 991	*Clavier Book for Anna Magdalena*, Book 1	Keyboard Music: 5 French suites, without prelude; assorted organ works and fragments	1722–5
846–869	*The Well-Tempered Clavier*, Book 1	Keyboard Music: 24 preludes and fugues	1722
772–801	*Upright Introduction* [*Aufrichtige Anleitung*]	Keyboard Music: 15 inventions and 15 sinfonias	*ca.* 1720; revised 1723
1046–51	*Brandenburg Concertos*	Ensemble: six concertos	1721
1007–12	*Cello Suites*	Six suites for solo cello	*ca.* 1720; some composed earlier; autograph missing

between 1723 and 1728 for use in Leipzig churches. Their texts, form, and content address the specific needs and liturgical practices of the Saxon town in which he worked. In the secular realm, Bach's chamber music shows an equally close bond to his employment and patrons. He composed a huge amount of instrumental music during his six years in Cöthen as director of the court orchestra, an appointment that demanded domestic music and teaching (Table 11.1).

Bach as Teacher, Composer, and Performer

Bach's skills as a composer, performer, and teacher developed in tandem over the course of his career. His lifelong interest in fugal counterpoint is a case in point. Bach's immersion in fugal technique began with childhood lessons and continued through his studies, as a young man, of the music of Georg Böhm, Buxtehude, Johann Adam Reinken, and Girolamo Frescobaldi (whose *Fiori musicali* Bach copied in 1714). Fugal writing pervaded his improvisational style in performance, his compositional technique, and his systematic approach to pedagogy. Johann Nikolaus Forkel's famous account of Bach's virtuoso organ playing, included in his biography of the composer, captures how central fugal technique was to Bach's performance style:

> First he made use of the theme in a prelude and fugue, with full organ; then there appeared his art of registration for [in the form of] a trio, quartet etc., still on the same theme; then a chorale followed. . . . Finally the conclusion on full organ was made with a fugue.[2]

Knowing how to play a fugue was also critical for young keyboard students. A revealing account of Bach's teaching method comes from Ernst Ludwig Gerber, whose father, Heinrich Nicolaus, studied with Bach for about two years beginning in November 1724, soon after Bach arrived in Leipzig. Ernst's account of his father's tutelage under Bach remarks upon the gradual progression from simple to more complex contrapuntal works:

> Bach accepted him with particular kindness because he came from Schwarzburg, and always thereafter called him "*Landsmann*" [compatriot]. He promised to give him the instruction he desired and asked at once whether he had industriously played fugues. At the first lesson he set his Inventions before him. When he had studied these through to Bach's satisfaction, there followed a series of suites, then the *Well-Tempered Clavier*. This latter work Bach played altogether three times through for him with his unmatchable art, and my father counted these among his happiest hours, when Bach, under the pretext of not feeling in the mood to teach, sat himself at one of his fine instruments and thus turned these hours into minutes.[3]

A fugal world view lies at the heart of Bach's keyboard collections from the Cöthen period: the *Clavier Book for Wilhelm Friedemann*, the first volume of *The Well-Tempered Clavier*, and the *Upright Introduction* (which includes the Two-Part Inventions and Three-Part Sinfonias). These three works reveal Bach's highly systematic approach to educating amateur keyboard players, including his own children. Written for his eldest son, Bach's *Clavier Book for Wilhelm Friedemann* (1720) opens with a compact review of clefs, pitches, registers of voices, ornamentation, and fingering patterns, before proceeding with preludes, chorale elaborations, stylized dances, fugue and contrapuntal works, three-part fantasias, suites, and short compositions by Wilhelm himself. Intended for novices, the *Upright Introduction* comprises two sets of fifteen contrapuntal pieces that spin out a single short idea, first for two parts, known as inventions, and then for three parts, called sinfonias. Bach frames this practical layout in a structure of ascending keys, creating a parallel between technical development and harmonic progression.

Bach took elements from both volumes to create the first book of *The Well-Tempered Clavier* (1722), drawing from some of the preludes in the *Clavier Book for Wilhelm Friedemann* and from the updated versions of praeambula and fantasias found in the *Upright Introduction*. The volume dates from his application to the post of cantor at St. Thomas's School, and it is likely that Bach used *The Well-Tempered Clavier* to promote his teaching credentials with the Leipzig town council and rector of the St. Thomas School, M. Johann Heinrich Ernesti. The image of Bach as the consummate pedagogue persists to this day. The title page highlights the systematic organization of the collection and its value for young students:

> The Well-Tempered Clavier, or preludes and fugues through all the tones and semitones. . . . For the use and profit of the musical youth desirous of learning as well as for the pastime of those already skilled in this study.[4]

Bach's use of the phrase "well-tempered" in the main title for both volumes of his preludes and fugues signals his participation in ongoing theoretical debates over tuning practices and harmonic relationships among such German theorists as Andreas Werckmeister, Johann Philipp Kirnberger, and Friedrich Wilhelm Marpurg. "Well-tempered" in Bach's day implied a system of tuning that allowed one to play in all twenty-four keys. It did not, however, refer to the system of equal temperament used on today's pianos. Bach's temperament included both pure and impure fifths, and thirds that were slightly sharper than pure thirds (yet generally narrower than an equal tempered third). Such a temperament preserves differences between the keys that would have been even more marked in earlier temperaments (and were often associated with particular affects or moods). In the first book of *The Well-Tempered Clavier*, Bach demonstrates the practicality of a twenty-four chromatic key system, which had previously existed only in theory, and provides a prelude and fugue pair for each of the twenty-four keys. The first prelude spells out its C major key in the clearest fashion in a series of arpeggiated harmonies (Ex. 11.5).

As a set, the variety, contrast, and pedagogical applications of the forty-eight preludes and fugues appeal to Baroque ideals on several levels. The fugue themes in the two volumes of the *Well-Tempered Clavier* vary widely in style and length, and are ideal for learning through pattern and example. There are extremely short subjects, such as that of Fugue no. 4, WTC I, in *stile antico* (Example 11.6a); chromatic subjects as in Fugue no. 6, WTC II (Example 11.6b); subjects with repeated notes that make the subject entries particularly easy to hear, as in Fugue no. 16, WTC II (Example 11.6c); subjects that express joyful affects, like the sprightly giga in Fugue no. 11, WTC II (Example 11.6d); subjects full of pathos, as in Fugue no. 24, WTC I (Example 11.6e); and even a fugue that mimics the gestures of a French overture, as in Fugue no. 5, WTC I (Example 11.6f). The variety of subjects demand a variety of treatments, and, as in any other movement in the Baroque era, the performer's first task is to discover the affect of the piece from the information provided in the music: meter signature, rhythmic profile, key, types of figures, degree of dissonance, and any references to dances or other genres.

The contrapuntal treatment of Bach's fugues ranges in complexity as well, from simple fugues in three voices with substantial episodes to complex double fugues in five voices. The preludes are even more diverse, exploiting multifarious meters and stylistic categories (whether aria, dance, concerto, trio sonata, or toccata), while the juxtaposition of improvisatory preludes with highly structured fugues provides maximum

Example 11.5 Bach, *Prelude no. 1 in C Major*, BWV 846/1, mm. 1–4.

Examples 11.6a–f Fugue subjects from J.S. Bach's *Well-Tempered Clavier*.

(11.a)

(11.b)

(11.c)

(11.d)

(11.e)

(11.f)

contrast. A representative example is the *Prelude and Fugue no. 21 in B-flat Major* (BWV 866). The prelude opens with a compact sequential melody in the left hand, accompanied in the right with an energetic three-note figure that completes the triad on each note in the bass (Ex. 11.7).

Cascading scalar passages contribute to the overall improvisatory feel of the prelude, which contrasts with the learned style of the fugue. These passages suggest a rhythmically flexible performance, common to improvised keyboard preludes, and described as early as Frescobaldi in his preface to *Fiori Musicale*. They occur sporadically in the preludes, and even occasionally at the end of the fugues as lead-ups to or elaborations on the final cadence. To play them in strict time would be to dilute their rhetorical function.

The fugue that follows is in many respects a textbook fugue. The easily recognizable subject (A) moves across the parts in a predictable way, in company with two countersubjects (B and C) and alternating with two episodes (those sections in which the subject does not appear) that modulate to related keys (Ex. 11.8). The exposition takes up the first sixteen measures; the first episode (mm. 17–26) modulates to the relative G minor; the second episode (mm. 30–37) moves to the submediant E-flat; and each episode is followed by subject entries in the new key. But what makes this fugue interesting is not the road map of subject entries and episodes but the implications of the subject itself and how Bach follows these through. Bach viewed his fugue subjects as challenges, as inventions with qualities to be revealed and potential to be realized, and with this in mind, the exposition alone tells us a great deal of Bach's compositional process. While the straightforward subject is typical of Bach's fugue subjects, closer inspection shows us a number of interesting features not the least of which is the implied counterpoint in its melody. The first four eighth notes of the subject, for instance, seem to be answered by the last two, and a similar gesture is made in the next measure. Also, the four-bar subject is symmetrical, and the last measure is essentially a repeat of the measure that precedes it. This has implications for the first of the two countersubjects, since countersubject one (B) reiterates the same pitch (the dominant) for most of its third measure, then does it again. The second countersubject (C) repeats in the same fashion. We hear all three voices, repeating themselves together in mm. 11–12.

The opening subject is also versatile: This is especially obvious when it enters, in the bass, at m. 9, where it feels very much like a standard, left hand bass line. The subject is not particularly forceful in stating the tonic: One could imagine F major (V) as the tonic at first; and the subject tails off with only a cadence on the dominant, F major, on the first beat of m. 9. This too contributes to its affect. Oddly, the tonal answer is where the tonic B-flat major triad is first outlined melodically; exploiting that, Bach lets us hear the tonal answer again in the soprano towards the end of the exposition (m. 13). Bach fools the listener, who expects to hear it as a fourth entry, as if there were four voices in this fugue when in fact there are only three; but it cements the B-flat with the tonic triad at the very moment it is heading into the dominant. Significantly, after the first episode (beginning m. 17) modulates to G minor, the first entry of the subject in the new key outlines the G minor triad as a tonal answer, a clear acknowledgement that the subject proper is ineffectual in declaring the key.

In typical fashion, the episodes exploit motives derived from the subject and countersubjects, which are used in sequence to move to or through other key areas. For instance, the first episode inverts the subject (m. 19) and repeats it in a descending sequence; the countersubjects follow in tandem; and together they effect a modulation to the relative minor, which is confirmed in m. 26.

Example 11.7 Bach, *Prelude no. 21 in B-flat Major*, BWV 866, mm. 1–3.

Example 11.8 Bach, *Fugue no. 21 in B-flat Major*, BWV 866, mm. 1–26.

The subject's non-committal quality relative to the tonic is integral to the key plan of the whole fugue, which spends much more time in the dominant and related keys (G minor and E-flat major) than it does in the tonic; even the confirmation of the home key at the end is brief—only seven measures (Ex. 11.9). It is in these last measures that Bach capitalizes on the repeated notes of his primary countersubject, first with repeated B flats (functioning as V/E flat major, mm. 39–40, tenor), then, drawing out the approach to the final cadence, with repeated Fs, in the soprano voice (mm. 43–44), and again in the bass (mm. 45–46). The opening gesture of the subject also makes a final appearance in the bass voice in the penultimate measure, but in a much more forceful version, as if it had suddenly come into its own. It is still recognizable, but octave Fs replace the original descending sixth, and it now makes a strong authentic cadence.

Example 11.9 Bach, *Fugue no. 21 in B-flat Major*, BWV 866, mm. 39–48.

There are dozens of recordings of Bach's *Well-Tempered Clavier*, and the variety in interpretations reflects a broader debate on how to perform Baroque music. The debate is polarized between those who wish to approximate a historical interpretation and those who prefer to approach the works entirely from a modern perspective. The former would advocate playing on replicas of early instruments and getting as close as possible to the tempos and stylistic niceties described in seventeenth- and eighteenth-century writings. The underlying premise of historically informed performance (abbreviated HIP) is that it will ultimately allow the music to speak most effectively. Those who approach Bach's music through a modern lens, however, would give the performer more creative autonomy, even if there is no indication that the composer would have sanctioned their choices. They are likely to consider the modern piano an acceptable substitute for harpsichord (or even an improvement upon it), and they would not hesitate to add pedalling, slurs, and dynamics if they felt these enhanced the original music and perhaps made its expressive potential more accessible to modern taste. The contrasting views are exemplified in recordings of Bach's Fugue no. 21 by Martin Gallin on harpsichord and by Glenn Gould, who was known for taking considerable subjective license in Bach, on piano.

Sacred Music

Lutheran music around 1700 comprised a wide range of repertory of sacred music for court chapels, town churches, and Latin schools, much of it geared directly towards congregational participation and the singing of simple chorales. Luther's vision had embraced more complicated forms of music-making too, however, and this provided ample opportunities for professional singers, who performed sacred showpieces at central moments in the liturgy. As well, organists were required to provide the musical glue for the Lutheran service. Bach's responsibilities as an organist accord with the general qualifications outlined in Andreas Werckmeister's influential *Harmonologia musica* (1702): musicianship, the ability to improvise a fugue on a given subject, to vary a chorale, to transpose a chorale, to read figured bass and tablature, and to care for the organ.

Bach's most significant contributions to sacred music came during his Leipzig years, when he composed the majority of some three hundred church cantatas, two Passions based on the Gospels of John and

Matthew, an elaborate Christmas Oratorio, a *Magnificat* setting, and the monumental *Mass in B Minor* (although the latter for the most part reworked existing pieces). His reputation as the supreme Lutheran cantor rests largely on these works, which also influenced the nineteenth-century image of Bach as "The Fifth Evangelist." If the twentieth century was less eager to view Bach in such a hagiographic light, the pendulum has swung back again. Recent scholarship affirms that the notes in Bach's handwriting in the margins of his personal Bible (and in his collection of sermons, Bible commentaries, and writings by Martin Luther) present persuasive evidence that Bach was deeply committed to the Lutheran faith.

How did Bach's music reflect his own beliefs and inspire devotion among listeners? Here it is important to consider Bach's music relative to broader religious debates in the Lutheran church during the seventeenth and early eighteenth centuries. The two issues most relevant to Bach were the role and value of music in worship, and the idea of personal faith, or the individual's direct relationship with God.

The writings of Martin Luther, as we read in Chapter 4, affirm the reformer's belief that music was a gift of God, one perfectly suited to moving the emotions of listeners and inspiring their devotion. The theological debate in the seventeenth century centered on the issue of personal faith. The period of Lutheran Orthodoxy that followed the hundredth anniversary of Luther's 95 theses led to attacks on church hierarchy and claims that it placed too much emphasis on the Book of Concord (1580) and not enough on personal faith. A spiritual reform movement emerged within the Lutheran Church; the movement was known as Pietism, after the influential treatise *Pious Desires* (Pia desideria, 1675) by Jacob Spener. Spener, and other reformers such as Johann Arndt, felt that direct experience was the key to union with God or Christ. To this end, they promoted the private devotional reading of mystical literature and gatherings outside the Church to read and study the Bible.

Music played a major part in the controversy between Orthodox Lutherans and reformers. Orthodox Lutherans viewed elaborate music as an offering to God and a powerful and invaluable means of communicating the meaning of the text. Reformers believed that musical forms and styles should be kept simple, serious, and easy to understand by the congregation, and they therefore favored simpler spiritual songs for the church and home. Theophil Grossgebauer's complaint, in 1661, of the excesses of music in the church is typical of the Reform position:

> Many would like to pray, but are so occupied with and bewildered by the howling and din that they cannot . . . so if an unbeliever were to come into our assembly would he not say we were putting on a spectacle and were to some extent crazy?[5]

The divide only intensified with the popularity of styles derived from Italian opera, which was automatically associated with the secular world. The church cantata, a genre in which composers were known to experiment with newer, operatic styles of writing, was most likely to display what were considered by many to be musical extravagances.

The Church Cantata in Leipzig

The cantata was the main musical work for the *Hauptgottesdienst* (high service) every Sunday and holiday of the year at Leipzig's two main churches: St. Nicholas and St. Thomas. According to Bach's own observation of the First Sunday of Advent in 1714, the entire service often lasted four hours, and the cantata was positioned after the prelude that followed the reading of the gospel. Each cantata was performed twice: once in the morning at the church of St. Thomas and again in the afternoon Vespers service at St. Nicholas Church (or vice versa). Between 1723 and 1727 Bach produced sacred cantatas on a regular basis, writing new works and revising existing ones.

Comprised of a series of sections that contrasted in both emotional content and imagery, the cantata was a musical counterpart to the sermon. Both exploited rhetorical principles, employing specific styles of composition and delivery to arouse an emotional response from the listener. Cantor and music director

Georg Motz of Tilsit, East Prussia, who incorporated operatic elements in his music in order to portray the affections of sacred texts, essentially defends that practice below:

> Thus, righteous composers, using all their qualities for expressing every word of a text artistically in a religious composition, show sufficiently that they are not concerned only about sweetness, but also about religious matters as true Christians. And therefore a well-worded piece of church music consists not only of a melodious exterior, but even more of true holy devotion and meditation.[6]

The musical style of cantatas was closely bound to the type of texts that were set, and these underwent significant changes during Bach's lifetime. While more dramatic styles of text—often in dialogue form—were popular after 1700, cantata texts from the late seventeenth century were often a mixture of biblical quotations, chorale texts, and free verses. The sectional format of the cantatas accommodated a great deal of variety, and the type of text influenced the choice of musical style. Free texts (those not bound to a textual source) offered the most flexibility and might be set as either recitative or aria, the latter using dance meters or ritornello techniques, and scored as vocal solos or duets. Chorale verses suggested contrapuntal settings and were set for chorus (implying the entire vocal ensemble, regardless of the number of voices per part).

German poet and theologian Erdmann Neumeister (1671–1756) occupies a central position in the development of the cantata text. Between 1695 and 1742 Neumeister completed nine cycles of cantata texts for all Sundays of the church year. These mixed biblical verses with madrigalesque poetry that was suitable for recitatives and arias. This earlier type of hybrid text, used for Sunday service, he called an *oratorio*.

In 1700 Neumeister experimented with a new type of cantata text. His *Geistliche Cantaten statt einer Kirchen-Musik* (Sacred Cantatas Instead of Church Music) abandons biblical quotations and chorales in favor of free poetry that alternates recitatives and arias. Neumeister likened his "cantatas" to "a piece out of an opera," a direct appeal to the craze for opera at the courts of Weissenfels and Naumburg in central Germany and in the towns of Hamburg and Leipzig. Indeed the metaphorical language of opera was easily adapted to sacred topics by substituting religious devotion for secular love. In the preface, Neumeister advised that an aria, akin to its function on the operatic stage, ought to present a single affect or primary expression; each successive aria, and its accompanying recitative, was designed to move the reader or listener through a progression of emotional states, from fear to acceptance, say, or from a state of sin to grace.

Neumeister provided a model for the standardization of Protestant sacred cantata texts. Building on his example, German poets Salomo Franck and Georg Christian Lehms wrote cycles of cantata texts in the hybrid form that mixed chorales and biblical quotations with free poetry for recitatives and arias. Neumeister's model was taken up by composers at the Saxon and Thuringian courts, where interest in opera was on the rise. From his Weimar period on, Bach used this type of text, either by Neumeister himself (only five have been authenticated) or by poets inspired by Neumeister's models.

Neumeister's cantatas reignited debates among German theologians and theorists over the role of music in the Lutheran church. Joachim Meyer, a cantor and academic in Göttingen, complained that the fast-moving lines of operatic style rendered the words unintelligible. Closer to home, Johann Kuhnau (1660–1722), Bach's immediate predecessor as cantor at the St. Thomas School in Leipzig, actively avoided "the madrigalian style [of poetry] that pertains to arias and recitatives," despite having proposed, in his "Treatise on Liturgical Text Settings" (1709), that music's two aims were to interpret the sacred words and to delight and move the spirit of the listener.[7] Bach's contract of 1723, we remember, had specifically warned against writing in operatic style: "In order to preserve the good order in the Churches, so arrange the music that it shall not last too long, and shall be of such a nature as not to make an operatic impression, but rather incite the listeners to devotion" (Document 1).

Yet operatic style also had its supporters. Theologian and poet Gottfried Ephraim Scheibel valued good poetry and good music, and promoted the union of poetry and music in the church as a logical extension of those values. Writing in 1721, Scheibel defends the suitability of operatic style for moving the emotions of worshipers when he writes:

The tone that gives me pleasure in an opera can also do the same in church, except that it has a different object. . . . I still think, however, that if our church music today were a little livelier and freer, that it to say, more theatrical, it would be more beneficial than the stilted compositions that are ordinarily used in churches. . . . I do not know what operas alone should have the privilege of squeezing tears from us; why is that not true in the church? (Document 3a)

For Scheibel, the spiritual ends justified the musical means.

The debate was taken to the highest level of literary circles by Bach's contemporary, Johann Mattheson, arguably the most influential German music critic of the first half of the eighteenth century. Writing in *Der musicalische Patriot* (The Musical Patriot, 1728), Mattheson argues that:

In church . . . I have precisely the same idea about music as in the opera, that is to say: I want to stir the listener's mind. . . . Especially here, during worship, intense, serious, long-lasting, and extremely profound emotions are needed.[8]

Bach's cantata *Wachet auf, ruft uns die Stimme* (Wake Up! Call the Voices, BWV 140) can be interpreted as the composer's musical response to the debate.

Wachet auf, ruft uns die Stimme (BWV 140)

Wachet auf was recognized early on by Bach enthusiasts and scholars as exceptional, for although the work is based on a chorale melody, it allows for considerable variation and freedom of expression in those movements that depart from the chorale text. We can pinpoint the first performance of the cantata to November 25, 1731, for the twenty-seventh Sunday after Trinity. Its position on the church calendar was dependent upon the date of Easter: There were only two possible dates for its performance during Bach's time in Leipzig: in 1731 and 1742—both years when Easter fell before March 27. *Wachet auf* is based on an anonymous libretto that builds on two interrelated biblical texts: Thessalonians 5:1–11, a plea to be ready for the Second Coming of Jesus, and Matthew 25:1–13, the parable of the ten virgins waiting for the bridegroom, here a stand-in for Jesus. The poet added references to the Song of Songs and Revelations, both sources of imagery rich in musical potential.

Musically, Bach's *Wachet auf* is exemplary in marrying contemporary musical style with the Lutheran chorale tradition. The cantata comprises seven movements: an opening chorale, recitative, aria duet, chorale, bass recitative, aria duet for soprano and bass, and chorale finale. Three chorale movements (movements 1, 4, 7) mark the beginning, middle, and end of the cantata; interspersed are recitatives and duets for Christ and his bride. Each movement is further differentiated by its unusual scoring—Bach's instrumental resources include two oboes, an oboe da caccia, violino piccolo, and a cornetto to double the chorale melody in the soprano voice, in addition to strings and continuo.

The chorale movements call for full chorus; the intervening arias and recitatives featured solo singers and instruments. We should note here that current (albeit still controversial) scholarship suggests that in Bach's day even choral movements probably required only one (male) voice per part. Instrumentalists out-numbered the singers: Bach's letter to the Leipzig town council of 1730 specified a total of at least eighteen instrumentalists, plus organ, for accompanying the cantatas. This group typically comprised a string body of eleven, and at least seven other instruments, including trumpets, woodwinds, and timpani as required. An ensemble of this size is essentially still chamber music, and in marked contrast to the massive choral and orchestral forces that a long tradition of performing and recording Bach's cantatas has made familiar to listeners. It is possible that Bach directed from the harpsichord while playing continuo; or he may have beat time or "conducted" in the modern sense. The range of approaches to performing this work reflect the performance history of much choral music of the Baroque period, and can be heard in recordings by the Mormon Tabernacle Choir, with its massive choral and instrumental forces, and Joshua Rifkin's The Bach Ensemble, with its trimmed down, one-singer-to-a-part aesthetic.

The opening chorale fantasia shows off Bach's contrapuntal technique at its finest. The text tells the parable of the ten virgins who await the bridegroom: Five have brought oil for their lamps and are ready to meet him, while the others have let their lamps go out. It's an apt metaphor, clearly illustrating the lesson that one must be ready for the kingdom of heaven and the coming of Jesus Christ.

Bach establishes an energetic mood at the start with an exchange—between two different instrumental groups—of a series of dotted rhythms that function formally as a rudimentary ritornello (Ex. 11.10).

These dotted rhythms also add momentum to a movement that has many affinities with the first movement of a concerto (note the vigorous running bass, melodic sequences, motor rhythms, and the presence of the ritornello itself). The instrumental activity is, however, but one contrapuntal layer of the movement. Superimposed on it is a vocal fantasia for four voices: the soprano voice carries the cantus firmus of the chorale tune; the other three voices engage in imitative counterpoint with their own material.

Bach positions the chorale—a well-known, three-verse melody by Philipp Nicolai (1599)—in augmented or prolonged note values in the soprano, doubling the melody with cornetto (or possibly horn) (Ex. 11.11).

Wachet auf, ruft uns die Stimme	Wake up! call the voices

The text of the opening movement, which contrasts the virgins who are awake and ready with those who are not, is represented by various dichotomies in the music: the two instrumental groups in alternation, one with oboes, one with strings; the chorale tune versus the vocal counterpoint; the traditional vocal counterpoint versus the up-to-date concerto style. This is a prime example of Bach's attention to musical symbolism. His music operates within a network of associations. Some of Bach's techniques, such as the opposing instrumental groupings in the opening chorale, "Wachet auf," are more abstract and subtle. Yet Bach has further established the *affect* with a recurring motive in the instrumental parts of two sixteenths plus and eighth—an urgent, energetic figure; and with short, two note ascending intervals (leaping up a fourth, fifth, even a seventh) in the vocal lines, a prime example of word painting to mimic the text "Wake up!" (Wach auf!) and "steht auf" (stand up) (Ex. 11.12).

Wohl auf, der Bräutgam kömmt;	Arise-then, the bridegroom is coming;
Steht auf, die Lampen nehmt!	Get up, take your lamps!

Bach balances the section's rich motivic texture with simple tonic and dominant harmonies.

The final "Alleluia" of praise is given more complex harmonic treatment in the relative key of C minor (Ex. 11.13); greater harmonic freedom is made possible by the absence of the chorale melody which largely dictates its harmonic underpinning. The dense, busy counterpoint reminds us of Scheibe's complaint that Bach "demands that singers and instrumentalists perform with their throats and instruments exactly what he is able to play on the keyboard." Yet, as Birnbaum retorts, "it is certain that the voices in pieces by this great master of music interact marvelously together, all without the least confusion" (Document 3b).

Example 11.10 Bach, *Wachet auf*, BWV 140, opening chorus, mm. 1–5, rhythm only.

Example 11.11 Bach, *Wachet auf*, BWV 140, opening chorus, chorale melody, mm. 17–26, soprano line.

Example 11.12 Bach, *Wachet auf*, BWV 140, opening chorus, mm. 117–134.

Example 11.12 (continued)

Example 11.12 (continued)

Example 11.12 (continued)

Example 11.12 (continued)

Example 11.13 Bach, *Wachet auf*, BWV 140, opening chorus, mm. 135–156.

Example 11.13 (continued)

Example 11.13 (continued)

Example 11.13 (continued)

Example 11.13 (continued)

The second movement, "Er kommt" (He Comes, (Ex. 11.14)), gives us a glimpse of Bach's recitative writing. Though Bach did not compose operas—arguably, he had little occasion to do so—a dramatic impetus consistently underlies his sacred music. This short recitative passage for solo tenor with continuo (a style known as *secco* or "dry" recitative) is indistinguishable from an operatic recitative in the way it expresses the text. Bach immediately establishes an aura of anticipation: the C pedal in the bass suggests the long wait for the bridegroom, while the shifting harmonies above it convey the imminence of his arrival. Bach uses word painting to depict Heaven, or the "heights" (with an ascent to a high note and a surprise move to the secondary dominant harmony of G minor). Similarly, as the bridegroom "leaps . . . like a young buck," the harmony springs from G minor to E-flat major; and "Wake up! and "rouse yourselves" are both rising melodic gestures, the latter in quicker note values. The recitative's disjunct melody, the irregular, speech-like rhythms punctuated by rests, and the restless harmonic progression give this recitative an edgy energy that effectively sets the stage for the aria that follows.

Er kommt, er kommt	He comes, he comes,[9]
Der Bräutgam kommt!	The bridegroom comes!
Ihr Töchters Zions, kommt heraus,	You daughters of Zion, come forth,
sein Ausgang eilet aus der Höhe	He hastens from the heights
in euer Mutter Haus.	Into your mother's house.
Der Bräutgam kommt, der einem Rehe	The bridegroom comes, who leaps like a roe
und jungen Hirsche	And young buck
gleich auf Deinen Hügeln springt,	Upon the hills
und euch das Mahl der Hochzeit bringt.	And brings you the wedding banquet.
Wacht auf, ermuntert auf!	Wake up, rouse yourselves!
Der Bräutgam zu empfangen;	So you can receive the bridegroom!
dort sehet, kommt er hergegangen.	There, lo, he comes approaching.

Bach gets closest to an operatic aesthetic in the two duets for soprano and bass, no. 3, "Wann kommst du, mein Heil?" (When Comest Thou, My Salvation?, (Ex. 11.15)) and no. 6, "Mein Freund ist mein" (My Friend Is Mine, (Ex. 11.16)). The mood is dramatically different in these movements where

Example 11.14 Bach, *Wachet auf*, BWV 140, "Er kommt," mm. 1–13.

earthly love stands as a metaphor for the heavenly union of Christ and the Soul. Interpreted in this way, the text "Wann kommst du, mein Heil?" is full of erotic symbolism, for the bride and groom represent Christ and the Church. The mood is set by the instrumental introduction for violin and *basso* continuo, a siciliano in a gentle rocking rhythm, around which the violin weaves expressive ornamental lines.

Wann kommst du, mein Heil	When comest thou, my Salvation?

Bach repeats the opening question, "wann kommst du," to imply a sense of urgency and pits the singers against each other in question and answer dialogue.

Wann kommst du, mein Heil	When are you coming my salvation?
Ich komme mein Teil	I come, your part

Bach specifies a violin *piccolo*, in this case an instrument with strings tuned a minor third higher than a standard violin (B-flat, F, c2, and g2), probably in order to facilitate playing such an active chromatic melody line in a high range; the choice enhances the arabesques that weave sinuously around the vocal lines. Note that the singers do not sing the same music in unison or together in thirds at any time, a standard means of conveying an amorous connection: that is yet to come, in the duet discussed below.

The text for "Mein Freund ist mein" (My Friend Is Mine) was cobbled together from four separate sources—the Song of Songs, Romans 8:35–9, Revelations 7:17, and Psalm 16:11—all of which contain

Example 11.15 Bach, *Wachet auf*, BWV 140, "Wann kommst du mein Heil," mm. 1–8.

Example 11.16 Bach, *Wachet auf*, BWV 140, "Wann kommst du mein Heil," mm. 8–14.

Example 11.17 Bach, *Wachet auf*, BWV 140, "Mein Freund ist mein," mm. 1–9, oboe solo.

erotic or amorous imagery that functions as a metaphor for divine love. The movement is a joyous one: the major key, rising lines, absence of dissonance, and the slurred (ascending) pairs that the voices harmonize together in parallel thirds and sixths in typical love-duet fashion, all point us to that affect. The da capo form (ABA) opens with a short obbligato oboe solo that introduces the melodic material for the singers (Ex. 11.17), and it is perhaps meaningful that the obbligato instrument shares that material with the singers, rather than providing an opposing counterpart.

Bach casts the oboe on equal footing with the singers: they share the same musical material and expressive dimension (Ex. 11.18). In typical love duet fashion, the singers respond antiphonally with ardent expressions ("Thy love is mine," "And I am thine!") before launching into a homophonic texture of harmonized thirds and sixths to a shared text.

Mein Freund ist mein!	My friend is mine!
Und ich bin dein!	And I am yours!
Die Liebe soll nichte scheiden, nichts scheiden	Nothing shall divide our love.

The final movement returns us to the chorus and chorale melody for "Gloria sei die gesungen." Bach sets the chorale's last verse in four-part harmonization, a fitting texture for the joyous foretaste of heaven (Ex. 11.19).

Gloria sei dir gesungen	Gloria be to thee sung[10]
Mit Menschen- und englischen Zungen,	With human and angelic tongues,
Mit Harfen und mit Zimbeln schon.	With harps and with cymbals (sweet).
Von zwölf Perlen sind die Pforten,	Of twelve pearls are the portals,
An deiner Stadt sind wir Konsorten	In thy city are we consorts
Der Engel hoch um deinen Thron.	Of angels high around thy throne.

Example 11.18 Bach, *Wachet auf*, BWV 140, "Mein Freund ist mein," mm. 8–27.

Example 11.18 (continued)

Example 11.19 Bach, *Wachet auf*, BWV 140, "Gloria sei dir gesungen," mm. 1–16.

After Bach

Johann Sebastian Bach is now regarded as one of the greatest composers in the European tradition, but it was not always so. After Bach's death, the aesthetic goals of elaboration, variety, and decoration—already in decline in the last decades of his life—fell out of fashion, to be replaced by taste for a more natural simplicity, as articulated by Jean-Jacques Rousseau. Musical style changed drastically after 1750, as French ideals of simplicity and clarity swept across the Continent in opera, symphony, and chamber music. The sharp shift in musical style associated with the Pre-Classical period charted an entirely different path from Bach's, one that did not go unobserved by contemporary critics. Writing in 1737, the music critic Johann Adolph Scheibe had already condemned Bach's music for its "turgid and confused style" and for an "excess of art" that "conflicted with Nature" (Document 3a). Scheibe's critique of Bach could stand as a critique of the entire Baroque period. Two years later Johann Abraham Birnbaum responded with a defense of Bach that argued that the composer applied artistry to the service of naturalness:

> Moreover, it is certain that the voices in pieces by this great master of music interact marvelously together, all without the least confusion. They proceed together and against each other, each in its proper place. They separate and reunite at the proper time. Each voice is distinguished by some specific variation, even though they often imitate each other. (Document 3b)

Birnbaum adheres to the contemporary standard of rational order to defend Bach.

Bach's reputation after his death was limited to German-speaking lands, particularly the southeastern regions of Saxony and Thuringia, where he grew up and spent most of his career. Bach's close contemporary George Frideric Handel was both more famous and more cosmopolitan—witness his early years in Italy and his long tenure in London. Handel also composed operas—a fashionable and prestigious genre—which Bach did not. What fame Bach had he owed to his extraordinary skills as an organist (Fig. 11.4). Thus it was for his organ playing that the flutist and theorist Johann Joachim Quantz praised Bach shortly after his death (1752):

> Finally the admirable Johann Sebastian Bach brought it [organ playing] to its greatest perfection in recent times. We can only hope that now, after his death, owing to the small number of those who still devote sufficient industry to it, it will not again fall into decline or even decay.[11]

As a composer, Bach was soon forgotten. Only a handful of his musical works—including the *Clavier-Übung* and *The Art of the Fugue*—were published during his lifetime, and this only added to the void upon Bach's death. Outside the circle of his students and offspring, most of the musical world after 1750 was unaware of his music.

The Bach Revival

Bach's music had lain in obscurity for decades when the Romantic cult of the past provided optimal conditions for its rediscovery. The Bach revival of the nineteenth century was launched by Johann Nikolaus Forkel (1749–1818), organist and music director at Göttingen University, who paved the way for future scholarship on the composer by publishing the first extended biography of Bach in 1802. Forkel interviewed Bach's two eldest sons, Wilhelm Friedrich (1710–84) and Carl Philipp Emanuel (1714–88), who offered biased accounts of their father's greatness. The pivotal event in the revival of Bach's music was Felix Mendelssohn's performance of the *St. Matthew Passion* in Berlin on March 11, 1829, after two years of rehearsals. This monumental performance—the choir comprised over 150 voices—set the tone for the reception of Bach's sacred music, and for the idealization of the composer as a genius of Protestant Germany's past.

Bach's music reached a wide community of performers, scholars, and the public through the efforts of the Bach Gesellschaft (Bach Society), a group founded in 1850 to mark the hundredth anniversary of the composer's death. The Bach Gesellschaft had as its mission the publication of Bach's complete works. Their

Figure 11.4 Bach playing the organ at the St. Thomas School, Leipzig.

volumes often appeared with an engraving of Bach based on Haussmann's portrait (Fig. 11.1), thereby creating an iconic image of the composer. The first edition of Bach's collected works appeared in 1900. The series made available for the first time all of Bach's music, in one unified edition, prepared under strict editorial guidelines by top scholars in the field of Bach studies. In 1950 German musicologist Wolfgang Schmieder assigned each piece a catalogue number (this is referred to as the BWV number, from the German, Bach-Werke-Verzeichnis) to indicate its placement in the thematic catalogue of Bach's works. Grouped by genre (rather than chronology), BWV numbers remain the standard system for numbering and identifying Bach's works.

Bach's posthumous fame escalated yet again in the second half of the nineteenth century with Philipp Spitta's massive biography of Bach (two volumes, 1873 and 1880). Published in an era of intense German nationalism, Spitta effectively elevated the composer to the status of national hero. New engravings of the composer appeared that idolized Bach's teaching and organ playing, as the master sits surrounded by adoring students and singers.

Bach's remains were even exhumed from burial (in a minor parish) and his brain was examined for signs of "genius." No matter that philosopher Friedrich Nietzsche attacked such monumentalization of Bach as a "mythical fiction" that obscured a true understanding of both past and present: Bach's pedestal was there to stay. Bach now lies at the high alter of St. Thomas Church in Leipzig, a fitting tribute to the composer's decades of service to the city.

Documents

Document 1. Johann Sebastian Bach to the Leipzig Town Council, Leipzig, May 5, 1723. "Bach's Final Undertakings." In *The Bach Reader: A Life of Johann Sebastian Bach in Letters and Documents*. Ed. Hans T. David and Arthur Mendel. New York: Norton, 1945. pp. 91–2.

1. That I shall set the boys a shining example of an honest, retiring manner of life, serve the School industriously, and instruct the boys conscientiously;
2. Bring the music in both the principal Churches of this town into good estate, to the best of my ability;
3. Show to the Honorable and Most Wise Council all proper respect and obedience . . .
4. Give due obedience to the Honorable Inspectors and Directors of the School in each and every instruction . . .
5. Not take any boys into the School who have not already laid a foundation in music, or are not at least suited to being instructed therein . . .
6. . . . faithfully instruct the boys not only in vocal but also in instrumental music;
7. . . . arrange the [church] music that it shall not last too long, and shall be of such a nature as not to make an operatic impression, but rather incite the listeners to devotion;
8. Provide the New Church with good scholars;
9. Treat the boys in a friendly manner and with caution, but in case they do not wish to obey, chastise them with moderation or report them to the proper place;
10. Faithfully attend to the instruction in the School and whatever else it befits me to do;
11. And if I cannot undertake this myself, arrange that it be done by some other capable person . . .
12. Not go out of town without the permission of the Honorable Burgomaster currently in office;
13. Always so far as possible walk with the boys at funerals, as is customary;
14. And shall not accept or wish to accept any office in the University without the consent of the Honorable and Learned Council;

Document 2. Gottfried Ephraim Scheibel. "That Church Music, in Comparison with Secular Music, Has Nothing Peculiar to It for Moving the Affections." Chapter 5 from "Random Thoughts about Church Music in Our Day (1721)." Trans. Joyce Irwin. In *Bach's Changing World: Voices in the Community*. Ed. Carol K. Baron. Rochester, NY: University of Rochester Press, 2006. pp. 238–41 (excerpts). Reproduced with permission of UNIVERSITY OF ROCHESTER PRESS in the format Republish in a book via Copyright Clearance Center.

1. My purpose in this chapter is to show that religious and secular music have no distinctions, as far as the movement of the affections is concerned, and therefore a composer must make use of the same kinds of modes for these. It is a common opinion that the two sorts of music must be different, and the best musicians and composers have affirmed this and have believed that church music must indeed look different from secular music, that one must not make the cadenzas so free, and other such matters. It always seems to me as if they themselves did not know what the movement of the affections is even though they are trying to move them.
2. I would grant them this opinion if they knew how to give me the divisions of joy, sadness, and other affections that they make in their brains perhaps without a basis. It remains one affection, only that the objects vary, that, for example, here a spiritual pain, there a worldly pain is felt, that here a spiritual, there a worldly good is missed, and so forth. Just as I can be saddened concerning worldly things, so I can be saddened about spiritual things; just as I can rejoice about these, so I can rejoice about those. The tone that gives me pleasure in an opera can also do the same in church, except that it has a different object.

3. I do not know what objection one will raise against this. I take a secular composition from a cantata, make a parody on it from religious material, and express precisely the affection which the composition brings with it. Then precisely this affection will be moved just as well as when it was directed toward a secular object, and for that reason it will not lose its power. . . . I will present one more aria from the opera "Artaxeris," which was translated from Italian and composed by Monsieur Vogler in Leipzig.

Oeffnet euch / ihr schönen Augen /   Open up, you lovely eyes,
Lasset euren Wunder Schein   Let your magic appearance
Meiner Seelen Pharus seyn   Be the lighthouse of my soul.
Haltet die beflammten Blicke   Keep the emblazoned looks
Länger nicht von mir zurücke   No longer back from me,
Denn ihr Glantz hemmt meine Pein.   For their shine checks my pain.
Da Capo

Could not a believing soul on the occasion of the unbelieving Thomas have the following thoughts, which would remain the same affect in the music:

Oeffnet euch ihr Glaubens-Augen   Open up your eyes of faith,
Lasset Jesu Friedens-Schein   Let Jesus' peace appearance
Eurer Hoffnung Pharus seyn   Be the lighthouse of your hope.
Haltet die beflammten Blicke   Keep the emblazoned looks
Von der Lust der Welt zurücke   Back from desire of the world
Denn ihr Ansehn bringt nur Pein.   For their sight brings only pain.
Da Capo

[. . .]

6. I do not know why operas alone should have the privilege of squeezing tears from us; why is that not true in the church? No, choral works have to be performed there where one hears counterpoint and whatever else that serves better for an organist playing a prelude than for edifying the listener. It is often said: this or that composer can set a good church piece, but he is not so successful in other matters. I turn it around: if a composer can move the affections in theatrical and secular music, he will be able to do this in spiritual matters, as witness the examples of Messieurs Keiser, Mattheson, and Telemann. Admittedly the lack of apt texts is also to blame, but of that at the end.

7. I gladly grant that minuets, jigs, gavottes, passepieds, and so on, are not appropriate in church because they induce idle thoughts in the listeners. One can be outraged about this, and a composer will have a thousand other fantasies without thinking of the same. But enough of this: I could write much more, but let me stop here; reasonable people will have to give their assent to me on this.

Document 3a. Johann Adolf Scheibe, Passage on Johann Sebastian Bach from a Letter of 1737, Sixth Issue of *Der critische Musikus*, May 14, 1737. 2nd ed. Leipzig, 1745, repr. Hildesheim: Olms, 1970. p. 62. In *Music and Culture in Eighteenth-Century Europe: A Source Book* by Enrico Fubini. Translated from the original sources by Wolfgang Freis, Lisa Gasbarrone, and Michael Louis Leone. Translation edited by Bonnie J. Blackburn. Chicago: University of Chicago Press, 1994. p. 272. © 1994 by the University of Chicago. Reprinted with permission of the University of Chicago Press.

This great man would be the admiration of entire nations if he had more pleasantness, and if he did not allow a bombastic and confused style to suffocate naturalness in his pieces, or obscure their beauty through excessive artifice. Since he judges according to his own fingers, his pieces are exceedingly difficult to play, for he demands that singers and instrumentalists perform with their throats and instruments exactly what he is able to play on the keyboard. This, however, is impossible. All styles of playing, every little embellishment, and everything that involves playing "by the method," as it is called, he writes out in actual notes; this deprives his pieces not only of the beauty of harmony, but it also renders the melody imperceptible. In short, he is to music what Herr von Lohenstein once was to poetry. Pompousness has led both from naturalness to artificiality, from sublimity to obscurity. One admires the onerous toil and the exceptional effort of both, but they have been applied in vain because they contend with reason.

Document 3b. Johann Abraham Birnbaum, from *Impartial Remarks on a Dubious Passage in the Sixth Issue of* Der critische Musikus (1738). In *Music and Culture in Eighteenth-Century Europe: A Source Book* by Enrico Fubini. Translated from the original sources by Wolfgang Freis, Lisa Gasbarrone, and Michael Louis Leone. Translation edited by Bonnie J. Blackburn. Chicago: University of Chicago Press, 1994. pp. 274–5. © 1994 by the University of Chicago. Reprinted with permission of the University of Chicago Press.

The court composer, in addition, is accused of depriving his pieces of naturalness through a "bombastic and confused style." These are harsh and obscure words. What does "bombastic" mean in music? Is it to be understood as in oratory, where bombast refers to wasting splendid adornments on trivial things, thereby underscoring even more their contemptuousness? If one draws on external and superfluous splendor without realizing the essential beauty? If one lapses into base, forced, and foolish trifles and confuses reasonable thoughts with childish ideas? I concede that such mistakes regarding music may be committed by those who do not understand or are unable to apply the rules of composition; yet to accuse the court composer of them would constitute the coarsest abuse. This composer does not, after all, squander his splendid ornaments on drinking songs or lullabies, or silly and galant pieces. His church compositions, overtures, concertos, and other musical works contain embellishments that are always appropriate to the theme he wishes to develop. Thus the author's contention is worthless, since it is obscure and cannot be proven. Consequently, the subsequent comparison of the court composer with [poet] Herr von Lohenstein is a notion belonging to the category of objectionable ornaments, and thus it is itself a pompousness of style.

What does "confused" mean in music? Inevitably one has to consult the definition of the word if one is to guess the author's opinion. As far as I know, "confused" refers to something having no order, and whose individual parts are intermixed and entangled so oddly that one cannot discern where each belongs. If this is what the author means, he must be reproaching the court composer for having no order in his compositions, and that everything is so bewildering that one cannot make sense of it. If the author is serious in passing such judgment, I am almost forced to believe that some confusion has affected his own thoughts that does not allow him to discern the truth. Wherever the rules of composition are followed to the letter, inevitably there must be order. I surely hope that the author does not consider the court composer to be a violator of these rules. Moreover, it is certain that the voices in pieces by this great master of music interact marvelously together, all without the least confusion. They proceed together and against each other, each in its proper place. They separate and reunite at the proper time. Each voice is distinguished by some specific variation, even though they often imitate each other. They flee and follow each other, without ever creating the impression of the slightest irregularity in their anticipation and pursuit of one another. If all this is executed as it should be, there is nothing more beautiful than this harmony. . . .

Now it has been demonstrated sufficiently that there is nothing bombastic or confused to be found in the court composer's pieces; consequently, they cannot be devoid of naturalness, that is, of pleasant melody and harmony, which is at issue here. Rather, the praiseworthy endeavors of the court composer are aimed at presenting this very naturalness with the help of artistry in its most splendid appearance to the world.

Notes

1 Hans T. David and Arthur Mendel, eds., *The Bach Reader: A Life of Johann Sebastian Bach in Letters and Documents* (New York: Norton, 1945), p. 121.

2 J.N. Forkel, *Über Johann Sebastian Bachs Leben, Kunst und Kunstwerke* (Leipzig, 1802), quoted in trans. in Peter Williams, *The Organ Music of J.S. Bach: III A Background* (Cambridge: Cambridge University Press, 1984), p. 51.

3 Quoted in Hans T. David and Arthur Mendel, eds., *The Bach Reader: A Life of Johann Sebastian Bach in Letters and Documents* (New York: Norton, 1945), pp. 264–5.

4 Quoted in Christoph Wolff, *Johann Sebastian Bach: The Learned Musician* (New York: Oxford University Press, 2002), p. 226.

5 Excerpt from Theophil Grossgebauer, *Wächterstimme aus dem verwüsteten Zion* (A watchman's voice from devastated Sion, Rostock, 1661), chapter 11, quoted in Joseph Herl, *Worship Wars in Early Lutheranism: Choir, Congregation, and Three Centuries of Conflict* (Oxford: Oxford University Press, 2004), p. 199.

6 Georg Motz, *Die vertheidigte Kirchen-Music* (Tilsit, East Prussia, 1703), p. 52, quoted in trans. in Ulrich Leisinger, "Affections, Rhetoric, and Musical Expression," in *The World of Bach Cantatas*, ed. Christoph Wolff (New York: W.W. Norton, 1997), p. 195.

7 Johann Kuhnau, "A Treatise on Liturgical Text Setting (1710)," trans. Ruben Weltsch and intro. Carol K. Baron, in *Bach's Changing World: Voices in the Community*, ed. Carol K. Baron (Rochester, NY: University of Rochester Press, 2006), p. 221.

8 Johann Mattheson, *Der musicalische Patriot* (Hamburg, 1728), p. 105, quoted in trans. in Ulrich Leisinger, "Affections, Rhetoric, and Musical Expression," in *The World of Bach Cantatas*, ed. Christoph Wolff (New York: W.W. Norton, 1997), p. 186.

9 Melvin P. Unger, *Handbook to Bach's Sacred Cantata Texts: An Interlinear Translation with Reference Guide to Biblical Quotations and Annotations* (Lanham, MD: Scarecrow Press, 1996), p. 486.

10 Melvin P. Unger, *Handbook to Bach's Sacred Cantata Texts: An Interlinear Translation with Reference Guide to Biblical Quotations and Annotations* (Lanham, MD: Scarecrow Press, 1996), p. 489.

11 Hans T. David and Arthur Mendel, eds., *The Bach Reader: A Life of Johann Sebastian Bach in Letters and Documents* (New York: Norton, 1945), p. 253.

Part IV
The Baroque Goes Global

12 The Americas

Nowhere were the processes of cultural exchange and transformation in the Baroque era more evident than in the New World. The Americas encompassed a huge and diverse area with strong native traditions and complex cultural interactions. Its development brought new products into the world economy, such as sugar, tobacco and corn, and instituted a massive, multicultural emigration of Europeans to the New World—part of the vast program of overseas expansion undertaken by European powers in the early modern period referred to as colonialism.

Discovery and colonization revitalized European powers. The years of discovery coincided with improvements to map-making and printing techniques. Print media spread news of the New World back home, and elegant maps of the New World appeared soon after the first discoveries. Theodore de Bry's engraving depicts the New World surrounded by portraits of explorers Magellan, Columbus, Vespucci, and Pizarro (clockwise from lower left). The map shows costumes and other cultural features which clearly mark it for European consumption (Fig. 12.1).

As the European settlers met various indigenous cultures for the first time, and as they met each other's cultures in unfamiliar contexts and altered social hierarchies, their encounters were anything but neutral. They were volatile, inspiring, fertile, and transformative, and they were sometimes destructive as

Figure 12.1. Theodore de Bry (1528–98), allegory of West Indies or Americas, 1590.

well. Between 1600 and 1750, the music produced in New Spain (Spanish-held territories centered around modern-day Mexico, colonial America, and New France) reflected the novel circumstances in which it was made.

It would be easy to see this as a somewhat passive, one-way process. Indeed the history of Baroque music in general is often told as a series of innovations absorbed and imitated across Europe and beyond: A new idea takes hold in one place, is heard and copied elsewhere, and gradually makes its way into the common vocabulary. However, at the same time that a new style was traveling east, another one might be traveling west, and rarely did either emerge in its new context unchanged: Local traditions and cultural exchange took place at every level. European models were never uniformly adopted as they moved outside their countries of origin. Rather, each model was actively adapted to suit new contexts, preferences, and purposes. The same type of multidirectional exchange and influence continued in the New World. It was often quite subtle and it took place over time; it was also dependent upon the attitude of the settlers themselves to their new situation and their new neighbours.

What role did European music and the arts play in these early settlements and colonies? The reception of European musical styles reflected broader patterns of intercultural contact between Europeans and indigenous groups that ranged from deliberate attempts to stamp out indigenous culture, to mutual coexistence and active engagement with indigenous song, to heavy reliance on musical genres and styles from back home. Adherence to European cultural norms reinforced social and racial hierarchies. At first there was a one-way flow of composers and music from Spain and France. But a second generation of musicians native to the New World eventually came into its own, leading musical establishments, driving culture of the late Baroque, and even becoming artistic models back in the homeland.

The Spanish Americas

Portugal and Spain were the first European nations to experiment with imperialism in the fifteenth century. Portuguese expansion took the form of a few strategic islands and chains of fortified trading posts, called *feitorias*, along the continental coastlines of Africa, Asia, and the New World. From the outset, the Spaniards adopted a highly structured administrative model. With the conquest of the Canary Islands of Gran Canaria, Tenerife, and La Palma in the 1480s and 1490s, the Spanish crown established each island as a municipality governed by a city council. This model reflected Spain's broader colonization strategy of founding cities. Between 250,000 and 300,000 Spaniards migrated to Spanish America and the Caribbean in the sixteenth century. And by 1620, Spain had founded 190 towns and cities. The Spanish presence pushed the indigenous populations into farming and mining trades, and from the mid-seventeenth century, sugar drove the economy, provoking a market for African slaves to provide plantation labor. With core activities based in New Spain, exploration and missionary activity also extended to present-day Florida, New Mexico, California, and Texas, beginning in the late sixteenth century and continuing through the early nineteenth century.

Spanish colonization of Mexico began in 1519 when Hernán Cortés landed on the mainland of North America. The principal Aztec city, known as Tenochtitlán, became the capital (present Mexico City), and the term Mexico was applied to the whole territory. Religion always played a central role in New Spain. Mexico comprised seven ecclesiastical dioceses, one for each of the major cities of the region: Mexico, Puebla, Valladolid (modern Morelia), Guadalajara, Oaxaca, Mérida, and Guatemala. Mexico City and Lima City rose to prominence as viceregal capitals: Over fifty percent of the populations of New Spain and Lima resided in these centers, respectively. Spain retained control through centralized governance, issuing an average of approximately 2,500 decrees on American colonial affairs annually. Mexico City was the seat of the archbishop, with each diocese hosting its own bishop.

The cathedral was the focus of religious life in urban centers. An archbishop and a council of clergymen (chapter, or *cabildo*) governed the cathedral. The chapter exerted a strong artistic influence through the hiring of musicians. The cathedral was the center for processions, civic display, and religious devotion in the Baroque period. The cathedrals of Mexico City and Puebla were particularly lavish. Started by the 1560s, the Mexico City cathedral was built on the site of Aztec ruins and modeled on the Cathedral of Seville (Fig. 12.2). It took over a century to build, and was not completed until 1667. A new organ built in Spain by the Aragonese Jorge de Semsa was installed in the Mexico City Cathedral between 1692–5 by Tiburtio Sanz who traveled from Spain with the instrument.

Music flourished at the Mexico City Cathedral under the leadership of such prominent chapel masters as the Spanish-born Juan Hernández (active around 1620) and Antonio de Salazar (*ca.* 1650–1715). The ascendancy of Mexican-born Manuel de Zumaya (*ca.* 1678–1755) to the post represents a significant shift in protocol, for it was customary to reserve positions of cultural, political, and religious leadership to Spaniards. There is also evidence that Indians sang and were employed as instrumentalists at the cathedral. An early music teacher, Pedro de Gante (1479?–1572), noted that Indians sang both songs in their Nahuatl language and Western polyphony in ceremonies—indicating a high degree of cross-cultural artistic mixing.

Of course, leadership for music came foremost from the archbishop, whose tastes and predilection for musical spectacle governed the size and quality of the cathedral's musical establishment. The short tenure of Fray García Guerra, who served as archbishop of Mexico (1608–12) and viceroy in 1612, left a remarkable stamp on musical culture of the city.[1] He brought with him the finest singers from Spain, retained talented Mexican singers, repaired and refurbished the organs, and continued the tradition of hiring Indian instrumentalists as permanent musicians to play shawms, sackbuts, and flutes. Shortly before his death, Fray García Guerra decreed in July 1611 that the best music of the cathedral be copied into lavish manuscripts for lasting cultural preservation.

Fray García Guerra's opulent burial in Mexico City in 1612 was a significant cultural, political, and religious event, the highlight of which was the procession. Processions were important markers of civic order in New Spain, for the order of procession reinforced religious, political, and social hierarchies.[2] At the head were ecclesiastics, followed by the viceroy and civil authorities of the colony and members of the nobility, with the third rank comprised of native leaders from surrounding regions. American historian and ethnologist Hubert Howe Bancroft (1832–1918) offers a romanticized account of the procession for Fray García Guerra. Bancroft describes the attendants' clothes in remarkable detail and lavishes attention on the hats, caps, insignia, and other symbols of religious hierarchy. Inhabitants and visitors to the city publically mourned the death of the chief of Church and State. The singing of masses and chants reinforced the splendor of the occasion (Document 2).

Figure 12.2 Metropolitan Cathedral, Mexico City. Ornate tower and carvings over the entrance to the cathedral.

The specifics of incorporating the chant melodies into the procession are detailed in the *Manuale Sacramentorum secundum usum ecclesiae Mexicanae* (Manual of the Sacraments According to the Mexican Use, 1560), among the first music books printed in the Americas. There were five key moments for musical responsories: They were sung after a series of prayers at each of five stations (preplanned locations where the procession would stop), culminating with the *Requiem aeternam* at the fifth station, and the singing of "Subvenite Sancti Dei" (Succour Him, Ye Saints of God) upon entering the church.

Cathedral music drew from both liturgical and popular traditions. By the mid-sixteenth century, thirteen liturgical music books had been printed in Mexico City. The formal liturgy of Mexico is preserved in the *Manuale sacramentorum* (1560) and *Missale Romanum Ordinarium* (1561). The *Missale* includes fifty-two pages of music notated on a single, red, five-line staff. Added to this are four graduals, two psalters, two antiphoners, a Passion-book, and a new edition of the *Manuale* that followed the decrees of the Council of Trent. Juan Navarro's *Quatuor Passiones* (Mexico City, 1604) consists of 105 leaves of music for the four Passions, the Lamentations, and the Prayer of Jeremiah. Stylistically, these works adopted European norms of music and rhetoric that reflected the aesthetic tastes of the cathedral's clergy and principle attendees: political leaders and wealthy merchants.

Alongside this liturgical tradition stands a rich practice of *villancico* performances. The term *villancico* has held multiple meanings over the centuries. Scholar Tess Knighton reduces the meanings of the term *villancico* to two main connotations. In the fifteenth and sixteenth centuries, *villancico* denoted a composition identified by formal traits, notably, the combination of *estribillo* and *coplas*. From the late sixteenth century until the early nineteenth centuries, however, *villancico* is used more broadly to denote all learned songs in the vernacular performed in a sacred context.[3] As a religious song, the *villancico* was performed in various contexts: at Mass during the Elevation of the Host; for the Office hour of Matins; or for Marian feasts, processions, and devotional purposes.

The *villancico* in New Spain

The *villancico* was an important genre of sacred music making in the Iberian and Latin American worlds of the seventeenth and eighteenth centuries. During this period of Counter Reformation, *villancicos* were cultivated in large numbers, and it was normal for chapel masters at large religious institutions in Spain, Portugal, and Latin America to produce as many as seventy-five during a typical tenure. *Villancicos* were performed for major feasts such as Corpus Christi and the Christmas season as well as for extraordinary events and occasions. Spanish composers such as Joseph Ruiz de Samaniego, Juan Bautista Comes, and Cristóbal Galán experimented with various current styles in their *villancicos*, including monody, trio writing, recitative, and aria.

But the New World *villancico* was not merely an offshoot of a Spanish prototype; there was a certain amount of cross-influence as well. Because a *villancico* was customarily performed only once, composers traded texts and music to assemble new *villancicos* from old ones. There is also evidence that texts were recycled: Several texts in *villancico* cycles by the Mexican poet Sor Juana Ines de la Cruz, which were used at the cathedrals of Mexico City and Puebla, survive in earlier Iberian sources from Madrid and elsewhere. The compositional processes of recombining and recycling music and texts helps explain the discrepancy between the large numbers of *villancicos* that we know were performed and their comparatively low survival rate in manuscripts.

Latin American composers combined the Spanish *villancico* with music and dance from different ethnic groups of Spanish-speaking America. Such "ethnic *villancicos*" include sections sung by one or more non-Castilian characters, including the *villancicos de negros*, a sub-genre performed by white singers in imitation of perceived speech patterns and mannerisms of black Africans. A prime example is Maitinez Natividad (1653), a set of nine Christmas *villancicos* by Juan Gutiérrez de Padilla (*ca.* 1590–1664), that features the Afro-Hispanic *negrillas*, *gallegos*, and *jácaras*. Such works offer insight into racial politics in Mexico City, where the black population outnumbered the white population by a ratio of 3 or 4:1 in the seventeenth century.[4]

Villancicos of the eighteenth century typically feature operatic styles of recitative, virtuosic arias and duets, and an orchestra of violins, wind instruments, and continuo. For such works, the traditional *villancico* sections were broken into subsections, called *cantadas*. Manuel de Zumaya (ca. 1678–1755) excelled as a composer of *villancicos* in this style.

Manuel de Zumaya

Born in or near Mexico City in 1678, Zumaya is the most important Mexican-born composer of the Baroque period. He excelled in all genres of music and produced *Partinope* (1711), the earliest known opera performed in North America. Zumaya's play *Rodrigo*, written to celebrate the birth of Prince Luis, was staged on August 25, 1707, possibly to his own music. His works show a mastery of styles, ranging from the *stile antico*—in the *Lamentations*, for instance—to the more up-to-date style of the concerted works and operatic cantatas of his later years. Zumaya spent most of his career at the Cathedral of Mexico City. He trained there as a choirboy, studied organ with the cathedral's principal organist, José de Ydiáquez, and composition with Salazar. Zumaya was promoted to the position of chapel master in 1715, after five years of service as his teacher, Salazar's, assistant in that role. The magnificent organ of the Mexico Cathedral was built and installed during Zumaya's twenty-four-year period as chapel master. Zumaya left the Cathedral in 1739 to serve as personal chaplain to Tomás Montaño, Bishop of Oaxada, remaining there as chapel master after Montaño's death in 1742. Zumaya's music survives in the cathedrals of Mexico City, Oaxaca, and Guatemala.

Zumaya, *Celebren, publiquen, entonen y canten* (Praise, Proclaim, Intone, Sing)

Celebren retains many elements of the traditional *villancico* as cultivated in Spain and the New World. Zumaya adopts the familiar choral and solo structure for the refrain. The refrain alternates with four-line stanzas set for an imitative vocal duet of alto and tenor, known as the *Coplas a dúo*. Hemiola and syncopation in triple meter, syllabic declamation, homorhythmic textures, and conjunct melodies—all typical of the *villancico* and common to theatrical and popular music of Spain and Portugal—are found here as well.

To this traditional framework, Zumaya adds modern elements of the eighteenth-century Baroque. The scoring reflects contemporary trends: three violins and partially figured basso continuo, in addition to the more traditional two choirs (ATB and *tiple* [treble or soprano] ATB), and cornet. The polychoral writing recalls the rich tradition of Giovanni Gabrieli's Venetian works. The transfer of the polychoral idiom from Baroque Europe to New Spain was also reflected in church design with spaces on either side of the central altar designed for groups of musicians to create a surround sound effect. Zumaya marks the start of the refrain with unison statements on violin and trumpet (Ex. 12.1).

Estribillo	Refrain[5]
Celebren, publiquen,	Praise, proclaim,
entonen y canten.	Intone and sing.

The first chorus (ATB) completes the theme. The final section of the refrain grows in rhythmic and textural intensity on the words "each one awaits reverently as the Pure One, as Queen, as Virgin, as Mother." The text may have been written for the Assumption of Mary, the principal feast of the Blessed Virgin Mary that celebrates her ascent to heaven (Ex. 12.2).

por pura, por reyna	As the chaste one, as queen,
por virgen, por madre.	As virgin, as mother.

Example 12.1 Zumaya, *Celebren*, mm. 1–6.

For the *Coplas a dúo*, Zumaya pairs the alto and tenor in a short imitative phrase that ends with an instrumental tag (Ex. 12.3).

Coplas a duo
1. Las tres altas jerarquías
en fiel controversia amable
amorosos solicitan
a la que sube triunfante.

1. The three high hierarchies
In friendly and faithful dispute
lovingly Call for the attention
Of Her who rises up triumphantly.

Zumaya's instrumentation is rich and varied. This was typical of *villancicos* from the eighteenth century. Surviving printed *villancico* booklets list fifteen instruments in the accompanying ensemble: clarion, trumpet, sackbut, cornett, organ, bassoon, violin, shawm, marine trumpet, zither, bass viol, vihuela, small rebeck, bandore, and harp. On occasion, composers noted details of specific groupings

Example 12.1 (continued)

Example 12.2. Zumaya, *Celebren,* mm. *41–45.*

Example 12.2 (continued)

for each stanza of the coplas; fifteen different instruments did not imply fifteen different players. It was expected that a cathedral instrumentalist have the ability to double on up to four different instruments.

Zumaya's *Celebren* is a large-scale sacred showpiece that reflects the versatility and malleability of the *villancico* as it absorbed influences from the late Baroque era. The *villancico* remained popular in Latin America to the end of the eighteenth century, although religious efforts to curtail the use of vernacular texts in church services in Spain may have led to the genre's decline in the New World as well.

Example 12.3. Zumaya, Celebren, mm. 1–6.

Music in New France

Explorer Giovanni da Verrazano (1485–1530) named the northeastern portion of North America "New France" in honor of his patron, King Francis I (1494–1547). In 1534, Jacques Cartier navigated the gulf of the St. Lawrence River and claimed the lands for the French king. French and Basque fur traders followed, establishing a lasting network of contacts with Indigenous peoples. The French remained strong allies with the Huron nations. Cartographer and explorer Samuel de Champlain (ca. 1570–1635) established the first permanent settlements: a colony at Port Royal, Nova Scotia in 1604, and another at Quebec in 1608 (Fig. 12.3).

The Company of New France operated the territory and formed alliances with indigenous nations to facilitate the beaver pelt trade. Further south, French lands prospered along the Mississippi River in the colony of Louisiana, prior to the Louisiana Purchase of 1803. French presence in the Caribbean included a Compagnie des Isles d'Amérique and the settlements of Martinique and Guadeloupe in 1635. These far flung islands proved important for growing sugarcane, and, later, tobacco and cotton.

Champlain, who served as governor of the colony of New France from 1633 until his death, chronicled the history of European exploration in his writings. *Voyages* describes the intense rivalry among European powers, the thrill of discovery, and the sense of adventure and danger that accompanied conquest. Religious justification for conquest plays a key role in Champlain's *Voyages*, and one that reminds us that such texts need to be approached and interpreted with special care (Document 1).

Little is known about music-making in New France during the first half of the seventeenth century. Although music certainly celebrated major events, the function of *A la claire fontaine*, reportedly sung by Samuel Champlain's men in 1608, the year they founded Quebec City, was more modest: For the *voyageurs* who transported goods and passengers by water, singing was a way for the paddlers to keep time. The many references to nature in the text complement the outdoor context in which it was sung, but they also contrast with a central theme of lost love. The poem is strophic, with stanzas of four lines and a two-line refrain at the end of each verse. The refrain structure supports performance by a soloist throughout, or the alternation of a soloist for the verse with a larger group for the refrain. Still popular in 1834, *A la claire fontaine* was adopted as the anthem of the St.-Jean-Baptiste Societies, a nationalist society of French-Canadians founded that year in Montreal, and it continues to be associated with French Canadian nationalism.

> By the clear fountain[6]
> Out strolling one day
> I found the water so lovely
> I bathed in it.
> *I have long loved you*
> *Never will I forget you.*

Montreal and Quebec City soon became centers of cultural life in their own right. Among the early settlers were wealthy merchants and military leaders who enjoyed aristocratic entertainment. These ranged from *ballets de cour* (theatrical spectacles with dancing) to the kinds of vocal and instrumental music associated with the French court. *Théâtre de Neptune*, the first theater spectacle in the New World, was produced in 1606 as a welcoming celebration for Baron de Poutrincourt, lieutenant governor of Port Royal. Early settlers collaborated with members of local native communities in producing *Théâtre de Neptune*, a common occurrence from early on in New France.

The Roman Catholic faith was perceived as a way to unite the early settlers, missionaries, and native converts. The founding of Quebec City in 1608 established the first church in the colony, and the cathedrals in both Quebec City and Montreal became centers for music-making in the Baroque period. The task of converting indigenous populations largely fell to the Jesuits, a Roman Catholic order of priests and brothers formed by Ignatius Loyola (1491–1556) and officially recognized as a group by Pope Paul III in 1540. The Jesuits dedicated themselves to the "progress of souls" doctrine and the spread of the faith; the ecclesiastical order had the greatest impact on music and cultural life in the New World. The first Jesuits arrived in Quebec in 1625, traveling from Quebec to the small colonies of Trois Rivières and Montreal and into the

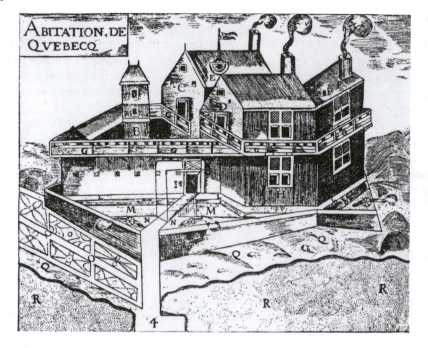

Figure 12.3 Quebec Colony, 1629.

Huron country, where a mission was established at Ste. Marie (Ontario). Jesuits gradually migrated west and south into the middle of the United States.

The Jesuits brought Catholic teachings to the native populations and tended to the spiritual needs of the colonists in the New World. Jesuit missionaries chronicled their efforts in diaries and in official reports, known as the *Jesuit Relations*, which were sent from Quebec City and Montreal back to France. One of the most important documents of early New France history was the diary of Father Paul le Jeune, who arrived in 1632 as superior of the Jesuit mission in Quebec. Recognizing the power of teaching the indigenous populations to sing religious songs in their native language, Le Jeune instructed both French and First Nations boys in singing: "It is a sweet consolation to hear them sing publicly, in our Chapel, the Apostles' creed in their own language. Now, as a greater incentive to them, our French sing a Strophe of it in our language, then the Seminarists another in Huron, and then all together sing a third, each using his own language, in excellent harmony."[7]

Jean de Brebeuf (1593–1649) adopted the custom of polyglot song when he became leader of the mission to the Hurons. Brébeuf arrived in Canada in 1625 and was sent to the Huron settlement near Georgian Bay, Ontario, the following year. He remained there for three years and learned the Huron language. When the Kirke brothers captured Quebec in 1629 and expelled the Jesuits—including Brebeuf—he went back to France. When Brebeuf eventually returned to Canada, he headed the mission at Ste. Marie in Huronia for much of the period from 1634 until 1649. In 1642, Brébeuf composed the text of the "Huron Carol" *Jesous Ahatonhia* in both Huron and French, and set it to the melody of the sixteenth-century French folk song, *Une jeune pucelle* (A Young Maid).

> Have courage, you who are humans[8]
> Jesus, he is born
> Behold, the spirit who had us as prisoners fled
> Do not listen to it, as it corrupts the spirits of our minds
> Jesus, he is born.

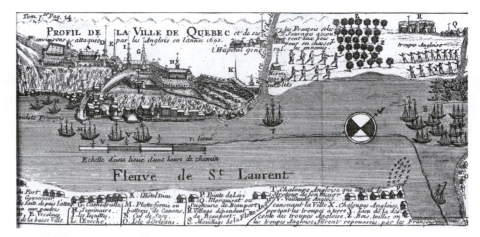

Figure 12.4. Quebec under attack by the English, 1691.

Famously, Brébeuf became a martyr of the Church when the Iroquois captured him at the St.-Louis mission and killed him at St.-Ignace on March 16, 1649. The depiction of his brutal torture and death became one of the most powerful pieces of propaganda distributed in the New World. Christophe Regnaut's (1649) vivid, yet problematic account of the event, which he heard from Huron Natives who had witnessed it and escaped, was verified by Regnaut himself in his examination of the martyr's body: "I saw and touched all the wounds of his body, as the savages had told and declared to us; we buried these precious Relics on Sunday, the 21st of March, 1649, with much Consolation."[9] Brébeuf was canonized on June 29, 1930.

In 1663, Louis XIV dissolved the Company of New France and assumed direct control of the colony, restructuring colonial administration and sending soldiers, settlers, and capital to foster a colony built on a European model. The towns of Quebec and Montreal served as cultural and economic capitals for the surrounding agricultural lands along the Saint Lawrence. It was a period of tremendous growth and immigration. In 1681, the population of French-Canadians numbered 9,742; at the end of French rule in 1760, it had multiplied to about 76,000. Quebec, as the capital of New France, captured the attention of onlookers near and far (Fig. 12.4). American engraver Thomas Johnston's view of the city highlights its unique and strategic situation.

Eighteenth-century tensions between the French and British in North America mirrored those back home. While the Anglo-Americans had greater numbers and a better economy, the French-Canadians had greater wilderness acumen, supported by a network of First Nations alliances. With parties of Natives and Canadian militia, New France waged a *"petite guerre"* (small guerrilla war), raiding vulnerable outposts on the frontiers of New England, New York, and Pennsylvania. After a series of French victories early in the Seven Years' War (1754–63), Britain mounted a major assault. The famous battle on the Plains of Abraham at Quebec City brought a dramatic conclusion to the eastern campaign. On September 8, 1760, the governor of New France surrendered. Britain absorbed the colony in 1763 with the Peace of Paris.

Efforts to recreate European culture intensified upon the change of government in 1663. From this point, Louis XIV operated New France as a royal province, under the jurisdiction of his personal representative, or intendant. The first intendants strove to replicate French social and political life in New France, modeling their balls, parties, and dances on those of Versailles, although much of this ephemeral party music is lost. What we do know is that their music, both secular and sacred, came primarily from France, and the music of French Baroque masters Henry Dumont, André Campra, Nicolas Bernier, and Jacquet de la Guerre reinforced the shared cultural bond between France and the colonists.

Remarkably, the largest collection of French organ repertoire exists in a New France source discovered only recently. Like the liturgy, music in the church replicated French practice, particularly after the Royal Government of 1663 established a quasi-national church under state supervision. The organ played a major

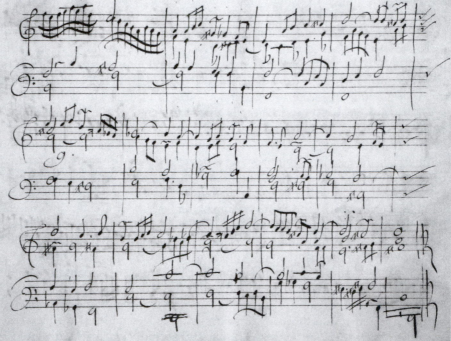

Figure 12.5 Anonymous, *Magnificat en D. Prélude*. Livre d'orgue de Montréal.

role in the French Catholic service, and in 1663, François Xavier de Laval brought a one-manual, seven-stop organ from Paris when he arrived in Quebec as its bishop. When Jean Giraud (1696–1765) emigrated from Bourges to Montreal to assume the post of organist at Montreal's Notre Dame Church in 1724, he brought with him a 540-page manuscript of organ music. This manuscript, known as the *Livre d'orgue de Montreal*, was rediscovered in 1978 by Canadian musicologist Elisabeth Gallat-Morin. It is the sole source for almost all of the music in this huge collection, and indeed the *Livre d'orgue de Montreal* is the largest surviving manuscript of French organ music. Its 398 works include six Masses, eleven Magnificats, Te Deums, and a series of *Tierces* or *Cromhornes en Taille, Dialogues de Récits*, and *Fugues*. The volume lacks a table of contents and there is no indication of authorship. The only composer who has been identified is Nicholas Lebègue (1630–1702), organist for the king of France, who contributed sixteen pieces (fifteen of which appear in his three organ books, 1676, 1678, 1685). Giraud, who had studied with Lebègue, grouped works according to the eight Church tones or by liturgical genre, making it easy for organists to select music for church services.

The *Livre d'orgue de Montreal* served a liturgical function: It contains six Masses, eleven Magnificats sung at Vespers, three Te Deums, one Pange lingua, and nine suites of pieces that could serve as Magnificats.[10] The music represents styles from the 1670s through the early eighteenth century, and these range from dance, vocal forms and recitative to more traditional plainchant and contrapuntal idioms. Giraud's organ at Notre-Dame in Montreal was a simple single manual instrument with a *Plein Jeu* registration, a *Jeu de Tierce* registration, and one or more reed stops. Several stops were divided between treble and bass, which highlighted the distinction between melody and accompaniment. The *Livre d'orgue de Montreal* is important for providing information about the registration of individual pieces (which stops to use).

The manuscript opens with a series of Magnificats. These would have been used to celebrate the Magnificat on Sundays at Vespers, a French custom retained by the churches in New France. The Magnificat comprises twelve verses, of which six to eight were suitable for organ performance. The opening *Magnificat in D* begins with a Prélude whose ornamentation, dotted rhythms, and stately tempo contribute to its ceremonial quality, reminding us of the role that music played in recreating the ritual and splendor of France in the New World (Fig. 12.5). Not surprisingly, the fashion for organ music in Quebec coincided with Louis XIV's assumption of direct control over the colony. The long arm of the state had become longer still, and music proclaimed it on both sides of the Atlantic.

Colonial New England

Britain's stake in the New World focused on the Caribbean and the North American mainland. Britain was also active on the other side of the globe, forming the East India Company in 1600. This highly lucrative trading organization paved the way for the British Parliament to appoint a governor general in Bengal in 1773 and to eventually occupy the whole of India in the nineteenth century.

In 1606 King James I divided the Atlantic seaboard into the north and south territories: the colonies of Virginia and Maryland prospered with tobacco crops and African slaves, while successful Puritan migration under the Massachusetts settlement generated new colonies to form New England. In 1664 King Charles II granted the territory between New England and Virginia to his brother, James, Duke of York, who absorbed Dutch settlements and renamed the area New York (Fig. 12.6). Charles II granted 45,000 square miles of land west of the Delaware River to William Penn, a Quaker whose colony of "Penn's Woods" attracted migrants from all over Europe. The Carolina colony, stretching south from Virginia to Florida and west to the Pacific Ocean, split into North and South Carolina in 1729, and the colony of Georgia was established in 1732. The population of European and African inhabitants of the Thirteen Colonies rose to 250,000 in 1700 and nearly 2.5 million by 1775.

Economic life was much more diversified than that based on either the Spanish or Portuguese models. The New England economy in the north was founded on commercial shipping, fishing, and timber, while southern plantations grew cereal grains, cotton, and, later, tobacco. Prosperity attracted large numbers of immigrants from Germany and Ireland in the eighteenth century, and expansion moved westward.

Figure 12.6 North America, Connecticut, Maine, Massachusetts, New Hampshire, New Jersey, New York, 1671.

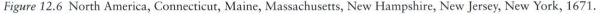

British-held islands in the Caribbean produced labor-intensive crops like sugarcane, while the outer islands of St. Kitts and Barbados were colonized as bases for further expansion.

This active phase of settlement in colonial America coincided with the rise of American popular psalmody. Sacred music in the colonies in the first half of the seventeenth century shared many common features with Protestant psalmody in England and Continental Europe, consisting primarily of unaccompanied congregational songs, occasionally supported by a bass instrument. Psalmody and metrical psalms united early settlers—Anglicans, separatists, and Puritans alike. British service books such as *The Book of Common Prayer* and *The Whole Book of Psalms* (1562), by Thomas Sternhold and John Hopkins, were the staples of colonial service and music. Indeed, psalmody in the American colonies formed part of a larger, transcultural Protestant ideology.

Puritan members of the Church of England founded the Massachusetts Bay Colony in 1629 with John Winthrop as its first governor. Opposed to the ritual of the English Church, the Bay colonists were less concerned with musical expression than with understanding the text. Nonetheless, the Puritans of Massachusetts Bay carved out their own musical legacy with *The Whole Booke of Psalmes Faithfully Translated into English Metre*, published in Cambridge, Massachusetts, in 1640. The brainchild of John Cotton, who led a team of thirty ministers to create a more literal translation of Sternfeld and Hopkins, the collection was popularly known as the *Bay Psalm Book*, and it was the first book of any kind printed in British North America (Fig. 12.7).

The *Bay Psalm Book* was revised in many editions over the next century and became the most important American versification of the psalms. It offers early evidence of the two-way flow of cultural and religious influence from America to Europe, for editions of it appeared in London, Scotland, and Amsterdam. A new third edition, published with revised versifications by Henry Dunster and Richard Lyon, came to be called the "*New England Psalter*" (Cambridge, Massachusetts, 1651).

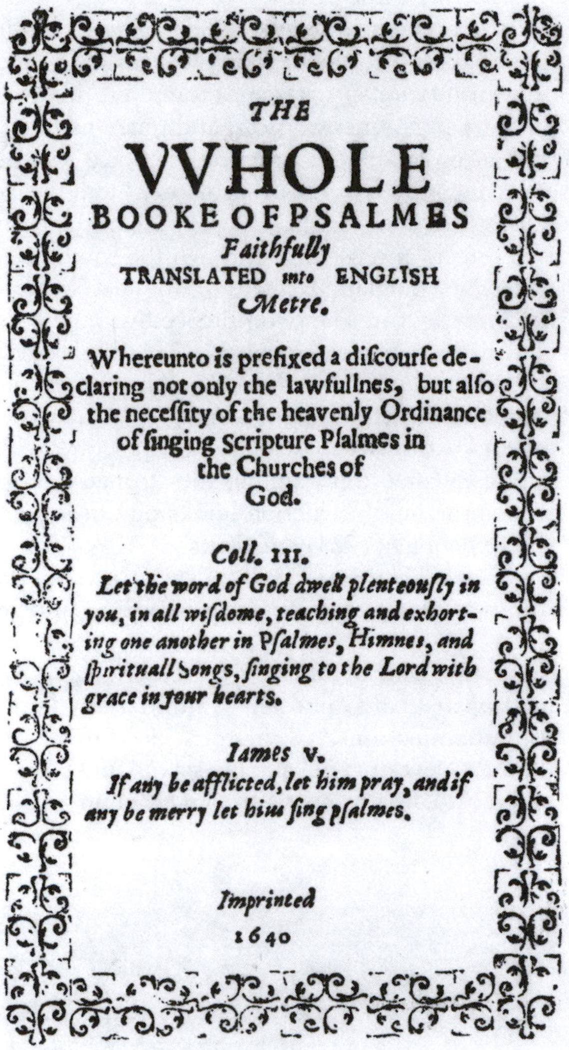
THE
VVHOLE
BOOKE OF PSALMES
Faithfully
TRANSLATED *into* ENGLISH
Metre.
Whereunto is prefixed a diſcourſe declaring not only the lawfullnes, but alſo the neceſſity of the heavenly Ordinance of ſinging Scripture Pſalmes in the Churches of God.

Coll. III.
Let the word of God dwell plenteouſly in you, in all wiſdome, teaching and exhorting one another in Pſalmes, Himnes, and ſpirituall Songs, ſinging to the Lord with grace in your hearts.

James V.
If any be afflicted, let him pray, and if any be merry let him ſing pſalmes.

Imprinted
1640

Figure 12.7 Bay Psalm Book, 1640.

The *Bay Psalm Book* (1640) first appeared without musical notation. The compilers listed forty-eight tunes at the back of the book that would accommodate the psalm texts, and the singer could simply fit the new words to the old, and usually familiar tunes. According to an "admonition to the reader," the newly versified psalms could be sung to thirty-nine tunes found in Thomas Ravenscroft's English psalter of 1621, and to others in Sternhold-Hopkins. In the "usual" or "common" way of performing these, the deacon chanted the psalm text one line at a time, and the congregation sang each line back antiphonally, a process known as "lining-out." The format is extremely accessible, and it made it easy for congregants to improvise and embellish their musical responses, one phrase at a time.

Musical tunes were printed above the texts in the ninth edition of the *New England Psalter* of 1698, making it the first musical notation printed in English-speaking America. The musical supplement consists of thirteen tunes named after their town of origin. These are set for tenor and bass using a solmization notation in which the letters F, S, L, and M—corresponding to *fa, sol, la*, and *mi* respectively—are placed directly under the staff notation. The tunes, the notation of so-fa letters, and the introductory notes were taken from John Playford's *A Brief Introduction to the Skill of Musick* (London, 1654). The ninth edition is also the first to add a bass part ("bassus") to the melody ("cantus'). The presence of a bass line suggests significant copying from Playford, for instruments were not found in American churches at this time.

The compiler arranged the tunes by pitch, meter, affect, and religious function of the psalms associated with each melody. For instance, the "directions for ordering the voice" stipulates that the Oxford, Litchfield, and Low Dutch tunes are for singing "to psalms consolatory" and the York and Windsor "to psalms of prayer, confession, and funerals." It reminds us that the purpose of the psalms was to inspire the appropriate religious sentiments in both singers and listeners through the combined impact of text and music.

The use of musical notation in the New England Psalter (1698) reflects a broader reform aimed at singing "by note" rather than the "usual" way by ear. The two practices—notated versus oral—reinforced urban, rural, social, and cultural divides in early American culture. Those who led the movement to introduce "regular singing," or singing with scores and musical rules, tended to be ministers who were highly educated; less literate rural parishes upheld the tradition of singing without scores. The conflict bubbled over in the 1720s in a series of pamphlets known as the Regular Singing Controversy.

Ministers John Tufts and Thomas Walter were among the strongest proponents of the New Way of singing using notation. They penned the first instruction books on music printed in the colonies: Walter's *The Grounds and Rules of Music Explained* (1721) and Tufts's *A Very Plain and Easy Introduction to the Art of Singing Psalm Tunes* (11 editions, Boston, 1721–44). They provided practical instruction on scales, notation, keys, so-fa letter notation (in the case of Tufts), and vocal technique, appending a large body of psalm tunes as well.

In the preface to *The Grounds and Rules of Music Explained* (1721), Walter laments that the tunes are "now miserably tortured, and twisted, and quavered . . . into a horrid medley of confused and disorderly noises." To counteract these "abominations," Walter provided three-part harmonizations of the tunes (Fig. 12.8). He started the first known New England singing school and concert performances in Boston in 1721. Singing schools caught on quickly, first in port cities and then in rural areas. The shift from oral to

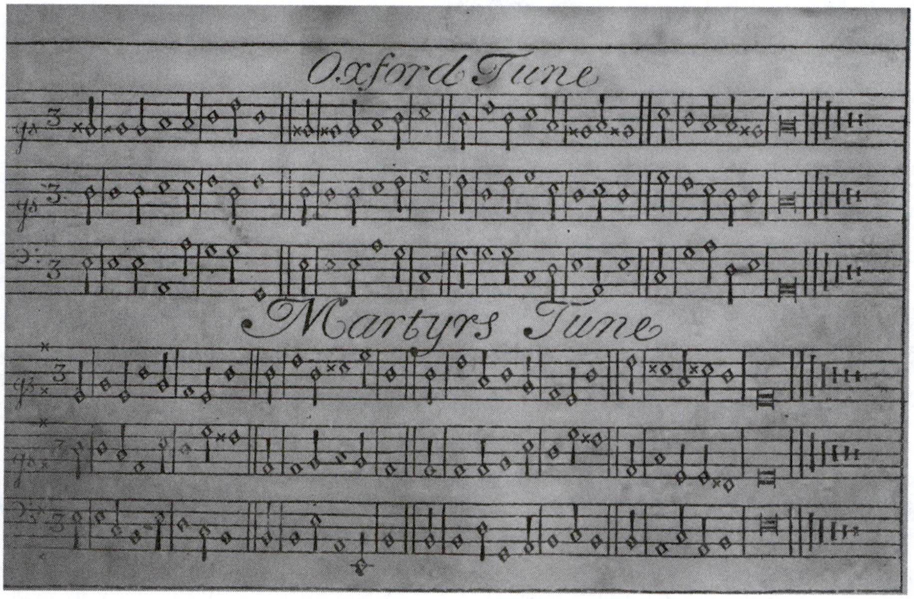

Figure 12.8 Oxford Tune from Walter, *The Grounds and Rules of Music Explained*, 1721.

Figure 12.9 John Collet (*ca.* 1720–80), *George Whitefield Preaching.*

written music was not without ramifications, for it effectively moved singing away from musically illiterate congregants to semi-professional church choirs.

The mid-eighteenth century saw the rise of a new evangelical spirit of worship that culminated in a series of spiritual revivals, known as the First Great Awakening, from 1740 to 1743 in the northern colonies. Revivals or awakenings referred to sudden, revelatory episodes of religious excitement and spiritual conversion among congregants. These were strikingly at odds with the Puritan understanding of conversion as a long, uncertain process, and the First Great Awakening had a profound impact on the colonial churches. It ushered in an incredible growth of evangelical Christianity across the United States and laid the foundation for American evangelical Christianity from the Civil War to the present day. Resistance to the evangelical movement was acute, however, and effectively divided the movement into three groups: moderate evangelicals, anti-revivalists, and radical evangelicals.

Singing played a prominent role in the First Great Awakening, whether it was used to arouse, elevate, unite, or pacify the feelings of a group of worshippers, and it remains a hallmark of evangelical spirituality and worship. George Whitefield, the greatest of the Awakening's itinerant preachers, began and ended his meetings with singing (Fig. 12.9). In his journal account of preaching to crowds at Basking Ridge, New Jersey, in 1740, Whitefield describes an atmosphere of near hysterical religious fervor, where members of the huge congregation—desperate for signs of God's mercy—wept for their sins and cried out at random (Document 3). Whitefield, adding his prayers above the noise of the crowd, then brings the meeting to a close with a hymn.

The impact of the Great Awakening was felt across the Atlantic. English psalmody responded to the individualistic style of American worship with a renewed approach to traditional forms of psalmody. English poet and theologian Isaac Watts created a new style of Anglophone Protestant worship, infusing metrical psalms and hymns with expressions of evangelicalism that reinforced the congregants' identity as a "covenanted community." Watts's *Hymns and Spiritual Songs* (1707) and *The Psalms of David Imitated in the Language of the New Testament* (1719) are full of exclamations in first person and biblical imagery. Both volumes appeared from presses across colonial America and England: Watts became the most published author in colonial America. His version of Psalm 4 from *The Psalms of David* is a representative example.

1. LORD, thou wilt hear me when I pray;
    I am forever thine:
    I fear before thee all the Day,
    Nor would I dare to fin.
2. And while I rest my weary Head
    From Cares and Business free,
    'Tis sweet conversing on my Bed
    With my own Heart and Thee.
3. I pay this Evening Sacrifice;
    And when my Work is done,
    Great God, my Faith and Hope relies
    Upon thy Grace alone.
4. Thus with my Thoughts compos'd to Peace,
    I'll give mine Eyes to sleep;
    Thy Hand in Safety keeps my Days,
    And will my Slumbers keep.

Music-making in the New World retained the general contours of music-making in Europe. Sacred music in particular, from Mexico, New France, and the colonies, showed a close tie to European traditions of worship and praise. But the actual music wasn't the only thing that crossed the ocean with the colonists. They also brought with them the assumption—so integral to Baroque era thought—that music could move the emotions of its listeners. More than any other single element, this united the music of New World and old.

Documents

Document 1. Samuel de Champlain, *The Voyages and Explorations of Samuel de Champlain (1604 1616) Narrated by Himself*. Trans. Annie Nettleton Bourne. Ed. Edward Gaylord Bourne. Vol. 1. Toronto: The Courier Press, 1911. Dedication, pp. xxxvi, xxxviii, and Chapter 2, pp. 9 10.

To Monseigneur, the most illustrious Cardinal, Duke de Richelieu, Head, Grand Master and Superintendent-General of the Commerce and Navigation of France.

Monseigneur: These narratives are offered to you as the one to whom they are chiefly due, not only because of your eminent power in the Church and in the State, as well as in the command of all navigation, but also that you may be promptly informed of the greatness, the fertility, and the beauty of the places that they describe. For it may be assumed that it was not without great and vital reasons that the Kings who were predecessors of His Majesty, and he also, not only raised the standard of the Cross in that land, in order to establish the faith there, as they did, but also wished to attach to it the name of New France. You will find here the great and dangerous voyages that have been undertaken thither; the discoveries that followed upon them; the extent of these lands, no less than four times as large as France; their situation; the facility with which a safe and important commerce can be carried on there; the great profit to be derived from it; the fact that our Kings have taken possession of a large part of the country; the missions that they have instituted there of various religious orders; their progress in the conversion of a good many savages; [the account of] the clearing of certain tracts of land, by which you will discover that they in no way fall short of the soil of France in fertility; and, finally, the settlements and forts which have been built there in the name of France.

[Chapter 2]

The most illustrious palms and laurels that kings and princes can win in this world are contempt for temporal blessings and the desire to gain the spiritual. They cannot do this more profitably than by converting, through their labor and piety, to the catholic, apostolic and Roman religion, an infinite number of savages, who live without faith, without law, with no knowledge of the true God. For the taking of forts, the winning of battles, and the conquests of countries, are nothing in comparison with the reward of those who prepare themselves crowns in heaven, unless it be fighting against infidels. . . . And if all this cannot move us to seek after heavenly blessings at least as passionately as after those on the earth, it is because men's covetousness for this world's blessings is so great that most of them do not care for the conversion of infidels so long as their fortune corresponds to their desires, and everything conforms to their wishes. Moreover, it is this covetousness that has ruined and is wholly ruining the progress and advancement of this enterprise, which is not yet well under way, and is in danger of collapsing, unless His Majesty establishes there conditions as righteous, charitable and just as he is himself; and unless he himself takes pleasure in learning what can be done to increase the glory of God and to benefit his state, repelling the envy of those who should support this enterprise, but who seek its ruin rather than its success.

Document 2. *The Conquest of Mexico: Volume 3, 1600–1803*, by Hubert Howe Bancroft. San Francisco: A. L. Bancroft, 1883, pp. 21–23.

The embalmed body, arrayed in pontifical robes of purple taffeta garnished with gold and silver, rested in the chapel on a catafalque, covered with black gold-bordered velvet, and surrounded with candles. The interior of the chapel was draped in black. The head of the corpse reclined on a black velvet cushion, ornamented with gold and silver, and bore on the brow a mitre. Close to it rose the guidon of the captain-general, a rank held by the deceased in virtue of his office as viceroy. At the left shoulder rested the pastoral staff, and in the right hand the archiepiscopal cross; at the feet were two royal maces of gilt silver, and between them the prelate's hat.

For three days a constant stream of visitors appeared at the chapel to give a last look at the beloved face, while friars and clergy held vigils, masses, and chants here as well as at other temples. The bells tolled solemnly all the while, and nearly every person exhibited some token of mourning, especially officials and men of means.

On the 25th a vast concourse gathered at the palace to escort the body to the cathedral tomb. First marched the school children with white lighted tapers; then came thirty-eight brotherhoods, according to age, with standards, crosses, and other paraphernalia; the different monastic orders, closing with the Dominicans, to whom belonged the deceased, followed by over four hundred members of the clergy, the prebendaries of the Chapter being last. Then came the coffin, having at the feet the prelate's hat, and a cap with white tassel, the insignia of a master of theology. Behind were borne the cross and guidon, draped in black, between two kings-at-arms. On either side of the coffin strode the viceregal guard, while halberdiers assisted in keeping back the crowd. Following the guard came the deacons; the commercial court; the university representation, with sixty-four of its graduated doctors bearing the insignia of the faculty; the municipality, preceded by their mace-bearers; the audiencia, with three nephews of the deceased; the royal officers, bearing a black standard with royal arms in gold; three companies of infantry in lines of seven, with arms reversed, marching to the sound of four muffled drums and two fifes; the maestre de sala of the viceroy, bearing aloft on a half-pike the arms of the deceased, gilded on a black surface; the master of horse and chamberlain, leading a steed in deep mourning with a long train; another gentleman of the court, on horseback, bore the guidon of captain-general, with royal arms on crimson velvet. The procession closed with the servants of the palace, led by the major-domo.

Between the palace and the cathedral five catafalques had been erected, to serve as resting-places for the coffin as it was transferred to different bearers. The oidores bore it from the chapel to the first station; then the cathedral chapter, the municipality, the university corporation, and the commercial representatives carried it successively, the oidores taking it from the last station into the cathedral, where it was placed in a lofty position, amid a blaze of lights. As the procession approached they lowered the standards, and placed them at the foot of the coffin. On the left rested Guerra's coat of arms; on the right were the cross and the guidon. After service the coffin was buried at a late hour by the high altar, on the evangel side. It was a grand and glorious casting-forth.

During the novenary each religious order came to chant masses, assisted by ecclesiastic and civil bodies. On March 7th the members of the procession marched in the same order as before to the cathedral, where the vigil was chanted, and funeral oration delivered in Latin. The following day the funeral sermon was preached by the Dominican provincial.

Document 3. George Whitefield, *Journals, 1735–1740.* Basking Ridge, NJ, November 5, 1740. In Thomas S. Kidd, *The Great Awakening: A Brief History with Documents.* New York: Bedford/ St. Martin's, 2008. p. 49.

Wednesday, Nov. 5. Set out at eight in the morning, and got to Baskinridge, the place where Mr. Cross exercises his stated ministry, about one o'clock. At the house where I waited in the way, a woman spoke to me under strong convictions, and told me "she was deeply wounded by my last night's discourse." When I came to Baskinridge, I found Mr. [James] Davenport had been preaching to the congregation, according to appointment. It consisted of about three thousand people. I had not discoursed long, when, in every part of the congregation, someone or other began to cry out, and almost all were melted into tears. A little boy, about eight years of age, wept as though his heart would break. Mr. Cross took him up into the waggon, which so affected me, that I broke from my discourse, and told the people that, since old professors were not concerned, God, out of an infant's mouth, was perfecting praise; and the little boy should preach to them. As I was going away, I asked the little boy what he cried for? He answered, his sins. I then asked what he wanted? He answered, Christ. After sermon, Mr. Cross gave notice of an evening lecture in his barn, two miles off. Thither we went, and a great multitude followed. Mr. Gilbert Tennet preached first: and I then began to pray, and gave an exhortation. In about six minutes, one cried out, "He is come, He is come!" and could scarce sustain the manifestation of Jesus to his soul. The eager crying of others, for the like favor, obliged me to stop; and I prayed over them, as I saw their agonies and distress increase. At length we sang a hymn, and then retired to the house, where the man that received Christ continued praising and speaking of Him till near midnight. My own soul was so full that I retired, and wept before the Lord, under a deep sense of my own vileness, and the sovereignty and greatness of God's everlasting love. Most of the people spent the remainder of the night in prayer and praises. It was a night much to be remembered.

Notes

1 See Robert Stevenson, "Mexico City Cathedral Music: 1600–1750," *The Americas* 21/2 (1964), pp. 111–35.
2 This outline is based on Grayson Wagstaff, "Processions for the Dead, the Senses, and Ritual Identity in Colonial Mexico," in *Music, Sensation, and Sensuality*, ed. Linda Phyllis Austern (New York: Routledge, 2002), pp. 171–2.
3 Tess Knighton, "Chapter 1, Introduction," in *Devotional Music in the Iberian World, 1450–1800: The Villancico and Related Genres*, ed. Tess Knighton (Aldershot, UK: Ashgate, 2007), p. 3.
4 Geoffrey Baker, "The 'Ethnic Villancico' and Racial Politics in 17th-Century Mexico," in *Devotional Music in the Iberian World*, ed. Tess Knighton (Aldershot, UK: Ashgate, 2007), pp. 399–408.
5 Translations for Examples 12.1–12.3 are by Astrid Topp Russell in Chanticleer, *Mexican Baroque: Music from New Spain* (Audio CD. 2564–69765–2 DDD LC 04281. Teledec Classics, 1994), booklet, pp. 30–1. The Spanish text appears in *Tesoro da la Musica Polifonica en México* (Mexico City: CENIDIM, 1983), vol. 3.
6 Trans. Leonard Doucette, in Timothy McGee, *The Music of Canada* (New York: Norton, 1985), p. 4.
7 Paul le Jeune, *Jesuit Relations and Allied Documents*, vol. 12 (1637), ed. Reuben Gold Thwaites (Cleveland, OH: Burrows Brothers, 1898), p. 66.
8 Trans. John Steckley/Hechon, in Timothy McGee, *The Music of Canada* (New York: Norton, 1985), pp. 13–14.
9 Paul Ragueneau, *Jesuit Relations and Allied Documents*, vol. 34 (1649), ed. Reuben Gold Thwaites (Cleveland, OH: Burrows Brothers, 1901), p. 35.
10 Élisabeth Gallat-Morin, "Livre d'orgue de Montréal," www.thecanadianencyclopedia.ca/en/article/livre-dorgue-de-montreal-emc/ (accessed August 26, 2014).

Glossary—Compiled by Elissa Poole

accompanied recitative   recitative that is accompanied by the orchestra, or by an ensemble larger than mere continuo.

affect   the *affect* of a movement in the Baroque era was the mood or emotion it represented or attempted to evoke.

agréments   a type of essential ornamentation originally associated with French music in the Baroque, usually comprising formulaic melodic shapes of relatively few notes, such as trills and turns, that could be notated using small signs.

air de cour   French "courtly air," usually strophic, composed in the late seventeenth and early eighteenth centuries in both polyphonic vocal settings and as solo songs with lute accompaniment.

alexandrine   the standard, twelve-syllable poetic line in French spoken tragedy.

allemande   originated in Germany as a quick dance in duple meter, but was standardized in instrumental suites as a much slower, more dignified abstract dance, usually the first movement (after the prelude), and often somewhat contrapuntal.

anthem   English sacred choral composition, related to the motet.

aria   lyrical setting of a poetic text in an opera, cantata, or oratorio or related genre.

arioso   a passage in a recitative that is more lyrical and melismatic.

ballad opera   a type of opera popular in eighteenth-century England, comprising spoken dialogue and short popular songs that have been provided with new texts.

ballet de cour   literally, "court ballet," an elegant staged spectacle of dance and vocal music in which members of the court participated, associated with the early reign of Louis XIV.

basso continuo   the bass line in Baroque music, usually provided with figures that indicate which harmony is to be realized by the lute or keyboard instruments of the "continuo" section; the bass line is often doubled by a bass melodic instrument, such as a cello or bassoon.

bass viol   a member of the viol family with up to seven strings and a range similar to that of a cello; it was popular, especially in France, as a solo instrument and for playing the bass line of the basso continuo.

binary form   a two-part musical structure, common in dance music, in which each part was normally repeated; the first part usually modulates to the dominant or relative major; the second part returns to the tonic.

cadenza   a section in an aria or instrumental movement, often towards the end, intended as an opportunity to display the soloist's imagination and virtuosity, in which the solo performer improvises a flourish of varying length in a free rhythm and without accompaniment.

Camerata   a group of Florentine intellectuals, poets, and musicians who gathered at the home of Count Giovanni de' Bardi to discuss humanist ideals and the means of recreating the theater of ancient Greece.

canon   the strictest form of imitative counterpoint, in which a theme is introduced in one melodic part and then duplicated by each voice in turn, either at the same pitch or in transposition.

cantata   a vocal piece with instrumental accompaniment, either sacred or secular, often alternating recitative with aria and duet sections, much like a small scene from an opera.

castrato   a male singer, castrated before puberty, whose voice maintained its childhood alto or soprano vocal range while achieving the power and projection of an adult; virtuosic, heroic roles were often designed for castrati, who were the superstars of Baroque opera, although castrati of lesser talents were used to reinforce the boys' voices in church choirs.

chaconne   a dance in variation form, usually in triple meter, written over a repeating bass line or harmonic pattern that may or may not modulate; the French chaconne often places a longer note value on the second beat which may be interpreted as either a slight stress or a lift.

chapel master   translation of the German "Kapellmeister," a term used to designate the director of a musical organization, not necessarily within the Church.

chittarone   a bass lute, frequently part of a continuo section.

chorale   monophonic settings of Lutheran hymn texts, some original, some derived from the Gregorian chant repertoire and hymns, or from secular sources, and the harmonizations of these melodies.

chorale partita   a series of variation movements based on a harmonized version of a chorale melody, usually composed for keyboard.

chorale prelude   a keyboard piece, often used to introduce congregational singing, that presents a single stanza of a chorale; the melody is prominently placed, although it may be embellished or embedded in different types of figuration.

ciaccona   a type of bass pattern used for variation, similar (and sometimes identical) to the chaconne bass.

clavichord   a small keyboard instrument of delicate sound in which the strings are activated by metal tangents that permit gradations in dynamic and vibrato.

clavier   a generic designation for a stringed keyboard instrument.

coloratura   virtuosic vocal music, usually featuring fast, melismatic passagework.

commedia dell'arte   improvised comedies originally performed by traveling Italian theatre companies, whose stereotypical characters and plots were often incorporated into eighteenth-century comic opera.

concertato style   a style originating towards the end of the Renaissance, in which two or more vocal or instrumental groups interact and compete, highlighting short-range contrast in timbre and volume; the style laid the groundwork for both early orchestration and the emerging concerto.

concertino   the solo instruments in a Baroque concerto grosso, sometimes used to refer to the vocal soloists in a choir as well.

concerto   a term used, in the seventeenth century, to refer to works that featured contrasting bodies of voices and instruments; in the eighteenth century the concerto standardized into a three movement form (fast-slow-fast) that contrasted solo instrument(s) and orchestra.

concerto grosso   a particular form of concerto that contrasts a small ensemble (the *concertino*) against a larger one (the *ripieno*).

consort   an English term for a group of instruments, either members of the same family, such as a viol consort, or members of different families (broken consort).

cori spezzati   literally "split choirs," it refers to the idea of contrasting different groups of voices and instruments by positioning them in separate parts of the musical or performing space.

cornett   (or cornetto) a family of wind instruments with a cup-shaped mouthpiece similar to that of a trumpet; in sacred music the cornett might double the voices; the highly skilled cornettist was especially prized in early seventeenth-century Italy, where such composers as Giovanni Gabrieli often wrote virtuoso parts for the instrument.

corrente   a dance in simple triple meter; the fast Italian *corrente* in 3/4 is sometimes confused in the eighteenth century with the more dignified French *courante* in 3/2 (J.S. Bach frequently mislabeled them).

Council of Trent   the body of Roman Catholic dignitaries who met in three sessions between 1545–63 to discuss ways of reforming the liturgy, its music, and various corrupt practices within the church that had contributed to the growing threat of the Protestant Reformation.

Counter Reformation   the Roman Catholic reaction to the Protestant Reformation, manifested in reforms in the liturgy and its music, and in church politics, organization and practice.

courante   originally a quick dance in triple meter, but standardized during the reign of Louis XIV as a stately dance of some complexity in slow 3/2 meter; a standard component of the instrumental dance suite.

da capo aria   an aria in ABA form, in which the second A is often elaborately embellished upon its return; the form is ubiquitous in opera, cantatas, and oratorios, and was sometimes transferred to choral and instrumental movements.

descending minor tetrachord   the stepwise diatonic descent from the tonic to the dominant of a natural minor scale; the pattern was often used as an ostinato bass and was associated with laments.

divisions   a late Renaissance method of improvising instrumental variations by sub-dividing the notes into patterns comprising successively smaller note values; the practice continued into the early Baroque.

dramatick opera   spoken plays with some recitative and interpolated music, preferred by the English to full-scale operas; later called "semi-opera."

episode   in a fugue, the part of the movement in which the fugue theme does not appear; in a concerto, the episodes are those sections that feature the soloist(s).

fantasia   an instrumental work that is either improvised or simulates the rhythmic and structural freedom typical of an improvisation. Also referred to as *stylus phantasticus*.

favola in musica   Italian for "fable in music"; often applied to the mythological tales of early operas.

figured bass   method of notating the harmonies with numbers indicating the intervals above the bass note which are part of the chord (see also basso continuo).

French overture   a type of overture, originating in seventeenth-century France and popularized by Lully, comprising a stately section in slow duple meter with dotted rhythms with a contrasting quicker section, often imitative.

fugue   a type of piece or procedure in which a theme in one voice is imitated by two or more voices that enter successively with the same subject; the subject is then manipulated in various ways, whether augmented, diminished, fragmented or imitated at different time intervals; most fugues have sections called "episodes" in which the subject does not appear.

galliard   an energetic dance with leaping steps of the late Renaissance, usually in compound duple meter, and often pared with the more dignified pavan.

giga   a brisk Italian dance in triple meter, often written in running eighth notes.

gigue   a quick French court dance in triple or compound meter with dotted rhythms; often the last movement of a standard instrumental suite.

grand motet   in France, a large motet for double choir and orchestra, performed during special services and ceremonies.

ground bass   a melodic pattern in the bass that is repeated many times, providing a structure for the voices above it.

harmonic rhythm   the rate at which the harmonies change in a given passage, piece, or style. Passages with a quick harmonic rhythm change harmonies more frequently than those with a slow harmonic rhythm.

hemiola   in pieces notated in triple meter, a passage in which the accentuation creates a feeling of duple meter, such that two measures in 3/4 will sound like three measures in 2/4.

inégalité (inequality)   the practice of dotting notes of even values below the level of the beat, most common in France, and applied to passages that move mostly by step; it is often compared to "swinging" the rhythms in jazz.

intabulation   arrangement of a vocal piece for keyboard or plucked string instrument, such as a lute.

intermedio   short dramatic piece with music performed between the acts of a spoken theatrical performance in the Renaissance and early Baroque.

libretto   the text of an opera, oratorio, cantata, or other musical work.

liturgy   the prescribed order and content of a religious service.

madrigal   songs set to vernacular poetry in Italy and England during the sixteenth and seventeenth century, usually polyphonic, and often including descriptive gestures in the music that illustrate the text. Seventeenth-century madrigals were also set for solo voice and continuo.

madrigalism   a way of depicting a word or phrase in a text, sometimes literally (using an upward scale on the word "climb"), sometimes figuratively (using a dissonance for the word "pain").

masque   in England, a type of courtly entertainment involving elaborate costumes, stage sets, music, and dance, and often performed by members of the court themselves; masques were often incorporated into "semi-operas" as an excuse for an extended musical scene.

menuet   French word for a minuet, a binary court dance in triple meter often included in instrumental suites.

monody   a solo song performed by a singer with basso continuo, sometimes featuring the declamatory rhythms associated with recitative, an innovation of the Baroque era.

motive   a small musical unit with a recognizable intervallic or rhythmic profile that often forms part of a larger theme.

opera buffa   comic opera, evolving in Italy in the eighteenth century, and featuring tenors and basses in male roles rather than the castrati of serious opera.

opera seria   serious opera of the eighteenth century, usually composed in three acts without comic characters, and featuring the *da capo* aria as its most common vocal form.

oratorio   sacred dramas performed in Latin in the seventeenth century, to texts based on biblical stories; evolved in the eighteenth century into what were essentially unstaged sacred operas that utilized the same musical means as secular dramatic forms.

Ordinary   the part of the Catholic Mass whose text did not change from week to week.

ornamentation   the practice of decorating or embellishing a vocal or instrumental part, according to particular local and national preferences.

partbook   a standard publishing format, in which each vocal or instrumental part was issued separately.

partita   another word for a suite.

passacaglia   an instrumental variation form constructed over a repeating harmonic progression or bass melody, usually in triple meter; the term is often used interchangeably with the *chaconne*.

Passion oratorio   musical setting of the events that lead up to the Crucifixion, as recounted in the New Testament.

pavane   a slow courtly dance in duple meter.

performance practice   a phrase used to describe the attempt, by musicologists and performers, to perform the music of a given age in the manner in which it might have originally been performed, using both period instruments and information from early prefaces, treatises, and tutors that discuss interpretation and notation.

prelude   the introduction to an instrumental suite or fugue, sometimes improvised, or written in a way that imitates an improvisation.

prima pratica   term coined by Monteverdi to describe Renaissance-style polyphony that followed strict rules for voice leading and the treatment of dissonance.

Proper   the texted part of the Catholic Mass that varies according to a yearly cycle.

psalm   a sacred song or hymn set to texts taken from the biblical Book of Psalms.

recitative   declamatory or speech-like singing that follows the rhythms and accentuation of natural speech, and an important component in dramatic music.

Reformation   the religious movement, initiated by Martin Luther in 1517, that marked the beginning of the Protestant reform movement, the birth of a repertory of chorale melodies and new forms of sacred music.

Restoration   refers to the restoration of the monarchy in England in 1660; with the return of Charles II to the throne, theatres reopened, with an expanded role for music, and the stage was set for the development of opera in England.

ricercare   an instrumental composition in imitative counterpoint.

ripieno   the large ensemble that plays the *tutti* sections of a concerto grosso.

ritornello   a musical theme or idea that returns several times in the course of a movement, usually contrasting with what comes before and after it.

ritornello form   a way of organizing a large-scale movement by contrasting sections with and without a refrain. In the eighteenth-century concerto, a ritornello in the tonic usually began and ended a movement, and might be repeated in part, and in different keys, elsewhere in the movement.

sarabande   a slow dance in triple meter, often featuring a longer (albeit not necessarily accented) note on the second beat of the measure; a standard member of the instrumental suite.

scordatura   the practice of tuning a string instrument an alternative way, which changes the timbre and the ease and availability of double and triple stops.

seconda pratica   term coined by Monteverdi to describe the new style at the beginning of the seventeenth century and its privileging of textual expression over the traditional rules for counterpoint and the treatment of dissonance.

sonata da camera   literally, "chamber sonata," and featuring a series of movements based on dance rhythms.

sonata da chiesa   literally, "church sonata," usually starting with a slow movement and including one or more contrapuntal movements in place of the danced-based movements of the *sonata da camera*.

Sprezzatura   Italian word meaning "elegant neglect" that refers to the ideal courtier's air of graceful nonchalance. Caccini used it to describe the rhythmic freedom an expressive singer will apply to a song's written notation in order to make it sound more natural.

stile antico   literally, "ancient style," and referring to the older style of equal-voiced polyphony of the late Renaissance, as opposed to the new "stile moderno" with basso continuo.

stile concitato   literally, "excited style," and referring to a texture characterized by the rapid repetition of a single pitch.

stile rappresentativo   literally, "representational style," one of the terms used in the early seventeenth century to describe an expressive style of singing closer in rhythm to speech and less lyrical than pure song.

stile recitativo   term used in the seventeenth century to describe the new style of speech-song.

stretto   the part of a fugue or piece in imitative counterpoint, usually building in intensity, in which the entries of the subject occur more closely together and thus overlap.

strophic   a piece in which every verse of the poetic text is set to the same or similar music.

style brisé   a "broken" style of writing that refers to the arpeggiated texture of compositions for lute, which was often transferred to keyboard works.

suite   an ordered series of instrumental dances or dance-like movements, often in the same key.

temperament   any system of tuning that adjusts the just intervals of the scale so that the most out-of-tune intervals can be avoided, although all or many intervals will be somewhat compromised as a result.

thoroughbass   another term for figured bass.

tragédie lyrique   France's answer to Italian serious opera, developed by Lully and his librettist, Quinault, on the model of French classical spoken tragedy in five acts, and incorporating recitative, airs, choruses, and dance.

transcription   a piece that has been arranged for another instrument, usually involving some changes in order to make the transcription idiomatic to the new instrument.

trio sonata   genre of chamber piece, notated in three parts, in which the texture comprises two melody lines plus a basso continuo. The most typical trio sonata would have been performed by two violins, keyboard, and violoncello.

tutti   Italian for "all" and referring to the full ensemble in a concerto grosso.

verse anthem   a motet-like genre of sacred music from seventeenth-century England in which a chorus and soloists, accompanied by orchestra, alternate verses.

villancico   genre of Spanish song in the Renaissance, usually set to a poetic form (also called a *villancico*) in which several stanzas are linked by a refrain. In the seventeenth century, the villancico for singers and orchestra became an important sacred genre in the Iberian peninsula and the New World, closer to the cantata in concept, and often mixing elements from popular theater with religious ones.

viol   family of stringed instruments, gradually replaced in popularity by the violin as the seventeenth century progressed, and differing from the violin family in its delicate timbre, the shape of the neck, the flat back, and the greater number of strings (usually six).

viola da gamba   member of the viol family closest in size to the violoncello and important as both a member of the basso continuo section and as a solo instrument, especially in France.

virginal   a small harpsichord, in which the sound is activated by a jack that plucks the string when the key is depressed.

Credits

Musical Examples And Translations

2.2 Giulio Caccini, "Amarilli mia bella" is published in *Giulio Caccini: Le nuove musiche*, edited by H. Wiley Hitchcock, vol. 9, Recent Researches in Music of the Baroque Era, Middleton, WI: A-R Editions Inc., 2009. Used with permission. All rights reserved; **2.4** Translation for excerpt from Claudio Monteverdi, "Combattimento" is published in *Claudio Monteverdi, Madrigals Book VIII (Madrigali Guerrieri et Amorosi)*, trans. Stanley Appelbaum and ed.Gian Francesco Malpiero, New York: Dover, 1991. Copyright 1991 by Dover Publications. Used by permission of Dover Publications; **3.1** Emilio de'Cavalieri, "Dalle più alte sfere," in *Ancient to Baroque*, vol. 1 of *Norton Anthology of Western Music*, ed. Claude Palisca, 2nd ed. New York: W. W. Norton & Co., 1988. Copyright © 1988 by W.W. Norton & Company, Inc. Used by permission of W.W. Norton & Company, Inc.; **3.2–3.6** *Claudio Monteverdi: L'Orfeo*, ed. and trans. Denis Stevens, London: Novello, 1967. Used with permission; **4.1** *Giovanni Gabrieli: "Hodie Completi sunt,"* in *Motetta: Sacrae Symphoniae*, ed. Denis Arnold, vol. 3 of *Opera omnia*, Rome: American Institute of Musicology, 1962, used with permission; **4.2–4.5** Giovanni Rovetta, "Quam pulchra es," ed. Shaun Pirttijarvi (submitted 2009-05-15) Copyright © 2000 *by CPDL*; **4.6–4.9** Emilio de' Cavalieri, *Rappresentatione di anima, e di corpo*, ed. Murray C. Bradshaw, vol. 4 of Early Sacred Monody, Middleton, WI: American Institute of Musicology, 2007, used with permission; **4.10–4.11** Heinrich Schütz: "Eile Mich Gott, zu erretten," in *Kleine geistliche Konzerte 1636/1639, Abteilung 1*, ed. Wilhelm Ehmann and Hans Hoffmann, vol. 10 of *Neue Ausgabe sämtlicher Werke*, Kassel: Bärenreiter, 1963. Used with permission; **4.12–4.13** Heinrich Schütz: "Mein Sohn, warum hast du uns das getan?" in *Symphoniae Sacrae III (1650)*, ed. Werner Breig, vol. 18 of *Neue Ausgabe sämtlicher Werke*, Kassel: Bärenreiter, 1989. Used with permission; **4.14** Orlando Gibbons, "This is the Record of John," in *Orlando Gibbons: Verse Anthems*, ed. David Wulstan, vol. 3 of *Early English Church Music*, London: Stainer and Bell, 1964. Reproduced with kind permission; **5.1** Orlando Gibbons, "The Queenes Command," reproduced by arrangement with The Broude Trust from *Parthenia or the Maydenhead of the first musicke that ever was printed for the Virginals*. Facsimile of London, [1612/13?] Edition. New York: Broude Brothers, 1972; **5.2** Transcribed from Ennemond Gaultier: "Tombeau de Mezangeau," in *Œuvres du Vieux Gautier*, ed. André Souris, Paris: Éditions du Centre national de la recherche scientifique, 1966; **5.3** Johann Hermann Schein, Courente from Suite 6 in *Banchetto Musicale 1617*, ed. Dieter Krickeberg, vol. 9 of *Neue Ausgabe sämtlicher Werke*, Kassel: Bärenreiter, 1967. Used with permission; **5.4–5.6** Dario Castello, *Sonata Sesta a 2*, ed. Andrea Fuggi, http://imslp.org/wiki/Sonata_No.6_(Castello,_Dario), used with permission; Dario Castello, Sonata Sesta a 2, ed. Andrea Fuggi, http://imslp.org/wiki/Sonata_No.6_(Castello,_Dario), used with permission; **5.7–5.8** Biagio Marini, "Sonata in Ecco" is published in *Biagio Marini: String Sonatas from Opus 1 and Opus 8*, edited by Thomas D. Dunn, series 2, vol. 10, Collegium Musicum: Yale University, Madison, WI: A-R Editions Inc., 1981. Used with permission. All rights reserved; **5.9** Giulio Caccini, "Preface" is published in *Giulio Caccini: Le nuove musiche*, edited by H. Wiley Hitchcock, vol. 9, Recent Researches in Music of the Baroque Era, Middleton, WI: A-R Editions Inc., 2009. Used with permission. All rights reserved; **6.1–6.5** Claudio Monteverdi: *L'incoronazione di Poppea*, ed. and trans. Alan Curtis, London: Novello, 1989. Used with permission; **6.6–6.8** Reproduced by arrangement with The Broude Trust from Francesco Cavalli, *Il Giasone*, in *Die Oper: Zweiter Teil*, ed. Robert Eitner, vol. 12 of *Publikation Aelterer Praktischer und Theoretischer Musikwerke*, New York: Broude Brothers, 1966; English translations from Francesco Cavalli, *Giasone*, Concerto Vocale, cond. Rene Jacobs. Harmonia Mundi, HMX2901282.84, trans. Derek Yeld, pp. 109, 111, 113, 177, 181. Used with permission; **6.9–6.10** Antonio Cesti, *Orontea*, Act I, "Intorna all'idol mio," in *Ancient to Baroque*, vol. 1 of *Norton Anthology of Western Music*, ed. and trans. Claude V. Palisca. 4th ed. New York: W.W. Norton & Co., 2001. Copyright © 2001 by W.W. Norton & Company, Inc. Used by permission of W.W. Norton & Company, Inc.; **7.1–7.4** Reproduced by arrangement with The Broude Trust from Jean-Baptiste Lully, *Phaëton*, vol. 10 of *The*

Photographs And Figures

of Lute-Lessons. Facsimile of the London, 1610 Edition. Performers' Facsimiles no. 159. New York: Performers' Facsimiles, 1997; **Figure 5.8** Bayerische Staatsbibliothek München **Figure 5.9** Girolamo Frescobaldi: Toccata Nono, Orgel- und Klavierwerke [Organ and Keyboard Works], ed. Pierre Pidoux, vol. 3 of Das erste Buch der Toccaten, Pariten usw. 1637 – The First Book of Toccatas, Partitas etc. 1637, Kassel: Barenreiter, 1949. Used with permission **Figure 6.1** Hulton Archive/Getty Images; **Figure 6.2** DeAgostini/Getty Images; **Figure 6.3** DeAgostini/Getty Images; **Figure 6.4** Lipnitzki/Roger Viollet/Getty Images; **Figure 6.5** GREG WOOD/AFP/Getty Images; **Figures 6.6–6.7** Francesco Cavalli, *Il Giasone*, manuscript n.d., http://imslp.org/wiki/Il_Giasone_(Cavalli,_Francesco), licensed under a Creative Commons Attribution-ShareAlike 4.0 International Public License, http://creativecommons.org/licenses/by-sa/4.0/ **Figure 7.1** DeAgostini/Getty Images; **Figure 7.2** © RMN-Grand Palais/Art Resource, NY; **Figure 7.3** DeAgostini/Getty Images; **Figures 7.4–7.7** Music Collections/Libraries of the University of North Texas; **Figure 7.8** Courtesy of the Library of Congress Music Division, Washington, DC; **Figure 7.9** Paris, Bibliothèque Nationale VM7-1854. Courtesy Bibliothèque Nationale, Paris; **Figure 7.10** Paris, Bibliothèque Nationale VM7- 1851. Courtesy Bibliothèque Nationale, Paris; **Figure 7.11** Paris, Bibliothèque Nationale VM-PHOT MIRI-4 (58). Courtesy Bibliothèque Nationale, Paris; **Figure 7.12** Paris, Bibliothèque Nationale AC P-3603. Courtesy Bibliothèque Nationale, Paris; **Figure 7.13** Paris, Bibliothèque Nationale V-689. Courtesy Bibliothèque Nationale, Paris; **Figures 7.14–7.16** Manuscript, Cauvin collection, 1741, Les Bibliotheques Versailles, http://imslp.org/wiki/De_Profundis,_S.23_(Lalande,_Michel_Richard_de), licensed under a Creative Commons Attribution-ShareAlike 4.0 International Public License, http://creativecommons.org/licenses/by-sa/4.0/ **Figure 7.17** Les Bibliotheques Versailles, http://imslp.org/wiki/De_Profundis,_S.23_(Lalande,_Michel_Richard_de), licensed under a Creative Commons Attribution-ShareAlike 4.0 International Public License, http://creativecommons.org/licenses/by-sa/4.0/ **Figure 8.1** Johan Closterman; **Figure 8.2** Copyright © The British Library Board, All Rights Reserved, Music Collections B.347.g **Figure 8.3** Copyright © The British Library Board, All Rights Reserved, Music Collections K.4.b.10 **Figure 8.4** Copyright © The British Library Board, All Rights Reserved, Music Collections K.4.b.10 **Figure 8.5** Copyright © The British Library Board, All Rights Reserved, Music Collections K.1.a.15 **Figure 8.6** Copyright © The British Library Board, All Rights Reserved, Music Collections K.4.g.10 **Figure 8.7** SSPL/Getty Images; **Figure 9.1** Historic Map Works LLC and Osher Map Library; **Figure 9.2** DeAgostini/C. Bevilacqua; **Figure 9.3** Snark/Art Resource, NY; **Figures 9.4–9.5** Music Collections/Libraries of the University of North Texas; **Figure 9.6** Universal History Archive/Getty Images; **Figure 9.7** Paris, Bibliothèque Nationale, *Traité de la police*, Paris, 1705. Courtesy Bibliothèque Nationale, Paris; **Figure 9.8** Paris, Bibliothèque Nationale, X-857. Courtesy Bibliothèque Nationale, Paris; **Figure 9.9** Paris, Bibliothèque Nationale, X-905. Courtesy Bibliothèque Nationale, Paris; **Figure 10.1** Stefano Bianchetti/Corbis; **Figure 10.2** Copyright © The British Library Board, All Rights Reserved, Music Collection f.17. **Figure 10.3** SLUB Dresden, Mus. 2389-0-43 **Figures 10.4–10.5** Copyright © The British Library Board, All Rights Reserved, Music Hirsch III.38 **Figure 11.1** Imagno/Getty Images; **Figure 11.2** © TOBIAS SCHWARZ/Reuters/Corbis; **Figure 11.3** Premium UIG; 7 **Figure 11.4** DEA/A. DAGLI ORTI/DeAgostini/Getty Images; **Figure 12.1** DEA/M. Seemuller; **Figure 12.2** Charlotte Hindle; **Figure 12.3** MPI/Getty Images; **Figure 12.4** Encyclopaedia Britannica/UIG; **Figure 12.5** Bibliothèque et Archives nationales du Québec, BAnQ Vieux-Montréal, Fonds Families Girouard et Berthelot CLG4_004–CLG4_005; **Figure 12.6** Historic Map Works LLC and Osher Map Library; **Figure 12.7** MPI/Getty Images; **Figure 12.8** Thomas Walter, *The Grounds and Rules of Musick Explained*, http://imslp.org/wiki/The_Grounds_and_Rules_of_Musick_Explained_(Walter,_Thomas), licensed under a Creative Commons Attribution-ShareAlike 4.0 International Public License, http://creativecommons.org/licenses/by-sa/4.0/ **Figure 12.9** John Collet/Getty Images.

Index